The Complete Works

A medieval illustration of a fictitious work, written sometime between the third and ninth centuries, entitled *The Dialogue between the Emperor Hadrian and the Philosopher Epictetus*. Note the philosopher's typically unkempt appearance.

EPICTETUS

The Complete Works

HANDBOOK, DISCOURSES, AND FRAGMENTS

*Edited and translated with introduction
and notes by* ROBIN WATERFIELD

THE UNIVERSITY OF CHICAGO PRESS
CHICAGO AND LONDON

The University of Chicago Press, Chicago 60637
The University of Chicago Press, Ltd., London
© 2022 by Robin Waterfield
Published 2022
Printed in the United States of America

31 30 29 28 27 26 25 24 23 22   1 2 3 4 5

ISBN-13: 978-0-226-76933-2 (cloth) ·
ISBN-13: 978-0-226-76947-9 (paper)
ISBN-13: 978-0-226-76950-9 (e-book)
DOI: https://doi.org/10.7208/chicago/9780226769509.001.0001

Library of Congress Cataloging-in-Publication Data

Names: Epictetus, author. | Waterfield, Robin, 1952–, editor, translator.
Title: The complete works : handbook, discourses, and fragments / Epictetus ;
    edited and translated with introduction and notes by Robin Waterfield.
Other titles: Works. English. 2022
Description: Chicago : University of Chicago Press, 2022. | Includes
    bibliographical references and index.
Identifiers: LCCN 2022008960 | ISBN 9780226769332 (cloth) | ISBN
    9780226769479 (paperback) | ISBN 9780226769509 (ebook)
Subjects: LCSH: Philosophy, Ancient—Early works to 1800.
Classification: LCC B560.E5 W38 2022 | DDC 180—dc23/eng/20220304
LC record available at https://lccn.loc.gov/2022008960

⊛ This paper meets the requirements of ANSI/NISO Z39.48-1992
(Permanence of Paper).

In memoriam WGD

Contents

Fragments *353*

Preface

It has been a great pleasure to work once again with Susan Bielstein and James Whitman Toftness (and then Dylan Montanari) at the University of Chicago Press, and it was also a pleasure to have the typescript assigned to a skillful copy editor, Lori Meek Schuldt. I received useful advice and suggestions from the readers who assessed the book proposal and the finished draft. Tony Long, the doyen of Epictetus studies and even of Stoic studies as a whole, was kind enough to act as one of the final readers, and I am particularly grateful to him for making me focus on the issue I address in the Note on the Translation. Charles Brittain also read the final draft of the book and gave me an extremely helpful and detailed report. Many improvements were made in the light of his comments.

This book was written under COVID-19 restrictions. It is in any case my usual practice when writing a book to ask friends and colleagues to send me offprints of articles of theirs that are unavailable in the online archives, but, denied access to libraries, it was especially important this time. I am particularly grateful to those—Brad Inwood, John Sellars, Ron Polansky—who sent me copies from their collections of articles written by others who were unavailable. William Stephens supplied a whole book (his translation of Bonhöffer's 1894 *Die Ethik des stoikers Epictet*), and I should also thank the publisher, Peter Lang, for letting me see an advance copy of the 2021 revised edition of the book. Alexander Meeus's generosity extended to making material available to me from his university library at

Mannheim. In the process of translating, I consulted Radcliffe G. Edmonds III on incantations, David Martinez on puzzling ethical datives, and Bill Murray on how to capsize a boat; I thank them for their help.

Note on the Translation

I have translated the following texts. For the *Handbook*: G. Boter, *Epictetus: Encheiridion* (Teubner, 2007); for *Discourses*: J. Souilhé and A. Jagu, *Épictète, Entretiens*, 4 vols. (Budé, 1945, 1949, 1963, 1965); for the fragments: W. Oldfather, *Epictetus: The Discourses as Reported by Arrian, The Manual, and Fragments*, 2 vols. (Loeb, 1928). These are the most recent available editions, but for *Discourses* I have also had on hand H. Schenkl's ground-breaking, but out-of-print *Epicteti Dissertationes ab Arriano Digestae*, 2nd ed. (Teubner, 1916). However, there are many places where I differ from the readings of these editors; they are marked in the translations by an obelisk, or dagger (†), which points to a note in the Textual Notes (pp. 431–433). An asterisk in the text indicates that there is a note on that passage in the explanatory Notes (pp. 367–430). The notes (and the introduction) are designed more for students and lay readers than professionals in ancient philosophy.

The translation that I consulted most is the one by R. Hard: *Epictetus: Discourses, Fragments, Handbook*, with introduction and notes by C. Gill (Oxford University Press, 2014).

My policy, as in all my translations, has been to try to combine accuracy with current English fluency and readability. In one important respect, however, I have not followed current English practice: I have not gender-neutralized Epictetus's pronouns. Epictetus often talks about or addresses an anonymous "he," who is either a fictional person acting as a foil or one of his visitors or students, who appear to have all been male. To neutralize this person would have misrepresented Epictetus and his world. He was writing two thousand years ago, at a time when male dominance was simply assumed. Nor was it possible in ancient Greek to write about people (as opposed to things) in a gender-neutral way; in fact, to neutralize their gender in some linguistic fashion was often an insult.

In any case, it is clear that the anonymous "he" that Epictetus talks about or addresses is meant to be masculine, because the people and creatures to whom he is likened are always masculine. It is not just that he is likened to Heracles and Theseus, for instance, but to people with professions or occupations that in the ancient world were exclusively masculine: wrestlers and other athletes, actors (there were actresses in Rome but not in Greece, and Epictetus assumes Greek culture), orators, soldiers. At one point he is likened to a fighting cock. He can be waylaid by sexual attraction to girls. He can be called a "son of God." He goes to the male bathhouse. He stands for office in Rome. So I have largely preserved Epictetus's usage in this respect.

Map of Greece by András Bereznay

Introduction

Four great expositors of Stoicism emerged in Rome in the first and second centuries CE: Seneca the Younger, Gaius Musonius Rufus, Epictetus, and Marcus Aurelius—an imperial courtier, a member of the equestrian order, an ex-slave, and an emperor. Despite being men of their time, their voices reach us clearly across the centuries because they speak always to our common humanity and our best aspirations. Since the work of earlier Stoics exists only in fragments, the surviving writings of these men constitute for us by far the most detailed record of Stoic philosophy.[1]

Seneca focused on writing, and his books, plays, and letters were widely disseminated in his lifetime. Musonius Rufus was a popular teacher, and some of his lectures were transcribed by students and published. Marcus wrote for himself, and his private notebooks, known to us as *Meditations*, did not become widely available until after the tenth century. Epictetus focused on teaching; he wrote nothing himself, but some of his lectures were transcribed or summarized and quickly became well known. Within fifty years of his death, he was praised at length in a rock-cut inscription from Pisidia (southern Turkey), and anecdotes about him were cropping up in other works of literature.[2] Within a hundred years, one writer asserted that Epictetus was more widely read than Plato.[3] The fundamental question that his teaching was designed to address is: How must we live if our lives are to be subjectively fulfilling and objectively worthwhile?[4] And his answer was: Get ever closer to yourself, your true self.

At the heart of his teaching is an easily understood and insightful distinction. Some things are not "up to us"—they are external to us and just happen to us—but our minds are our own, and we can control our internal states and our responses to events: our desires, inclinations, choices, judgments, and intentions; in short, all the things that make up our characters. These things are up to us and cannot be thwarted by anyone or anything else. We need to learn to accept experiences and events over which we have no control, to recognize them as "indifferent" (neither good nor bad, and with no contribution to make to our happiness or misery) and to use them as the materials on which to practice virtue and appropriate action; we need to see them as gifts of the providential God who steers and arranges everything in the universe, great and small. In this way, fated events become opportunities, not constraints.

If we understand that our happiness does not depend on our bodies and possessions and careers, but on the mental faculties that are up to us, we will free ourselves of negative emotions (those that are not supportive of our natural potential for goodness), and our rational faculty, the distinctive part of a human being, will begin to work better, now that it is uncluttered by unnecessary reactions. It will begin to judge things correctly, and since everything bad that happens to us is the result of our own wrong judgments, we will start to live well. It is a fact of our human nature that we have all the resources we need to achieve happiness and a smoothly flowing life. No one empowers or disempowers us except ourselves. Moment by moment, we need to assess our mental condition to make sure that we are focusing only on things that are up to us and not letting externals worry us. That way we can take control of our lives.

This focus on what is up to us increasingly aligns us with the Reason that guides the universe, which is God. For the human soul, in its rational aspect, is a fragment of God. Rationality is our birthright and an inalienable human capacity. When our rational faculty is working well, we can act freely as independent and responsible moral agents, perpetuating the divine plan for the world by always acting virtuously. And virtue, which is the proper functioning of the soul in accord with its nature under the guidance of reason, always fulfills and benefits us and those around us, so that virtue is the essential prerequisite of happiness and peace of mind. If we are virtuous, nothing external to our minds can make the slightest difference to our happiness—not poverty or ill health, or even the imminent prospect of violent death. We therefore need to safeguard what is ours, our mental faculties, and turn away from everything else.

Since it is our nature's goal to be rational and to act virtuously, it is the job of philosophy to help us realize this potential by curing us of attachment to everything about us that is not conducive to this end. By relying on reason and focusing only on what is up to us, we will be fulfilling our nature as human beings, which is happiness, and there is no one in the world who does not want to be happy.[5] It will take hard work and total commitment, and no one should undertake the work unless they are prepared to change. A teacher such as Epictetus can show the way, but he cannot do the work for us. Theory, information, and advice from others are useless unless they are acted on and put into practice by the student.

EPICTETUS'S LIFE

Little is known of Epictetus's life beyond what we can read in his discourses. He lived from c. 50 to c. 130 CE. He was born a slave in the city of Hierapolis in what is now southwestern Turkey. Hierapolis ("Sacred City") was famous for its hot springs and its temple of Cybele, the great Mother Goddess of Anatolia. How and when Epictetus came to Rome is unknown, but he worked there in the household of a powerful man, Tiberius Claudius Epaphroditus, perhaps as a kind of personal assistant to his master. Epictetus was a Greek, a Mediterranean person, and he was enslaved to another Mediterranean person; although slavery might be based on race in the ancient world (and so-called inferior races were despised as such), most ancient slavery was different from the modern version in this respect, that it was far less likely to be based on race. Generally, people were either born into slavery, as Epictetus was, or became slaves after defeat in warfare.

Epaphroditus was himself a freedman, a former slave, who had risen to be one of the emperor Nero's secretaries, responsible for receiving and sifting petitions. Epictetus mentions an Epaphroditus three times in *Discourses*. One of these mentions is indifferent (1.1.20), but the other two come with a sneer (1.19.19–21, 1.26.11–12). The Epaphroditus of 1.19 is certainly Epictetus's master, but the other two might be different men: the name was not uncommon.

Epictetus comments caustically on life in the imperial court, but it is unlikely that he experienced it directly.[6] He arrived in Rome after Nero's suicide in 68, and Epaphroditus was probably not employed by any emperors after Nero. Epaphroditus played a role in Nero's suicide by holding the emperor steady as he thrust the dagger into his own throat.[7] For this, he was condemned to death many years later by the emperor Domitian, sometime around 95.[8]

Epictetus's experience of slavery marked him for life. More than any other ancient philosopher, he insisted that, however else one describes the goal of life, it must be a state of freedom, where everything that happens to a person is "in accord with his will and no one is able to impede him" (1.12.9). Slavery most frequently occurs in the discourses in this metaphorical sense, but Epictetus reflected on literal slavery as well. At 1.13, he claims that the institution of slavery is not natural but a matter of human convention; by nature, all human beings, whatever their status, are equal just because they all possess reason. Despite this claim, however, Epictetus seems to accept slavery as an institution (e.g., 1.18.19, 2.20.29–31, 2.23.24, *Handbook* 14a). If he was no active abolitionist, that was presumably because, for a Stoic, one's station in life is a matter of little or no relevance to one's moral progress or ultimate happiness.[9]

Even while enslaved, Epictetus was permitted to attend the lectures of the foremost Stoic in Rome, Musonius Rufus (1.9.29), but otherwise, as a slave, his education may have been rather sketchy. We should probably think of him as self-taught to a great extent—or even as contemptuous of much learning: his speech in the discourses has few of the flourishes that embellish the work of educated orators and writers; his cultural allusions are limited largely to myth, Homer, and popular drama; and his references to writers such as Plato and Xenophon are largely limited to paraphrases of popular passages that had already featured in other Stoic writers. The few historical figures to whom he alludes were household names.

Given that Musonius Rufus was often away from Rome (exiled first by Nero and then by Vespasian), it was not until the reign of Titus, which began in 79, that we can safely say that he was back in Rome and that Epictetus could have been attending his lectures. Musonius Rufus wrote nothing, but we have transcripts of a few of his discourses by a student and a collection of shorter fragments. He seems to have specialized in offering Stoically tinged advice on everyday topics such as marriage, family life, and self-presentation. Of particular interest is the fact that he treated women as equal to men, in the sense that they have the same capacity for rationality. They are just as capable as men of striving for and attaining virtue, and marriage and raising children are not incompatible with a life devoted to philosophy.[10]

Epictetus may have agreed with his teacher on this, but it is not a topic on which he touches in the extant discourses, and there is only one hint, at 4.11.35, that any of his students might be female. His attitude toward women appears to have been conventional—that women's roles are of lesser importance than men's (*Handbook* 40, *Discourses* 2.4.9, 3.7.20). But Epictetus was a true follower of his teacher in that both were popularizers of Stoicism. Epictetus talks not just of how to cope with tyrants and banishment but about family life, friendship, clothing, cleanliness, and dinner table manners. Nothing, however trivial, lies beyond the reach of his teaching. A true Stoic puts his philosophy into practice whatever he is doing.

Sometime after he was given his freedom by Epaphroditus (in 80 or thereabouts), Epictetus set himself up as a philosophy teacher under Rufus's patronage. But, probably in 93, Domitian ordered all philosophers out of Rome, suspecting them of republican sympathies.[11] Epictetus, who was by then a successful teacher, moved to the west coast of Greece, easy to reach from Italy, where his main client base was, and set up his school in Nicopolis, the largest city in western Greece and the capital of the Roman province of Epirus.[12] Athens was the traditional center of learning in Greece, but Epictetus chose Nicopolis because it was closer to Italy. A secondary reason might have been that he did not want his students to be distracted by the fabled beauties of Athens, of which he thought little (2.16.32–33, 3.24.73).[13]

Epictetus thought little of Rome either. In the discourses Rome comes across as a place of false values and loose morals (1.10, 1.26.10, 2.12.17, 3.23.27, Fragment 15), where flattery rather than ability is the best way to get promoted (e.g., 3.17.2, *Handbook* 25.4); a place where people are constantly in danger of being executed or sent into exile (e.g., 1.1.22–24, 1.1.30, 1.2.21, 1.10.2, 1.25.20, 2.1.38, 2.6.20–22, 2.7.8); a place therefore that is seething with hostility toward the emperor

(3.4.7–8), and where secret policemen entrap people into treason (4.13.5, and see 3.4.8); and above all a place dominated by the emperor, who is often called a tyrant (especially in 1.19 and 4.7).[14]

After Domitian's death in 96, Epictetus probably could have returned to Rome, and passages such as 1.29.37–39 might imply that he made the occasional voyage back (though, with Epictetus, it is often difficult to separate fact from one of his flights of fancy). But essentially Nicopolis remained his home for the last thirty-five or so years of his life. He was less well off than he had been as a teacher in Rome (3.5.9, 3.26.31), but he seems to have attracted enough students to make a living. In keeping with his teaching, he probably lived frugally.[15] When he was elderly (by which time, we happen to know, he was lame: 1.8.14, 1.16.20),[16] he retired from teaching and took up a family life by adopting a child and taking in a female housekeeper to look after himself and the child.[17]

ARRIAN AND EPICTETUS'S *DISCOURSES*

Epictetus, like his hero Socrates and his teacher Musonius Rufus, wrote nothing and confined himself to live teaching. But students took notes, and one of them turned his notes into *Discourses* and then prepared a digest of his mentor's ideas, which is the *Handbook* or *Manual*. This student's name was Lucius Flavius Arrianus, or Arrian to us, and he is also famous for other books, including what is widely regarded as the most authoritative account of the eastern conquests of Alexander the Great. Arrian considered himself a second Xenophon. Not only did he call his Alexander book *The Anabasis of Alexander* (*Alexander's Eastern Expedition*) in homage to Xenophon's most famous historical work, *The Anabasis of Cyrus*, but he also wrote a "supplement" to Xenophon's treatise on hunting and, like Xenophon, wrote a book *On Cavalry Command*. In writing up Epictetus's lectures, he was performing the same service as Xenophon in his *Memoirs of Socrates* (*Memorabilia*). Later writers sometimes refer to *Discourses* as *Memorabilia*.[18]

We have four books of discourses, but we know that originally there were more. Other writers, including Marcus Aurelius, preserve a few fragments from the missing books, and a Byzantine encyclopedist tells us there were originally eight books.[19] Moreover, the *Handbook*, which is supposed to consist of extracts or summaries of entries in *Discourses*, contains quite a few entries that correspond to nothing in the extant discourses. Simplicius of Cilicia, the Platonist scholar who wrote a commentary on the *Handbook* in the sixth century, says, "Practically all the material [in the *Handbook*] can be found in the same words at various points in Arrian's *Discourses of Epictetus*" (*On Epictetus's Handbook* 192). He does not seem to have had a copy of *Discourses* on hand as he was writing his commentary, so there may be some exaggeration in his "in the same words," but he still corroborates the evidence that there was originally more to *Discourses*.

In the preface to *Discourses*, Arrian claimed that they are verbatim records of his master's voice. There is no reason to suspect him of being disingenuous: stenography had been practiced in Rome since the first century BCE.[20] Without stenography, the task would have been impossible. It is plain from the lectures that Epictetus's delivery could be rapid. Even if Arrian had checked his memory against that of his fellow students, and even consulted Epictetus himself, it would have been impossible to get it all down—to recover, to a satisfactory degree of accuracy, what would originally have been more than 250,000 extemporized words. However, some of Epictetus's talks might already have been transcribed (see 2.17.30), creating a certain stock for Arrian to draw on.[21] And a final reason for confidence that we are hearing Epictetus's voice is that the style of *Discourses* is unique in Arrian's corpus. The rest of his works are written in literary Greek—he wrote in the dialect that Xenophon had used hundreds of years earlier—whereas *Discourses* is written in Koine, the supraregional dialect of Greek that everyone spoke at the time.[22]

Nevertheless, Arrian must have introduced some differences. His main contributions were probably a bit of scene setting (e.g., the beginning of 2.4, 2.14, 3.9), the titles of the discourses,[23] and the order of the discourses.[24] He might have undertaken some amalgamation too. That is, if he found discourses delivered by Epictetus on different days but on the same topic, he might have put them together; there are some awkward transitions in the talks that could be explained in this way (e.g., 2.23.16, 4.6.25), and three of the discourses are perhaps too long to have been delivered comfortably in a single session (3.22, 3.24, 4.1). But otherwise he did not organize the material by topic; there is no overall plan to the order of the talks.[25] However, the fact that each of the four books is about the same length suggests that Arrian might have arranged the discourses to reach this satisfying result. His playing around with the order makes no difference because, as any reader will quickly learn, Epictetus typically circles around the same topics, the central insights that I summarized at the start of this introduction and will develop subsequently.

THE *HANDBOOK*

We know from Simplicius (*On Epictetus's Handbook* 192) that there was originally a letter prefacing the *Handbook*, as there still is for *Discourses*. Arrian addressed the letter to someone called Messalenus, and in it he said that he had selected from Epictetus's talks the principal and most necessary elements of his thought—"those that are most likely to move the souls of readers." If Arrian interfered little in the discourses, then, the same cannot be said for the *Handbook*. As well as selecting what to include, he must have paraphrased, abridged, and rewritten much of the material. Although we are missing four books of the discourses, it is remarkable how little direct correspondence there is between the content of the *Handbook* and the discourses. This again suggests that Arrian did more than just excerpt bits of the discourses. On some occasions he may have lifted phrases and ideas from different discourses and put them together as a *Handbook* entry. So *Handbook* 47, for instance, if it is not a report of a lost discourse, seems to consist of several snatches from *Discourses* 3.12, but with elements of 3.14 and possibly 4.5. The philosophy of the *Handbook* is Epictetus's, but the way it is told is due to Arrian.

The *Handbook*, then, is Arrian's distillation of the essence of Epictetus's teaching, with an emphasis on practice rather than theory. It is a "handbook" in the sense that it contains reminders that Epictetus wanted his students to have "at hand"—a repeated phrase in both the *Handbook* and *Discourses*. In *Discourses*, Epictetus often illustrates his point with anecdotes; almost all of these were omitted from the *Handbook*. Whereas the discourses were addressed to Epictetus's students, the *Handbook* addresses the reader, so Arrian omitted the teacherly aspects of the discourses, especially those many occasions when Epictetus reprimands and criticizes his students. No one can deny that Arrian did a good job in composing the *Handbook*. It serves its introductory purpose well, but it is thinner fare than *Discourses*.

The *Handbook* became very popular. The usual way books were published in medieval times was that a customer approached a monastery to commission a scribe to make a copy of the book he wanted. We have almost sixty manuscripts of the *Handbook*, with many more lost than surviving. The earliest of the survivors date from the fourteenth century, but they stand at the end of a long, invisible tradition, demonstrating considerable demand for the work. Passages were included in the fifth-century anthology of John of Stobi (commonly known as Stobaeus), and in the sixth century the Platonist Simplicius, the most learned scholar of the time, wrote a commentary on it. Perhaps in the seventh century the first of the extant Christian adaptations of the *Handbook* was written. At least two others followed over the centuries, written as guides for monks and nuns. They Christianized Epictetus's work by, for instance, substituting "Paul" for "Socrates" and "God" for "the gods"; they undertook some judicious rewriting, omitting words, phrases, and sentiments that they found distasteful.[26]

Did Arrian also impose structure on the entries of the *Handbook*? In his *On Epictetus's Handbook*, Simplicius thought he could detect structure, and even that each entry developed material left unfinished by earlier entries, but this notion seems fanciful. More recently, a number of scholars have been attracted by the idea that the book is structured by the three "domains"—the three areas of life where training is needed to perfect oneself (more on this later). But this idea does not work either. The first domain is that of desire and aversion, the second that of inclinations and appropriate (that is, ethical) behavior, and the third that of logic and rational thinking. Given that the thrust of the *Handbook* is practical, there can be little doubt that the three domains underlie much of its content, but it would be more realistic to see them scattered throughout the book, and they certainly do not occur in blocks.[27] Even casual reading disproves this idea. The impression of randomness that one gets on reading the book is correct.

So there is no fine structure to the *Handbook*, but it does have a beginning, a middle, and an end. The first two entries are programmatic, laying out the objectives and the means of attaining those objectives, and introducing and explaining the technical terms that are employed. Then almost all the rest of the entries illustrate the practical applications of this theoretical model. Themes are treated at random or in a kaleidoscopic fashion throughout the book, with the final entries, 48a–53, forming an epilogue, covering the philosophical life and providing some essential maxims for students to remember as they set out to cope with the real world. Each entry makes its point clearly and simply, avoiding theoretical technicalities.

If the *Handbook* gives an overview of the practical work a would-be Stoic philosopher needed to undertake, it was probably written for both beginners and more advanced students. Beginners would glimpse the kind of work to which they would be committing themselves and the goals for which they would aim, and more advanced students, such as Arrian, would be reminded of what they should be doing. It could be read, then, either before or after *Discourses*. Since I think Arrian intended the primary audience to be beginners (see *Handbook* 1.4), those who had heard of Epictetus and were curious about what he demanded of a student, I have placed it first in this book, before the discourses and the surviving fragments of the lost books.

EPICTETUS'S SCHOOL

It is clear that the discourses constitute only a fraction of the teaching that went on in Epictetus's school in Nicopolis. They are his extracurricular talks, delivered in the afternoon,[28] when he addressed his students' personal issues, rather than the impersonal, systematic teaching that made up the core curriculum. They were probably not a regular feature of the school, and the letter with which Arrian prefaced the discourses suggests that they were impromptu, as does the whole tenor of the talks. Nevertheless, there are hints in the discourses that allow us to discern the regular curriculum at least in outline.

The Stoics divided philosophy into three major fields: logic, physics, and ethics. Logic covered not only the rules of correct argumentation and thinking but also grammar, linguistics, rhetorical theory, epistemology, and all the tools that might be needed to discover the truth of any matter. Physics was concerned with the nature of the world and the laws that govern it, and so it included ontology and theology as well as what we would recognize as physics, astronomy, and cosmology. Ethics was concerned with how to achieve happiness, or the conditions for living a fulfilled and flourishing life as a human being. As a teacher of Stoicism, Epictetus taught all three subjects at his school.

There are plenty of references to logic throughout the discourses (see the index under "argument"). They show that Epictetus's students received a substantial grounding in the subject. He expected his students to understand and be proficient at definition, and at syllogisms (formally valid arguments) and their analysis. They were to be familiar with various modes of argumentation, which Epictetus calls "changing arguments," "hypothetical arguments," and arguments that proceed by question and answer.[29] And they studied various specific arguments, such as the Master Argument and other sophisms, where the point was to be able to spot invalid argumentation. As for epistemology, they would have examined human rationality, to discover "what its constituent parts are, and how they're related and interconnected" (4.7.38). That is, they learned to distinguish knowledge and belief, what impressions are and how they affect the soul, and the mechanics of how we gain reliable knowledge of the world. And they would have come to know "the elements of reason: what each of them is, how they fit together, and what their consequences are" (4.8.12).

There is no such abundance of references when it comes to physics, but we can be certain that the subject formed part of the school curriculum. In Fragment 1, Epictetus asks whether there is any point to studying physics, and by the end of the fragment it is clear that he expects the answer "Yes, it is worthwhile—but don't get lost in the details." The whole of Epictetus's teaching is founded on assumptions that fell within the province of Stoic physics, and in his formal lectures he would not have left those assumptions unexamined or poorly understood (3.12.15). He assumes, for instance, that the world is perfect and is run by a providential God (1.6, 1.10.10, 1.12, 1.14, 1.16, 2.14.11, 3.17, Fragment 23), and he discusses theological issues (1.12.1–6, 2.8.1–2, 2.14.11, *Handbook* 31). He makes claims about the human constitution—that we are rational beings and that we are fragments of the Reason that guides the universe (1.14, 1.17.27, 2.8.11). He claims that we are made up of the four elements (earth, water, air, fire), and that these elements are constantly being recycled into new forms of matter (2.1.18, 3.13.14–15, 3.24.10, 4.7.15, Fragment 8). He talks of a human being as "a part of the universe" (1.12.26, 2.5.13, 2.5.25–26, 2.10.2, 4.7.7) and assumes a *scala naturae* (great chain of being; 1.16.2) and familiarity with the doctrine of eternal recurrence (3.13.4). These are all issues that would have been included in a general course on Stoic physics, along with broader topics that are not touched on in the extant discourses, such as the corporeality of all things, causation, and cosmology (mentioned at 1.10.10).

Along with logic and physics, the systematic study of ethics and moral psychology would have formed the final part of the curriculum. The students would have learned, above all, why virtue is the only good and vice the only thing that is bad, how all actions follow from what the Stoics called "inclinations" (*hormai*), why passions are misleading, and what it is appropriate or proper for us, as human beings, to do.

So logic, physics, and ethics were all represented in the school curriculum. The chief means of acquainting students with these fields was the study of classic Stoic texts, especially those of Chrysippus. A student would be set a chunk of one of these texts to study, and the next day it would be read out either by him or by Epictetus, and then one or both of them would explain the text, answer questions, and defend the content against the theories of rival philosophical schools (1.10.8, 1.26.1, 2.1.30, 2.14.1, 2.21.11, 3.21.6–7), or it might be opened up for general discussion (2.16.20). As well as this oral work, written work was required (2.6.23, 2.17.35, 4.4.17).

But even if all three parts of philosophy formed the curriculum that was taught in the school in the mornings, the basic thrust of the discourses, delivered in the afternoons, is ethical. In the discourses, Epictetus assumes and argues that logic and physics, and theory in general, are not goals in themselves, but they help aspirants gain the conviction that they should live life rationally and in accord with nature. Some Stoics held that all three branches of philosophy were equally important, but others contended that logic and physics were subordinate to ethics.[30] It looks as though Epictetus—or at least the Epictetus of *Discourses*—belonged to this latter group (see

1.8.5-6 and *Handbook* 52). The core curriculum consisted of all three branches equally, but in the discourses Epictetus asserts time and again that the work is pointless unless it changes a student's character and behavior. And this, he insists, is not something theory alone can do: it must be put into practice. Theory alone cannot bring *ataraxia* (peace of mind, tranquility, serenity); theory is not dispensable, but it alone does not make a philosopher.

His most forceful assertions along these lines concern logic and the study of Chrysippus's treatises. Quite a few passages give the impression that he dismissed logic and theoretical work in general as useless.[31] But he clearly did not think logic useless, otherwise it would not have constituted a third of the regular curriculum of his school. And so there are also passages, such as 1.7.12 and 1.17.8, where he argues for its usefulness and importance. This apparent contradiction can easily be resolved. What Epictetus is saying is that theoretical studies are useless on their own (1.29.35, 2.9.13–17, 2.16.20–21, Fragment 10). Meaning must be given to them by putting the ideas into practice, so that they take root and change your life, rather than just being clever bits of information that enable you to show off at dinner parties (e.g., 1.26.9, 2.19.8, 2.21.17). Theory is merely the preliminary to practice (1.26.3–4, 2.9.13–22, 2.23.46, 4.4.11, 4.4.30); hence throughout the discourses Epictetus offers advice about how to cope with the real world, and he talks in this context even about apparent trivia, such as how to eat or bathe properly. Practice enables one to digest theory and put it to work (2.9.18, *Handbook* 46.2, Fragment 16), while undigested theory is nothing but vomit (1.26.16, 3.21.1–6). "If you didn't learn the theory so as to be able to put it into practice, what was the point?" (1.29.35).

Transformation of character and behavior was the ultimate goal of Epictetus's teaching, then, not the mere imparting of information. "It isn't arguments that we're short of these days; books written by Stoics are full of them. What's missing is someone to put them to practical use, someone who testifies to the arguments by his actions" (1.29.56). Logic is not an end in itself; it is a tool, a measuring instrument (1.17, 3.26.19). The point of reading texts is to learn how to judge things correctly, and then to apply those judgments in real-life situations (1.4.18–24, 2.9.13–14, 2.17.29–33, 2.19.21–24, 3.21.23, 4.4.11–18).

So once in a while, after the regular classes were over, Epictetus tried to hammer home the importance of grounding and realizing the theory in daily practice. The audience for these impromptu talks, the discourses, were mainly students who were enrolled at the school, but there were more casual visitors as well (1.10, 1.11, 1.15, 1.19.26–29, 2.2, 2.4, 2.6.20, 2.14, 2.24, 3.1, 3.4, 3.7, 3.9, 3.24).[32] Some came with sincere questions, but Epictetus's fame had also made him something of a tourist attraction (3.9.14). Most of the students were rounding off their education by attending a school of philosophy, but some intended to become professional philosophers themselves (3.21).

On applying to the school, a prospective student was assessed by Epictetus (2.24, 3.1, 3.6.9–10). For the application to be accepted, the student had to be open-minded and willing to change (3.15.8–13, 4.2.2, *Handbook* 29.7). Epictetus would present the starting point of philosophy in perfectly general terms, not specifically Stoic (2.11). Any student who was accepted was first entrusted, at least in part, to the care of an older student (1.26.13), perhaps one of those who intended to make a career out of philosophy. The students would mostly have been in their late teens or early twenties, but some of the visitors were older. Epictetus may even have been visited by the emperor Hadrian in 125 or thereabouts; at any rate, the emperor certainly passed through Nicopolis and, given his love of all things Greek, it is hard to imagine that he did not visit the most famous contemporary teacher of Greek philosophy. Some of the talks were clearly delivered in some kind of classroom, and those would have been exclusively for students, but some were delivered in the open air,[33] and that is when Epictetus became available to casual visitors.

The students we meet in the discourses are all male. Only young men from the elite strata of society had the time and money for higher education in rhetoric and philosophy, so it is no surprise to find that Epictetus's students were generally well off. They assume the existence of enslaved people to wait on them (1.13.3, 1.18.19, 2.21.11, 3.19.4–5, 3.26.21–22); they have enough leisure time to travel as sightseers (1.6.23); they receive allowances from their parents (2.21.12–14); they frequent gymnasia, baths, and the elite dinner parties known as "symposia" (1.26.9, 2.4.8, 2.16.27–29, 2.21.14, 3.16.1, 3.16.14); when they leave the school, they expect to engage in the affairs of their city (2.10.10), to move in senatorial circles in Rome

(1.30, 3.3.15, 4.1.55), and even to hold high office and be close to the imperial court (1.25.26, 2.6.20, 2.23.38, 3.5.3, 3.14.11, 4.1.60, 4.1.94–95, 4.1.149, 4.1.173, 4.4.47, 4.7.23, 4.10.11, 4.10.18–21). The number of times in the discourses that Epictetus advises his students how to think of exile or execution suggests that they were the kind of people who might find themselves condemned by the emperor for political crimes (e.g., 2.19.17). Humankind had to wait many centuries for the ideal of universal access to education; in Epictetus's time it was almost entirely for the rich.

EPICTETUS AS A TEACHER

In Epictetus's day, there was no Stoic school as such—no particular person recognized as the head of the school or particular city where one went to study this brand of philosophy—so you became a teacher without official accreditation and made a living at it only if you became recognized as good at it. To claim that you were a teacher of Stoicism, you based your teaching firmly on the early Stoics and, above all, on the works of Chrysippus, the third head of the school in the third century BCE, who was its primary and most important theoretician. This is exactly what Epictetus did. Chrysippus is mentioned many times in the discourses, and his written work formed the basis of the curriculum.

Philosophy in Epictetus's time differed in certain respects from its modern counterpart. Modern philosophy is pursued in classrooms, seminars, and the written word, and much of it consists of analyzing abstract concepts and arguments, but much ancient philosophy, especially in the postclassical centuries, was philosophy to live by and practice daily. It was supposed to purge you from your base attachments and make you a better person. It was supposed to help you cope with difficulties you encountered and things that might disturb your equanimity, and so over the decades before Epictetus, certain topics—old age, death, anger, poverty, exile—were regularly discussed and analyzed, with a view to finding out how to cope with them. This therapeutic and consolatory philosophy is what Epictetus taught in the afternoons. Throughout *Discourses*, we find him encouraging his listeners to regard illness, death, and so on as "indifferents"—as things that should not trouble us or contribute in any way toward our happiness or misery.[34] His framework was Stoicism, and he was teaching in rivalry to Epicureans, Skeptics, and Cynics. He explicitly attacks Epicureanism and Skepticism (1.5, 1.23, 1.27.15, 2.20, 2.22.21, 2.23.20–22, 3.7), but along with many other Stoics, he thought highly of Cynicism, the most ascetic and radical of the philosophical traditions (3.22). All the schools agreed on the therapeutic aim of philosophy, so a student would attach himself to Stoicism not just because it was advertising its therapeutic effectiveness but because of what distinguished it from the other schools, its entire worldview. Moreover, unlike its chief rival, Epicureanism, Stoicism encouraged participation in public life,[35] and that would have been attractive to some students.

Over the centuries before Epictetus's time, then, philosophy had gone in two directions. High philosophy, as we may call it, was the impersonal presentation of often very subtle ideas and arguments; some of the work of the Stoics, for instance, on logic and epistemology is as challenging as philosophical work of any era. Low philosophy, on the other hand, was the attempt to make philosophy practical and accessible to the common man and woman. Both high and low philosophy were taught at Epictetus's school, as we have seen, but only his discourses remain, and in these Epictetus was focused entirely on therapeutic or low philosophy: on his students' ethical development, or in other words, on curing the erroneous judgments that were causing their attachment to the external world. His students were sick, and his teaching held the cure (2.21.15–22, 3.23.30–32); Epictetus is liberal with his analogies, but those based on the field of medicine are among the most striking.

Since Epictetus believed that everyone has the natural capacity to develop and perfect reason, which is the route to happiness, his teaching methods are designed to elicit that realization in his students and then to put it to work. He is always concerned to encourage students, or to eradicate their false beliefs, or to get them to accept advice. To these ends he naturally used argument, especially of a Socratic kind (question and answer), but also less rational and more rhetorical methods.[36] Most strikingly, he employed the shock tactics of reproof and abuse. He could be merciless even with some of the casual visitors (2.4, 2.14, 2.24, 3.7). He tears into members of his audience, serious students and laymen alike, exposing their pretensions, pricking the bubbles of their conceit and complacency, grounding them in reality. He addresses them as "slaves" or "wretches" and calls them "blind."[37] He makes it clear to his students that none of them is the ideal student that he would like to have (2.16.17, 2.17.29–30, 2.19.20–28, 3.6.4).

This abrasiveness is justified at 3.1.10–15: it is a philosopher's duty to make a potential student see the "disgraceful state" he is in. Epictetus *wanted* to upset his students. "If a philosopher's words fail to produce [the realization that the listener is in a bad way], they're lifeless, and the speaker's a corpse too" (3.23.28). One should leave the "doctor's office" in pain (3.23.30–32). The effective teacher is one like Musonius Rufus, who enables people to see their flaws (3.23.29). A good talk is one that makes a student "worried about himself" and determined to change his ways (3.23.37). Epictetus believed that every human being has an innate sense of "self-respect" (*aidōs*), close to our notion of a conscience, and tried to use that as a trigger to get his students to correct their lives. He also believed that all of us, whatever our circumstances, are innately programmed to form certain moral conceptions that give us, among other things, the ability to distinguish good from bad (see especially 1.22). These two beliefs meant that he placed the burden of the work on his students themselves. It was his job in the discourses to arouse in them the desire to undertake the work that was required for them to correct themselves. Work on oneself must take place not only in a school environment but, more importantly, at every moment of every day.

Epictetus comes across as a forceful personality, and the discourses are intense and fast-paced—so fast, occasionally, that it is hard to follow the train of thought. Sentences are short, even staccato. His Greek is colloquial (see the ironic comment at 3.9.14), conversational, and often powerfully expressive and metaphorical. Analogies abound from the natural world, and, like his hero Socrates, he employs homely examples to illustrate his points: the arts and crafts, games and sports, cracked jars, chamber pots, runny noses, ears of wheat, dinner parties, hunted deer. Anecdotes concerning famous people from the past demonstrate that people with political power are not as powerful as they think, and characters from myth and legend demonstrate that the events of their lives were due to faulty judgments. Socratic-like dialogue, often rapid-fire, is a common idiom, as he answers his own questions or puts objections into the mouths of imaginary interlocutors and refutes them.[38]

His tone of voice frequently changes, and we have to remember that originally these were live talks, some even delivered while strolling in the open air. The talks would have been accompanied by gestures, pauses, facial expressions, and other body language. Epictetus uses irony a lot, and without hearing him in person, it is sometimes hard to know whether or not a given passage is ironic. He argues logically less than he makes use of parallels, so the validity of many of his points depends on the validity of the parallels. The anecdotes, quotations, and examples leaven the serious subject matter, as do occasional flashes of humor (which can be quite acerbic: 2.20.29–30), but there are also considerable stretches of argument.

His constant and somewhat heavy-handed employment of imperatives and pointed rhetorical questions, peppered with insults, frequently makes him sound like a street preacher and turns his talks into harangues. His listeners must sometimes have felt pummeled by his relentless questioning and driving home of consequences, and his repetition of key points. But Epictetus was not claiming to be perfect himself. He is merely God's mouthpiece (3.1.36). He is capable of laziness (1.10.8, 12) and weakness (2.8.24), he has not achieved freedom (4.1.151), he does not altogether put theory into practice (*Handbook* 49), and in general there is still work to do (4.8.43, 4.10.13). Sometimes, when he is pointing out faults, he includes himself along with his students by saying "we" (e.g., 2.9.21, 2.16.2, 3.23.10, 4.5.36). All in all, the discourses bear the marks of a passionate and effective teacher.

STOICISM: A SKETCH

Epictetus was an orthodox Stoic. He introduced a few innovations, but they are changes in emphasis or terminology rather than substantial changes in doctrine.[39] To say that he was orthodox is to say that he looked back to the first founders of Stoicism in the third century BCE, especially Chrysippus. Sometimes he offered his audiences plain, commonsensical advice (this was also the specialty of his teacher, Musonius Rufus), for which no knowledge of Stoicism was needed (e.g., 2.11, *Handbook* 25, 33). But generally speaking, he is not fully understandable without some knowledge of Stoicism. Given the ethical thrust of *Discourses*, in what follows I shall focus on Stoic ethics and moral psychology, rather than on logic and physics.

The fundamental Stoic ethical tenet is that the only thing that is good and beneficial is moral virtue or human excellence, and the only thing that is bad and truly harmful is moral vice or imperfection. Everything else falls into the class of "indifferents," and it is careless talk to describe an indifferent as good or bad (as, for instance, Epictetus's interlocutors do from time to time [e.g., 1.22.12, 1.28.26–27, *Handbook* 24]). This is a radical thought, since it accuses almost all of us, along with our laws and institutions, of being misguided in our judgment of what is good and bad.

However, we cannot be completely indifferent to the external world. In the first place, it provides us with what Epictetus calls the materials on which we can practice living appropriately and virtuously. Virtue is a kind of craft knowledge, knowledge of "the art of living" (1.15.2–3, 1.26.7, 4.1.118), and consists in making skillful use of one's experiences, which are the raw material of virtue, as leather is a cobbler's raw material (e.g.1.4.20, 1.15.2, 1.29.2). In the second place, many indifferents can be rated on a scale of value, even if they cannot be rated as good or bad.[40] Their value depends on whether they are in accord with nature and aid an aspirant's progress toward virtue, and so consideration of the value of things allows us to draw distinctions within the infinite class of indifferents, such that some of them are "preferred indifferents," while others are "dispreferred."[41]

For example, health is neither good nor bad, since it is neither virtue nor vice; we can be happy whether we are healthy or unhealthy. But health is still to be preferred to sickness because it is natural to us as human beings, or in other words, it is the bodily condition that God established for human beings. Since happiness depends on our being in harmony with nature in all respects, and since health is our natural condition, it is a preferred indifferent. By the same token, moderate wealth and some degree of status in society are also preferred indifferents; not surprisingly, since they reflect our nature as human beings, Stoic preferred indifferents coincide to a considerable degree with the ordinary values of society. There may be special circumstances, recognizable by an advanced student, that make poverty or ill health right for you, but until you are in a position to recognize such circumstances, you had best follow the guidelines laid down by God in your nature. You should do all you can to acquire preferred indifferents for yourself and for others, but whether or not you succeed in doing so is a matter of indifference. It is playing the game well that counts, not winning or losing, because although an action is up to us, its consequences are not.

Preferred indifferents and the appropriate actions to take in relation to them are in accord with our nature; it is perfectly natural to prefer health to sickness, a moderate degree of wealth to poverty, and so on. So why not just call them good? Chiefly because they can be used for bad purposes and are not always good for us (3.20.4). But, more subtly, another reason is that we want things that are good, but we should not want an indifferent, though we may "select" or "choose" it. That leads to a further thought: if we want something, we feel pleasure when we get it, but pleasure is generally to be avoided anyway and is certainly an inappropriate response to something that is indifferent. If we find pleasure in anything that is not a genuine good, we are further mired in our attachment to the things of this world. Acting with virtue is pleasant in a way, the Stoics acknowledged, but one's focus should be entirely on the virtuous act, not on the incidental concomitant pleasure.

Following Socrates's lead, the Stoics held that virtue was knowledge. They recognized four primary virtues and analyzed each as a kind of knowledge. *Prudential wisdom* is knowledge of good and bad; *courage* is knowledge of what to fear and what not to fear; *moderation* is knowledge of what to pursue and what to avoid; *justice* is knowledge of what to give or not give others. Virtue is the goal, virtue is perfected rationality, and rationality is the only fundamentally human quality, one that we share with no other creatures but only with the gods. So a rational, virtuous person is one who has fulfilled his potential as a human being, and such fulfillment is both necessary and sufficient for happiness. Progress in Stoicism is not the acquiring of new faculties or powers but learning to trust and depend on your rational faculty.

If virtue is knowledge, it follows that behaving non-virtuously is a product of ignorance. As Socrates insisted, people always want what is good for them; the Stoics claimed that this was obvious from birth and was the fundamental human motivation, shared with animals.

So even people who behave non-virtuously think that what they are doing is good for themselves, and it is just that they are objectively wrong, because what they are doing will not fulfill them as human beings (that is, make them happy). They are denying their potential because they have a mistaken belief or judgment. Since all actions thus depend on beliefs, it is critical to get one's belief-set right.

What is more, reason, according to the Stoics, is the spark or splinter of divinity in us. Not only are the gods rational beings, but reason is God, the helmsman who steers the whole universe. The Stoics, again following Socrates, employed an argument from design to demonstrate this: the orderliness of the universe, and especially the fact that in many ways it seems to have been made for the good of humankind, shows that it was created and is maintained by a cosmic Reason. For instance, the world has been given a hierarchical structure, from inanimate objects such as stones, to plants, to animals, to human beings as rational creatures, and each lower level has been made to serve the higher ones. If the world is running on a program, there must have been a programmer.

It was a Stoic custom to describe the goal of human life as "living in accord with nature."[42] The final word is deliberately ambiguous between "Nature" (that is, Nature at large) and "nature" (that is, human nature), because they come to the same thing. Since universal nature is rational, and since the core of one's human nature is rationality, living in accord with one's human nature is at the same time living in accord with Nature. To live in accord with nature is to live a smoothly flowing life—and so we see how it dovetails with Epictetus's constant insistence that we can live a life free of impediment and constraint.[43]

What makes an act appropriate (*kathēkon*), and therefore the material for virtue, is whether it is in accord with nature and admits of rational justification. Thus self-regarding actions such as self-preservation are also appropriate, according to Stoicism, since they are in accord with human nature. But it is also in our natures to look out for other people: witness the way a mother takes care of her offspring. In this context the Stoics spoke of "appropriation" (*oikeiōsis*, literally "the process of making something one's own"), the natural preference all creatures have for what is good for themselves. A creature first and fundamentally appropriates itself to itself; hence the lifelong instinct for self-preservation (see 1.25.4). Gradually, in the case of rational creatures, the circle consisting of what it considers to belong to it, of what it appropriates to itself, widens to include family, friends, neighbors, fellow citizens, and eventually all other rational creatures, so that the motivation provided by appropriation is simultaneously self-regarding and other-regarding (1.19.13–14).[44] Hence, other-regarding virtues, such as justice, are good for the agent. So Epictetus insists that human beings are social creatures (e.g., 1.23.1, 1.28.20, 2.20.13, 4.11.1), by which he means that it is natural for us to take thought for others and to do them good. He repeatedly stresses other-regarding virtues such as kindness and trustworthiness.[45]

All the virtues arise out of natural human tendencies. Why, then, are there so many bad people in the world? Since badness is assenting to the wrong propositions, there are as many forms of badness as there are wrong propositions, but one widespread error is, according to the Stoics, the result of upbringing. Many people never grow out of the infantile trap of judging things in terms of pleasure and pain, and so their aim in life is to seek pleasure and avoid pain. Although it is a natural human tendency to want what is good for oneself, most people mistakenly think that what is good for themselves is pleasure, and that leads them to inappropriate and non-virtuous behavior. This argument lies at the root of Epictetus's distaste for Epicureanism: in claiming that pleasure was the goal of human life, it supports this mistaken, infantile view of the world.

The Stoics were determinists. The rational mind of God, or Nature, or Reason (all terms for the same thing), has a plan for the universe and is seeing it through. A virtuous person—every little virtuous act, in fact—is an assistant in the plan. Everything that happens is a link in endless networks of sequential causes. Yet determinism is a contentious doctrine. What scope does it leave us for freedom of action? What is the point of trying to behave as rational moral agents when we appear not to be free agents at all? Does determinism not encourage laziness, on the grounds that nothing we do makes any difference anyway?

The Stoics came up with a pretty good response. They claimed that, although everything has antecedent causes, things are not always necessitated by their antecedent causes. A cylindrical roller has the capacity to roll downhill. When someone pushes it, he has started it rolling, but he has not given it the capacity to roll, which is simply an attribute of what it is to be a cylinder. So, when an impression of some kind impinges on us, it is bound to make a mark, but we do not have to assent to it, nor do we all assent to the same impressions. The sight of a beautiful woman provokes lust in a heterosexual man who lacks self-control; her beauty is the antecedent cause, but his reaction is still up to him because it is part of his makeup, not part of the antecedent cause.

In effect, then, there are two kinds of causes, external and internal. The external cause is the person pushing the roller; the internal cause is the nature of the roller. The external cause is the impression that impinges on me; the internal cause is my individual nature or character. So, while the things that just happen to us are entirely predetermined, our responses to these events are not. They are up to us, and therefore things that are up to us, or within our power, or subject to our will, are the domain of morality and culpability. An important implication of the roller analogy is that if you change your disposition, you will react differently: the source of virtue is internal.

I have used the term "assent" a few times. This was a key term in Stoicism. When a mature, rational human being receives an impression (which may be an externally arriving sense-impression or something internally generated, such as a thought, a memory, a fancy, or a hope), it is assessed by the "command center," a Stoic term for the mind, seen as the faculty that processes impressions and initiates action. The incoming impression presents itself as providing information about the world; it comes in the form of a proposition. If the proposition seems true, the command center will assent to it (e.g., 1.18.1, 1.28.1–2, 3.3.2); otherwise, it will withhold assent or suspend judgment. If it assents, and if the proposition to which it assents contains value terms (such as "it is right for me to do such-and-such"), an "inclination" is generated that leads to action. Another way of saying this is that assent gives rise to desire, the belief that something is worth doing or pursuing. If we withhold assent, no inclination arises; in other words, the withholding of assent gives rise to an "aversion," the desire to avoid or not do something, or the belief that something is not worth doing or pursuing.

Non-rational animals, mad people, and children (under the age of about fourteen) differ in that action follows directly on the impression, without an act of assent. Adult human beings have a choice as to whether they react to stimuli and how they do so; this is precisely the choice Epictetus stresses with his emphasis on the will (as will be discussed in the next section). This element of choice is the result of our developing a disposition not to assent to immediate impressions. So when we see something that comes with the proposition "A snake: I'd better be careful," we do not immediately assent to this impression, and that creates a space for a further proposition, along the lines of, "I had the impression that there was something dangerous here, but it may not in fact be dangerous." To do this, we have to be alert and observant every moment of our lives because at every moment a host of impressions is crowding in on us.

It is immediately clear how assent is critical for morality.[46] Assent is a mirror of our moral being because we assent to what we think is true and will lead to our acting in an expedient way. Appropriate, rationally justifiable behavior results from assenting to impressions that correctly judge the value of the source of the impression, which leads one to desire to do the right thing. The soul, being material (even if made of refined matter), has the ability to move the body to action. So appropriate behavior takes place when the soul assents to correct propositions, leading to inclinations that initiate action in the real world.

The Stoics were as notorious in their own time as they still are for holding out as an ideal the state of *apatheia*, complete freedom from passion;[47] we still use the word "stoical" for rational calmness in the face of situations that would normally generate an emotional reaction. As a form of inclination, passions should be under our control; we should not get carried away by them. Given that inclination always leads to action, correcting passions should lead one to act more rationally and more in accord with nature.

The Stoics held that a passion was the product of a judgment formed by assent to an impression. Distress, for instance, is triggered by the judgment that something bad is present (4.1.84). To correct a passion, therefore, you have to correct your judgments. In the Stoic view, the problem with the passions is not just that they are likely to disturb the cool processes of rationality and therefore dislodge one from the path of virtue but that they are, or come with, mistaken beliefs about the value of whatever it is to which the passion attaches. They are a form of overhasty assent to a mistaken proposition. In short, the passions are in fact value judgments, and they assign importance to things that are indifferent.

If you are afraid of something, for instance, you think that it is going to be bad for you, when in fact, since it is neither virtue nor vice, it is neither good nor bad.[48] Even your child's death is actually a matter of indifference and should be treated as such. You love your child (as Epictetus acknowledges at 1.23.5), but you know that neither it nor your love for it are ultimate goals for a human being. Replacing incorrect and harmful propositions about death counteracts the tendency toward passion. So a Stoic is still aware of the passion and its propositional content ("My child's death is going to upset me") but withholds assent from it by substituting a more rational proposition ("I always knew that my child was mortal"). A dispassionate or impassive person, in the Stoic sense, is not an unfeeling zombie but rather someone who has changed his mind about the value of passions and who experiences only sane passions.

However, some feelings were acceptable. Thinking that an indifferent is good or bad is false; so a sage, who has no false beliefs but only knowledge, experiences no passion. He does, however, experience three "good feelings" (*eupatheiai*): volition (the rational pursuit of something), caution (the rational avoidance of something), and joy (rational elation). Each of the three has subspecies that were therefore considered acceptable passions: kindness/benevolence, which is constantly stressed by Epictetus, was considered a form of volition, as was friendliness; modesty and reverence were forms of caution; a sense of humor and cheerfulness were forms of joy.

EPICTETUS'S STOICISM

All these Stoic doctrines appear in the foreground or background of *Discourses*. Whether Epictetus emphasizes a particular aspect of Stoicism or plays it down, his purpose is always pedagogical and his focus always on practical application rather than theory. Above all, he wants to cut through the complexities of Stoic theory to the simplicity at its core, and he wants to show that, thanks to God's providential benevolence toward humankind, we have all the resources we need to change and achieve happiness and peace of mind. Whenever he treats topics such as death, exile, fear, or anxiety, he always explains how they fit into the big picture—how just a few basic principles justify the Stoic approach to such matters.

The simplest and most fundamental point is the one with which Arrian rightly starts the *Handbook*: "Some things are up to us and some are not." This was not a new idea in Stoicism. For instance, in claiming that the world we live in and the events we experience are all predetermined, facets of an endless chain of necessary causation, the Stoics left only our inner life as the sphere where we could exercise choice and be considered responsible. The occurrence of impressions is not up to us, but our response to those impressions is. What is different in Epictetus (as far as we can tell, given the loss of most earlier Stoic literature) is the emphasis he puts on this idea.

What does it mean to say that things are up to us? At 1.1.12, Epictetus summarizes the faculties that constitute the inner life of a human being: the "faculty of inclination and disinclination, of desire and aversion, or, to generalize, the faculty of making use of impressions."[49] By "making use of impressions," he means that we do not have to be taken in by appearances. We need to test them with our rational minds to see whether or not they deserve assent.[50] This message is strongly urged through constant repetition. If we assess impressions correctly, we will assign the correct value to everything we come across in our lives, which in turn means that we will feel only the right kinds of inclinations, and we will therefore act only in appropriate ways. It is entirely up to us to see that our actions are motivated by correct judgments and to avoid being motivated by bad judgments. And being motivated by correct judgments is the source of all that is good.

Whether or not we use impressions correctly is a matter of what Epictetus calls "will" (*prohairesis*).[51] The central importance he places on correct use of impressions led Epictetus to give will far greater prominence than his predecessors had. Will is the faculty that makes use of impressions (2.23.5–13). It gives us the freedom to assent or not to an impression; the root of the word *prohairesis* implies choice. In itself, will is unstoppable, in the sense that if we correct our beliefs and judgments, we will always get what we want and act as we intend. If it seems far-fetched to suggest that all our desires can be satisfied, it must be remembered that aspirants are supposed to reduce their desires (e.g., 3.9.22) until they want only good things, and that in any case they always act with reservation, tuning what they desire to their circumstances (see the note to *Handbook* 2.2).

Since nothing and nobody can either compel or hinder our will, it is entirely up to us to choose one action rather than another. Put this way (as at, e.g., 1.1.23, 2.15.1, and 3.26.24), it sounds as though Epictetus was getting close to the notion of free will—that is, the power to do otherwise. This is not quite right, however. Free will is something that everyone is supposed to have, but the kind of freedom Epictetus is talking about is hard-won, not an automatic aspect of what it is to be human. Since the will is free if it consists of a perfectly consistent set of true beliefs about the value of things, only the Stoic sage truly has freedom of will, while the rest of us compromise its freedom by enslaving ourselves, more or less, to the external world by false beliefs and wrong judgments. Freedom of will is something we should aim for, but it is not a birthright. And another reason for not equating Epictetus's concept of will with free will is that *prohairesis* is a rational faculty—or, rather, it is *the* rational faculty, operating with the mental faculties and activities that are up to us. So for Epictetus, will is not entirely free because he does not allow for our choices being determined by anything other than right reason, such as hopes or feelings. To Epictetus's way of thinking, will is free only in the sense that it is not constrained by external circumstances (4.1.128–131).

Since we are essentially rational, self-conscious, purposive, decision-making agents, *prohairesis* is equivalent to our moral selves (1.18.17, 1.19.8, 3.18.3, 4.5.11, 4.5.23, *Handbook* 9)[52] because it makes use of all the other faculties (2.23.6, 2.23.28); it is the sum of all the faculties that are entirely up to us and make each of us who and what we are. Will can even be bad or corrupted, if someone uses these faculties to identify with his body or external possessions rather than things that are up to us—that is, if he makes bad use of externals, misjudging their value (1.17.26, 1.25.1, 1.29.1, 2.1.6, 2.16.1, 2.23.19, 2.23.40, 3.5.2, 4.5.32, 4.12.7). Will can be ruined (4.4.23), and it may need purifying (2.23.40), improving (3.5.2), or freeing (1.4.18, 3.5.7). Everything we consciously do, however trivial, stems from our will and is therefore indicative of our moral character.

As part of this program of cutting through to the core of Stoicism,

Epictetus pushed into the background the controversial distinction between preferred and dispreferred indifferents—controversial because it allowed a critic to charge a Stoic with admitting that some indifferents might be good—and put greater emphasis simply on aspiring to virtue. "Things are good, bad, or indifferent. The virtues and everything in which the virtues play a part are good, and their opposites are bad. Indifferents are things like wealth, health, and status" (2.9.15). This perspective served his pedagogical purpose of focusing his students on their ultimate goal, without confusing them with possible distractions.

A final difference of emphasis between Epictetus and his Stoic predecessors is the significance he gives to our roles in life. He talks little of the four cardinal virtues because he substitutes talk of roles and of acting in accord with nature.[53] He does not say, for instance, that, as citizens, we should behave with justice toward our fellow citizens; he just says that we should act as citizens properly should. Since virtue is what is good, since we strive for the good in all things, and since we cannot help but be entwined in certain social relationships, we have to bring virtue to bear on those relationships.

I have a role as a human being, but I also have a role as a particular human being (3.23.4), and this role divides into numerous subroles because the particular person I am is also a son, a husband, a father, a citizen, and so on (2.10.1–14, 3.23.3–5, *Handbook* 30).[54] In addition, I must also adapt myself to the roles that fortune assigns me (Fragment 11), or that I choose after due consideration of my native abilities (1.6.37, 2.6.3, 3.22.7, 3.23.1–6, *Handbook* 29.5, 37). Epictetus never offers advice as to how to behave as a brother, say, or as a son. He assumes his students already know—in other words, it is the behavior sanctioned by Roman tradition or common humanity. Hence, for instance, he counsels deference to a father (2.10.7, *Handbook* 30).

In addition to talking about the plurality of roles that each of us has, he also talks about one's role in the singular (1.2, *Handbook* 37). He means the face or facade (that is the literal meaning of the Greek word for "role," *prosōpon*) that we present to the world—the part that we play on life's stage (the word also means "theatrical role," as in 1.29.46 and *Handbook* 17). He does not take this role to be something superficial but rather an aspect of our integrity, the kind of person we have chosen to be, or that fate has cast us to be, and a reflection of our true nature. In the terms of a pervasive metaphor employed by Epictetus, it is our station in life, where we have been posted by the divine commander in chief (e.g., 1.16.21, 1.29.39, 3.24.34, 3.24.95). But it needs training to acquire it (1.2.32, *Handbook* 33) and practice to stay true to it. It is what makes one unique, not just the same as all the other threads in the toga, as he puts it at 1.2.18 and 3.1.23. It therefore—and this is the underlying message of 1.2—has ethical implications, in that different people need to develop or tone down different aspects of their personality in order to act appropriately and progress toward virtue.

Whether Epictetus is talking about roles in the singular or plural, they have the same function: when it comes to making ethical decisions, we should refer to our roles. Whether or not you assent to an impression is determined in part by the kind of person you are or take yourself to be. Roles have consequences, and once we have accepted a role, we should accept as reasonable anything that follows from that role. Appropriate behavior is living in accord with nature or focusing only on things that are up to us, subject to our will (3.1.25–26), and treating all other human beings as kin—that is, with kindness and justice (e.g., 2.4.1–5, 2.9.1–7, 4.1.122). Along with his development of the concept of *prohairesis*, this "role ethics" is Epictetus's most distinctive contribution to Stoicism.

There is a tension in Epictetus's thought between the claim that even family members should be nothing to us (e.g., 1.1.14 and 3.3.5–7) and the frequently repeated claim that it is an aspect of morality to foster our relationships with family members and others (e.g., 2.14.8, 3.2.4, 4.4.16, 4.10.15). The solution is given by 3.3.8 (see also 2.17.19, 2.22.18–21). We maintain our relationships without thinking that father, brother, and other relatives and friends are the good. The good, our goal, is purely internal. If our focus is on the good, we can fulfill our duties toward our kin without being as "unfeeling as a statue" (3.2.4), but also without making the mistake of thinking that family members are ultimately that important. In the same way, we look after our bodies (1.2.37, 4.11, Fragment 23) while not identifying ourselves with our bodies.

As a teacher, Epictetus kept his focus on his students and their moral development. So he does not ban all passions, nor does he stress the remote ideal of the enlightened sage. He often talks in more or less everyday terms about everyday issues. He also—along with the other Roman Stoics—stresses the importance to the individual of social responsibility. He expects his students to engage not just with the political life of their communities but also with the everyday life of friendship, marriage, and parenting. This move was not incompatible with traditional Stoicism, but it represented a swerve or a shift of emphasis. If the earlier Stoics had claimed that true friendship can subsist only between and among people who are wise, the four Roman Stoics emphasized that, as rational creatures, *all* human beings are kin. You could say that in abandoning the more austere aspects of Greek Stoicism, they were substituting reality for utopia. That would be true, but at the same time all the Stoics of the Roman period retained what was at the heart of Stoic ethics—the insistence on training until the rational self was the source of all one's actions.

EPICTETUS ON PHILOSOPHICAL TRAINING

For Epictetus, philosophy was not just the construction of doctrinal systems but a way to meet life's contingencies with equanimity and to make use of them for self-improvement. Philosophy offers a glimpse of a better state, encouraging one to change, and then supplies the theoretical tools to understand what is involved in such work and the practical tools to progress toward that state. Philosophy is the way to gain expertise at the art of living. As with any art, it is not enough just to know the principles; one must also be able to put them into practice. As we saw earlier, Epictetus saw theory as a preliminary to practice, and specifically to the practice of virtue. But virtue, for a Stoic, was knowledge. Epictetus is therefore saying that knowledge does not come from reading and understanding theory but from putting that theory into practice. Only then will you transform information into knowledge and truly know what the books tell you.

Will, as we have seen, is the faculty that determines for each of us what we believe and so influences our activities: assent, inclination/disinclination, and desire/aversion. These, then, are the three faculties that need to be trained until they are "in accord with nature." At a number of points in the discourses, Epictetus outlines or refers to a training course designed for these three faculties (1.4.11, 1.17.22–24, 1.21.2, 2.8.29, 2.17, 3.2, 3.12, 3.21.23, 3.26.14, 4.1.69, 4.4.13, 4.10.13,

Fragment 27).[55] As several of these passages make clear, it is a progressive course: he consistently labels the three domains (as he calls them) "first," "second," and "third" (which is also called the "last" of the domains at 3.26.14), and he talks of moving on from one domain to the next (especially at 2.17.31–33). The first domain is that of desire, the second that of inclinations, and the third that of judgment or assent. Desire, inclination, and assent are the three areas of life where training is needed to make a person free and unconstrained by external hindrances. But the hindrances differ in each domain. The division of practical work into these three domains is original to Epictetus, his adaptation of Stoic material to practical training.[56]

People who have trained their desires (that is, brought them under rational control) will never fail to get what they desire (3.12.4) because they will have reduced their desires to reasonable levels and appropriate objects. They will have learned to properly apply their preconceptions about good and bad, and understood that if they direct their desires toward things such as health, fame, wealth, and the avoidance of death, they are bound to be frustrated. Since frustrated desire is the source of all the passions (e.g., 1.27.10, 2.17.17–18, 3.2.3), by eliminating desire for these things, people will gain control over their lives rather than be subject to their whims (1.1.31). Completion of this phase of the training will rid a person of false conceptions of good and bad, so that one wants only what is morally good and wants to avoid all that is morally wrong. Epictetus calls this phase of the training, the elimination of attachment to the external world, the most urgent (3.2.3) and says that mastery of it would make one almost a complete philosopher (3.14.10).

Since inclination leads to action, training the second domain is supposed to supply us with the tools to act appropriately in all our various roles. Having learned, during the first phase of training, that virtue is the goal in all life's circumstances, this second stage applies that lesson in the domain of our roles—that is, in our everyday lives. It teaches students to recognize and fulfill their duties toward parents, gods, the community, and so on.

So completion of training in the first domain brings inner tranquility (the elimination of frustration), and completion in the second brings appropriate outward behavior. Together they constitute the training of character, which is the field of ethics, as distinct from the third domain, which has to do with certainty of judgment. In terms of the Stoic theory of appropriation, in the first stage we replace our instinctive desire for things such as health with the understanding that these things are indifferent compared with virtue, and in the second stage we move from wanting to do good to ourselves to wanting to do good to others as well. We learn in the first phase to assess external things correctly, and that enables us to learn to act appropriately toward others in the second phase. At 2.14.8–9, Epictetus says that mastery of the first two domains makes one a true philosopher.

The third phase, the training of assent or judgment, is designed to enable us to assent only to true or beneficial impressions—to avoid being deceived, as Epictetus occasionally puts it (1.4.11, 3.2.7), even when "asleep, drunk, and in a black mood" (2.17.33; see also 3.2.5). For this phase, rigorous training in logic is required, since logic (in the capacious Stoic sense of the term) enables us to think clearly and transforms the true beliefs gained in the first two phases into secure knowledge. Now, as we have seen, logic, along with physics and ethics, formed part of the formal curriculum of Epictetus's school. But the point then was proficiency at argument (2.13.21), whereas the emphasis in this third phase of training is on observation of the way one's mind is working (3.2.5), so that one does not too readily give assent to impressions. The outcome will be that all one's ethical views, value judgments, and so on are coherent and consistent. This result will enable one to be unassailable in the first two domains (2.17.33). Thus completion of training in the third domain consolidates the moral progress we have made by mastering the first two domains.

Mastery of all three domains makes people "educated," in Epictetus's terms: they will always make correct use of their impressions (3.21.23).[57] It also fulfills the requirement, constantly stressed in the discourses, that ideally one should never be impeded or constrained. The first domain guarantees that one's desires will never be disappointed; the second makes one's inclinations unerring (1.19.2); the third makes one incapable of being deceived or carried away by impressions. Probably only a sage completes all three phases (3.2.1), and it would not be surprising if Epictetus, along with all other Stoics, doubted whether a sage could exist. Mastery of the three domains would make one an expert in the art of living, and, as any craftsman knows, improvement goes on for as long as one practices the craft; it is a lifelong, never-ending process.

Epictetus nowhere tells us the particular exercises that constitute this three-phase training course, but quite a few exercises are mentioned in the discourses, and I list some of them here.[58] Most of them can readily be assigned to one or another of the three phases.

General exercises:
1. To have at hand and to repeat to ourselves important theoretical principles and maxims until they have been absorbed (1.1.25, 1.27.7, 2.1.29, 3.10.1–5, 3.11.5, 3.24.103, 3.24.115, 4.4.29, 4.4.39, 4.12.7, 4.12.15; *Handbook* 1.5, 4, 16, 53; Fragment 16), and we can put them into practice on all occasions (1.4.20, 1.13.1, 2.1.29, 2.8.12–13, 3.10.1, 4.4.8, 4.8.20, 4.12.7–9).
2. To foresee possibilities, especially negative ones, either in general or at the start of the day, so as to be able to preempt disturbances (4.5.8, 4.6.34, *Handbook* 4, 12, 33.13, 21), and at bedtime to review with a critical eye the events of the day (3.10.2–3, 4.6.33–35).
3. To assess one's progress (2.18.12–18, 3.13.8, 3.25.1, 4.4.18, 4.4.46).
4. To act always with reservation, so that one is never thwarted (*Handbook* 2, 4, Fragment 27).[59]

Phase 1 exercises—that is, exercises that help us to see the indifference of everything except virtue and vice, until we no longer desire anything else:
1. To bring our bodily needs and desires under our control (3.13.21, *Handbook* 47).
2. To practice responding correctly to things, and if necessary to change habitual responses to the opposite responses (1.27.4–6, 2.16.1–3, 3.12.6–7, 3.13.21).
3. To undertake the gradual elimination of attachment to anything other than virtue (1.18.18, 3.13.20–21, 3.24.84–88; 4.1.111–14; *Handbook* 3, 12, 15, 26).

Phase 2 exercises—that is, exercises designed to manage our inclinations so that we always act appropriately and, ultimately, virtuously:

1. To look for the appropriate response in all situations (1.6.32–37, 1.24.1–2, 3.20.9–15, *Handbook* 10).
2. To check our instinctive inclination to act in ways that are pleasant by imagining the pleasure we will get from refraining from such actions and the sense of regret we will experience if we do not refrain (*Handbook* 34).
3. To ask ourselves what a completely virtuous agent such as Socrates, Diogenes, or Heracles would do when faced with a situation like the one we are faced with (1.29.57, 2.18.21–23, 4.1.152, 4.1.169–170, *Handbook* 33.12).

Phase 3 exercises—that is, exercises that train our faculty of judgment:

1. To pause and catch the act of assent before it happens, so that we can check whether the impression is something to which we really want to assent (1.20.7–12, 2.18.24–26, 3.3.14–17, 3.8.1–6, 3.12.15, *Handbook* 1.5, 20, 34).
2. To assess, before every decision, what it demands of us and whether we can actually see it through (*Handbook* 29.1–3 = *Discourses* 3.15.1–5).
3. To relabel and reframe situations in more positive ways (1.12.20–21, 4.4.24–6, *Handbook* 11, 43), such as seeing ourselves as parts of a whole (1.12.26, 2.5.25, 4.7.7).

Epictetus's work is truly valuable in preserving for us these sketches of the kinds of exercises that supported Stoic theory. They are all supposed to be daily exercises (2.16.27, 3.3.16, 3.8.1, 3.24.103, 4.1.111), and Epictetus also frequently tells his students to remember or bear in mind their precepts, to pay attention, and to observe themselves. To follow Epictetus's training regime, students needed to develop constant self-awareness, monitoring their internal states all the time (4.3.6, 4.9.16). These practical exercises were additional to studying the regular curriculum; theory and practice went on in parallel. We can see why the work as a whole—not just studying the regular curriculum, but also attending the impromptu talks that make up *Discourses* and practicing all the exercises—was considered arduous (1.2.32, 1.7.30, 1.11.40, 1.20.13, 2.21.14, 2.21.19, 3.15.11, 4.1.171, 4.8.35). Epictetus demanded a lot of his students, but there can be little doubt that if they put in the work, they would get the results he promised: freedom from all the emotional and other drawbacks of attachment to external things, a well-functioning and unstoppable will, and the ability to act appropriately and do good to others.

NOTES TO INTRODUCTION

1. For Marcus Aurelius, see R. Waterfield, *Marcus Aurelius, Meditations: The Annotated Edition* (Basic Books, 2021). For Seneca, see the seven volumes of translations by various hands published by the University of Chicago Press. For Musonius Rufus, see C. Lutz and G. Reydams-Schils, *Musonius Rufus: That One Should Disdain Hardships; The Teachings of a Roman Stoic* (Yale University Press, 2020).

2. Inscription: *Supplementum Epigraphicum Graecum* 47–1757. Anecdotes: Lucian, *Demonax* 55.

3. Origen, *Against Celsus* 6.2.

4. I owe this neat formulation to A. A. Long, "Epictetus," in *The Meaning of Life and the Great Philosophers*, ed. S. Leach and J. Tartaglia (Routledge, 2018), 79–86.

5. The Greek word, *eudaimonia*, literally implies "having one's inner being (or *daimōn*) in a good state" and is generally (but not entirely happily) translated "happiness." I have retained this translation, rather than "well-being," because "well-being" has no corresponding adjectival form. Greek philosophers generally agreed that *eudaimonia* was the goal in life, but they differed over what constituted it.

6. For an attempt to extract useful historical information from Epictetus's references to the imperial court and to historical personages, see F. Millar, "Epictetus and the Imperial Court," in *Rome, The Greek World, and the East*, vol. 2, *Government, Society, and Culture in the Roman Empire* (University of North Carolina Press, 2004), 105–19.

7. Suetonius, *The Lives of the Caesars: Nero* 49.

8. Suetonius, *The Lives of the Caesars: Domitian* 14.

9. For discussion, see J. Hershbell, "Epictetus: A Freedman on Slavery," *Ancient Society* 26 (1995): 185–204.

10. See E. Asmis, "The Stoics on Women," in *Feminism and Ancient Philosophy*, ed. J. Ward (Routledge, 1996), 68–92.

11. See J. Penwill, "Expelling the Mind: Politics and Philosophy in Flavian Rome," in *Flavian Rome: Culture, Image, Text*, ed. A. Boyle and W. Dominik (Brill, 2003), 345–68.

12. Nicopolis had been founded only about 120 years earlier by the emperor Augustus—its name and location celebrate his final victory over Antony and Cleopatra in the civil war—but he transferred the populations of numerous towns and villages to the new foundation. It was always intended to be a major

city in western Greece, and that is how Epictetus found it. Wonderful ruins remain and testify to the original splendor of the place.

13. A visit to Athens by Epictetus is attested by Philostratus, *Letters* 1.69.

14. C. Starr, "Epictetus and the Tyrant," *Classical Philology* 44, no. 1 (1949): 20–29, suggests that when Epictetus speaks of tyranny, he is thinking chiefly of the emperor Domitian. Although he was no longer emperor, he was the one who was responsible for Epictetus's banishment from Rome, and for the persecution and execution of a number of other philosophers and Stoically inclined public figures.

15. Toward the end of his life, he might have been supported by the emperor Hadrian: *Historia Augusta: Hadrian* 16. Philosophers were generally exempt from taxes, so that would have helped as well.

16. There were two strands to ancient speculation about Epictetus's lameness. In one, he was crippled by his cruel master; in the other, he was born lame. More recently, scholars have been inclined to think it might have been an affliction of his old age.

17. He was not asexual: in Fragment 23 he hints at sexual activity "when I was younger." Perhaps he chose a life of teaching over domestic comfort.

18. Another precedent for Arrian's compilation was the *Memorabilia of Crates*, written (according to Diogenes Laertius, *Lives of the Eminent Philosophers* 7.4) by Zeno, the founder of the Stoic school and a former student of the Cynic Crates.

19. Photius, *The Bibliotheca*, codex 58. But Photius is not always an accurate recorder of details. The Fragments are translated on pp. 353–365.

20. Plutarch, *Life of Cato Minor* 23.3.

21. At *Meditations* 1.7.8, Marcus Aurelius mentions that the person who turned him on to Stoicism, Quintus Junius Rusticus, lent him his personal copy of "Epictetus's *Discourses*." We have no way of knowing whether this was the *Discourses* as we have them, Arrian's compilation, or perhaps Rusticus's own notes. The former is the most likely option, but if the latter were correct, Arrian may have been able to get hold of Rusticus's and others' notes to aid his compilation.

22. If we assume that Arrian attended Epictetus's school for some months when he was a young man of twenty, c. 108, then what we have are talks from Epictetus's "late middle period"; we have no way of knowing whether his views or emphases changed in the last twenty years of his life. Arrian was probably writing up the discourses in the early 110s: A. B. Bosworth, "Arrian's Literary Development," *Classical Quarterly* 22, no. 1 (May 1972): 163–85. He went on to have a distinguished political career under Hadrian.

23. Epictetus himself had no reason to give his talks titles. Quite a few of the titles are somewhat careless or vague. They might pick out a relatively insignificant feature of the talk rather than the main topic: 1.13 is more about the correct treatment of enslaved people than "How to do whatever we do in

a way that pleases the gods"; there is not much about "the indispensability of logic" in 1.17; the title of 2.6, "On indifference," applies only to the first two sentences of the discourse; and so on.

24. The order is apparently random or, in some cases, triggered by minor factors. For instance, hypothetical arguments provide the link between 1.25 and 1.26. Wild beasts and sheep occur at the start of 2.9 and then again at the start of 2.10. The Master Argument is mentioned in 2.18 and then discussed in 2.19. The beginning of 2.24 features some reflections on the art of speaking, which was the main topic of 2.23. And so on.

25. However, for an attempt to argue that the first book, at least, is carefully structured, see P. de Lacy, "The Logical Structure of the Ethics of Epictetus," *Classical Philology* 38, no. 2 (1943): 112–25.

26. Epictetus's Stoicism has a strongly religious flavor (the same goes for many Stoics). His God, often called Zeus, was certainly the Stoic god—the supreme guiding, providential, immanent Reason of the universe (e.g., 1.1.17)—but he is not a mere abstraction. He hears prayers, for instance, and cares for each of us personally (1.12.3, 1.14, 1.17.27, 2.16.14, 2.18.29, 2.23.5–6, 3.22.53, 3.24.2, 3.26.28, 4.6.32), like a father (1.3.1, 1.6.40, 1.9.7, 1.13.3, 1.19.12, 3.22.82, 3.24.3, 3.24.15–16, 4.1.102); he deserves praise and gratitude (1.4.32, 1.16.15–21, 2.23.5, 3.26.30) and receives sacrifices (2.18.13). Our highest goals are to follow God, to please him, and to bear witness to him (1.9.16, 1.12.5, 1.29.47, 1.30.1, 2.19.26–27, 3.22.69, 3.24.114). Epictetus also speaks of gods in the plural, as though he were a traditional polytheist, but he saw them as servants of Zeus, carrying out his will, or perhaps as abstract forces of nature. Epictetus's Zeus is also a force of nature—*the* force of nature—but he is so personalized that he inspires devotion and gratitude: he has designed the world for the benefit of humankind, and he has given us the mental tools with which we can free ourselves. Despite some discrepancies (there is no room for grace in Epictetus's theology, for instance, nor is his god supernatural), it is not surprising that Epictetus was one of the few pagan authors (Seneca was another) whom some Christians found congenial.

27. This is the opinion of J.-B. Gourinat, *Premières leçons sur le Manuel d'Épictète* (Presses Universitaires de France, 1998), and J. Sellars, *The Art of Living*, 2nd ed.(Bristol Classical Press, 2009). But all such attempts are, in my opinion, refuted by G. Boter, "From *Discourses* to *Handbook*," in *Knowledge, Text and Practice in Ancient Technical Writing*, ed. M. Formisano and P. van der Eijk (Cambridge University Press, 2017), 163–99.

28. At any rate, we know from 1.10.8 that the formal teaching took place in the mornings.

29. What Epictetus means by these terms is obscure, but understanding is greatly aided by J. Barnes, *Logic and the Imperial Stoa* (Brill, 1997).

30. They came up with nice images to express this. If logic is the wall and physics the orchard protected by the wall, ethics is the fruit (Posidonius, frag-

ment 88 Edelstein/Kidd). Or, if logic is the skeleton and muscles, and physics flesh and blood, ethics is the soul (Diogenes Laertius, *Lives of the Eminent Philosophers* 7.40).

31. 1.4.5–17, 1.8, 1.17.13–19, 1.29.55, 2.1.38, 2.3.4–5, 2.13.26, 2.16.34, 2.17.27, 2.17.34, 2.17.40, 2.19.9–10, 2.23.41, 2.23.44, 3.2.6, 3.2.13–18, 3.21.7–10, 3.24.80–81, 3.26.13, 3.26.19, 4.4.14, *Handbook* 49, 52.

32. Epictetus also offers advice or assistance to people who seem not to be students of the school at 1.9.27–28, 2.2.17, 2.15.4–13, and 3.17.4–6.

33. There are occasional indications. At 3.21.4 he gestures toward a nearby house; at 4.11.10 he refers to the dirt of the ground where they are; at 4.1.26 he points to some birds; and at 4.1.113 he gestures toward a nearby gymnasium.

34. So, for instance, on death, following up the many entries in the index shows the several ways in which Epictetus urged his students to treat it as an indifferent: it comes to everyone; it is no more than the dissolution of our constituent elements; our bodies are not our selves; universal nature is good and death is a natural part of it—in other words, it is God's will, and we should submit to God in everything.

35. Despite a potential contradiction, since strictly it is a matter of indifference which party or faction has political power. But *Handbook* 24 argues that a person of integrity is of value to his community just because of his integrity, even without holding office or supporting this faction or that.

36. I suspect that this was closer to how he had taught in Rome: see the note to 2.12.25.

37. I cannot help thinking that it must have given him a certain satisfaction, as an ex-slave, to tongue-lash his upper-class students. In calling them "slaves," however, perhaps there was an underlying suggestion that all enslaved people were potentially free, like himself.

38. For the influence of Socrates on Stoicism in general, see A. A. Long, "Socrates in Hellenistic Philosophy," in *Stoic Studies* (Cambridge University Press, 1996), 1–34; and E. Brown, "Socrates and the Stoa," in *A Companion to Socrates*, ed. S. Ahbel-Rappe and R. Kamtekar (Blackwell, 2006), 275–84. For his influence on Epictetus in particular, see A. A. Long, *Epictetus: A Stoic and Socratic Guide to Life* (Oxford University Press, 2002), 67–94, and other items in the Recommended Reading section at the end of the book.

39. See the Introduction, 25–35, on *prohairesis* (will), roles, and the three domains of practical work, and see 1.22, 2.11.1–12, 2.17.1–13, and 4.1.41–45, with the note to *Discourses* 1.22.3, for his view of preconceptions. However, one always has to qualify assertions such as this. So little of the copious writings of the earlier Stoics has survived that it is hard to be certain what might count as novel in the later Stoics whose work survives.

40. This scale does not apply to all indifferents, some of which are completely and utterly indifferent, such as whether the number of hairs on my head is even or odd. Not everything has value, but many things do. For a thor-

ough study of indifferents, see J. Klein, "Making Sense of Stoic Indifferents," *Oxford Studies in Ancient Philosophy* 49 (2015): 227–81.

41. The distinction between preferred and dispreferred indifferents occurs implicitly rather than explicitly in Epictetus, but it underlies 1.1.26–27 and much of 1.2, for instance, where the choice is between indifferents such as life and death, or pain and pleasure. Otherwise, Epictetus generally operates with the bare distinction between things that are up to us and subject to will, and things that are not up to us, which are therefore indifferents (1.30.3). He argues that they cannot be good or bad, just because good and bad subsist only in will and the use to which it is put (e.g. 1.30.4, 2.16.1, 4.12.7, *Handbook* 32.1).

42. For a thorough study, see G. Striker, "Following Nature," in *Essays on Hellenistic Epistemology and Ethics* (Cambridge University Press, 1996), 221–80.

43. Living in accord with nature means chiefly two things for Epictetus: first, accepting all that happens, because everything has come from God, who is the same as nature; second, keeping one's will in its natural state of freedom—attentive not to the external world but to things that are up to us.

44. There is conflict here between aiming for one's own happiness and aiming for the happiness of the community, which Epictetus seems to have done his best to avoid by claiming that even when benefiting others, we are in fact aiming for our own happiness because our happiness lies in virtuous action and in preservation of our rationality. See S. Magrin, "Nature and Utopia in Epictetus' Theory of *Oikeiosis*," *Phronesis* 63, no. 3 (2018): 293–350. On the topic in general, see B. Inwood, "L'*oikeiōsis* sociale chez Épictète," in *Polyhistor*, ed. K. Algra, P. van der Horst, and D. Runia (Brill, 1996), 243–64.

45. We are social beings, but that does not mean that we should *need* others. We should strive for self-sufficiency (e.g., 3.13).

46. "Our whole life is entirely a matter of what we assent to and what not. For our beliefs are a matter of assent, and so are our desires, which are just special forms of belief. Ensuring our life will come out well is entirely a matter of giving assent when that is appropriate and refusing to give assent when it is inappropriate." M. Frede, *A Free Will*, ed. A. A. Long (University of California Press, 2011), 43.

47. I have translated *pathos* as "passion" rather than "emotion," because it is more literal (passion is something that happens to one as a passive, reactive subject, and so, according to the Stoics, is *pathos*) and, as the more forceful term, helps to explain why the Stoics saw many *pathē* as forms of psychic sickness. Epictetus talks less about the danger of passion than the advantages of being free from it: it disturbs one's peace of mind and compromises one's dignity as a human being. But he completely subscribes to the ideal of *apatheia*: if Odysseus wept, he must have been a poor, unfulfilled human being (3.24.18–20; see also 4.1.52).

48. The Stoics recognized four categories of passion: fear (*re* an apparent

bad in the future), longing (*re* an apparent good in the future), pleasure (*re* what we believe to be good and believe we now have), and distress (*re* what we believe to be bad and believe we now have). The other passions were regarded as subspecies of these four. It is less clear how they accommodated passions that are focused on the past, such as guilt and shame, but see M. Graver, *Stoicism and Emotion* (University of Chicago Press, 2007), 191–211. Whether we feel pleasure or distress, fear or longing, depends on whether or not we accept the way things present themselves to us, our impressions. Hence, in one and the same situation, one person will feel pleasure while another will not. But what makes reason weaker in one person than another? Largely upbringing, and so the Stoics stressed the importance of a good education. But upbringing was not the only factor: innate biases, inherited from parents and becoming habitual by repetition, also played a part. See Graver, *Stoicism and Emotion*, 149–71.

49. The fullest account is 4.1.68–75.

50. Hence making correct use of impressions is in accord with nature (2.23.42, 2.24.19, 3.3.1, 3.16.15, 4.10.8, 4.10.26) because it is a rational procedure and we are naturally rational.

51. For demonstration that "will" is the correct translation of *prohairesis* in Epictetus, see Frede, *A Free Will*. The word scarcely occurs in earlier Stoicism; Epictetus's main contribution to philosophy was to put it at the heart of his system. The word or its cognates occur more than 150 times in the discourses.

52. When Epictetus talks as if "I" and my will were separate (as at 4.12.12), he means only that will is not the totality of what I am. See also 2.8.21–23, 2.18.19, 4.6.7, and 4.9.13 for this manner of speaking.

53. This is the main thesis of B. Johnson, *The Role Ethics of Epictetus* (Rowman & Littlefield, 2014). On roles in Epictetus, see also A. A. Long, *Epictetus: A Stoic and Socratic Guide to Life* (Oxford University Press, 2002), 232–44.

54. Only a fully committed Cynic is free of the obligations that go with a plurality of roles because he has only one: 3.22.69.

55. These are just the passages that outline the threefold training course. But on all the dozens of occasions when Epictetus talks about getting our desires right, he is implicitly talking about the first domain; likewise for all the times he talks about correctly directed inclinations and our roles in life (the second domain), and assent and correct judgment (the third domain). The three domains have been widely discussed; the most useful studies are E. Asmis, "Choice in Epictetus' Philosophy," in *Antiquity and Humanity*, ed. A. Collins and M. Mitchell (Mohr Siebeck, 2001), 392–406, and Long, *Epictetus*, 112–18 (with 126–27).

56. The word I have translated "domain" (*topos*) is occasionally translated "field of study." This is misleading, because the domains are concerned with practice, not theory.

57. "Educated" is thus a synonym for "philosopher." This is the Platonic

conception of the function of education: to turn the mind away from the sensible world and toward the proper objects of a philosopher's attention.

58. The references I supply in what follows should not be taken to be comprehensive because the emphasis on practice over theory underpins the discourses in their entirety, and every entry in the *Handbook* can be read as recommending some exercise or other. But following up the references I have given will make it easier for readers to spot the same or similar notions in their own reading.

59. These are the only extant passages that explicitly refer to reservation, but it underlies the idea that we should only want to happen what actually happens: *Handbook* 8, *Discourses* 1.12.15, 3.4.11, 4.1.89, 4.1.99.

Handbook

1

[1] "Some things are up to us and some are not. Up to us are judgment, inclination, desire, aversion*—in short, whatever is our own doing. Not up to us are our bodies, possessions, reputations, public offices— in short, whatever isn't our own doing.* [2] Moreover, the things that are up to us are naturally free, unimpeded, and unobstructed, while the things that aren't up to us are weak, enslaved, subject to impediment, and not ours.* [3] So remember this:* if you regard things that are naturally enslaved as free, if you regard things that are not yours as yours, you'll be obstructed, dejected, and troubled, and you'll blame both gods and men. But if you regard as yours only what is yours, and as not yours only what is not yours, which is the way things are in reality, no one will ever constrain you, no one will impede you, you'll blame no one, you'll reproach no one, you'll never act reluctantly, no one will harm you, and you'll have no enemies, because you'll never suffer harm.

[4] "In setting yourself such great goals, then, bear in mind that no moderate effort is required as you set about attaining them. You'll have to let some things go altogether and postpone others for the time being. But if you want not only these great goals but also political power and wealth, the chances are that, in aiming at the former, you won't get even the latter; and you'll certainly fail to get the former,* which are the only things from which we get freedom and happiness. [5] So take up the practice right now of telling every disagreeable impression, 'You're an impression, and not at all what you appear to be.' Then go on to examine it and assess it by these criteria

of yours, and first and foremost by this one: whether it has to do with the things that are up to us or the things that are not up to us. And if it has to do with the things that are not up to us, have at hand the reminder that it's nothing to you."

2

[1] "Remember that desire holds out the prospect of getting what you desire, and aversion the prospect of not experiencing what you want to avoid, and that the person who fails in his desire suffers disappointment, while the one who experiences what he wants to avoid suffers misfortune. So if you try to avoid only things that are contrary to nature among the things that are up to you, you'll meet with none of the things you want to avoid, while if you try to avoid illness or death or poverty, you'll be miserable. [2] Withdraw aversion, then, from everything that isn't up to us and redirect it to things that are contrary to nature among the things that are up to us.* As for desire, abolish it altogether for the time being,* because if you desire something that isn't up to us, you're bound to become miserable, and because none of the things that are up to us, that it would be right for you to desire, are yet within your reach. Make use only of inclination and disinclination,* but do so with a light touch, with reservation, and with detachment."*

3

"When faced with anything you find attractive, useful, or lovable,* remember to tell yourself what kind of thing it is. Start with the least important things. If it's a jug you like, say, 'I like a jug,' because then you won't be upset if it gets broken. If you kiss a child of yours or your wife, tell yourself that you're kissing a human being, because then you won't be upset if they die."*

4

"Whenever you're about to start on some activity or other, remind yourself of its characteristic features. If you're going out to bathe, rehearse in your mind what typically happens in a bathhouse—getting splashed and jostled and abused and robbed. It's safer to set about an activity if you tell yourself: 'I want to bathe *and* to keep my will in accord with nature'—and so on for every activity. Then, if something happens that obstructs your bathing, you'll have at hand the reminder that 'That wasn't the only thing I wanted; I also wanted to keep my will in accord with nature. And I won't be doing that if I resent what's happening.'"*

5a

"People are troubled not by things but by their judgments about things. Death, for example, isn't frightening, or else Socrates would have thought it so.* No, what frightens people is their judgment about death, that it's something to fear. So whenever we're obstructed or troubled or distressed, let's blame no one but ourselves—that is, our judgments."

5b

"Blaming others when things are going badly for him is what an uneducated person does. Blaming himself is what a partially educated person does. Blaming neither others nor himself is what a fully educated person does."*

6

"Don't take pride in any distinction that isn't your own. If a horse were proudly to say 'I'm beautiful,' that would be acceptable. But when you proudly say, 'I own a beautiful horse,' you must realize that what you're taking pride in is a *horse's* good quality. So what is yours? Making use of impressions. And so, when you're in accord with nature in the use you make of impressions, that can be a source of pride, because then you'll be taking pride in something good that's yours."

7

"Suppose you're traveling by sea and the boat puts in somewhere, and you disembark to get some water. While you're at it you might also pick up a bit of shellfish and a few bulbs,* but you have to keep your mind fixed on the boat and pay constant attention in case the captain calls you back, and, if the call comes, you have to leave all those things behind to avoid being tied up and hoisted on board like the sheep.* The same goes for life too. Suppose you've been given, not bulbs and shellfish, but a wife and child. All well and good, but if the captain calls, run to the boat, leaving all those things behind, without paying them any mind. And, if you're elderly, you also shouldn't ever stray far from the boat, in case the call comes and you get left behind.""*

8

"Instead of wishing that things would happen as you'd like, wish that they would happen as they do, and then you'll be content."

9

"Illness may impair the body, but it doesn't impair the will unless the will wishes it. Lameness is an impairment of the leg, but it doesn't impair the will. Whatever happens to you, tell yourself this and you'll find that it's always something else that's impaired, not yourself."

10

"In every situation, remember to turn to yourself and try to find what means you have for dealing with it. If you see an attractive man or woman, you'll find that self-control is the appropriate faculty. If you're in pain, you'll find it to be fortitude. If someone's maligning you, you'll find it to be patience. If you make this your habitual practice, you won't be carried away by your impressions."

11

"Never say 'I've lost it' about anything, but 'I've returned it.' Has your child died? It has been returned. Has your wife died? She has been returned. Has your estate been confiscated? So that too has been returned. 'But the person who confiscated it is a bad man.' What difference does it make to you whom the donor used as the agent of its return? As long as they're in your charge, treat them as things that belong to someone else, as travelers treat an inn."

12

[1] "If you want to make progress, discard thoughts such as 'If I neglect my affairs, I'll have nothing to eat' and 'If I don't punish my slave, he'll turn out badly.' It's better to starve to death without distress and fear than to live in affluence with a troubled mind, and it's better for your slave to be bad than for you to be unhappy. [2] Start with trivial things, then.* A little olive oil is spilled, a little wine is stolen. Tell yourself: 'This is the price I pay for equanimity and peace of mind. Nothing comes for free.' And when you call for your slave, bear in mind the possibility that he might not respond, or that he might respond but do something quite different from what you want.* But he's not important enough for your peace of mind to depend on him."

13

"If you want to make progress, put up with being thought foolish and simpleminded about outward things. Don't yearn to be regarded as any kind of expert. Even if others take you to be a person of some importance, doubt yourself. For it's not easy, believe me, to keep your will in compliance with nature and also to secure external things for yourself. If you care about the one, you're bound to neglect the other."

14a

"It's foolish to want your children, your wife, and your friends to live no matter what, because you're wanting things that aren't up to you to be up to you, and things that aren't yours to be yours. By the same token, it's stupid to want your slave not to do wrong, because that's wanting badness not to be badness but something else. But if you want to get what you desire, that's in your power. So confine your efforts to what's in your power."

14b

"An individual's master is the person who has the power of procuring for him or denying to him what he wants or doesn't want.* So anyone who wants to be free must neither want nor try to avoid anything that's up to others. Otherwise, he's bound to be unfree."

15

"Remember that you ought to behave in life as you do at a dinner party. Something is making the rounds and comes to you: reach out your hand and modestly take some of it. It moves on: don't hold it back. It hasn't arrived yet: don't project your desire onto it in advance, but wait your turn. That's how to behave toward children, wife, high offices, wealth. Then you'll deserve to dine with the gods someday. And if you don't even take these things when they're offered to you but scorn them, then you won't only dine with the gods but share their rule. It was by acting like this that Diogenes, Heraclitus,* and others like them earned the right to be and be recognized as godlike men."*

16

"Whenever you see someone† weeping out of grief for the departure of a child or because he's lost some property, make sure you don't get carried away by the impression that his external circumstances really are bad. Instead, have at hand the reminder that 'It's not what's happened that's distressing him (otherwise it would distress everyone), but his judgment about what's happened.' Don't hesitate, however, to sympathize with him verbally, and even to mourn along with him, if that is what the occasion calls for. But make sure that you don't mourn inwardly as well."*

17

"Remember that you're an actor in a play that is just as the producer wants it to be. If he wants it short, it's short; if he wants it long, it's long. If he wants you to play a beggar, see that you play even this part proficiently—or a cripple, or a ruler, or a nobody. It's your job to act the role you've been assigned well, but the role was chosen by someone else."*

18

"When a raven croaks ominously,* don't let the impression carry you away, but immediately draw a distinction in your mind and say: 'None of these omens have any significance for me, but only for my body, my property, my reputation, my children, or my wife. But every omen is propitious for me if I so wish, because, whatever the outcome, it's up to me to benefit from it.'"

19a

"You have the potential to be invincible. All you have to do is never enter a contest where victory isn't up to you."*

19b

"When you see someone being preferred for an official position ahead of you, or possessing great power, or in general enjoying high status, make sure that you never get carried away by the impression and think him fortunate. If the essence of goodness is one of the things that's up to us, there's no room for envy or jealousy, and you won't wish yourself to be a praetor, a senator, or a consul, but a free man. And there's only one route to that, which is regarding things that aren't up to us as unimportant."

20

"Remember that what's making you feel insulted isn't this person's rudeness or that one's blows, but your judgment that they're insulting you. Whenever someone irritates you, then, realize that it's the belief that's irritating you. It follows that the first thing to do is to try not to be carried away by the impression. Once you pause and bide your time,* you'll find it easier to control yourself."

21

"Make it a daily practice to picture to yourself death, exile, and everything else that seems terrifying—especially death. Then you'll never have a contemptible thought or crave anything too much."

22

"Anyone with philosophical aspirations must immediately accept the fact that he's going to meet with a lot of ridicule and mockery. 'Look who's back!' they'll say. 'And now he's a philosopher all of a sudden!' And 'How did he get so hoity-toity?' You mustn't act superior, then, but hold fast to the things that seem best to you, knowing that where you are is where you've been assigned by God. And remember that if you keep this up, the people who formerly mocked you will come to admire you. But if you let them get the better of you, you'll make yourself doubly ridiculous."

23

"If you should ever find yourself turning outward because you want someone to think well of you, you can be sure that you've lost your bearings. Be satisfied, then, with always being a philosopher. And if you also want to be thought to be one, you don't need anyone else but yourself to think so."*

24

[1] "Don't distress yourself with thoughts such as 'I shall live a life without public honors, a complete nobody.' Even supposing that lack of honor is a bad thing..."

"Which it is."†

"...no one other than yourself can be responsible for your being in a bad state, just as only you can be responsible for your being in a shameful state. Now, it's not up to you to be appointed to public office or invited to a banquet, is it?"

"Of course not."

"Therefore, if dishonor is bad, this can't constitute being dishonored, can it? Moreover, you won't, of course, be a nobody everywhere, seeing that the only place where you have to be is where things are up to you, and there it's possible for you to be number one."

[2] "But I won't be in a position to help my friends."†

"What do you mean by that? They won't receive any cash handouts from you and you won't get them Roman citizenship. But from where did you get the idea that these are among the things that are up to us, not someone else's doing? And can anyone give anyone else something that he himself doesn't have? [3] 'Get money, then,' someone says, 'so that we can have some too.' If I can get it while retaining my self-respect,* trustworthiness, and high-mindedness, show me the way and I'll get some. But if you're asking me to lose my good qualities so that you can get things that aren't good, you can see how unfair and unfeeling you're being. What would you rather have, money or a trustworthy and self-respecting friend? Better for you to take me as I am, without asking me to act in ways that will cause me to lose these qualities."

[4] "But my country will be deprived of all the help I could have given it," he said.

"Again, in this regard too, what kind of help do you mean? You won't have provided it with porticoes or bathhouses, but so what? I mean, the blacksmith doesn't supply its footwear or the cobbler its weaponry. It's enough if everyone does their own job.* And if you were to equip it with another trustworthy and self-respecting citizen, wouldn't you be doing it good?"

"Yes."

"So you wouldn't be of no use to it either."

[5] "So what position shall I hold in it?"

"Any position you can hold while at the same time preserving your trustworthiness and self-respect. But if in your desire to do it some good you lose those qualities and end up untrustworthy and with no sense of shame, what use would you be to it?"

25

[1] "If someone has been preferred to you at a banquet or a reception line or in being called on for advice, you should be pleased at his success, if these accolades are good to have. And if they're bad,

don't be angry that the success wasn't yours. And remember that you can't think you deserve an equal share unless you act the same way as others do in pursuit of things that aren't up to us. [2] If someone doesn't regularly make his way to a patron's door,* or join his retinue, or sing his praises, how can he have the same share as someone who does all these things? It would be unfair and greedy of you not to pay the going price for these distinctions and to want to get them for nothing. [3] How much does a head of lettuce cost? Let's say an obol. So if someone pays the obol and gets a lettuce, while you don't have a lettuce because you haven't paid for it, you shouldn't think that you have less than him. After all, although he has the lettuce, you have the unspent obol. [4] It's the same for the accolades we're talking about. You weren't invited to someone's banquet? That's because you didn't give the host the price he demands for the meal. He sells it for flattery, for service. Pay the going price, if it's in your interest to do so. But if you want to have the goods without paying for them, you're being greedy and stupid. [5] Do you have nothing, then, in place of the dinner? Well, what you've gained is that you didn't flatter the man you didn't want to flatter, and didn't have to suffer the people at his doorway."

26

"It's possible to understand what nature wants from situations where we're no different from other people. For example, when a slave breaks someone else's cup, we're instantly ready to say 'These things happen.' So when it's a cup of yours that gets broken, appreciate that you should have the same attitude as when it's someone else's cup. Transfer the principle to things of greater importance. Has someone else's child or wife died? There's no one who wouldn't say 'So it goes.' But when it's one's own child or wife who's died, the automatic response is 'Oh, no!' and 'Poor me!' It's essential to remember how we feel when we hear of this happening to others."

27

"Just as a target isn't set up in order to be missed, so also badness isn't a natural feature of the world."*

28

"If someone gave your body into the keeping of a passerby, you'd be furious. But you give your mind into the keeping of any random person, so that, if he maligns you, it becomes troubled and confused. Doesn't this make you feel ashamed?"

29*

[1] "In every project you undertake, consider what preliminaries are required and the consequences before proceeding to act. Otherwise, you'll make an enthusiastic start, because you won't have given any thought to what comes next, and then later you'll shamefully† abandon the project when faced with some of the consequences. [2] You'd like to be a victor at the Olympic Games? Good heavens, so would I! That would really be fine! But consider the project from start to finish before setting about it. You have to be disciplined, maintain a strict diet, give up sweet pastries, undergo a strict training regime, exercise regularly every day however hot or cold it may be, refrain from cold drinks, drink no wine except when prescribed. In short, you have to submit to a trainer as you would to a doctor. Then, during the contest, you have to wield a spade,*† risk dislocating a wrist or spraining an ankle, swallow a lot of sand, possibly get flogged,* and, as if all that wasn't enough, possibly suffer defeat as well.

[3] "Once you've taken all this into consideration, go and compete if you still want to. If you don't, your behavior will be comparable to that of children, who at one moment pretend they're wrestlers and at another gladiators, then they're blowing trumpets, and then they're actors in a play. That's what you're like as well: at one moment an athlete, at the next a gladiator, then an orator, then a philosopher—without committing yourself wholeheartedly to anything. Like an ape, you imitate every passing thing you see, and one thing after another attracts you. You don't think through any of your projects or look at them in the round; you act without purpose and without really wanting anything.

[4] "This is no different from how some people, after seeing a philosopher and hearing one of them speaking as persuasively as Euphrates* (not that anyone can really speak like him), want to take up

philosophy themselves. [5] Man, first consider what kind of venture it is and then your own nature, to see if you've got what it takes. You'd like to be a pentathlete or a wrestler? Look at your arms, your thighs, your loins. Different people are naturally suited for different things. [6] Do you think that, doing what you do now, you can <be a philosopher? Do you think you can>* eat and drink as you do now, or get angry or irritated as you do now? As a philosopher, you have to go without sleep, work hard, and withdraw from friends and family; you'll find yourself sneered at by slaves, mocked by everyone, and inferior in everything—in honor, in political power, in the courts, and in every worldly enterprise. [7] Once you've taken all this into consideration, see if you want to exchange these external things for equanimity, freedom, and peace of mind. And if you don't, steer clear of philosophy. Don't act as children do and be a philosopher today, a tax collector tomorrow, then an orator, and then an imperial procurator.* These things don't fit well together. You must be one person, whether good or bad. You have to choose between cultivating your† command center* or the outside world—between exercising your ingenuity on inner things or outer things, or in other words between taking up a stance as a philosopher or as a man of the world."

30

"The actions it's appropriate for us to take* are generally given by our relationships.* He's a father: this means that we have to look after him, let him have his way in everything, and put up with his rebukes and beatings. 'But he's a bad father.' Do you really think you have affinity only for a good father, and not just for a father? Is your brother doing you wrong? Then don't let that affect your stance toward him. Don't think about *his* behavior but about what you can do to keep your will in accord with nature. After all, no one can harm you unless you let him; you'll have been harmed only when you believe yourself to be harmed. In this way, then, if you get into the habit of considering your relationships, you'll learn from a fellow citizen, from a neighbor, from a commanding officer what actions it's appropriate for you to take."

31

[1] "You should know that the most important aspect of piety toward the gods is having correct beliefs about them—that they exist, and that they govern the universe well and justly—and the second most important thing is to have set yourself to obey them, or in other words to submit and willingly accommodate yourself to everything that happens, knowing that it's being brought about by a flawless intelligence. In this way, you'll never either criticize the gods or accuse them of neglecting you. [2] But it's impossible for this to happen unless you detach goodness and badness from things that aren't up to us and locate them only in things that are up to us. You can be sure that if you believe anything that isn't up to you to be good or bad, it's absolutely inevitable that, when you fail to get what you want and meet with what you don't want, you'll blame and curse those who are responsible. [3] The point is that it's natural for every creature to flee and turn away from things that it takes to be harmful and what is responsible for them, and to pursue and value beneficial things and what is responsible for them. So it's as inconceivable for anyone who thinks he's being harmed to welcome what he believes is harming him as it is impossible for him to welcome the harm itself. [4] That's why even a father is maligned by a son when he doesn't let the boy have something that he judges to be good; and Eteocles and Polynices were the product of the belief that sole rule is a good thing.* It is also why farmers curse the gods, as do sailors, traders, and men who've lost their wives and children. Self-interest and piety are inextricably linked.* So whoever takes care to have the proper desires and aversions is at the same time taking care to be pious. [5] But there's no one for whom the traditional practices of pouring libations, performing sacrifices, and offering first fruits are inappropriate, if he carries them out after purifying himself, not in a perfunctory or slipshod manner, and without either being stingy or spending beyond his means."

32*

[1] "Whenever you consult a seer, remember that, although you don't know what future will be predicted (that's what you've gone to find

out from the seer), you're already in a position, if you're a philosopher, to know what *kind* of future it will be. I mean, since it's something that isn't up to us,* there can be absolutely no doubt that it'll be neither good nor bad. [2] So don't bring your desires and aversions to the seer (otherwise you'll approach him trembling with anxiety), but go to him in the knowledge that any outcome, whatever it may be, will be a matter of indifference and nothing to you. The point is that you'll be able to make good use of it and no one can stop you doing so. Approach the gods with confidence, then, regarding them as counselors, and from now on, whenever you've been given a piece of advice, remember whom you've accepted as your counselors and whom you'll be ignoring if you don't take the advice.

[3] "Have recourse to divination in a way that would meet Socrates's approval*—that is, for cases where the whole purpose of the inquiry is to learn what the future holds, and neither reason nor skill of any kind supplies one with the resources to find out about the matter in question.* So, when you have to share the risk faced by a friend or your country, don't expect divination to tell you whether you *should* share the risk. I mean, even if the seer warns you that the omens are unfavorable, clearly portending death, the mutilation of some part of your body, or exile—nevertheless, reason requires that, even in the face of such risks, you should stand by your friend and play your part at this time of danger for your country. Pay attention, then, to the greatest seer, Pythian Apollo, who threw out of his temple the man who failed to help when his friend was being killed."*

33

[1] "Starting now, prescribe a certain character and form for yourself which you'll maintain both when you're by yourself and when you're with other people.*

[2] "Keep silence for the most part, or speak only when necessary and briefly. On those rare occasions when the situation requires you to say something, speak,† but not about just anything—not about gladiatorial shows, horse races, athletes, food, or drink, the ubiquitous topics of conversation. Above all, don't talk about other people: don't criticize them, praise them, or compare them to others.* [3] If you can, redirect your conversation and that of the people you're with

onto an appropriate topic, but if you happen to find yourself alone among people who are of a different kind than you, remain silent.

[4] "Laugh little—that is, at few things and discreetly. [5] Avoid swearing oaths altogether, if that's possible, or at least as much as you can.* [6] Steer clear of parties where the guests are outsiders and non-philosophers. But if you find yourself at one, take great care not to slip back into unphilosophical ways. After all, you can be certain that anyone who brushes against a companion who's dirty is bound to get dirty, even if he happens to be clean.*

[7] "In things relating to the body, such as food, drink, clothing, housing, and household staff, limit yourself to what satisfies your basic needs, and cut out everything that's pretentious or self-indulgent. [8] As for sex, keep yourself as chaste as possible before marriage, and if you do engage in it, keep it within conventional bounds. But don't abuse or criticize those who are sexually active, and don't advertise your own abstinence all over the place.

[9] "If you're informed that someone or other is speaking ill of you, don't defend yourself against the allegations, but respond by saying: 'Well, he must be unaware of my other faults, otherwise these wouldn't have been the only ones he mentioned.'

[10] "You shouldn't feel obliged to go often to the public games, but if you find yourself there, make it clear that you favor no one except yourself. By this I mean that you should want only what happens to happen and want only the winner to win, because then you won't be frustrated. But refrain altogether from shouting and laughing at anyone, or getting overexcited. And after you've left, don't discuss what happened at any length, because that kind of thing makes people think that you found the show admirable. Confine yourself to bringing up those experiences that were relevant to your own moral improvement.*

[11] "Don't go casually, without having some purpose, to people's public readings and lectures, but if you do go, preserve your dignity and self-possession, while making sure at the same time that you don't give offense.

[12] "When you're about to meet someone, especially someone thought to be important, ask yourself what Socrates or Zeno would have done in this situation, and then you won't be at a loss as to how to make appropriate use of the occasion. [13] And when you go to call

on someone high and mighty, tell yourself that you won't find him at home, that you'll be shut out, that the door will be slammed in your face, and that he won't take any notice of you. If, despite all this, it's appropriate for you to go, then go; put up with what happens and never tell yourself that it wasn't worth so much aggravation. That's what a non-philosopher would do, someone who misconceives the external world.

[14] "In company, avoid frequent and excessive mention of your own activities and ventures. It may be enjoyable for you to talk about your ventures, but it's less enjoyable for others to hear what's happened to you. [15] Also, don't try to be funny. It's a slippery slope that easily descends into vulgarity, and at the same time it's a good way to lessen the respect you receive from those around you. [16] It's also dangerous to lapse into lewdness. When anything like that occurs, if the opportunity arises, you should even scold the person who introduced it into the conversation. If you can't do that, you should at least demonstrate by your silence, blushing, and frowning that you find what's been said distasteful."

34

"Whenever an impression of a pleasure occurs to you, make sure, just as with all other impressions, that you don't get carried away by it. Let the thing wait; allow yourself a pause. Then think about both times—the time when you'll be enjoying the pleasant feeling, and the time after that, the time of subsequent regret and self-criticism—and compare them to the gratification and self-satisfaction you'll feel if you abstain. But if you do think that it's the right time for that particular action, be careful not to be overwhelmed by its charm and allure. Set against its attractions how much better it is to be conscious of having won this victory."

35

"When you've decided that something needs to be done and you do it, never try to conceal the fact that you're doing it, even if it's something that most people are going to have a negative opinion about. I mean, if what you're doing is wrong, avoid doing it altogether, but if it's right, why worry about misplaced criticism?"

36

"Just as the propositions 'It is day' and 'It is night' are valuable for asserting a disjunction but have negative value for a conjunction,* so likewise taking a larger portion of food may have value for your body, but it has disvalue for preserving the friendly atmosphere of a dinner party as one should. So when you're dining in company, remember to consider not only the value for your body of the dishes but also the value for your host of your being properly restrained."†

37

"If you take on a role that's beyond your capabilities, you not only disgrace yourself in that one, but you've also passed up the role that you *were* capable of performing well."

38

"When you go for a walk, you're careful not to step on a nail or twist your ankle, and you should be just as careful to avoid harming your command center. If we're on our guard in this respect, we'll set about whatever we do in greater safety."

39

"Everyone's body is the measure of his property,* just as a foot is the measure of a shoe. If you abide by this rule, you'll preserve due measure, but if you transgress it, you're bound to end up walking off a cliff, so to speak.* It's the same as with a shoe: if you go beyond the requirements of the foot, you get a gilded shoe, and then one dyed purple, and then an embroidered one. Once you go beyond the measure, there's no end to it."

40

"Women are addressed by men as 'mistress' as soon as they're fourteen years old, and so, when they see that their only lot is to become men's bedfellows, they begin to beautify themselves and pin all their hopes on their looks. So it's worth making sure that they realize that the only thing that will earn them men's esteem is their appearing modest and self-respecting."*

41

"It's a sign of coarseness to spend a lot of time on bodily functions such as exercising, eating, drinking, defecating, and copulating. These are things to be done incidentally; all your attention should be on your intellect."

42

"Whenever anyone does you wrong or speaks ill of you, remember that he acts and speaks as he does because he thinks it's appropriate for him. He can only conform to his own views, not to yours. So if his views are wrong, he's the one who's harmed, because he's also been deceived. If someone takes a true conjunctive statement to be false, it's not the conjunctive statement that has been harmed but the person who's mistaken. If your inclinations to act are based on these principles, you'll be gentler with anyone who maligns you, because whenever that happens you'll tell yourself: 'That's what he thought it best to do.'"

43

"Everything has two handles, one of which makes it bearable, the other unbearable. If your brother's treating you badly, don't take hold of the fact that he's mistreating you, because that's the handle that makes it unbearable, but take hold rather of the fact that he's your brother, that you grew up together. Then you'll be holding the situation by what makes it bearable."

44

"These statements are invalid: 'I'm richer than you, and that means I'm superior to you'; 'I'm more eloquent than you, and that means I'm superior to you.' On the other hand, the following inferences are valid: 'I'm richer than you, and that means my property is superior to yours'; 'I'm more eloquent than you, and that means my diction is superior to yours.' But you yourself are neither your property nor your diction."

45

"Someone is bathing hurriedly: don't say that he's bathing 'badly,' only 'hurriedly.'* Someone is drinking a lot of wine: don't say that he's drinking 'badly,' only 'a lot.' Until you know how he judges things, how can you know if he's acting badly? Then the upshot will be that you won't be receiving cognitive impressions* of some things while giving your assent to others."

46

[1] "Under no circumstances call yourself a philosopher, and when you're among non-philosophers, talk little about philosophical theories. Just act in accordance with those theories. At a dinner party, for instance, don't talk about the proper way of eating, but just eat properly. Remember that Socrates had so thoroughly eliminated display that people used to come to him because they wanted him to introduce them to philosophers,* and he would effect the introduction in person. That's how little it bothered him to be unrecognized himself. [2] If, when you're among non-philosophers, a philosophical theory crops up in the conversation, say very little, because there's a good chance that before very long you'll be spewing up undigested material. And when someone accuses you of ignorance, if it doesn't bother you, then, believe me, you've made a start on the work. Sheep don't produce grass to show their shepherds how much they've eaten, but they digest their food inwardly, and produce wool and milk outwardly. You too, then, shouldn't flaunt your theoretical views to non-philosophers, but show them only the actions that result from those theories once they've been digested."

47

"When you've become accustomed to reducing your bodily needs, don't flaunt it. If you're a teetotaler, don't seize every opportunity to let people know that you're a teetotaler. If you want to train yourself to endure physical hardship, do so for yourself, not for others. Don't hug statues!* Instead, when you're parched with thirst, take cold water into your mouth and spit it out again—without telling anyone."*

48a

"The position and character of a non-philosopher: never expect benefit or harm to come from oneself, but only from the outside world. The position and character of a philosopher: only ever expect benefit and harm to come from oneself."

48b

[1] "The signs that a person is making progress: no criticism of others, no praise of others, no blaming others, no reproaching others, and no talking about himself as though he had any standing or knowledge. When he's obstructed or impeded, he finds fault with himself. If someone praises him, he laughs inwardly at the person doing so. If he's criticized, he doesn't defend himself. He treats himself like an invalid, taking care not to move any of his healing limbs before they've set. [2] He has rid himself of every desire* and has transferred his aversion entirely onto things that are contrary to nature and up to us. He manages all his inclinations with a light touch. If people take him to be simpleminded or ignorant, he doesn't care. In a word, he treats himself with circumspection, as though he were an enemy intriguing against himself."

49*

"When someone prides himself on his ability to understand and explain Chrysippus's works, tell yourself: 'If Chrysippus hadn't written so unclearly, this person wouldn't have anything to feel proud about.'* But let's look at my case. What is it that I want? To understand nature and make it my guide. So I look for someone to explain things to me, and because I've heard that Chrysippus does that, I turn to him. But I don't understand what he's written, so I look for someone to interpret it. So far, nothing to be proud of. But when I've found an interpreter, there's still the matter of putting the precepts into practice; that's the only thing to be proud of. But if what I prize is just the interpreting itself, haven't I ended up as a literary critic rather than a philosopher, with the only difference being that I explicate Chrysippus rather than Homer? So when someone asks me to expound some passage of Chrysippus, I blush at my inability to show him that my actions reflect and are consistent with the words I'm reading."

50

"Stick with every goal you set yourself as you would abide by laws—that is, regarding it as wicked to transgress any of them. Don't worry about what people will say about you, because that's no longer your business."

51

[1] "For how long will you go on deferring the time when you demand the best of yourself and put an end to transgressing right reason? You've accepted the theories. You've subscribed to the views to which you ought to subscribe. What kind of teacher are you still expecting, that you postpone the correction of yourself until he's there to do it for you? You're not a child anymore but a grown man. If you're remiss and lazy now—if you constantly find one reason after another for delay and make each successive day the day when you'll start working on yourself—you'll imperceptibly fail to make progress, and in the end you'll have lived and died without committing yourself to philosophy. [2] Now is the time, then, for you to choose to live as an adult and as one who is making progress as a philosopher. Now is the time for you to regard everything you know to be best as a law that you're bound to obey. And, in the event that you're faced with something painful or pleasant, or something that will enhance or damage your reputation, remember that the contest is on—that here, now, are the Olympic Games, that procrastination is no longer an option, and that just one defeat and surrender determines whether your progress is ruined or remains intact. [3] That's how Socrates got to be

the person he was, by urging himself under all circumstances to pay attention to nothing other than reason. You may not yet be Socrates, but you ought to live as someone who wants to be Socrates."

52

[1] "The first and most necessary aspect of philosophy is the one that has to do with the application of theories such as 'Don't tell lies.' The second has to do with proofs, such as why one shouldn't lie. The third confirms and analyzes the proofs by asking what makes this particular argument a proof: what is it to be a proof, what is entailment, incompatibility, truth, falsehood? [2] So the third aspect is necessary because of the second, and the second because of the first, and the one that's most necessary, and is therefore the one over which we should be spending time, is the first. But we get it all back to front. We linger over the third aspect and put all our efforts into that, while utterly neglecting the first. And the upshot is that we tell lies, while being thoroughly conversant with how to prove that we shouldn't lie."*

53

[1] "We must always have at hand the following sentiments:*

'Lead me, Zeus, both you and Destiny,
Wheresoe'r you have ordained for me,
And I shall gladly follow. And if I am unwilling
Out of wickedness, still I shall follow.'

[2] 'Whoever complies nobly with necessity
We count as wise and expert in the ways of the gods.'

[3] 'Well, Crito, if this is pleasing to the gods, so be it.' [4] 'Anytus and Meletus may be able to kill me, but they cannot harm me.'"

Discourses

Preface

Arrian to Lucius Gellius,* greetings. I did not write these talks by Epictetus in the sense that one might normally be said to "write" such things, nor did I publish them under my own name, seeing that I am not claiming to be the author. What I did was try to write down everything I heard him say in his own words, as far as possible, so as to have a record of his ideas and his blunt way of talking for my own future use. Their style, then, is what one might expect of spontaneous speech, rather than a careful composition for people to read later. This is the form in which they have somehow ended up, without my consent or knowledge, in the public domain. It hardly matters to me if I come across as an incompetent writer, and it matters little to Epictetus if the style of the discourses is disparaged, since there can be no doubt that his sole purpose in speaking was to incline the minds of his listeners toward goodness. So if these discourses were to have the same effect, they would, I think, be doing what the words of philosophers should do. And even if they fail in this respect, readers should appreciate that, whenever Epictetus spoke, his listeners inevitably felt exactly what he intended them to feel. If the discourses on their own prove not to have this effect, that is either my fault or possibly unavoidable. Farewell.

Book 1

1.1
*What is and is not up to us**

[1] "Generally speaking, you'll find no faculty that has the ability to examine itself, and therefore none that has the ability to assess itself and see whether or not it's acceptable.* [2] Take grammar: how far does its power of examination extend? Only as far as making decisions about writing. What about musicology? Only as far as making decisions about tunes. [3] So does either of them contemplate itself? Certainly not. Now, if you're writing to a friend, grammar will tell you how best to express yourself, but it won't tell you whether or not you *should* be writing to your friend.* It's the same with musicology and tunes: it won't tell you whether now is the time for you to be singing and playing the lyre or whether, at this moment you should be neither singing nor playing the lyre.

[4] "Which faculty, then, will give you this information? The one that examines both itself and everything else. And which is that? The faculty of reason, because it's the only one we've been granted that considers both itself—what it is, what it's capable of, what value it comes with—and all the other faculties. [5] What else is it that tells you that gold is beautiful? It isn't the gold itself. It must be the faculty that makes use of impressions. [6] Is there anything else that decides about musicology, grammar, and all the other faculties, that assesses their uses and shows when it's the right time for them? No, there's not.

[7] "Fittingly, then, the only faculty the gods made up to us was the best of them all, the master faculty—that is, the right use of impressions—but they made none of the others up to us. [8] Is this because they didn't wish to? In my opinion, they'd have entrusted those

others to us as well if they'd been able to, but there was absolutely no way they could. [9] Here we are on earth, shackled to our bodies and the people around us: how could we not meet with obstruction from outside in these respects?

[10] "But what does Zeus say? 'Epictetus, if it had been possible, I'd have made your body and your possessions free and unobstructed. [11] But as things are, don't forget that your body isn't yours but only artfully molded clay. [12] Since I couldn't do that, however, I've given you a portion of myself, this faculty of inclination and disinclination,* of desire and aversion, or, to generalize, the faculty of making use of impressions. If you care for it and place what's yours in it, you'll never be impeded, never obstructed, you won't complain, you won't find fault, and you won't court anyone's favor. [13] Now, do these gifts seem petty to you?' 'Hardly.' 'So you're satisfied with them?' 'I pray to the gods that I may be.'

[14] "But now, although it's possible for us to make just one thing the object of our care and devotion, we prefer to care for and be attached to many things—body, possessions, brother, friend, child, slave. [15] And this attachment to many things weighs and drags us down. [16] That's why, if the weather stops us from setting sail, we sit and fume, constantly peering outside: 'Which direction is the wind from?' 'The north.' 'Damn! When is it going to blow from the west?' In its own good time, my friend, or when Aeolus decides. After all, it was Aeolus, not you, whom God made the steward of the winds.* [17] So what must we do? Make the best of what's up to us and take everything else as it comes. And how does it come? As God wishes.*

[18] "'So am I the only one who's going to be decapitated today?'* What are you saying? Would you want everyone to have their heads cut off? Would that make you feel better? [19] Shouldn't you stretch out your neck as Lateranus did*† when Nero ordered his head removed? He stretched out his neck and was struck, but the blow was feeble and he reacted to it by shrinking back a little—but then he stretched it out again. [20] And before that, when Epaphroditus went up to him and asked him about his conflict with Nero, he said, 'If I have anything to say, I'll speak to your master.'*

[21] "So what resources do we need to have at hand for circumstances like these? Just the knowledge of what is and isn't mine, and of what is and isn't possible for me. [22] I am condemned to death.

Do I have to die moaning and groaning as well? To incarceration. Do I have to complain about it? To exile. Is there anyone stopping me from going with a smile, joyful and content? [23] 'Divulge your secrets.' I refuse, because that's something that's up to me. 'I'll clap you in irons.' What are you talking about, man? Me? You'll shackle my leg, but not even Zeus can conquer my will. [24] 'I'll throw you in prison.' My body. 'I'll cut off your head.' Well, have you ever heard me suggest that I'm unique in having a non-detachable head? [25] These are the ideas to which people who take up philosophy should apply themselves, which they should write about every day, and in which they should train themselves.*

[26] "Thrasea used to say, 'I'd rather be killed today than sent into exile tomorrow.' [27] And how did Rufus respond to him? 'If you're choosing death as the harsher of the two options, what an idiotic choice!* And if you're choosing it as the less harsh alternative, who was it that gave you the choice? Shouldn't you practice being satisfied with what's been given to you?'

[28] "By the same token, what was it that Agrippinus used to say?* 'I'm not going to make obstacles for myself.' He was informed that his case was being heard in the Senate. [29] 'That's as may be. But it's the fifth hour now'—this was when it was his custom to exercise and take a cold bath—'so let's go and exercise.' [30] Afterward, someone came up to him and said, 'You've been condemned.' 'To exile,' says he, 'or death?' 'Exile.' 'What about my property?' 'It's not been seized.' 'So let's go to Aricia and have breakfast there.'*

[31] "That's what it's like to have trained oneself properly, to have made desire immune to impediment and aversion immune to encountering what it wants to avoid. [32] I am condemned to death. If it happens straightaway, I die. If after a short delay, I eat first, since the time has come for it, and then I'll die later. How? As is proper for someone who's giving back what was not their own."

1.2
*How to preserve conformity with one's role in every situation**

[1] "For a rational being, the only unbearable thing is unreasonableness, but anything reasonable is bearable. [2] Being beaten isn't in itself unbearable."

"What do you mean?"

"Look at it this way: the Spartans submit to being flogged once they've realized that it's a reasonable thing to do."*

[3] "But being hanged is unbearable, isn't it?"

"Except that when a person feels that it's a reasonable thing to do, he'll go and hang himself. [4] In short, if we look carefully, we'll find that nothing distresses a rational being as much as what is unreasonable and, conversely, that nothing attracts it as much as what is reasonable. [5] But people's views of what's reasonable and unreasonable differ, just as their views of good and bad do, and what is or is not expedient. [6] This, above all, is why we need education, so that we learn how to adjust our preconceptions of what's reasonable and unreasonable until they fit particular instances in a way that conforms with nature.*

[7] "In order to determine what is and isn't reasonable, we not only take account of the values of external things, but each of us also takes his role into consideration. [8] For one person it's reasonable to fetch someone else's chamber pot, because he's focused on the fact that, if he doesn't do it, he'll be flogged and denied food, while, if he does, nothing unpleasant or painful will happen to him.* [9] But another person not only considers it unbearable to do that but can't stand even the idea of someone else's doing it.* [10] So if you ask me, 'Should I or shouldn't I fetch the chamber pot?' I'll reply that being fed is preferable to being denied food, and that being thrashed is less preferable than not being thrashed, and that therefore, if these are the criteria by which you measure what's in your interest, you should go and fetch it. [11] 'But that's not the kind of person I am.' That's something for you, not me, to take into account in your deliberations. After all, you're the one who knows himself, which is to say you know how much you're worth to yourself and at what price you sell yourself. The price differs for different people.

[12] "That's why, when Florus was wondering whether or not he should attend Nero's theatrical spectacle* and even play a part in it himself, Agrippinus said, 'Go!' [13] But when Florus asked him why he wasn't going himself, Agrippinus replied, 'Because I don't even stop to consider it.' [14] The point is that, as soon as someone starts to deliberate about this kind of thing, weighing up the relative values of externals and making a decision on that basis, he's not far off be-

ing one of those people who are unaware of his own role. [15] I mean, what are you asking me? Which is preferable, death or life? Life, of course. Pain or pleasure? Pleasure, of course. [16] 'But if I refuse to take part in the tragedy, I'll lose my head.' 'Go ahead, then. Take part. But I won't.' [17] 'Why me and not you?' 'Because you're thinking of yourself as just one thread in the toga.' 'Meaning what?' 'You're bound to care about how to be similar to other people, just as a thread too wants to be no different from all the other threads. [18] But I'd like to be purple, the little bit of brightness that makes all the rest seem fair and lovely.* So why are you telling me to conform to the majority? How, in that case, would I be purple?'

[19] "Helvidius Priscus saw this, too, and acted on the insight. When Vespasian told him not to attend a meeting of the Senate, he replied, 'You have the power to disqualify me as a senator, but as long as I am one, I'm obliged to attend meetings.' [20] 'All right, then, attend the meeting,' says Vespasian, 'but don't say anything.' 'Don't ask me for my opinion and I'll keep quiet.' 'But I'm bound to ask you.'* 'And I'm bound to say what seems right.' [21] 'But if you speak, I'll have you killed.' 'Did I ever tell you that I was immortal? You do your job and I'll do mine. Yours is to put me to death and mine to die fearlessly. Yours is to send me into exile and mine to leave without grieving.'*

[22] "So did Priscus do any good? After all, he was just a single individual. But what 'good' does the purple do the toga? All it does is stand out in it as purple and serve as a model of beauty for the rest of the threads. [23] If someone else had been told by Caesar in such circumstances not to attend a meeting of the Senate, he'd have said, 'Thank you for letting me off.' [24] Not that Caesar would have stopped that sort of person from attending. He'd have known that he'd either just have sat there like a stoppered jug or, if he did open his mouth, it would only be to say what he knew Caesar wished him to say, and even improve on it.

[25] "A similar case is that of the athlete who was likely to die if his genitals weren't amputated. His brother, who was a philosopher, came up to him and said, 'All right, then, brother, what's it to be? Do we cut off the affected parts and carry on going to the gymnasium?' But the athlete refused to submit to the operation, and instead remained true to himself and died."*

[26] Someone asked whether this man had acted as an athlete or

a philosopher. "As a man," Epictetus replied, "a man who had competed in the Olympic Games and been proclaimed a victor, after
spending his life in that kind of setting, rather than merely being
oiled up at Baton's gymnasium.* [27] And someone else might even
have let himself be decapitated, if he could have lived headless. [28]
This is what it is to act in accordance with one's role, and this is the
degree of importance it has for those who habitually take this aspect of themselves into account in their deliberations. [29] 'All right,
now, Epictetus, shave off your beard.' As a philosopher, I reply, 'No, I
won't.'* 'I'll remove your head.' 'If that seems best, go right ahead.'"

[30] Someone asked, "So how will each of us come to realize what
is in accord with his own role?"

"How is it," Epictetus replied, "that on the approach of a lion only
the bull is aware of his aptitude and takes up a forward position in
defense of the whole herd? It's obvious, isn't it, that the possession of
aptitude is directly and simultaneously accompanied by awareness
of it? [31] The same goes for us too: if any of us has such aptitude, he
won't be unaware of it. [32] But a bull doesn't get to be a bull overnight, and a person doesn't acquire excellence all at once either. Winter training is called for;* one has to be prepared and not rush into
situations for which one is ill suited.

[33] "The only thing you need to take into consideration is the
price at which you sell your will. Listen, man, whatever else you do,
don't sell it cheap! But it may be that exceptional greatness belongs
to others, to Socrates and others like him."

[34] "So if we're equipped by our natures for greatness, why don't
all of us, or even many of us, achieve it?"

"Does every horse turn out swift? Does every hound become a good
hunter? [35] Well, then, am I to stop trying just because I lack natural ability? Perish the thought! [36] Epictetus won't be a greater
man than Socrates, but I'm satisfied with his not being too bad.† [37]
I won't be Milo, either, but that doesn't mean I neglect my body.* Nor
will I be Croesus, but that doesn't mean I neglect my possessions.* In
short, in any field of endeavor, we don't let the recognition that we
won't reach the peak make us stop trying."

1.3
How one may proceed from the fact that God is the father of humankind to its consequences

[1] "If one could fully and properly assimilate the idea that we're all principally children of God—that God is the father of both human beings and gods—I doubt he'd ever think of himself as base or despicable. [2] If Caesar were to adopt you, you'd be insufferably arrogant, so how could it fail to be a source of pride if you knew you were a son of God? [3] But, as things are, that's not what happens. Two components are intermingled in us at birth—the body, which we have in common with animals, and reason and intelligence, which we have in common with gods—and while most of us gravitate toward a relationship with the body, a wretched and lifeless thing,* few incline toward the divine and blessed component. [4] So, since all of us, whoever we may be, can only regard things on the basis of our opinions about them, those few who think they were born for trustworthiness, self-respect, and unassailability in their use of impressions don't think of themselves as despicable or base, while most people do.* [5] 'What am I, after all?' they cry. 'A miserable little creature.' And 'Oh, my wretched body!' [6] You're right, it is wretched, but you also have something better than the body. So why are you ignoring that and clinging to the body? [7] This kinship with the body is the reason why some of us, having gravitated in that direction, become like wolves—deceptive, cunning, and pernicious—and others like lions—fierce, brutal, and wild—while most of us are foxes and other forms of wretched animal life. [8] I mean, isn't 'fox' the perfect description of a scurrilous and malicious person—unless he's some lower and more wretched creature? [9] So be careful, and make sure that you don't turn out to be one of these wretched creatures."

1.4
*On progress**

[1] "A person who's making progress—who has learned from the philosophers* that desire is for good things and aversion is the response to bad things, and also that contentment and equanimity are attainable only if his desires aren't disappointed and, where his aversions

are concerned, he doesn't experience what he wants to avoid—such a person has uprooted desire from himself altogether and set it aside,* and feels aversion only for things that are subject to will. [2] That is, he knows that if he seeks to avoid anything that isn't subject to will, he'll meet with it at some point, in spite of his aversion, and be miserable. [3] Now, if virtue holds out the prospect of causing happiness, equanimity, and contentment, then, of course, progress toward virtue is also progress toward each of these states. [4] After all, whatever the end may be toward which perfection in anything conducts us, it's always the case that to progress is to draw nearer to that end.

[5] "How is it, then, that, while agreeing that virtue is like this, we look for progress elsewhere and demonstrate how much progress we've made in other areas? [6] What is the product of virtue? Contentment. Who is making progress, then? Is it the person who's read many of Chrysippus's treatises?* [7] Virtue can't consist in understanding Chrysippus, can it? If that were so, we'd have to acknowledge that progress consisted in understanding many of Chrysippus's works. [8] But in that case we'd be acknowledging that the product of virtue is one thing and at the same time asserting that progress, drawing nearer to virtue, is something else."

[9] "What about someone who's already able to read Chrysippus without any help?"

"Oh, yes indeed: you're making excellent progress, man! Wonderful progress!"

[10] "Why are you mocking him?"

"Why are you distracting him from an awareness of his defects? Shouldn't you just show him what virtue's product is, so that he can understand where to look for progress? [11] Look for it in things that are up to you, you pitiful creature. Where is that? In desire and aversion, so as not to be disappointed or to encounter what you want to avoid; in inclination and disinclination, to avoid going wrong; in the application of assent and suspension of judgment, to avoid being deceived.* [12] Look first in the most important and essential places. But if you're fearful and downcast in your quest for perfection, in what sense are you making progress?

[13] "So show me what progress you're making in this regard. Suppose I were talking to an athlete and said, 'Show me your shoulders,' and then he said, 'Look at my weights!' You and your weights can

see to yourselves; I want to see what the weights have done for you. [14] 'Get the treatise *On Inclination* and you'll see how thoroughly I've read it.' That's not what I'm trying to find out, slave! What I want to know is how you manage your inclinations and disinclinations, and your desires and aversions; how purposeful, intentioned, and prepared you are; whether or not you're in harmony with nature. [15] If you're in harmony with nature, prove it to me and I'll agree that you're making progress. If you're out of harmony with nature, go away and, rather than just interpreting books, write similar ones yourself. [16] And yet, what good will that do you? Don't you know that the whole book costs only five denarii? Do you suppose, then, that an interpreter of the book is worth more than five denarii? [17] So never look for your work in one place and your progress in another.

[18] "Where is progress to be found, then? If any of you has turned away from external things and is focused on cultivating and working on his own will, so as to bring it into accord with nature, upraised, free, unimpeded, unobstructed, trustworthy, and self-respecting; [19] if he has understood that anyone who longs for or tries to avoid things that aren't up to him compromises both his trustworthiness and his freedom, and is bound to find himself too changed and tossed about along with them, and is also bound to make himself subservient to other people, those who are able to procure these things for him or deny them to him; [20] and if, finally, when he gets up in the morning, he keeps to and observes these principles, bathes as a trustworthy and self-respecting person, eats as a trustworthy and self-respecting person, putting his guiding principles to work on whatever material comes his way, as a runner does in his running and a voice trainer in his voice training—[21] this is the one who's truly making progress, and the one whose journey here hasn't been pointless.

[22] "But if his efforts are directed toward acquiring what can be got from books, if this is what he works at and what he hoped to gain by coming here, I suggest that he go straight back home and stop neglecting his affairs there, [23] because he left home for nothing. No, a student should apply himself to ridding his life of gloom and grief, cries of 'Alas!' and 'Poor me!', misery and wretchedness, [24] and to learning what death, exile, prison, and hemlock really are, so that while in prison he's able to say, 'Well, Crito, if this is what the gods

want, so be it,' and not 'Pity me in my old age! Was this what I kept going for until my hair was gray?'* [25] 'Who talks like that?' you ask, thinking that I'll reply with the name of some obscure and lowly individual. But doesn't Priam speak that way? And Oedipus? Don't all the kings there have ever been speak that way?* [26] Isn't this exactly what tragedies are: versified portrayals of the suffering of people who valued externals? [27] I mean, even if it took deception for one to learn that externals, things that aren't subject to our will, are nothing to us, speaking for myself I'd want to be deceived like that, if as a result I'd be living a life of contentment and tranquility.* As for what you want, that's for you to decide.

[28] "So what *can* we learn from Chrysippus? 'If you want to know,' he says, 'that those things are not false, from which contentment ensues and equanimity comes, [29] take up my books and you'll discover that those things that deliver me from the turmoil of passion are in compliance† and harmony with nature.'* What great good fortune! And what a great benefactor is he who shows us the way! [30] And yet, although people have established shrines and altars to Triptolemus all over the world, because he gave us our nourishment in the form of cultivated crops,* [31] they have not done so for the man who discovered, published, and made available to all of us the truth that gives us not mere life but a life lived well. I mean, have any of you raised an altar to him or a temple? Have any of you dedicated a cult statue to him? Do any of you bow down before God in gratitude for him? [32] We perform sacrifices to the gods for their gifts of vine and wheat,* but they have also brought forth this wonderful fruit in the human mind, by means of which they wanted us to see the truth about happiness. Shall we not thank God for this?"

1.5
Against the Academics*

[1] "If someone refuses to accept what's plainly obvious, it's not easy to find an argument that will make him change his mind. [2] This isn't due to his strength, nor to the weakness of his would-be instructor, but once someone turns to stone because he's cornered, how can one hope to get through to him with rational argument?

[3] "This petrifaction comes in two forms. One is a hardening of the intellect, when someone stubbornly refuses to acknowledge what is totally obvious, and the other is a hardening of the sense of shame, when he refuses to abandon his inconsistencies.* [4] Most of us dread necrosis of the body, and we do all we can to ensure that it doesn't happen, but are supremely unconcerned about this necrosis of the soul. [5] In fact, by Zeus, if someone's mind has become deadened in a way that makes him unable to follow or understand an argument, we think, 'Here's another one who's in a bad way,' whereas if someone's sense of shame and self-respect have died, we even go so far as to call that strength of character!*

[6] "Do you know that you're awake? 'No,' replies the Academic, 'no more than when I have an impression of being awake in a dream.' So there's no difference between one impression and the other? 'No, none.' [7] Why am I even talking to this fellow? What fire or steel* can I bring to bear on him to get him to realize that he's become deadened? If he does realize it, he makes out that he doesn't, in which case he's deader than a corpse. [8] One of them doesn't even see the point in contention; he's in a bad way. Another sees it, but isn't moved and doesn't move on from his position; he's in an even more pitiable state. [9] His self-respect and sense of shame have been cut out of him, and although his rationality hasn't been amputated, it's become dehumanized. [10] Should I call this strength of character? Hardly! Unless I'm also to say that sex addicts have strength of character, thanks to which they both do and say in public everything that occurs to them."

1.6
*On providence**

[1] "Everything that happens in the universe readily moves one to praise providence, as long as he has within himself the following two attributes: the ability to see each particular event in the context of the whole, and a sense of gratitude. [2] Otherwise, one will either fail to see the usefulness of events or fail to be grateful for them even if one does see it.

[3] "If God had created colors but hadn't created the faculty of

sight, would that have served any useful purpose? None at all. [4] Conversely, if he'd created the faculty of sight but hadn't ensured that things were such that they impinge on it, would *that* have been useful? Not at all. [5] What about if he'd created both these things, but hadn't created light? That would have been no use either. [6] Who is it, then, who has harmonized one thing with another like this? Who is it who has fitted the sword to the scabbard and the scabbard to the sword? No one? [7] But it's usual to look at the design of artifacts like these and conclude that they were produced by some craftsman or other, and didn't come about by accident.*

[8] "So do swords and scabbards reveal the hand of a craftsman, while visible things, sight, and light don't? [9] What about male and female, and the appetite they have for sex with each other, and the serviceability for them of the organs that have been designed for that purpose? Doesn't all this seem to be the work of a craftsman as well? [10] But, leaving that aside, what about the way the mind is constituted? I mean, it's not just the case that sensible things imprint themselves upon us when they come our way, but we also select from among them, subtract from them and add to them, and form combinations out of them by ourselves—yes, and even, by Zeus, pass from some of them to others that are in some way related.* Is even this not enough to stir people, and get them to change their minds and admit the existence of a craftsman? [11] Otherwise, let them explain to us what it is that does cause all this, or how it is that such wonderful contrivances could come about accidentally and by chance.*

[12] "Well now, is this phenomenon restricted to human beings? There are many things that are unique to us—those that are peculiar to the needs of a rational animal—but you'll find that we also share many features with non-rational animals. [13] So do they, too, understand what happens? Certainly not. 'Making use of' and 'understanding' are different things. God wanted them to make use of impressions, but he wanted us to understand the use we make of impressions. [14] Hence it's enough for them to eat, drink, rest, mate, and do all the other things that animals of every kind do, but that's not enough for us because he also gave us the faculty of understanding. [15] No, in our case, unless we act fittingly, consistently, and in conformity with our individual natures, we won't be able to attain our proper end. [16] Creatures with different constitutions, you see,

have different functions and different ends. [17] So, if a creature is constitutionally capable only of use, mere use is sufficient, but a creature that's constitutionally capable of understanding use will never attain its end unless that capacity is properly employed.

[18] "So what about the animals? God makes one of them to be eaten, another for farm work, another to produce cheese, another for some other similar function, and for them to carry out these functions, what need do they have for the capacity to understand impressions and distinguish between them? [19] But he introduced human beings to be spectators of himself and his works, and not just to observe them but also to interpret them. [20] That's why it's shameful for a person to begin and end where non-rational animals do. He should begin where they begin and finish where nature finished in *our* case—[21] in contemplation, in understanding, and in living a life that's in harmony with nature. [22] Make sure, then, that you don't die without having been spectators of his works.

[23] "You travel to Olympia to see the work of Phidias,* and every one of you regards it as a misfortune to die without having informed yourselves about such things. [24] So when there's no need for you to travel anywhere, when you're already there, with the works before your eyes, won't you feel an urge to observe and understand them? [25] Won't you then come to recognize who you are, what you're born for, and the reason why you've been granted the spectacle? [26] 'But unpleasant and harsh things happen in life.' Don't they happen in Olympia? Isn't it blazingly hot? Isn't it crowded? Isn't it difficult to bathe? Don't you get soaked when it rains? Don't you get sick of the noise, the shouting, and all the other irritations? [27] But I'm sure that, weighing the remarkable nature of the spectacle against all these discomforts, you put up with them and endure them. [28] Tell me: haven't you been endowed with faculties that enable you to endure all your experiences? Haven't you been granted greatness of soul?* Haven't you been granted courage? Haven't you been granted fortitude? [29] If I have greatness of soul, why should I worry about what might happen? What can derange me or upset me or seem in any way distressing? Shall I fail to employ this faculty of mine for the purposes for which I've been granted it, and instead let events cause me grief and sorrow?*

[30] "'Yes, but my nose runs.' So what do you have hands for,

LE JUPITER OLYMPIEN,
VU DANS SON TRÔNE ET DANS L'INTÉRIEUR DE SON TEMPLE.

FIGURE 1. Antoine-Chrysostome Quatremère de Quincy (1755-1849), *Le Jupi-ter Olympien vu dans son trône*. Frontispiece to A.-C. Quatremère de Quincy, *Le Jupiter Olympien, ou l'art de la sculpture antique* (Paris, 1814). This is a somewhat fanciful reproduction of Phidias's famous statue of Zeus for the temple at Olympia. The scale is about right, however: the statue, made largely of ivory and gold on a wooden frame, was enormous. It was recognized as one of the Seven Wonders of the World.

slave? Isn't it, among other things, so that you can wipe your nose? [31] 'But is there any good reason for there to be runny noses in the world?' How much better it would be for you to wipe your nose rather than find fault! [32] I mean, what do you think Heracles would have amounted to if there'd been no great lion, no hydra, stag, and boar, and none of the evil and brutal men he drove off and cleared away? [33] What would he have done if there'd been nothing like that in the world? The answer's obvious, isn't it? He'd have wrapped himself up and gone to sleep. In the first place, then, he wouldn't have become Heracles if he'd dozed his life away in this kind of peaceful comfort.* And even if he had, what good would it have done him? [34] What use would he have made of his arms and his strength in general? What would have been the point of his fortitude and nobility if there'd been no difficulties such as he faced, no materials to stir him to action and train him? [35] So should he have arranged these conditions for himself? Should he have brought a lion from somewhere into his homeland, and a boar and a hydra? [36] That would have been stupid, even crazy. But they did exist and there they were, and so they served a very useful purpose in revealing Heracles's caliber and training him up.

[37] "All right. Now that you too appreciate all this, consider the faculties that you have and then say, 'Bring it on now, Zeus, any situation you wish, because I have your gift to me, the aptitude and resources to use my experiences to shine come what may.' [38] But no, you sit trembling with fear in case certain things happen, and lamenting, grieving, and moaning because certain other things did happen. And then you blame the gods, [39] because such a small-minded attitude can only lead to impiety. [40] Yet not only has God given us these faculties, that make it possible for us to tolerate everything that happens without being diminished or crushed by any of them, but he has also—as a good king and, in truth, our father—given them to us unimpeded, unconstrained, and unobstructed. He has made them entirely up to us, without even reserving for himself the power to impede or obstruct them at all. [41] Although you possess these faculties, and they're free and yours, you make no use of them and you fail to realize what it is you've got and who gave them to you. [42] Instead, you sit mourning and deploring your circumstances, some of you with no sense of who gave you these things and no recognition of your benefactor, and others misled by their small-mindedness into blaming and finding fault with God. [43] In fact, I shall show you that you have the resources and aptitude for greatness of soul and courage, and you . . . why don't you show me the resources you have for blaming and fault-finding?"

1.7

On the use of changing arguments, hypothetical arguments,
and the like

[1] "It's not generally recognized that the study of changing arguments, hypothetical arguments, arguments that proceed by questioning,† and, in fine, the study of all such arguments,* is relevant to acting appropriately. [2] Whatever the material we're dealing with, we want to find out how a truly good person may discover the course he should adopt and the appropriate thing to do. [3] There are various options, then. Perhaps a good person won't engage in questioning and answering, or perhaps he will, but without caring if he goes about it in a casual and haphazard fashion. [4] Or, if neither of these alternatives is acceptable, it must be granted that the topics with which question and answer are chiefly concerned do warrant investigation.

[5] "What is it that reason professes to do? Establish the truth, eliminate falsehood, and suspend judgment in uncertain cases. [6] Is that enough, all we need to know?"

"Yes."

"So is it also enough for someone who wants to avoid making mistakes in his use of coined money to be told 'Accept good coins and reject fakes'?"

"No."

[7] "What else is required, then? It must be the ability to assay the coins and tell genuine from counterfeit, mustn't it? [8] So, in reasoning as well, what's been said isn't enough on its own, but one must also know how to assess it and distinguish what's true, what's false, and what's uncertain. Is that right?"

"Yes."

[9] "Apart from this, what else does reason prescribe? To accept what follows from what you've already rightly granted. [10] All right, but here again, is it enough just to know this? No, it's not. One must also learn how something follows as a consequence of certain other things, and how sometimes one thing follows from one thing, but sometimes from a number of things in conjunction. [11] So isn't knowing this also necessary if someone is to conduct himself intelligently in argument, and is to prove each point that he himself brings

up, follow others' proofs, and not be misled into taking sophisms as proofs? [12] That's why in our school we have taken up the study of valid arguments and their modes, and why we train ourselves in them. This has shown itself to be indispensable.

[13] "But of course there are occasions when we've rightly granted the premises and a certain conclusion follows from them, which, though false, is still formally a valid inference from them. [14] What's the appropriate response? To accept the falsehood? That's out of the question. [15] Then should I say that I was wrong to grant the premises? That's not allowed either. Or should I say, 'That's not a valid inference from the premises'? No, that's not allowed either. [16] So what should one do in such cases? Might it not be that, just as the fact that someone has in the past borrowed money isn't sufficient to prove that he's still in debt, but one must add that he remains committed to the debt and hasn't discharged it, so our having granted the premises isn't sufficient to make it necessary for us to accept the inference, but we must also remain committed to accepting the premises? [17] Moreover, if the premises remain to the end as they were when we accepted them, it's absolutely necessary for us to remain committed to our acceptance of them and to accept what follows from them. [18] <But if they don't, we don't have to,>* [19] because from our point of view, and as far as we're concerned, the inference no longer follows once we've withdrawn our acceptance of the premises. [20] So we must also consider these kinds of premises and the way they shift and change like this, because if such a shift happens actually in the course of asking questions, answering them, drawing conclusions, or whatever, it makes it possible for unwary people to get into trouble if they fail to see the consequences. [21] And the reason why we need to carry out this investigation is so that our conduct in this regard is not inappropriate, purposeless, or confused.

[22] "The same is true of hypotheses and hypothetical arguments as well. It's sometimes necessary to postulate a hypothesis as a foundation, so to speak, for the subsequent argument. [23] So should we accept every hypothesis that's proposed, or only some of them? And if only some, which ones? [24] And once we've accepted a hypothesis, should we remain committed to assuming it forever, or should we sometimes abandon it? And should we accept what follows from it and reject what's incompatible with it?"

"Yes."

[25] "But someone might say, 'If you've accepted something possible as a hypothesis, I shall force you to infer something impossible.'* Will a wise man refuse to engage with this person? Will he abstain from examining and discussing the issue with him? [26] But who else is good at argument, skilled at questioning and answering, and, by Zeus, proof against trickery or sophistry? [27] So he'll engage with him, but will he do so without caring if he goes about the argument in a casual and haphazard manner? That would make him a different kind of person from how we conceive him to be. [28] But without the appropriate training and aptitude, is he capable of guarding against the consequences? [29] Let it be demonstrated that he is, and all the theory turns out to be redundant—irrelevant and incompatible with our preconception of a good person.

[30] "Why are we still indolent, lazy, and torpid? Why do we look for excuses to avoid the hard work and lack of sleep involved in training our rational faculty?"

[31] "Well, if I go wrong in an argument, I haven't killed my father, have I?"

"Where was your father, slave? Was he here for you to kill? What did you do? The only wrong you could have done in this context. [32] I mean, look, I too responded in exactly the same way to Rufus when he was telling me off for having failed to find the single omission in a syllogism. 'It's not as if I burned down the Capitol,'* I said. And he replied, 'Here, slave, the omission *is* the Capitol.' [33] I mean, are setting fire to the Capitol and killing one's father the only faults there are? What about using one's impressions in an aimless, vain, and haphazard fashion? What about failing to follow an argument, a proof, or a sophism—or, in a word, failing to see, in the course of questioning and answering, what's consistent with one's position and what isn't? Are these not faults?"

1.8

That our faculties are not without danger for uneducated people

[1] "There are as many ways in which it's possible for epicheremes and enthymemes* to be substituted for one another in the course of arguments as there are for equivalent terms to be substituted for one

another. [2] Look at it this way: 'If you've borrowed money from me and haven't paid it back, you owe me money'—'It is not the case that you've borrowed money and haven't paid it back, and yet don't owe me money.'† [3] And there's no one better fitted for making this kind of substitution in a skillful way than a philosopher. After all, if an enthymeme is an incomplete syllogism,* obviously someone who's trained himself on complete syllogisms is going to be just as competent at the incomplete version as well.

[4] "So why don't we train ourselves and one another in this way? [5] It's because at the moment, despite the fact that our training is not concerned with these matters (and in fact we aren't being distracted at all from ethical studies, or at least not by me), we're still making no progress toward true goodness. [6] So imagine what it'll be like if we take on this task as well—and it's particularly important to note that not only would it mean extra work that would take us away from more essential matters, but it would also make it incredibly easy for a person to become proud and conceited. [7] This is because the ability to argue credibly and plausibly is a very powerful tool, especially if it's deployed after a lot of training and gains in addition a certain elegance from its use of language. [8] Generally speaking, in fact, no faculty is without its dangers for people who are uneducated and weak, in the sense that they give themselves airs and preen themselves on it. [9] I mean, how might one go about convincing a young man who excels at argument that he shouldn't be accessory to his skill, but it should be accessory to him? [10] Doesn't he treat all such arguments with contempt and walk among us filled with pride and vanity, deaf to anyone who undertakes to remind him of his shortcomings and where he's gone astray?"

[11] "Well, wasn't Plato a philosopher?"*

"Yes, and wasn't Hippocrates a doctor? But you can see how well Hippocrates expresses himself. [12] But it isn't by virtue of his being a doctor that Hippocrates expresses himself so well, is it? So why are you confusing attributes that are only incidentally found together in people? [13] If Plato was handsome and strong, should I set to and work at becoming handsome and strong as well, as though that were an essential aspect of philosophy, just because a certain philosopher happened to be both handsome and a philosopher at the same time? [14] Shouldn't you recognize what it is that makes people philosophers and distinguish it from their incidental attributes? Tell me: supposing I were a philosopher, would you have to become lame like me?

[15] "So, what? Am I rejecting these faculties? Not in the slightest! Nor would I reject the faculty of sight. [16] Nevertheless, if you ask me what is truly good for people, I can only reply that it's the right kind of will."

1.9

How one may proceed from the fact of our kinship with God to its consequences

[1] "If what the philosophers say about the kinship of God and men is true, we can only follow the example of Socrates, and if someone asks where we're from, never say 'I'm an Athenian' or 'I'm a Corinthian,' but 'I'm a citizen of the universe.'* [2] I mean, why do you describe yourself as from Athens, rather than merely from that corner of Athens into which your body dropped at birth? [3] Isn't the reason obvious? It's because you choose the more dominant place, the one which includes not only that little corner of yours, but also your whole house—the place, in short, where your ancestral line has its origins—and it's on that basis that you call yourself Athenian or Corinthian. [4] So anyone who's paid attention to the way the universe is managed and has learned that the greatest, most dominant, and most all-inclusive community is the one made up of human beings and God, and that God is the source of the seeds that have come down not just to my father or grandfather* but to everything that is born and grows on earth, [5] and especially to rational beings, because only they are equipped by nature to partake of fellowship with God, since they are bound to him by their rational faculties*— [6] why shouldn't such a person call himself a citizen of the universe? Why shouldn't he call himself a son of God? And why should he fear anything that happens in the world of men? [7] I mean, if kinship with Caesar or some other powerful man in Rome is enough to enable people to live in safety, secure against contempt and free from all fear, will having God as our creator, father, and protector not deliver us from distress and fear?"

[8] "And where am I to get food from," someone asked, "if I have nothing?"

"Well, how do slaves eat, runaways? What do they rely on when they leave their masters? On their fields, their servants, their silverware? No, they rely on nothing but themselves, but they don't go short of food. [9] Will our philosopher, when he's away from home, have to trust and depend on others, rather than take care of himself? Will he be more craven and cowardly than the non-rational creatures of the wild, every one of which is self-sufficient and doesn't go without either its proper food or the way of life that suits it and accords with its nature?

[10] "In my opinion, it's not the job of your elderly teacher to sit here and try to work out how to stop you underrating yourselves or reckoning yourselves base and despicable creatures. [11] No, he should be trying to make sure that awareness of your kinship with the gods and of how we're shackled, so to speak, to the body and its possessions (that is, all the things which, because of these bonds, become necessary to us for the maintenance and perpetuation of our lives), doesn't make any of you, young as you are, wish to discard these things as irksome and useless burdens and depart to their kin.* [12] This is the struggle in which your teacher and instructor should be engaged, if he's a genuine teacher.

"You would come to him and say, 'Epictetus, we can no longer stand being bound to this body, feeding and watering it, resting it and cleaning it, and moreover being compelled by its needs to associate with this person and that. [13] Aren't these things indifferents?* Aren't they nothing to us? Isn't it the case that death is no evil? And that we have some kind of kinship with God and originally came from there? [14] Allow us to go back to where we came from. Allow us to be released at last from these burdensome bonds with which we're chained. [15] Here on earth, robbers and thieves, law courts and those we call tyrants plainly have power over us because of this poor body of ours and its possessions. Allow us to prove to them that in fact no one is in their power.' [16] And in response I'd say, 'My friends, wait for God. You're free to return to him only when he gives the signal and releases you from your service here on earth.* For the time being, resign yourselves to residing here, at the post to which he's assigned you. [17] The time of your stay here is short, and easy to endure for people with your convictions. What tyrant or thief or law court can strike fear in those who regard the body and its possessions as of no importance? Stay. Don't leave for no good reason.'

[18] "That's the kind of advice that should pass from a teacher to gifted young men. [19] But what happens at present? The teacher's a corpse and you are corpses. Once you've eaten today, you sit and whimper about where you'll get food from tomorrow. [20] Slave, if you get hold of some, you'll have food to eat. If you don't, you can leave; the door is open.* Why are you so downcast? What place is there for tears? What occasion is there for flattery? What will make one person envy another? What will make anyone respect others because of all the possessions they have or because they're in positions of power, especially if they have both strength and short tempers? [21] What are they going to do to us? We won't be bothered by anything they're capable of doing, and they're incapable of affecting the things that *do* matter to us. Who can exercise power over someone with these convictions?

[22] "What was Socrates's position on these matters? Exactly what you'd expect from someone who was convinced of his kinship with the gods. [23] 'If,' he says, 'you were now to tell me, "We will acquit you provided that you stop pestering us, young and old, by engaging us in conversation as you have been up until now," [24] I'd reply that it's ridiculous of you to think that I should hold and defend a post assigned to me by one of your generals, and should be prepared to die ten thousand times before abandoning it, but should abandon a post and a way of life assigned to me by a god.'* [25] There you have someone who's truly a kinsman of the gods. [26] But we . . . as bellies, as guts, as genitals—that's how we think of ourselves, that's how we are fearful, that's how we have cravings.† We flatter those who are able to help us in these respects, and these are the people we also fear.

[27] "I was once asked by someone to write to Rome on his behalf since he had suffered what most people would take to be a misfortune: although he had formerly been famous and rich, he subsequently lost everything and was living here. [28] I wrote a humble letter on his behalf, but when he read it, he gave it back to me and said, 'I wanted your help, not your pity. I'm not badly off at all.' [29] Likewise, Rufus used to say to me, by way of a test, 'Your master's go-

ing to do such-and-such to you.' [30] And if I replied by saying 'That's life,' he'd say, 'So why should I bother to plead with him when I can get the same result from you?'*

[31] "After all, it's truly pointless and futile for someone to get from someone else what he can get from himself. [32] So since I can get from myself greatness of soul and honor, am I going to get from you a plot of land or some money or an official position? Hardly! That would mean that I didn't appreciate what I had. [33] But there's nothing one can possibly do for a cowardly wretch except write, as though he were a dead man: 'Could we please have his carcass and his pint of blood?' [34] Because, in truth, there's nothing more to that kind of person than a carcass and a pint of blood. If there was anything more to him, he'd appreciate that a person's misery is never anyone else's doing."

1.10
To those who are intent on advancement at Rome

[1] "If we had put as much serious effort into our work as senators put into what they're intent on, we too would probably have achieved some degree of success. [2] I know a man, older than me, who's currently responsible for the grain supply in Rome. I met him when he passed this way while he was returning to Rome from exile, and I was struck by what he said to me. He decried the life he had lived there in the past and assured me that from then on, after his return, he'd devote himself exclusively to spending his remaining years in untroubled peace. 'How many years remain to me, after all?' he said. [3] And I said, 'No, you won't. At the first scent of Rome, you'll totally forget these resolutions of yours.' I told him that if he was granted access to the palace, he'd push his way in exulting and giving thanks to God. [4] 'Epictetus,' he said, 'if you find me setting one foot inside the palace, feel free to think what you like about me.' [5] So what did he actually do? Before he had got to Rome, letters from Caesar reached him, and on receiving them he totally forgot his resolutions and ever since he has given himself a whole heap of trouble, one thing after another. [6] I wish I could be with him now, so that I could remind him of what he said as he passed this way. I'd point out how much better a prophet I am than him!

[7] "What am I saying, then? That man is an animal made for in-activity? Far from it. But I am saying that elderly people like him and me aren't made for activity. [8] I'm a prime example: at the break of day, I briefly remind myself of the text I have to interpret, but then I say to myself, 'Why should it bother me how well or poorly so-and-so reads?* The crucial thing is that I should get some sleep!'

[9] "Still, do activities in Rome bear comparison with ours? If you look at what people there do, you'll see. All day long, they do nothing but make decisions, debate issues, and consult about grain, land, and other such sources of profit. [10] So is there no difference between receiving a petition from someone that reads 'I would like permission to export some grain,' and one that reads 'I would like you to consider what Chrysippus says about the governance of the universe and the place that rational beings have in it, and also who you are and what kinds of thing are good and bad for you'? [11] Are these requests similar? Do they deserve the same degree of attention? Is it just as shameful to neglect the one as the other?

[12] "Anyway, is it only people like me and him who are lazy and sleepy? No, you young men are way ahead of us there. [13] I mean, look: we old-timers are eager to join in when we see youngsters at *play*, so I'd be far more eager to join you in a *serious* activity, if I saw you wide awake and going eagerly about your work together."

1.11
*On family affection**

[1] Once, when he was visited by a government official, after inquiring about this and that, Epictetus asked him if he had children and a wife. [2] He said that he did, and Epictetus next asked, "And how do you find family life?"*

"It makes me miserable," he said.

[3] "How can that be?" asked Epictetus. "I mean, that's not why men marry and have children. They expect it to make them happy, not miserable."

[4] "Well, in my case," the man replied, "it's my young children who make me miserable. The other day, for instance, when my daughter was ill—dangerously ill, apparently—I couldn't bear even to be with

her while she was sick, but I left and stayed away until I was told she was all right."

[5] "Well, do you think you were right to have done that?"

"I think it was a natural reaction,"* he said.

"Well, if you convince me that it was the natural thing to do," said Epictetus, "I'll convince you that everything that's in accord with nature is rightly done."

[6] "I did what any father would have done," he said, "or most of them, at any rate."

"For my part," said Epictetus, "I don't dispute that that's what happens, but the point at issue is whether it's right. [7] You see, on your way of thinking, you'd have to say that tumors are good for the body, just because they happen, and, to generalize, that mistakes are natural, because most of us—almost all of us, in fact—make mistakes.* What you have to show me, then, is how your behavior was in accord with nature."

[8] "I can't," he said. "Why don't you show me instead how it isn't in accord with nature and isn't right?"

[9] "All right," said Epictetus. "If it were white and black that we were investigating, what criterion would we call on to distinguish between them?"

"Sight," he said.

"And if it was hot and cold, or hard and soft?"

"Touch."

[10] "So, since our dispute concerns things being in accord with nature, and being right or wrong, what criterion should we employ?"

"I don't know," he said.

[11] "And yet, although not knowing the criterion may not be very harmful in the case of colors and smells, and flavors too, what about not knowing the criterion by which to judge what's good and bad, and whether or not something is in accord with nature? Do you think that, if a person is ignorant in these cases, he'll get off lightly?"

"No, quite the contrary."

[12] "Tell me, then: when people believe something to be good and the proper thing to do, are they always right? For example, are the views about food of Jews, Syrians, Egyptians, and Romans all correct?"

"That's impossible."

[13] "In fact, I suppose, it's absolutely inevitable that if Egyptian opinions are correct, those of the others aren't. And if the Jews are right in this respect, the others aren't.*

"Of course."

[14] "Now, where there's ignorance, there's also lack of learning and lack of education in matters of fundamental importance."

He agreed.

[15] "Well, if you appreciate this," Epictetus said, "in the future there's only one thing that you'll take seriously and to which you'll apply your intelligence, and that's getting to know the criterion by which to judge whether or not things are in accord with nature, and putting this knowledge to use to decide about particular cases. [16] But for the time being, the only way I can help you have the kind of family life you want is this. [17] Do you think that family affection is natural and good?"*

"Of course."

"Well, then, granted that it's natural and good for family members to love one another, what about reasonableness? Is that good?"

"Of course it is."

[18] "So there's no incompatibility between reasonableness and loving family members?"*

"No, I don't think so."

"Otherwise, if they were incompatible, it would necessarily follow that, if one of them was in accord with nature, the other would be contrary to nature. Isn't that right?"

"Yes," he said.

[19] "So if we find anything that involves family affection and at the same time is reasonable, we can confidently declare it to be right and good, can't we?"

"Agreed," he said.

[20] "Well, I doubt you'd deny that leaving a child when it's sick and then staying away isn't a reasonable action. But we still have to consider whether it's an affectionate thing to do."

"Let's do that."

[21] "So, given your affection for the child, was it right for you to run away and leave her? What about the mother? Doesn't she feel affection for the child?"

"She certainly does."

[22] "So should the mother also have deserted the child, or not?"

"She shouldn't."

"What about the nurse? Is she fond of the child?"

"She is."

[23] "So should she too have deserted her?"

"No."

"What about the child-minder? Isn't he fond of her?"*

"Yes, he is."

"So should he too have deserted her and gone off, so that the child would have been left alone and unsupported thanks to the great affection you, the parents, and her attendants felt for her, and might even have died in the arms of those who weren't fond of her and didn't care for her?"*

"God forbid!"

[24] "But isn't it unfair and unfeeling of a person to deny to those who feel no less affection than he does the action that he regards as the proper thing for him to do because of his affection?"

"Absurd."

[25] "All right, but tell me: if it were you who was ill, would you have wanted your family—children, wife, and all—to display their affection for you by deserting and abandoning you?"

"Certainly not."

[26] "Would you pray for your relatives to be so fond of you that, moved by their excessive affection, they always left you alone when you were ill? Wouldn't you rather have prayed, therefore, to be loved by your enemies instead (let's assume that makes sense), so that it would be they who left you alone? If so, we're forced to conclude that your behavior was in no way prompted by affection.

[27] "So was there nothing that moved and inclined you to desert the child? There must have been, of course. Perhaps it was the kind of thing that moved a certain fellow in Rome to cover his head while a horse he favored was running (and then when it won against the odds, he needed sponges to bring him round from his faint). [28] And what was it that moved him? This is perhaps not the occasion for precision, but it's enough for us to be convinced that, if what the philosophers say is sound, we shouldn't be looking for the answer anywhere outside ourselves. They say that it's only ever one and the

same thing that moves us to act or not, to speak or keep silent, to be elated or depressed, to avoid or pursue things, [29] and this is what even now is motivating you and me—you to come here and sit and listen to me as you are doing now, and me to say what I'm saying. [30] And what is this? Can it be anything other than that we judged it the right thing to do?"

"It can only be that."

"And if we changed our minds, we'd still be doing what seemed right to us, wouldn't we? [31] So wasn't Achilles too moved to grief not by Patroclus's death (after all, not everyone feels grief at the death of a comrade), but because he thought it right to grieve?* [32] And in your case, on the occasion in question, you ran away because it seemed the right thing to do, and if you'd stayed, you'd have done so because it seemed the right thing to do. And now you're on your way back to Rome because you judge it the right thing to do. And all it would take would be a change of mind for you not to go back there. [33] In a word, it isn't death or exile or pain or anything like that that moves us to do or not do something, but our beliefs and our judgments.* [34] Are you finding what I'm saying persuasive?"

"Yes," he said.

"It's a general principle, in fact, that the type of result depends on the type of cause. [35] So from this day on, if we ever do something wrong, we'll attribute it entirely to the judgment that led us to act as we did, and we'll put more effort into eliminating and extirpating this judgment than we put into ridding our bodies of tumors and growths. [36] But by the same token, we'll also acknowledge judgments to be the cause of anything we do right. [37] We'll stop blaming our slaves, neighbors, wives, and children for any of the bad things that happen to us, because of our conviction that it's judging things in a certain way that causes us to carry out the corresponding actions. And it is we who are responsible for judging something to be so or not so, not anything outside us."

"You're right," he said.

[38] "So from today on we won't examine and scrutinize the state or status of anything else, such as our land, our slaves, our horses, or our hounds, but only our judgments."

"I hope so," he said.

[39] "You can see, then, that you have to become a student, that

butt of universal mockery, if you really want to look into your judgments. [40] And even you recognize that this is not the work of a
single hour or day."

1.12
On contentment

[1] "On the subject of the gods, there are some who deny their very
existence, and others who admit their existence, but say that they're
ineffective and don't exercise any care or forethought.* [2] A third
group admits both their existence and their providence but only with
regard to large-scale, heavenly phenomena, not to anything that
happens on earth. A fourth group claims that they also take thought
for things on earth and human affairs, but only in a general way, and
that their providence doesn't apply to individuals. [3] Then there's a
fifth group, among whom are Odysseus and Socrates, who say, 'Nor
am I hidden from you as I go on my way.'*

[4] "We must therefore make it our top priority to examine each
of these positions to see whether or not they're sound. [5] I mean, if
there are no gods, how can it be the goal of life to follow the gods?*
And how can that be a sound goal also if they exist but exercise no care
for anything or anyone? [6] And if they exist and exercise care, but
there's no transmission of that care from them to human beings—
from them to *me*, by Zeus!—how, again, is that a sound goal?

[7] "After a thorough examination of these matters, then, a truly
good person subordinates his intellect to the power that governs the
universe, just as good citizens submit to the laws of the city. [8] A student ought to approach his education with this objective: 'How can I
follow the gods in everything? How can I be content with the divine
dispensation? How can I become free?' [9] Because someone is free
if everything that happens to him is in accord with his will and no
one is able to impede him."

[10] "So are you saying that freedom consists in losing one's
mind?"

"Far from it. Insanity and freedom don't go together. [11] 'But my
wish is for everything to turn out just as I want it to, no matter what
it is.' [12] That's insane! You're out of your mind! Don't you know
that freedom is a fine and admirable thing? But for me to randomly

want my every random whim to come to pass is not only not admirable, but probably the most shameful thing there is. Look, how do we go about writing? [13] Do I get to write the name 'Dion' in any way I like? No, I'm taught to want to write it as it should be written. And what about music? The same. [14] What about in general, wherever some skill or expertise is involved? It must be the same, otherwise expertise would be quite worthless, if it changed according to every individual's wishes.

[15] "Is it only here, then, in the case of freedom, the most important and consequential thing in the world, that I'm allowed random wishes? Absolutely not, because education consists precisely in learning to want everything to happen as it does happen.* [16] And how do things happen? As the ordainer has ordained. And for the harmony of the universe he has ordained summer and winter, plenty and scarcity, virtue and vice, and so on for all the opposites, and has given each of us a body and its parts, possessions, and other people to associate with. [17] We should bear this dispensation of his in mind as we approach our education. Its purpose isn't for us to be able to change existing conditions (which is neither possible nor desirable) but rather, given that things around us are as they are and as they're constituted to be, for us to learn how to keep our intellects in harmony with everything that happens.

[18] "After all, is it possible to escape from people? No, that's quite impossible. But is it possible to change them just by being with them? No, we haven't been given that ability. [19] What's left, then? Where should we look for an expedient for coping with people? It has to be such that they can act as they see fit without threatening our accord with nature. [20] But you can't stand hardship of any kind; you're always dissatisfied. If you're on your own, you call it loneliness, and if you're with people, you say they're schemers and thieves. You find fault even with your parents, children, brothers, and neighbors. [21] When you're on your own, you should call that peace and freedom, and think of it as a godlike existence; and when you're in a crowd, you shouldn't call it a mob or focus on the noise and discomfort, but think of it as a celebration and a festival, and so accept and be contented with everything.

"How are people who don't accept their situations punished? By remaining as they are. [22] Does someone find it hard to be contented on his own? Let him remain lonely. Does someone find it hard to be contented with his parents? Let him remain a bad son and disconsolate. Does someone find it hard to be contented with his children? Let him remain a bad father. [23] Throw him in prison. What prison? The one he's in now. I mean, he doesn't want to be where he is, and any place where someone doesn't want to be is a prison for him. That's why Socrates wasn't in prison,* because he was there by his own choice.

[24] "'But my poor crippled leg!'* Slave, are you really damning the whole world because of one little leg? Won't you donate it to the universe? Won't you give it up? Won't you happily surrender it to what gave it to you in the first place? [25] Are you going to be angry and discontented with Zeus's arrangements for your life, which were determined and ordained by him with the help of the Fates, who were present at your birth and spun the thread of your destiny?* [26] Don't you realize how small a part you are compared to the whole—in respect of your body, I mean: as far as your reason is concerned, you're no worse than or inferior to the gods, because the greatness of reason is not assessed by length and height but by the quality of its judgments. [27] So shouldn't you locate your good in that which makes you equal to the gods?

[28] "'Oh, poor me! What terrible parents I have!' So what? Were you given the right to choose your parents in advance and say, 'Let that man have intercourse with that woman at such-and-such time, so that I may be born'? No, of course not. [29] Your parents were bound to exist first, and then you were bound to be born as you were. From what *kind* of parents? From exactly the kind they are.

[30] "So, given what your parents are like, are you endowed with any coping mechanism? Suppose you didn't know why you have the faculty of sight: you'd cut a sorry and pathetic figure if you closed your eyes when colors presented themselves. But won't you be even more sorry and pathetic if you don't know that you have greatness of soul and nobility that make it possible for you to cope with every difficulty? [31] Things that are congruent with the faculty you possess present themselves, but you shut it off, just when you ought to have it wide open and observant. [32] Shouldn't you rather give thanks to the gods for having allowed you to be beyond the reach of everything they made not up to you, and for making you accountable only for

things that are up to you? [33] They released you from accountability for your parents, your brothers, your body, possessions, death, life. [34] So for what have they made you accountable? Only for what's up to you, which is the proper use of impressions. [35] So why are you taking on things for which you're unaccountable? You're just making trouble for yourself."

1.13
How to do whatever we do in a way that pleases the gods

[1] When someone asked if there was a way of eating that pleased the gods, he said, "If you eat in a way that's just, polite, fair, moderate,† and decent, isn't that also pleasing to the gods? [2] And if you call for warm water and the slave doesn't respond, or he responds but the water he brings is tepid, or he isn't even to be found in the house, isn't not getting angry, not blowing up, the way to please the gods?"

[3] "But people like that slave are intolerable."

"Slave, won't you tolerate someone who's your own brother? He has Zeus for a father, so that† he's a son born from the same seed as you and from the same heavenly sowing. [4] Just because you've been assigned a somewhat higher station, is your immediate reaction despotism? Won't you remember what you are and who these people are over whom you have authority—that they're kinsmen, brothers by nature, offspring of Zeus?"

[5] "But I own them, and they don't own me."

"Do you see where you're looking? You're directing your attention to the earth, to the pit, to these debased laws of ours, corpse-laws,* not to the laws of the gods."

1.14
That the Deity watches over us all

[1] When someone asked him for a convincing argument that everything anyone did was watched over by God, he said, [2] "You believe in the unity of the universe, don't you?"

"Yes," he said.

"And you believe that heavenly things are in a sympathetic relationship with things on earth?"*

"Yes," he said.

[3] "Yes, because how else could there be such regularity? It's as if God were issuing orders. When he tells trees to flower, they flower; when he tells them to propagate, they propagate; when he tells them to produce fruit, they produce fruit; when he tells them to ripen, they ripen. And again, when he tells them to let their fruit drop, shed their leaves, and, reduced now just to themselves, to stay quiet and rest, they stay quiet and rest. [4] And how else could the waxing and waning of the moon, and the approach and withdrawal of the sun, affect to such a degree the alternation and changing of opposites that we observe on earth? [5] But if plants and our bodies are so connected to the universe that it causes sympathetic changes in them, won't this be even more true for our souls? [6] But if our souls are connected and coupled with God in this way, since he is the greater whole of which they are fragments and splinters, won't he perceive every movement of our souls, since it will be his own movement and integral to him?

[7] "Now, *you* have the ability to apply your mind not only to the divine dispensation and every single aspect of it, but also to human affairs; you have the ability to be moved by countless things both sensually and mentally at the same time, and in such a way that you give your assent to some and reject others or suspend judgment; [8] you preserve in your mind numerous imprints, formed by a great many things of all kinds, and when you're moved by them, ideas occur to you that are of the same kind as those initial imprints; and so from countless sources you derive and retain the various skills, one after another, and your memories as well. [9] Is God, then, incapable of watching over everything, being simultaneously present everywhere, and receiving what everything transmits, so to speak? [10] When the sun is capable of lighting up such a large part of the universe, leaving unlit only the small part that is covered by the shadow cast by the earth, is he who made the sun (which is no more than a small part of him, compared to the whole) and causes it to revolve* not capable of perceiving everything?"

[11] "But *I* don't have the ability to attend to all these things at once," he said.

"Who says your abilities are equal to those of Zeus? [12] Nevertheless, he has also furnished every individual with a custodian in the form of an individual guardian spirit,* and has entrusted him to the protection of this unsleeping and undeceivable being. [13] Is there any better or more caring guardian to which he could have entrusted each of us? And so, when you people close your doors and make it dark inside, remember never to think that you're by yourselves, [14] because you aren't: God is there with you and so is your guardian spirit. And what need do they have of light to see what you're doing? [15] This is the God to whom you should swear allegiance as well, as soldiers do to Caesar. They swear that while they're on the payroll they'll make Caesar's safety their top priority, so won't you, who've been granted so many great blessings, take the oath and honor it thereafter? [16] And what will your oath be? Never to disobey, never to criticize, never to find fault with any of God's gifts to you, and never to be unwilling to do or endure whatever you must. [17] Is this oath similar to the military one? The soldiers swear not to hold anyone in higher honor than Caesar, but we swear to honor ourselves above all."

1.15
The prospect held out by philosophy

[1] When someone asked Epictetus to tell him how he could get his brother to stop being angry with him, [2] he said, "Philosophy doesn't promise to help anyone get anything external. If it did, it would be taking on something extraneous to the material that's proper to it. Just as wood is a carpenter's material, and bronze a sculptor's, so each individual's life is material for the art of living."

[3] "What about my brother's life, then?"

"Again, that's the material for *his* art of living, but as far as *your* art of living is concerned, it's an external, like farmland, health, and popularity. Philosophy doesn't hold out the prospect of your getting these things. [4] 'Under all circumstances, I shall keep the command center aligned with nature.' Whose command center? 'That of the individual in whom I am to be found.'"

[5] "So how am I to stop him being angry with me?"

"Bring him here and I'll talk to him, but I've nothing to say to *you* about *his* anger."

[6] At this, the man who was consulting him said, "What I want to

know is how I can remain in accord with nature even if he refuses to make peace with me."

[7] "Anything of any importance takes time," said Epictetus, "even a bunch of grapes or a fig. If what you were telling me now was 'I want a fig,' I'd reply, 'Be patient. First let the tree flower and then fruit, and then wait for the fruit to ripen.' [8] So given that it takes time for even a fig tree's fruit to mature, and it doesn't happen overnight, are you wanting to get the fruit of human intelligence so quickly and easily? You shouldn't expect that, even if I were to promise you it myself."

1.16

On providence

[1] "It should occasion no surprise that all other creatures have their bodily needs provided for them—not just food and drink, but a place to sleep as well—and that they have no need of footwear, bedding, or clothing, while we need all these things. [2] They don't exist for themselves, you see, but for service,* so there'd have been no point in creating them with other needs. [3] I mean, imagine what it would be like for us to have to care not only for ourselves but also for our sheep and donkeys—to make sure that they had clothing and footwear, food and drink! [4] No, just as soldiers report to their commanding officer already shod, clothed, and armed, and it would be dreadful if the tribune* had to go around finding shoes and clothing for his men, so when nature created animals for service, it made sure that they were equipped and ready, in need of no further care. [5] That's why one small child with a stick can drive a flock of sheep.

[6] "But as things are, instead of being grateful because we don't have to care for these creatures as much as we do for ourselves, we accuse God of failing us. [7] And yet, by Zeus and all the gods, take any single feature of creation, and on its own it's enough evidence of providence to satisfy anyone, as long as he's a respectful and appreciative kind of person. [8] I'm not talking about large-scale phenomena at the moment, but consider just the fact that milk comes from grass, cheese from milk, and wool from an animal's hide. Who made this happen? Who thought it up? No one? What a benighted and disgraceful state must one be in to say that!

[9] "All right, but let's leave aside nature's obvious works, and look

FIGURE 2. Representation of the Great Chain of Being from Diego de Valadés (1533–1582), *Rhetorica christiana* (1579). This is a medieval illustration of the *scala naturae* that lies in the background of some of Epictetus's remarks. Typically, in medieval times, the Great Chain of Being (as it was called then) ran as follows: God, angels, monarchs, commoners, animals, plants, inanimate objects.

at its more incidental products. [10] What could be more useless than the hairs on a chin? Well, but hasn't nature made even them serve the most fitting purpose possible? Don't they allow us to tell male from female? [11] Doesn't this natural endowment automatically enable each of us to call out from afar, 'I'm a man! Approach me as a man, talk to me as a man! No need to look any farther: the signs are plain to see!' [12] And what about women? Not only has nature made the tone of their voices more delicate, but it has also done away with their chin hair. You disagree? Humans should have been left without distinguishing marks, with each person having actually to declare his manhood? [13] But how fine and fair and grand a sign chin hair is! How much more beautiful it is than a cock's crest, how much more magnificent than a lion's mane! [14] And so we should preserve the signs given us by God, not discard them.* Insofar as it's up to us, we shouldn't confuse the sexes but keep them distinct.

[15] "Are these the only works of providence that relate to us? The question is rather whether there's any way to praise them all or describe them in words that do them justice. If we were in our right minds, isn't that precisely what we should be doing, in public and in private—glorifying God, singing his praises, and recounting all the ways in which he has benefited us? [16] As we dig and plow and eat, shouldn't we be glorifying God? 'Great is God, who supplied us with these tools with which we work the land. [17] Great is God, who gave us hands, and the ability to swallow, and a stomach; who gave us the ability to grow without being conscious of it and to breathe while we're asleep.' [18] That's how we should sing his praises in every instance, and the most important and most sacred of the hymns we should sing is the one thanking him for his gift to us of the ability to understand all this and make methodical use of it.

[19] "So, what? Since most of you are blind, there has to be someone to stand in for you, doesn't there? Someone to praise God on everyone's behalf? [20] After all, what else can a lame old man like me do except sing God's praises? If I were a nightingale, I'd do what nightingales do; if I were a swan, I'd sing like a swan. But as it is, I'm a rational being, and so I must glorify God in hymns of praise. [21] That's my work and I carry it out. That's what I've been assigned to do, and I shan't give up as long as I'm allowed to continue. And I invite you to join me in my singing."

1.17

On the indispensability of logic

[1] "Since it's reason that analyzes and processes everything else, and since it shouldn't go unanalyzed itself, what is it that analyzes it? [2] The answer, obviously, is that it is either reason itself or something else. Now, this 'something else' must either be reason or something superior to reason, but there's nothing superior to reason. [3] So, if it's reason, the question again arises: what will analyze it? If it's a case of reason analyzing itself, the reason we started with can do that. Otherwise, if once more we call on 'something else' to do the analyzing, we'll find ourselves in an unresolvable, interminable regress."*

[4] "True, but therapy and all that it entails are much more pressing needs."

"You want my response to that? Here it is. [5] Suppose you were to tell me 'I'm not sure that your argument is valid (or invalid),' or suppose I use a term in an equivocal way and you ask me to disambiguate it. I won't comply; I'll just tell you, 'There are more pressing matters.' [6] That, I imagine, is why logic is given priority; it's the equivalent of considering the measure before weighing grain. [7] If we don't first determine what a modius is,* and if we don't first determine how a pair of scales works, how will we be able to weigh or measure anything? [8] The same goes here. If we don't have full and precise knowledge of the criterion by which we assess everything else and which enables us to gain full knowledge of everything else, how will we be able to gain full and precise knowledge of anything? It'll be impossible, won't it?"

[9] "All right, but a modius is just a piece of wood.* Nothing comes of it."

"But it's good for measuring grain."

[10] "And nothing comes of logic either."

"Well, we'll come to that later. But even were that to be granted, it's enough that logic should enable us to draw distinctions and investigate everything else—to measure and weigh them, as it were. [11] According to whom? Only Chrysippus, Zeno, and Cleanthes?* [12] But doesn't Antisthenes say so too?* And who was it who wrote 'Education begins with the examination of terms'? Doesn't Socrates say as much?* And who's Xenophon writing about when he says that he made his starting point the examination of terms—that he inquired into the meaning of everything?"*

[13] "So is this a great and admirable achievement, to be able to understand or interpret Chrysippus?"

"No one's saying that."

"What is admirable, then?"

"Understanding the will of nature. [14] So where does that leave us? Is that something you can do by yourself? If so, what more do you need? I mean, if it's true that all wrongdoing is involuntary,* and you have full knowledge of the truth, you're bound to be acting correctly already."

[15] "Good heavens! Of course I don't understand the will of nature."

"Who can explain it, then? It's said that Chrysippus can. [16] I go and try to find out what this interpreter of nature says. At first, I don't understand his meaning, so I look for someone to explain it to me. 'Here,' I say. 'What do you make of this? What do you think it means? Treat it as though it were written in Latin.'* [17] So is there anything here for the interpreter to take pride in? It wouldn't be right for even Chrysippus himself to feel proud if all he does is interpret the will of nature, but doesn't follow it himself. The same goes even more emphatically for his interpreter. [18] Look, we don't need even Chrysippus for himself; what we want is his help in understanding nature. After all, we don't need a diviner for himself either, but because we expect him to help us understand the future and the signs sent by the gods; [19] nor do we need the entrails as such, but because they are the channels of communication; nor is it the crow we think important, or the raven, but the god who uses these birds as his messengers.

[20] "So I approach this interpreter, this diviner, and I say, 'Examine the entrails for me, please. What message do they hold for me?' [21] He takes them, spreads them out, and interprets them as follows: 'My friend, you have will, which is in itself unimpeded and unconstrained. So it is written here, in the entrails. [22] I shall prove it to you, first in the domain of assent. Can anyone stop you assenting to a truth?' 'No, no one can.' 'Can anyone compel you to accept a falsehood?' 'No, no one can.' [23] Do you see that in this domain you have a faculty of will that is unimpeded, unconstrained, and un-

obstructed? [24] And what about the domains of desire and inclination? Isn't it just the same? Who or what can overcome one of your inclinations except another of your inclinations? Who or what can overcome a desire or an aversion, except another desire or aversion?"

[25] "But if someone threatens me with death, that's a kind of constraint."

"No, it's not the threat of death that's constraining you, but the fact that you judge it better to act in ways that enable you to avoid death. [26] Once again, then, we find that it's your judgment that's constraining you—which is to say that your will constrained your will. [27] After all, if God had made the part of himself—the fragment of himself that he gave to us—such that it could be impeded or constrained by him or anyone else, he would no longer be God, nor would he care for us as he should.

[28] "'This is what I find in the entrails,' continues the diviner. 'This is God's message to you. If you so wish, you are free. If you so wish, you'll blame no one, find fault with no one, and everything will be in accord not just with your own will, but with God's.' [29] This is the prophecy that makes my visit to this philosophical diviner of ours worthwhile, not because I admire him for his interpretation, but because I recognize the importance of the content of his interpretation."

1.18
That one should not get angry with people for their mistakes

[1] "If what the philosophers say is true, and not only is assent only ever prompted by the feeling that something is the case, and the withholding of assent by the feeling that something is not the case, and, by Zeus, suspension of judgment by the feeling that something is uncertain, [2] but also an inclination to do something is prompted by the feeling that it's expedient for me to do it; and if it's impossible for me to judge something as in my best interests and yet desire something else, and impossible to judge one action as appropriate and yet have an inclination to do something else—if all this is true, why are we still so commonly angry with people?"

[3] "But there are thieves and robbers, aren't there?"

"What does it mean to call people thieves and robbers? They're mistaken about good and bad. So do they deserve anger or pity?* [4] Show them where they've gone wrong and you'll see them desist from their mistakes. If they don't see what you're getting at, they remain bogged down in their mistaken beliefs."

[5] "But shouldn't a thief or an adulterer be eliminated, just for being who he is?"

"No, and you'd do better to phrase your question like this: [6] 'Should we do away with this person because he's mistaken and misled about matters of supreme importance, and because he's become blind—not in the sense that he's lost the ability to distinguish white and black by sight, but because he's lost the mental ability to distinguish good and bad?' [7] If you put the question like this, you'll realize how inhumane it is, and see that it's no different from saying, 'So shouldn't we kill this blind person, or this deaf person?' [8] If a person is injured most by the loss of the most important things, and if the most important thing in every individual is right will, what's the point in getting angry with someone if he loses it?

[9] "Listen, man. If, unnatural though it is, you feel obliged to adopt an attitude toward someone else's troubles, you should pity him rather than hate him.* Let's have no more of this readiness to take offense and hate people. [10] Think who you are, man. Do you really want to express sentiments that one expects to hear only from the masses, such as 'Curse these vile and loathsome people'? Well, all right. But how come you've suddenly abandoned good sense and are now angry with other people?

[11] "Anyway, why do we get angry? Because we value the stuff others take from us. I mean, look: place no value on your clothes and you don't get angry at someone for stealing them; place no value on your wife's attractions, and you don't get angry at someone for seducing her. [12] You need to appreciate that thieves and adulterers don't fall into the category of what's up to you, but into the category of things that are external to you and aren't up to you. If you dismiss them and consider them worthless, who can make you angry? And for as long as you give them significance, be angry with yourself, not with them. [13] Consider the following scenario. You have nice clothes, your neighbor doesn't. You have a window onto the street and you want to dry them. Your neighbor, in his ignorance about what constitutes the good for a human being, thinks (as you do too)

that it consists in having nice clothes. [14] So he'll come and steal them, won't he? If you let greedy people see that you've got a cake and you start to gobble it down on your own, aren't you inviting them to snatch it away from you? Don't tempt them; do without a window onto the street; don't put your clothes out to dry.

[15] "Something similar happened to me, too, just the other day. There's an iron lamp by my household shrine, and I heard the window make a noise and ran downstairs to find the lamp had been stolen. I reasoned that the thief had been moved by an inclination he found compelling. 'All right, then,' I said. 'Tomorrow I'll buy one of clay.'* [16] The point is that one can only lose what one has. 'I've lost my toga.' Yes, because you had a toga. 'I've got a headache.' But you don't have a horn-ache, do you? So why are you annoyed? Only things we possess can be lost or ache.*

[17] "'But the tyrant will chain...' What? Your leg. 'He'll remove...' What? Your head? So what can't be chained or removed? Your will. That's why men of old recommended the precept 'Know yourself.'* [18] What we have to do, then, by the gods, is practice on little things, and move on from this starting point to greater things. [19] 'My head aches.' Don't say, 'Poor me!' 'My ear aches.' Don't say, 'Poor me!' I'm not saying you don't have the right to complain, but don't complain inwardly. And if the slave is slow in bringing the poultice, don't cry out and lose your composure. Don't say, 'Everyone hates me!' Who wouldn't hate someone who carries on like that? [20] From now on, rely on these principles and walk upright and free. Don't rely on the size of your body, like an athlete. You don't have to be invincible in the way that a donkey is.

[21] "Who is invincible, then? Anyone who isn't sidetracked by things that aren't subject to his will. And so next I set myself to understand what might happen in every possible situation, as I would for an athlete. 'He's powered his way through the first round. What about the second? What if it's blazing hot? How will he perform in the Olympics?' [22] So likewise for our invincible person. All right, if you offer him money, he'll reject it. But what if it's a girl that's on offer? What if it's after dark? What if it's fame? What if it's an insult? What if it's praise? What if it's death? He can't be defeated by any of these. [23] What if it's blazing hot or—the effect is the same—

he's had some wine? What if he's in a black mood? What if he's asleep? This is the man I'd call an invincible athlete."

1.19
The proper attitude to have toward tyrants

[1] "Arrogance is absolutely inevitable in a person—an uneducated person, that is—who enjoys some advantage, or at least thinks he does, even if he doesn't. [2] A tyrant, for example, claims to be the most powerful man in the world. So what can you do for me with your power? Can you ensure that my desires are never impeded? How could you, when you can't do that for yourself? That my aversions effectively prevent the occurrence of things I want to avoid? No, because you can't do that for yourself. That my inclinations never lead me astray? I don't see that as one of your gifts. [3] Tell me: when you're on a ship, do you place your trust in yourself or in the expert? When you're on a wagon—yourself or the expert? [4] What about any other area of expertise? Same story. So what does your power amount to?

"'I'm the focus of everyone's attention.' Yes, and I attend to my plate; I wash it and dry it, and I drive a peg into the wall for my oil flask. Does that make these things more powerful than me? No, but they're useful to me, and that's why I attend to them. Don't I also attend to my donkey? [5] Don't I wash its feet and rub it down? Can't you see that everyone attends to his own needs, and attends to you as he does his donkey? I mean, who cares for you as a person? Point him out to me. [6] Who wishes to be like you? Who takes you as a role model, as they do Socrates? 'But I can have you beheaded.' You're right. I'd forgotten that I should attend to you in the same way that I attend to a fever or cholera—that I should set up an altar to you, just as Fever has an altar in Rome.*

[7] "What is it that's usually found troubling, even frightening? The tyrant? His bodyguards? Is that possible? Hardly! It's impossible for something that's naturally free to be troubled or impeded by anything except itself. [8] Only his own judgments trouble a person. When a tyrant tells someone, 'I'm going to chain your leg,' only a person who has come to value his leg says, 'Please, no! Have mercy!' But anyone who judges his will important says, 'Go ahead, if you think

that's the most expedient thing for you to do.' 'Don't you care?' 'No, I don't.' [9] 'I'll show you that I'm your master.' 'How will you do that? Zeus has set me free. Do you really think he's going to let his own son be enslaved? You're the master of my carcass: take that.' [10] 'You mean to say that when you're in my presence, I'm not the focus of your attention?' 'No, I'm attending to myself. If you want me to tell you that I attend to you as well, here's what I say: I give you the same kind of attention that I give my kettle.'

[11] "This isn't selfishness; the creature in question was born like this. It does everything for itself.* Even the sun does everything for itself, and so, for that matter, does Zeus himself. [12] But sometimes Zeus wishes to be 'the Bringer of Rain,' 'the Fruitful,' and 'Father of Gods and Men,' and you can see that he can't perform these functions and deserve these titles unless he makes some contribution to the common good. [13] And (without going into details) he equipped the rational creature with a nature which is such that its own particular goods are unattainable unless it makes some beneficial contribution to the common good. [14] In which case, doing everything for oneself isn't selfish. [15] Anyway, do you seriously expect someone to neglect himself and his own interest? In that case, how could all living creatures share the same fundamental drive; namely, appropriation to themselves?

[16] "It follows, then, that when someone entertains uncouth views about things that aren't subject to will—that is, when he labels such things good and bad—he is absolutely bound to dance attendance on tyrants. [17] If only it was just the tyrants, and not their chamberlains as well! How does a person become wise all of a sudden when Caesar puts him in charge of his closestool? How come we suddenly say, 'Felicio had some wise words for me'? [18] I'd like to see him demoted from his dung heap, so that you'd regard him once more as a fool. [19] Epaphroditus had a shoemaker who was so useless that he sold him. But then it so happened that the man was bought by a member of Caesar's household and became Caesar's shoemaker. You should have seen the respect Epaphroditus showed him! [20] 'What's up, Felicio, my very dear friend?'* [21] Moreover, if one of us asked, 'What's the master doing?' he was told, 'He's in a meeting with Felicio.' [22] But hadn't he sold him as useless? So

who suddenly made him wise? [23] This is what happens when someone regards as important anything other than what is subject to will.

[24] "'He's been made a tribune.' Everyone who runs into him offers his congratulations. One kisses his eyes, another his neck, slaves kiss his hands. He goes home and finds lamps being lit for him.* He goes up to the Capitol and offers a sacrifice. [25] But who has ever performed a sacrifice in thanks for the fact that his desires went well, or because his inclinations were in accord with nature? After all, it's things we count as good for which we thank the gods.[26]

"Someone was talking to me today about the priesthood of Augustus.* 'Steer well clear of it, man!' I advised him. 'You'll incur considerable expenses for nothing.' [27] 'But when bills of sale are drawn up, they'll be inscribed with my name.' 'But you won't actually be there when people read these contracts, will you? "Look: that's my name written there." [28] And then, even supposing that you were in fact able to be physically present at every signing, what will you do after your death?' 'My name will survive me.' 'Carve your name on a rock and it'll survive you. But tell me: who will remember you beyond Nicopolis?' [29] 'But I'll wear a golden crown.' 'Well, if you really want a crown, get a crown of roses and put it on. That'll look more chic.'"

1.20
*On reason and its ability to examine itself**

[1] "Every art and every faculty has the ability to examine certain specific objects. [2] When it's of the same kind as its objects, it necessarily becomes capable of examining itself as well. When it's of a different kind from its objects, it's unable to examine itself. [3] Take shoemaking, for example. It occupies itself with leather, but it's not at all leatherlike itself, and so it's unable to examine itself. [4] Or take grammar. Its concern is grammatically correct language, but that's not to say that it is itself grammatically correct language, is it? No. So it can't examine itself. [5] Now, why has nature given us reason? For the correct use of impressions. Well, what is reason in itself? A systematic arrangement of impressions of various kinds. So it's natural for it to be capable of examining itself as well. [6] Now consider

wisdom: it comes with the ability to look at what objects? Things that are good, bad, and indifferent. And in itself, what is it? A good thing. And lack of wisdom? A bad thing. Evidently, then, it necessarily has the ability to examine both itself and its opposite.

[7] "It follows that a philosopher's most important and crucial work is to assess impressions and distinguish between them, and only ever to accept an impression if it has been assessed. [8] In the case of coined money, which is supposed to be of interest to us, you can see that we've actually invented an art, covering all the ways in which an assayer tests coins—sight, touch, smell, and, last but not least, hearing. [9] He throws the denarius down, listens to the sound it makes, and so far from being satisfied by hearing it ring just once, he listens again and again, until he becomes a regular musician! [10] So, in areas where we think it makes a lot of difference whether or not we're misled, we're very diligent about trying to spot things that are likely to mislead us, [11] but in the case of our poor command center, we yawn and doze, and carelessly accept every impression because it doesn't occur to us that any harm will come of it. [12] So if you wish to know how casually you treat things that are good and bad, and how seriously you treat things that are indifferent, compare your attitude toward going blind with your attitude toward being in intellectual error. Then you'll see how badly you misjudge where goodness and badness lie."

[13] "But that needs a lot of aptitude, hard work, and study."

"So what? Do you think it takes only a little effort to acquire expertise in the most important art there is? [14] It's true that it takes hardly any time to state the core philosophical principles. If you're curious, read Zeno and you'll see. [15] I mean, how much time does it take to say, 'The goal of life is to follow the gods,' or 'The essence of goodness is the right use of impressions'? [16] But ask, 'What is a god?' and 'What is an impression?', or 'What is the nature of a particular individual?' and 'What is the nature of the universe?', and these questions take time.

[17] "If Epicurus happened by and told us that goodness must be something that involves the body, that again is a lengthy matter, for which you need to understand what the principal faculty in us is— that is, what the substantial and essential part of us is. It doesn't seem likely that goodness for a snail has to do with its shell, so is this a

plausible thing to say about a human being?* [18] Consider just your own case, Epicurus: What faculty do you have that's more authoritative than the body? What is it in you that deliberates, that thinks about everything, that considers the body itself and concludes that it's our principal component? [19] Why do you light your lamp and work so hard for our sakes, writing so many books?* Isn't it to make sure that we're not ignorant of the truth? Who are we? What are we to you? That's how the discussion becomes lengthy."

1.21
To those who want to be admired

[1] "When a man occupies his proper station in life, he doesn't yearn for anything more. [2] What would you like to happen, man? Speaking for myself, I'm satisfied if my desires and aversions are in accord with nature, if I manage my inclinations and disinclinations as my nature requires, and if my intentions,† objectives, and acts of assent are in compliance with nature. So why are you walking around letting us see that you've swallowed a skewer?* [3] 'I want to be universally admired. I want people to follow me around, crying out, "What a great philosopher!"' [4] Who are these people, the ones whose admiration you want? Aren't they the same people that you usually call mad?* So you want to be admired by mad people?"

1.22
On preconceptions

[1] "Preconceptions are common to all people, and there's no conflict between one preconception and another. Is there anyone who doesn't believe that anything that's good is advantageous and choiceworthy, and that we should make it our goal and aim in every situation? Is there anyone who doesn't believe that anything just is honorable and fitting? [2] So when does conflict occur? In the application of preconceptions to particular instances. [3] For instance, when someone says, 'He behaved honorably; he's a brave man,' and someone else says, 'You're wrong. In fact, he's out of his mind.'* That's how conflict occurs between people.* [4] Hence the conflict that exists between Jews, Syrians, Egyptians, and Romans is not over the

principle that holiness should always be one's top priority and should be one's goal in all circumstances, but whether the particular act of, say, eating pig meat is holy or unholy.*

[5] "You'll find that the same goes for the conflict between Agamemnon and Achilles as well.* Call them to testify. What do you think, Agamemnon? Shouldn't one do what is right and behave honorably? 'Of course.' [6] And what do you think, Achilles? Do you agree that one should behave honorably? 'Yes, absolutely.' So now apply these generalizations to the particular case; that's where the conflict arises. [7] One of them says, 'I'm not obliged to return Chryseis to her father,' and the other one says, 'Yes, you are.' It goes without saying that one or the other of them is misapplying the preconception of what it's right to do. [8] Again, one of them says, 'Well, if I have to give Chryseis back, it's only right that one of you should give me his war prize.' And the other says, 'So is it my concubine you want to take?' 'Yes, yours,' comes the reply. 'Am I alone to be without a war prize?'*† 'But am I alone to have nothing?' That's how conflict arises.

[9] "So what is education? Learning to apply your natural preconceptions to particular instances in accord with nature, [10] and also gaining the ability to recognize that some things are up to us and some aren't. Up to us are will and everything that results from will; not up to us are the body, the parts of the body, possessions, parents, brothers, children, the country of our birth, and in short, all the people with whom we associate. [11] So where will we find what's good for us? To what should we apply the concept? To what's up to us."

[12] "But then, where does that leave health, an unimpaired body, and life? Aren't they good? Do you really mean that not even our children, parents, or homeland are good things? Do you expect to get away with saying that?"

[13] "All right, then, let's apply the concept to the things you mentioned instead. So, is it possible to be happy if one's body is impaired and one fails to get good things?"

"No, it's not."

"What about treating one's associates right? How is that possible when it's natural for me to look out for my own interests? [14] If it's good for me to have a plot of land, it's also good for me to take my neighbor's plot of land. If it's good for me to have a toga, it's also good for me to steal one from the bathhouse. This is how war starts, and civil strife, tyranny, intrigue. [15] Moreover, it'll be impossible for me to worship Zeus appropriately, won't it? If my body's impaired and I'm a wretched failure, he doesn't care for me. And so: 'Damn him if he can't help me!' Or again: 'Damn him if it's his will that I'm doing so badly!' And then I begin to hate him. [16] 'Why do we build temples for Zeus and set up cult statues, when he treats us as evil spirits do, or as Fever does? How can he possibly be the Savior, the Bringer of Rain, the Fruitful?' But if we locate the essence of goodness in externals, all these consequences necessarily follow. [17] What are we to do, then? Getting to the bottom of this issue is what a true philosopher does, one who's in labor.* At present I can't see what's good and what's bad. Am I out of my mind, then? Yes.

[18] "But if I locate goodness here, among the things that are subject to my will, everyone will mock me. Some white-haired old man, his fingers dripping with gold rings, will come up to me, and then with a shake of his head he'll say, 'Listen to me, child. There's nothing wrong with doing philosophy, but you've got to keep your head. What you're doing at the moment is stupid. [19] Philosophers can teach you how to argue, but you know better than they do what you should be doing.' [20] So why are you telling me off, sir, if I know that? What can I say to this slave? If I say nothing, he loses his temper. [21] So I'd better say, 'Please excuse me as you would someone who's in love. I can't help myself, I'm out of my mind.'"

1.23

Against Epicurus*

[1] "Epicurus understands as well as anyone that it's in our natures to be social, but since he's committed to locating what's good for us in the shell that is our body, he can't say anything that contradicts this,* [2] because he next resolutely insists—and he's right in this respect—that we shouldn't value or accept anything that's unrelated to the nature of the good. [3] So why, if it's not natural for us to feel affection for our offspring,* do we regard with suspicion your suggestion that a wise man won't have any children of his own? Why are you worried that children will cause him distress? [4] Does the mouse that's growing up in his household causes him distress?* Why should it bother him if a little house mouse bursts into tears in his presence?

[5] No, Epicurus knew that, once a child is born, it's impossible for us not to love it and care for it.* [6] This also explains why he says that a sensible person won't have a public career; he knows what a public career necessarily entails. I mean, after all, if you intend to treat the company of other people as though they were flies, there's nothing to stop you. [7] Nevertheless, even though he's well aware of what I've been saying, he still has the audacity to say that we shouldn't raise children. But sheep don't abandon their offspring, nor do wolves—and a human does? [8] Take your pick: are people as foolish as sheep? Sheep don't abandon their offspring. Or are they as savage as wolves? Wolves don't abandon their offspring either.* [9] Tell me: does anyone who sees his child crying after falling to the ground find this idea of yours plausible? [10] It's my opinion that even if your parents had guessed that one day you'd think as you do, they still wouldn't have thrown you out of the house."

1.24
How to combat difficult circumstances

[1] "A person's caliber is revealed by difficult circumstances, and so, when a difficulty occurs, think of it as God pitting you, as a trainer might, against a tough training partner."

[2] "To what end?" someone asked.

"To help you become an Olympic victor,* which takes sweat. Anyway, it seems to me that no one has ever had a better difficulty than the one you have now, if you're prepared to use it as an athlete uses a training partner. [3] Now, we're currently in the process of sending you off to Rome as a spy. But no one sends a coward out on such a mission, someone who's terrified by the slightest noise or glimpse of a shadow, and comes running back to report that the enemy has already arrived. [4] So, in the present instance, suppose you too were to return to us and say, 'The situation in Rome is very frightening. Death, banishment, abuse, poverty—all are terrifyingly widespread. Run for your lives, men, the enemy's here!' [5] If you do that, we'll say to you, 'Go away! Save your predictions for yourself! Our only mistake was to have entrusted the mission to a coward like you. [6] Your predecessor as a spy, Diogenes, brought us back a different report.* "Death is no evil," he says, "since it involves no shame." "Disfavor is just noise produced by crazy people," he says.* [7] And see what this spy has to say about pain, pleasure, and poverty: "Simple clothing is better than any purple-trimmed toga"; "There's no bed more comfortable than the bare ground." [8] And as proof of each of his claims, he offers his courage, his serenity, his freedom, and also his body, hardened and glowing with health. [9] "There's no enemy nearby," he says. "Peace prevails everywhere." "How can you say that, Diogenes?" "Look at me," he replies. "Have I been hit by any missile? Have I been injured? Have I fled before anyone's assault?" [10] That's what it is to be a proper spy, but you bring us back a totally different kind of report. Why don't you go back and take a closer look, without succumbing to cowardice?'"

[11] "What am I to do, then?"

"What do you do when you leave a boat? You don't take the rudder or the oars with you, do you? What do you take? The things that belong to you—your oil flask and bag. In the present case, too, all you need to do is remember what's yours and you won't claim anything that isn't. [12] 'Take off your senatorial toga,' he says.* 'See? Now I'm wearing an equestrian toga.' 'Take that off too.' 'See? Now I'm wearing a plain toga.' 'Take it off.' 'See? Now I'm naked.' [13] 'But I'm still envious of you.' 'Take my entire body, then.' If I'm capable of flinging my body at someone, what reason could I have to fear him?

[14] "'But he won't remember me in his will.' So what? Have I forgotten that none of these things is mine? The only sense in which they're mine, then, is the sense in which we say that a bed in an inn is mine. So if on his death the innkeeper leaves you his beds … But if he leaves them to someone else, they'll be his and you'll have to look for another bed. [15] If you don't find one, you'll sleep on the ground, but be sure to do so free of care, snoring away, and bearing in mind that tragedies are played out among the rich, among kings and tyrants, while no one who's poor plays a part unless he happens to be a member of the chorus. [16] Kings start out from prosperity—'Deck the palace with garlands!'—but then, round about the third or fourth act: 'O Cithaeron, why did you receive me?'* [17] Slave, where are your garlands? Where's your diadem? Where's the help from your bodyguards? [18] So when you approach any of these people, remember this about them, that you're approaching a character in a tragedy— not the actor, but Oedipus himself."

[19] "But he's blessed with good fortune. I mean, wherever he goes, he's surrounded by people."

"Me too. I join a crowd and I'm surrounded by people wherever I go. [20] But the crucial point is this: remember that the door is open. Don't show yourself to be more of a coward than children are, but just as they say, 'I shan't play anymore,' when they don't like a game, so when you feel that things have got too difficult, say, 'I shan't play anymore,' and take your leave.* But if you stay, no complaining."

1.25
The same topic

[1] "If this is true, and we're not being frivolous or putting on an act when we say that what's good and bad for us lies in our will, and that everything else is nothing to us—if this is so, why are we troubled? What is there to fear? [2] The things we value aren't in anyone else's power, and the things that are in others' power we're not interested in. What is there to trouble us?"

[3] "Give me some guidance."

"What guidance am I to offer? Hasn't Zeus offered you guidance already?* Hasn't he made it so that what's yours is unimpeded and unobstructed, while what's not yours is subject to impediment and obstruction? [4] What guidance, what instructions, did you have from him when you came into this world? 'Do all you can to preserve what's yours and don't chase after things that aren't yours.' Your trustworthiness is yours; your self-respect is yours. These are not things that anyone can take from you. No one but you can stop you making use of them. How? When you're intent on things that aren't yours, you lose the things that are.

[5] "When Zeus has given you these kinds of directions and guidelines, what more do you want from me? Am I greater than him? Am I more deserving of your trust? [6] If you keep his commandments, do you need any others?* If there's any doubt that he's given you this guidance, look to your preconceptions, the proofs of the philosophers, the many talks you've attended, your own assertions, the books you've read, the subjects you've studied. [7] For how long is it right to obey his rules and not break up the game? As long as it's be-

ing conducted in a pleasing fashion. [8] At the Saturnalia* a king is chosen, because that's the game it's been decided to play. He issues orders: 'You, drink! You, prepare the wine! You, sing! You, go! You, come!' I obey, so as not to be responsible for breaking up the game. [9] 'You, believe yourself to be in a bad way.' I believe no such thing, and no one can make me do so. [10] Here's another example. We've agreed to act out the story of Agamemnon and Achilles.* The actor chosen to play Agamemnon tells me, 'Go to Achilles and take Briseis from him.' Off I go. [11] 'Come here,' he commands, and I go to him.

"What I'm getting at is that we should behave in life as we do in the case of hypothetical arguments. 'Let's assume, hypothetically, that it's night.' All right. 'So is it day?' No, because I've accepted the hypothesis that it's night. [12] 'Let's assume, hypothetically, that you suppose it to be night.' All right. 'Now also think that it actually is night.' No, that's inconsistent with the hypothesis. [13] So also in the present case. 'Let's assume, hypothetically, that you're in a miserable state.' All right. 'So you're wretched.' Yes. 'And unhappy, then.' Yes. 'Now believe yourself actually to be unhappy as well.' No, that's inconsistent with the hypothesis. Also, someone else* makes it impossible for me to believe that. [14] So for how long should one obey Zeus's rules? As long as it's worthwhile, or in other words, as long as I can continue to act in ways that are fitting and appropriate.

[15] "Anyway, there are some people, severe and dyspeptic types, who say, 'I'm incapable of dining with him. Every day he recounts his exploits during the war in Mysia* and I can't stand it. "I've told you, brother, how I made my way up to the top of the hill. The siege was renewed there..."' [16] But another person says, 'I'd rather have the meal and listen to him babbling on as much as he likes.' [17] You'd better choose between these two perspectives. Just don't do anything when you're feeling down or distressed, or when you believe yourself to be badly off—which no one is forcing you to do.

[18] "Has someone made the house smoky? If it's not too bad, I'll stay; if it's too much, I leave. What you need to remember and keep in mind is this: the door is open. [19] 'You're not to live in Nicopolis.' All right. 'Nor in Athens.' All right, not in Athens either. 'Nor in Rome.' Not in Rome either, then. 'You're to live on Gyara.'* [20] All right. But living on Gyara seems to me to be a lot of smoke. So I take

myself off to where no one can stop me residing, because it's open to all. [21] And once I've shed the last item of clothing, my body, no one has any way to get at me. [22] That's why Demetrius said to Nero,* 'You're threatening me with death, the same thing you're threatened with by nature.' [23] If I consider my body important, I turn myself into a slave; likewise if I value my possessions. [24] You see, I thereby betray myself by showing what can be used to capture me. When a snake pulls back its head, I say, 'Hit it there, because that's the part it's trying to protect.' And so, believe me, whatever you want to protect is where your master will attack you. [25] If you bear this in mind, whom are you going to flatter? Whom will you fear?"

[26] "But I want to sit in the senatorial seats."

"Can't you see that you're hemming yourself in, oppressing yourself?"

[27] "But otherwise, how will I get a clear view of what happens in the amphitheater?"

"Just don't go to the show, man. Don't oppress yourself. Why are you making trouble for yourself? Alternatively, wait a bit, and after the show's over go and sun yourself in the senatorial seats. [28] The basic point to remember is this: we oppress ourselves, we hem ourselves in—which is to say that our judgments oppress us and hem us in. [29] What, for instance, is this thing we call being abused? Stand by a stone and abuse it. Will you have any effect? So if you listen like a stone, what good will abuse do an abuser? But if he can use the weakness of the person he's abusing to gain a purchase, then he'll get somewhere. [30] 'Strip him.' What do you mean, 'him'? Take his *clothes* and strip him of them. 'I've insulted you.' Much good may it do you! [31] These are the principles that Socrates put into practice, and that's why he always wore the same calm expression. But we prefer to study and train ourselves in anything rather than how to become unobstructed and free."

[32] "'Philosophers speak in paradoxes.'* Are there no paradoxes in other arts? What could be more paradoxical than lancing people's eyes to enable them to see? If someone who was ignorant of medicine was told about this procedure, wouldn't he laugh at the person who was telling him about it? [33] So why is it surprising if many of the truths of philosophy seem paradoxical to the ignorant?"*

1.26

What is the law of life?

[1] Someone was reciting the hypothetical arguments when Epictetus remarked that one of the rules governing them was that one had to accept anything that's consistent with the hypothesis. "Much more important, however," he went on, "is the law of life that one has to act in a way that's consistent with nature. [2] It therefore plainly follows that, whatever the issue and whatever the conditions, if we want to remain in accord with nature, we must always aim to neither shun what's consistent with nature nor accept what conflicts with it. [3] That's why philosophers start our training with theory, where there's less difficulty, before introducing the harder matters. I mean, there's nothing in theoretical work that holds us back from following what we're being taught, but there's plenty in life to distract us. [4] So anyone who expresses a wish to get straight down to practical matters is making a fool of himself, given that it's not easy to start with what's more difficult.

[5] "And here's the defense to use with parents who are angry with their children for studying philosophy: 'Very well, father. I'm making a mistake. I don't know where my duty lies and what it's proper for me to do. Now, if this is something that can be neither learned nor taught, what grounds have you got for telling me off? But if it's teachable, teach me, and if you can't, allow me to learn it from those who claim expertise in the field. [6] I mean, do you suppose that I'm deliberately embracing what's bad for me and depriving myself of what's good? Hardly! So what has caused my mistake? It must be ignorance. [7] So don't you want me to lose my ignorance? Has anger ever taught anyone the art of navigation or music? So do you think that your anger will teach me the art of life?'

[8] "These words can be spoken only by someone whose objective is to learn the art of life. [9] However, if someone merely wants to show off his knowledge of hypotheticals at a dinner party, and that's why he reads books on the subject and attends philosophers' lectures, all he's doing is trying to win the admiration of the senator sitting beside him, isn't he? [10] It's there in Rome that the truly great fortunes are to be found, and riches here seem child's play to people there. That's why it's difficult to control one's impressions in Rome, since

powerful forces disconcert you. [11] I know someone who clasped Epaphroditus's knees in supplication,* with tears in his eyes, and told him that he was badly off because he'd lost everything—except a million and a half sesterces! [12] And what did Epaphroditus do? Laugh at the man as you are now? No. In an astonished tone of voice, he said, 'Your poor man! Why didn't you say anything? However did you keep going?'"

[13] The student reciting the hypotheticals was unsettled by this, and when the person who had set him to read them laughed, Epictetus said, "You're laughing at yourself for your failure to provide the young man with any preliminary training. You didn't find out whether he was capable of following these arguments, and yet you let him give a reading.

[14] "Why," he went on, "when a mind is incapable of following and assessing a complex argument, do we trust it to assign praise or blame—to assess whether someone has done well or badly? When someone who can't discern what comes next in something as trivial as an argument says that something was badly done, does the person he's criticizing care? If he says it was well done, does the person he's praising feel proud? [15] The first step in philosophy, then, is to recognize what kind of condition one's command center is in, because recognition of its weakness will make a person hesitate to apply it to the important matters. [16] At the moment, however, people who are incapable of swallowing a morsel buy whole treatises for their consumption. This makes them throw up and gives them indigestion, and then there follow stomach cramps, diarrhea, and fever. What they should have done is consider whether it was beyond their capabilities. [17] In theoretical work, it's easy to refute someone who's ignorant, but in life no one willingly submits to that kind of examination, and we hate anyone who puts us through it. [18] Socrates used to say that the unexamined life was not worth living."*

1.27
How many ways are there for impressions to arise, and what resources should we make sure we have at hand to help us with them?

[1] "There are four ways in which impressions occur to us. Either things that exist also appear to exist, or they don't exist and don't ap-

pear to exist, or they exist and don't appear to exist, or they don't exist and yet appear to exist.* [2] So it's the job of a trained philosopher to avoid error in all these cases. Whatever it is that's causing us difficulties, we must apply the appropriate remedy. If it's the sophisms of the Pyrrhonists and Academics* that are causing us difficulties, we must apply the appropriate remedy to them. [3] If it's the specious plausibility of things, so that some things appear good when they aren't, we must look for the appropriate remedy for that. If it's a habit that's troubling us, we must try to find the appropriate remedy to use against that. [4] So what's the remedy for a habit? The opposite habit. [5] You hear non-philosophers saying, 'Oh, I'm really sorry that he died! His father's crushed and so is his mother. He was cut down before his time in a foreign land.' [6] Listen to the opposite sentiments, free yourself from these habitual ones, counter a habit with the opposite habit. Countering sophisms requires logic, so study and practice logic. To counter the speciousness of things, clear preconceptions are required, polished and ready for use.

[7] "When death seems bad, the idea we need to have at hand is that it's appropriate for us to avoid things that are bad, but death is unavoidable.* After all, what shall I do? Where shall I run to escape it? [8] Suppose that I'm Sarpedon, the son of Zeus, so that I may echo his noble words:* 'When I left home, my intention was either to distinguish myself in battle or to enable someone else to do so. If I can't achieve any kind of success myself, I won't resent it if someone else performs nobly.' [9] Even if such greatness of mind is beyond us, the idea I mentioned before is available to us, isn't it? Indeed, where shall I run to escape death? Show me the country, show me the people I could go to who are beyond the reach of death. Show me a charm against it. Since I have no such charm, please tell me what to do. [10] I can't avoid death, but might I not avoid being frightened by it? Am I bound to die grieving and trembling with fear?

"The point is that the root cause of passion is wanting something and not getting it.* [11] That's why, if I'm able to alter my external circumstances to suit my wishes, I do so, and if I can't, I'm ready to gouge out the eyes of the person who's obstructing me. [12] It's because it's human nature to find it unbearable to be deprived of something good or to experience something bad. [13] And then the upshot is that, when I'm unable to alter my circumstances or blind someone for obstructing me, I sit and moan, and curse anyone I can—Zeus and

the rest of the gods—because if they don't care for me, damn them!
[14] 'All right, but that attitude will make you impious.' So will I be
any worse off than I am now? It's a general principle, worth remem-
bering, that unless piety and self-interest coincide in a person, piety
is unsustainable. A compelling argument, don't you think?

[15] "Pyrrhonists and Academics can come and offer battle all
they want. For my part, I don't have time for their nonsense, and I
refuse to act as advocate for normality. [16] Even if I were engaged
in a lawsuit for a plot of land, I'd have asked someone else to plead
my cause. [17] What will satisfy me, then, in this context? How does
perception occur? Does it involve the whole body or only a part? I
may not know how to defend one position or the other, though both
views trouble me. But I'm perfectly sure that you and I are not one
and the same person. [18] How can I be so certain? Because when I
want to swallow a bit of food, I never take it there but here.* And when
I want bread, I never grab a broom, but I always head straight for the
bread, as an arrow goes straight for the target. [19] What about you
people who deny the evidence of the senses? Don't you do the same?
Which of you goes to a mill when he intends to go to a bathhouse?"

[20] "But then shouldn't we do our best to stay true to our position—to defend normality and ward off arguments that contradict it?"

[21] "Is anyone disputing that? But only someone who has the
time and the ability should engage in such debates. Anyone who's
timid and troubled and has a weak heart should devote his time to
something else."

1.28
*That we ought not to get angry with people, and what is trivial or
important in human life*

[1] "Under what circumstances do we assent to something? When it
appears to be the case. [2] So it's impossible for us to assent to something that appears not to be the case. Why? Because it's the nature of
the mind to assent to truths, to find falsehoods unacceptable, and to
suspend judgment in uncertain cases. [3] Is this demonstrable? Accept the impression that it's now nighttime."

"I can't."

"Refuse to accept the impression that it's daytime."

"I can't."

"Accept or refuse to accept the impression that the stars are even in number."

"I can't."*

[4] "So whenever someone assents to a falsehood, you can be sure that it's not the falsehood to which he wished to assent—for no soul, as Plato says, is willingly deprived of the truth*—but that he judged something false to be true.

[5] "All right. Now, in the sphere of action, what is it that corresponds to truth and falsehood in the realm of belief? Appropriateness and inappropriateness, advantage and disadvantage, right for me and wrong for me, and so on and so forth."

[6] "So is it impossible to think an action personally advantageous but still choose not to do it?"

"Yes."

[7] "What about the woman who says, 'I recognize that what I plan to do is evil, but my counsels are ruled by anger'?"*

"That's just the point. She thinks it more advantageous for her to gratify her anger and punish her husband than to keep her children safe."

[8] "Yes, but she's wrong."

"Make her fully aware of her mistake and she won't act on it. But until you point it out to her, what can guide her except her impression of what's best for her? Nothing. [9] So why are you angry with her? The poor thing has gone astray in matters of supreme importance, and has changed into a viper instead of a human being. Doesn't she more deserve pity, then, if that's the case?* Just as we pity the blind and the lame, shouldn't we pity those who've been blinded and crippled where matters of supreme importance are concerned?

[10] "So whoever bears clearly in mind the fact that every action anyone takes is determined by an impression—and impressions, moreover, may be right or wrong; if they're right he's blameless, and if they're wrong he pays the penalty himself, since there's no way in which one person makes a mistake and another is harmed by it—such a person won't get angry with anyone, won't be irritated by anyone, won't curse anyone, won't blame anyone, won't hate anyone, and won't be offended by anyone."

[11] "So even great and fearful deeds stem from impressions?"

[12] "Absolutely. The *Iliad* consists of nothing but people's impressions and their use of impressions. Abducting Menelaus's wife seemed a good idea to Paris, and going away with Paris seemed a good idea to Helen. [13] So if an impression had led Menelaus to feel that he was better off without such an unfaithful wife, what would have happened? We'd have lost not only the *Iliad* but the *Odyssey* as well!"*

[14] "So events as great as those depend on such a slight matter?"

"What are these 'great events' of yours? Warfare, civil strife, the loss of many lives, towns razed to the ground? What's 'great' about them?"

"Nothing, you think?"

[15] "Is there anything great about killing large numbers of cows or sheep, or setting fire to and demolishing numerous swallows' or storks' nests?"

[16] "Are you saying that the two cases are similar?"

"They're identical. Human lives are lost; cow and sheep lives are lost. Human housing is set on fire; storks' nests are set on fire. [17] What's 'great and fearful' about these events? Or show me how a human house qua place of habitation differs from a stork's nest. The only difference is that humans build their houses out of timbers, tiles, and bricks, and storks out of sticks and mud."

[18] "So you're assimilating storks and human beings?"

"Of course. In everything that relates to their bodies they're identical."

[19] "You're saying that there's no difference between a human being and a stork?"

"Of course there is, but not in that respect."

"How do they differ, then?"

[20] "A little investigation will show you that the difference lies elsewhere. Might what makes the difference not be that a human being understands what he's doing, and is socially minded, trustworthy, self-respecting, honest, and intelligent? [21] So where do we find what's important in human life? Where is what's bad and good for us to be found? Precisely where humans differ from storks. If this part of us is kept safe, if it remains well defended, and if a person's self-respect, trustworthiness, and intelligence aren't destroyed, then he's

kept safe as well. But if any of these qualities is destroyed, if this Troy is besieged into submission, then he too is destroyed. That's where what's important in human life is to be found.

[22] "Did Paris's great failure occur when the Greeks arrived? When they put Troy under siege? When his brothers were killed? Not at all. No one is ever responsible for another person's failure. [23] No, that was just storks' nests being destroyed. He failed when he lost his self-respect, his trustworthiness, his respect for the laws of hospitality, his decency. [24] And what about Achilles? When did he fail? When Patroclus died? Hardly! It was when he lost his temper, when he shed tears over a mere girl, when he forgot that he wasn't there to acquire concubines but to make war. [25] It's when right judgments are eliminated, when they are destroyed, that people fail, that they are under siege, that they are razed to the ground."

[26] "Are you saying that it isn't bad for women to be taken away for enslavement, for children to be made captives, and for the men themselves to be slaughtered?"

[27] "What's your reason for adding this judgment? Tell me."

"No. What's *your* reason for denying that these things are bad?"

[28] "Let's turn to our standards for an answer: refer to your preconceptions.* Now you can see why I find it impossible to express enough astonishment at the way people behave. When we want to assess the weight of something, we don't do so at random; when we want to decide whether something is straight or warped, we don't do so at random. [29] To generalize, when it's important for us to know a relevant truth, none of us ever does anything at random. [30] It's only when it comes to what is not just the primary but the sole cause of doing right or wrong, of contentment or discontent, of failure or success, that we act at random and in haste. There's no equivalent to a balance or a standard to be seen: no sooner has some impression struck me than I immediately act upon it. [31] I mean, if impressions suffice for me,† am I better than Agamemnon or Achilles, seeing that they were led by impressions to do terrible things and suffer terribly? [32] Doesn't every tragic plot have the same starting point? What does Euripides's *Atreus* consist of? Impressions. Sophocles's *Oedipus*? Impressions. The *Phoenix*? Impressions. The *Hippolytus*?* Impressions. [33] So what kind of person pays no attention to this matter, do you think? What do we call people whose behavior is

guided by every passing impression? Insane. Is our behavior different, then?"

1.29
On self-possession

[1] "Goodness is essentially a certain state of will and so is badness.
[2] What part do things external to us play, then? They are the materials on which will works, and it will get what is good for itself, or what
is bad, depending on how it deals with them. [3] Under what circumstances will the outcome be good for it? If it doesn't count the materials as important. Will is good if we judge materials correctly and bad
if we judge them in a warped or distorted fashion. [4] This is a law,
established by God, and he says, 'If you want something good, get it
from yourself.' But you say, 'No. Get it from someone else.' Wrong!
Get it from yourself. [5] So suppose a tyrant threatens me and summons me to his presence. 'What am I threatened with?' I ask. If he
says, 'I'll clap you in irons,' I say, 'He's threatening my hands and feet.'
[6] If he says, 'I'll cut off your head,' I say, 'He's threatening my neck.'
If he says, 'I'll throw you in prison,' I say, 'Now it's my whole body.'
And I give the same response if he threatens me with banishment."

[7] "So he doesn't actually threaten *you* at all?"

"Yes, that's right, as long as I feel that these things are nothing to
me. But if any of those prospects makes me afraid, then he threatens
me. [8] So what would make me fear anyone? Over what would he
have to have control to make me fear him? Over things that are up to
me? They're not subject to anyone else's control. Over things that ar-
en't up to me? And what concern are they of mine?"

[9] "So are you philosophers telling us to hold kings in contempt?"

[10] "Far from it. Does any philosopher tell you to dispute the
claim of kings to the things over which they have authority? Take
my body, take my property, take my reputation, take my family and
friends. If I try to convince anyone to dispute a monarch's claim to
these things, I'd really be liable to be indicted. [11] 'Yes, but I want to
control your judgments too.' Who gave you that power? How can you
prevail over another person's judgment? [12] 'By making him feel
fear.' You fail to realize that a person's faculty of judgment prevails
over itself and can't be defeated by anyone else. And nothing can pre-

vail over will, either, except itself. [13] That's why there's no law of God's more powerful and fair than this one: what is superior shall always prevail over what is inferior."

[14] "Ten men are superior to one."

"For what? For clapping someone in irons, killing him, dragging him off wherever they like, taking his property. So ten men can prevail over one in the respect in which they're superior."

[15] "Well, in what respect are they inferior?"

"If their victim has true judgments while they don't. Can they prevail over him in this respect? Of course not. If you and I are weighed in a balance, the heavier one is bound to draw down the scale, isn't he?"

[16] "But wasn't that how Socrates came to be treated as he was by the Athenians?"

"Slave, why say 'Socrates'? State the facts as they are: that was how Socrates's *body* came to be arrested and hauled off to prison by those who were physically stronger; that was how his *body* came to be given hemlock to drink; that was how his *body* came to breathe its last. [17] Does this strike you as remarkable, as unjust? Is it for this that you rail at God? Well, did Socrates get nothing in exchange for them? [18] What, to his mind, was the essence of goodness? Should we listen to you or to him? And what does he say? 'Anytus and Meletus can kill me, but they cannot harm me.' And 'If this is what God wants, so be it.'*

[19] "No, you need to prove that a person with worse judgments prevails over someone who's his superior in judgments, but you won't be able to prove that or even come close. I mean, there's the law I mentioned, the law of nature and of God that what is superior shall always prevail over what is inferior. [20] In what respect? In whatever respect it's superior. One person is physically stronger than another, several people are stronger than one, a thief is stronger than a non-thief. [21] That's how I lost my lamp,* because the thief was better than me at doing without sleep. But he paid dearly for it: in return for a lamp, he has become a thief, untrustworthy, less than human. And he thought he was turning a profit!

[22] "So someone has grabbed me by the toga and is pulling me into the agora, and then other people are shouting at me, 'So, philosopher! What good have your judgments done you? Look, you're

being hauled off to prison! Look, you're going to be beheaded!' [23] But what kind of *Introduction to Philosophy* could I have studied that would have enabled me not to be pulled when a stronger man takes hold of my toga, and to avoid being thrown into prison if ten men drag me there? [24] So what else have I learned? I've learned to see that everything that happens is nothing to me unless it's something that's subject to my will. [25] Hasn't that lesson done you good? Why, then, do you look to be benefited by anything other than what you've learned? [26] So as I sit in prison I say, 'This person who's shouting these things at me is missing the point. He doesn't get it. He just hasn't bothered to find out what philosophers say or do. Don't mind him.'

[27] "'Now come out of prison again.' All right, if my imprisonment is of no further use to you; if it ever becomes useful to you again, I'll go back in. [28] For how long? For as long as reason chooses that I associate with my body. And when it chooses to end that association, take my body, and may you fare well with it. [29] Just so long as I don't relinquish it irrationally, or out of weakness, or for a trivial reason. Again, that's not what God wants, because he needs the universe to be as it is and the earth to be populated by creatures such as us. But if he sounds the retreat, as he did for Socrates, I must obey him as a soldier obeys his commanding officer."*

[30] "So should we spread these notions far and wide?"

[31] "What for? Isn't it enough just to believe them oneself? When children come up to us clapping their hands and saying, 'Hurray! Today's the Saturnalia!'* do we respond by saying, 'There's nothing to cheer about'? Of course not. We clap back at them ourselves. [32] You should do the same. When you're finding it impossible to get someone to change his mind, you should think of him as a child and clap back at him. If you don't want to do that, just say nothing.

[33] "We need to bear these ideas in mind, and when we're called on to cope with a difficulty such as those I've been talking about, we should be aware that the time has come to show whether we've been well educated. [34] You see, a young man, fresh from school and faced with a difficulty, is like someone who's trained himself in how to reduce syllogisms* and, if offered an easy syllogism, says, 'I'd rather you offered me a subtle and complicated one. I need the practice.' Wrestlers, too, don't like to be matched against lightweight training partners: 'He'll never get me off the ground.' [35] That's what a gifted

student does. Not you. When opportunity knocks, you're bound to weep and say, 'I want to continue with my education.' To learn what? If you didn't learn the theory so as to be able to put it into practice, what was the point? [36] I imagine that there's someone sitting here today who, feeling himself to be in labor, says, 'Is there no difficulty coming my way that's comparable to the one that came to him? Am I to waste my time sitting in a corner, when I could be winning a crown at Olympia? When will someone bring me word of that kind of contest?' That's the attitude you all ought to have.

[37] "Even among Caesar's gladiators* there are some who chafe because no one is sending them out into the arena that day or arranging an opponent for them, and they pray to God and go to their handlers begging for a fight—but will none of you display the same mettle? [38] That's exactly why I wanted to make a voyage. I wanted to see what my favorite contestant* was doing, how he was applying himself to his assignment. [39] 'I don't like this kind of assignment,' he said. Is it up to you to get the kind of assignment you like? You've been given a particular body, particular parents and brothers, a particular country and a particular station in it, and then you come to me and say, 'Please change my assignment.' So don't you have the resources for putting what you've been given to use? [40] 'It's your job to set the assignment and mine to carry it out well.' But that's not what you say. You say, 'Don't set me this kind of compound proposition to analyze,* but that. Don't push me toward this kind of conclusion, but that.'

[41] "The time is nearly upon us when tragic actors will take their masks and boots and robes to be themselves. Man, they're your materials, your assignment. [42] Say something to let us know whether you're a tragic actor or a clown, because otherwise we've no way of telling the two apart. [43] That's why... I mean, if you take away an actor's boots and mask and have him play an apparition, is that the end of him or is he still there? If he has a voice, he's still there. [44] The same goes in life too. 'Accept a governorship.' I accept it, and use the role to display how an educated person behaves. [45] 'Take off your senatorial toga, dress in rags, and step forward in that role.' All right. Isn't a fine voice one of my gifts?"

[46] "In what role, then, are you taking the stage now?"

[47] "As a witness with his assignment set by God: 'Go and bear

witness for me. You are my choice for playing the part of witness. Is anything not subject to will either good or bad?' 'No.' 'Do I harm anyone?' 'No.' 'Have I made what's good for each individual up to anyone other than himself?' 'No.' [48] What testimony will you offer God? 'I'm ill-fated, Lord, and miserable. No one cares for me, no one gives me anything, everyone blames me and speaks badly of me.' [49] Is that how you're going to testify? Is that how you're going to disgrace the assignment he gave you when he conferred this honor on you and made you his choice to act as his witness in such an important matter?

[50] "But someone with the authority to do so declares, 'I judge you to be impious and sacrilegious.' What has happened to you? 'I've been judged impious and sacrilegious.' Is that all? Yes. [51] Suppose it was a hypothetical argument he'd passed judgment on, and he'd declared, 'I judge the proposition "If it is day, it is light" to be false.' Would that have any effect on the argument? Who's being judged here? Who's being condemned? The argument or the person who's mistaken about it? [52] And this person who has the authority to make pronouncements about you: does he know what piety and impiety really are? Has he studied the matter? Has he learned about it? Where? From whom? [53] In any case, a musician would simply ignore him if he declared that the D string was the E string, as a geometrician would if he judged that the lines that extend from the center of a circle to the circumference aren't all equal. [54] Is a truly educated person going to pay any attention to the judgments of an uneducated person about what is and isn't sacrilegious, or about what is and isn't just? 'Oh, the injustice of educated men!'* Is that what you've learned here?

[55] "Shouldn't you just leave arguing about these matters to others, the work-shy gnomes, so that they can sit in a corner and collect their petty fees or complain that no one is giving them anything to do, while you step up and put what you've learned to use? [56] I mean, it isn't arguments that we're short of these days; books written by Stoics are full of them. What's missing is someone to put them to practical use, someone who testifies to the arguments by his actions. [57] Please, for my sake, take on this role, so that we can stop relying in our school on examples from long ago, and will instead have an exemplar from our own day.

[58] "Whose job is it, then, to contemplate these matters? Anyone who has the time, because the human creature is given to contemplation. [59] But it's shameful to contemplate these matters as a runaway slave might. People should sit and listen with undivided attention to a tragic actor or a minstrel, as the case may be; they shouldn't behave like a runaway slave, who pays attention to the actor and appreciates his skill, but at the same time is always looking around apprehensively; and then at the slightest mention of the word 'master' he panics and gets flustered. [60] It's also disgraceful for philosophers to contemplate the works of nature in that way. After all, what is a master? No person is the master of another person, but death and life are, and pleasure and pain. [61] Bring Caesar to me without these things, and you'll see how self-possessed I am; but when he comes with these things, in thunder and lightning, if they make me afraid, I'm no different from a runaway slave acknowledging his master. [62] But as long as I have only a kind of respite from these things, my attention is like that of a runaway slave in a theater. I wash, I drink, I sing, but I'm always frightened and miserable. [63] But if I free myself from my masters—which is to say, if I free myself from those things that make masters frightening—how could I still be troubled, and how could I still have a master?

[64] "So, should we proclaim these ideas to everyone? No, we must indulge a non-philosopher and say, 'All he's doing is recommending to me what he thinks good for himself. I forgive him.' [65] Even Socrates, when he was about to drink the hemlock, forgave his weeping jailer and said, 'A noble spirit, to have wept for us.'* [66] But it wasn't to him, was it, that Socrates said, 'That's why we sent the women away'? No, it was to his friends, who were capable of getting the point. He indulged the jailer as he would a child."

1.30

What we should have at hand in difficult circumstances

[1] "If you're ever in the presence of a powerful man, remember that someone else is looking down from on high at what's going on, and that it's him you have to please rather than that man. [2] So he asks you,* 'In your school, what did you call exile, imprisonment, shackles, death, and disfavor?' 'I called them indifferents.' [3] 'And how

are you thinking of them right now? Have they changed at all?' 'No.' 'Well, have you changed?' 'No.' 'So tell me what indifferents are, and also what the consequences are.' 'Indifferents are things that aren't subject to will, and the consequence is that they're nothing to me.' [4] 'Now tell me what things you took to be good.' 'Right exercise of will and right use of impressions.' 'And what is the goal?' 'To follow you.' [5] 'And do you think the same way even now?' 'Yes, I do.'

"Go into him, then, with confidence, bearing all this in mind, and you'll see what it is for a young man who's been properly trained to be among people with no education. [6] I imagine, by the gods, that your experience will be something like this: 'Why do we bother with such long and complicated preparations when it's all for nothing? [7] Is that all power is? Is that all there is to the antechambers, the chamberlains, the armed guards? Was it for this that I listened to so many lectures? They all amount to nothing, but I prepared myself as though they were important.'"

Book 2

2.1
That confidence and caution are not incompatible

[1] "There's one particular claim made by the philosophers that probably seems paradoxical to some people, but let's still do the best we can to see if it's true to say that throughout life we should act with a combination of caution and confidence. [2] Caution, after all, seems somehow to be the opposite of confidence, and opposites never co-exist.

[3] "The paradox that's commonly detected here is, in my opinion, related to the fact that if we expected a person to treat the same matter with both caution and confidence *at once*, we would rightly be charged with combining things that are incompatible. [4] But is there, in fact, anything odd about the actual saying? If the assertions that you've often heard stated and proved are sound, that the essence of goodness lies in the use of impressions, and the essence of badness likewise, and that things that aren't subject to will don't take on the qualities of either badness or goodness, [5] why is it paradoxical for the philosophers to say, 'Where things aren't subject to will, you should act with confidence, and where they are subject to will, you should act with caution'? [6] The point being that if badness lies in the bad use of will, it's only things that are subject to will for which caution is required; and if things that aren't subject to will and aren't up to us are nothing to us, we should approach them with confidence. [7] Then we'll be both cautious and confident—and, by Zeus, our caution will make us confident. I mean, as a result of exercising caution toward things that are genuinely bad, we'll be confident in approaching things that aren't.

[8] "But instead we behave like deer. When deer are frightened by the feathers and run from them,* where do they turn? Where do they flee in the hope of finding safety? To the nets. That's how they lose their lives, by confusing objects of fear with objects of confidence. [9] We suffer from the same kind of confusion. What causes us fear? Things that aren't subject to will. And, conversely, what do we deal with confidently, as though none of them could be frightening? Things that are subject to will. [10] Mistaken beliefs, thoughtless action, disgraceful behavior, and shameful cravings are treated by us as of no importance, as long as nothing goes wrong in matters that aren't subject to will. But death, exile, pain, and disfavor—these are the feathers we flee from, these are the things that make us panic.

[11] "What follows is what one might expect from people who are mistaken about matters of supreme importance: our natural confidence becomes rashness, recklessness, impulsiveness, and shamelessness, and our natural caution and self-respect become cowardice and submissiveness, shot through with fear and mental turmoil. [12] If instead someone applies caution to the sphere of will and the works of will, no sooner does he wish to act cautiously than, hard on its heels, he gains the power of aversion. But if he applies caution to the sphere of things that aren't up to us and aren't subject to will, he's employing aversion on things that are not up to him, and so he's bound to be frightened, unsettled, and troubled. [13] The point being that it's not death or pain that's frightening, but the fear of pain or death. That's why we approve of the line 'It's not dying that's dreadful, but dying in disgrace.'*

[14] "Death should therefore be the object of our confidence, and the fear of death the object of our caution. At the moment, we do the opposite: we treat death as something to flee from, while we're careless, negligent, and unconcerned in forming a judgment about it.† [15] Socrates was right to call death and so on 'bogeys.'* Masks appear terrifying to young children and frighten them with their weirdness, and we too are affected in much the same way by events, for exactly the same reason that children are frightened by bogey masks. [16] After all, what is a child? A creature of ignorance and incomprehension. I mean, if a child had knowledge, it would in no way be our inferior. What is death? A bogey mask. [17] Turn it around and you'll see it for what it is. Look! Now it can't bite! Now or later your body is

bound to be separated from your spirit, just as it was separated before.* If it's now, what is there to complain about, seeing that, if not now, it'll be later? [18] Why is there such a thing as death? For the cyclical perpetuation of the universe. The universe needs not only the things that currently exist in it but also those that are to come and those that have already been and gone.* [19] What is pain? A bogey mask. Turn it around and you'll see it for what it is. Your body experiences rough movements and then again smooth ones.* If you don't find this existence in your best interests, the door is open. If you do, put up with it. [20] After all, come what may, the door is bound to be open, and we can remain untroubled.

[21] "What is the fruit of these ideas? There could be no finer or more suitable fruit for people who are receiving an authentic education—tranquility, fearlessness, and freedom. [22] In other words, on these matters we shouldn't trust the masses, who say that only free men can be educated, but rather the philosophers, who say that only those who've been educated are free."

[23] "What do you mean?"

"I mean that nowadays freedom is nothing but the ability to live as we want. Don't you agree?"

"Yes."

"Tell me, then, people. Do you want to live in error?"

"No, we don't."

[24] "So no one who's in error is free. Do you want to live with fear, grief, and a troubled mind?"

"Of course not."

"So no one who's frightened or grieving or troubled is free, and anyone who's been delivered from grief and fear and anxiety has by the same process been delivered from slavery. [25] So, dearest rule makers, how can we go on trusting you? Do we allow only the free to be educated? I mean, the philosophers say that they don't allow people to be free unless they've been educated—which is to say that God doesn't allow it. "

[26] "So when someone has turned his slave around in front of the praetor,* he's done nothing?"

"No, he's done something."

"What?"

"He's turned his slave around in front of the praetor."

"Anything else?"

"Yes, he also owes the state 5 percent of the slave's value."

[27] "But hasn't the slave become free as a result of this process?"

[28] "He's no more become free than he's acquired peace of mind. I mean, what about you, the one with the power to turn others around? Do you serve no master? Isn't money your master, or a girl or a boy, or a tyrant or a member of the tyrant's inner circle? If not, why do you tremble when faced with a situation involving such things? [29] That's why my constant refrain is: study these teachings and have them at hand, so that you know what to approach with confidence and what to approach in a cautious frame of mind—so that you understand that you should approach things that aren't subject to will with confidence and things that are subject to will with caution."

[30] "But I haven't been reading my work to you. You don't know how I'm doing."

[31] "In what respect? In the field of fine phrases? Keep your fine phrases! Show me how you stand in relation to desire and aversion; show me that you never fail to get what you want and never experience what you don't want. As for your carefully constructed sentences, prove your good sense by taking them away and erasing them."

[32] "So did Socrates not write?"

"No one wrote more.* But how did he write? Since there wasn't always an interlocutor around to challenge his ideas and to be challenged in his turn, he used to challenge and investigate himself, and was always practicing seeing what could be made of one preconception or another. [33] That's what a philosopher writes. As for fine phrases and 'he said . . . I said,'† he leaves them to others, to the foolish or the blessed—either those who have the time thanks to their serenity, or those who are too stupid to be able to follow an argument.

[34] "And now, when opportunity knocks, will you go off and conduct public readings of your work? Will you boast, 'See how well I compose dialogues!'? [35] Don't do it, man! A better boast would be: 'See how my desires always succeed in attaining their object! See how my aversions enable me not to encounter what I don't want to encounter! I'll prove it to you: bring on death, pain, prison, disfavor, condemnation in the courts.' [36] That's the show a young graduate of the school should put on. Leave everything else to others. Don't ever let anyone hear you talk about these matters, and don't ever let

anyone think that you have these abilities, but present yourself as an ignorant nobody. [37] Make it clear by your actions alone that you know how to prevent disappointment and how to avoid encountering what you don't want to encounter. [38] Leave the study of law court arguments, hypothetical problems, and syllogisms to others, while you focus on how to face death, imprisonment, torture, and exile. [39] Approach all these things with confidence, trusting in the one who has called you to experience them and has judged you worthy of this post—an assignation that will enable you to show what a rational command center is capable of when it confronts forces that aren't subject to will.

[40] "And so the paradox we started with, the idea that we should act with a combination of caution and confidence, will no longer seem untenable or paradoxical. One can act with confidence where things aren't subject to will and with caution where things are subject to will."

2.2
On tranquility*

[1] "If you're ever involved in a lawsuit, you need to consider what you want to preserve and what you want to accomplish. [2] If you want to keep your will in its natural state, you'll be completely unassailable, everything will go smoothly, and you won't meet any difficulties, [3] because if what you want to safeguard are the things that are entirely up to you and naturally free, and if you're satisfied with them, what else is there for you to worry about? Who is their master? Who can take them from you? [4] If you want to be self-respecting and trustworthy, who can stop you? If you want to be unimpeded and unconstrained, who can compel you to desire something that doesn't seem desirable to you, or to feel aversion toward something that doesn't seem to you to need avoiding? [5] Now, the judge is going to deploy things against you that are widely supposed to be frightening, but it's impossible for him to make you feel aversion toward them. [6] So, since desire and aversion are up to you, what else is there for you to worry about? [7] Let this be your introduction, your narration, your proof, your victorious conclusion, your epilogue,* and the foundation of your renown. [8] That's why, when someone was reminding him

to prepare for his trial, Socrates said, 'Don't you think I've been preparing for this all my life?' 'What form has this preparation taken?' [9] 'I've safeguarded the things that are up to me.' 'What do you mean?' 'I've never wronged either another individual or the state.'*

[10] "But if you also want to safeguard things that are external to you—your body, your property, your reputation—my advice to you is that you'd better immediately make a start on preparing yourself in every possible way. Try, that is, to find out what kind of people the judge and your opponent are. [11] If you need to clasp their knees in supplication, clasp them; if you need to shed tears, shed them; if you need to whimper, go ahead and whimper. [12] Once you've subordinated what's yours to externals, you must act the slave from then on. Don't chop and change; don't be prepared to act the slave at one time and then refuse to do so at another, [13] but unambiguously and wholeheartedly be one thing or the other—either free or slave, either educated or uneducated, either a noble fighting cock or an abject one. Either put up with being thrashed to death or offer no resistance at all. God forbid that you should first receive a thorough thrashing and then give up! [14] But if you'd be ashamed to be a slave, you need immediately to decide where the essence of goodness and badness are found. That's where you'll find truth also.'*

[15] "I mean, do you really think that if Socrates had wanted to safeguard externals, he'd have stepped forward and said, 'Anytus and Meletus can kill me, but they cannot harm me'?* [16] Was he too stupid to see that this road doesn't lead there, but elsewhere? Why, then, did he belittle them and provoke them? [17] My friend Heraclitus was involved in a lawsuit in Rhodes about a piece of land, and after proving to the jury that his case was just, when he came to the epilogue of his speech he said, 'But I'm not going to plead with you, nor do I care what verdict you bring. It's you who are being judged more than me.' And so he lost the suit. [18] What was the point of that? Don't plead, Heraclitus, to be sure, but also don't add 'I'm not going to plead with you,' unless it's the right time for you, as it was for Socrates, to deliberately provoke the judges.* [19] The same goes for you too. If you're getting ready to deliver that kind of epilogue, why rise to speak? Why answer the summons? [20] If you wish to be crucified, wait and the cross will come your way. But if reason decides that you should answer the summons and do the best you can to con-

vince the jury, you should act accordingly, while, of course, preserving your integrity.

[21] "By the same token, it's also ridiculous to say, 'Give me some advice.'* What advice am I to give you? Better to say, 'Make my mind capable of adapting itself to whatever happens.' [22] I mean, there's little difference between your asking for advice and an illiterate person saying, 'Tell me what I should write when I'm set the task of writing a certain name.' [23] If I tell him how to write 'Dion,' and then the teacher comes along and sets the task of writing 'Theon' rather than 'Dion,' what will happen? What's he going to write? [24] If you're an experienced writer, you're ready for every test, and if you're not, what advice can I give you now? I mean, if circumstances test you in a different way, what will you say or do? [25] Remember this general principle,* then, and you'll never be short of advice. But if you yearn for externals, you'll inevitably be whirled here and there according to your master's wishes. [26] And who is your master? Anyone who controls anything that you're interested in having or avoiding."

2.3
To those who recommend people to philosophers

[1] "Diogenes made an excellent reply to someone who was asking him for a letter of recommendation. 'That you are a human being,' he said, 'he'll know as soon as he sees you. Whether you're good or bad, he'll know if he's capable of distinguishing good people from bad, and if he doesn't know how to do that, ten thousand letters from me to him won't make any difference.' [2] It's rather as though a drachma coin were to ask to be recommended to someone so as to be assayed. If the person you want me to write to is a good appraiser, you'll recommend yourself.

[3] "We ought to have something in life that's similar to the way we deal with silver, and then I'd be able to say what the assayer says: 'Bring me any drachma you want and I'll appraise it.' [4] Now, where syllogisms are concerned, I say, 'Bring me any syllogism you like and I'll show you the difference between one that's reducible and one that isn't.' Why? Because I know how to reduce syllogisms. I have the ability that's required if one is to recognize successful syllogisms.* [5] But when it comes to life, what happens? I can't decide whether a

thing is good or bad. What causes this? The opposite of my expertise with syllogisms: ignorance and inexperience."

2.4
To a man who had once been caught in adultery

[1] Epictetus was talking about how human beings are born to be trustworthy, and how anyone who compromises this quality compromises his humanity, when a man came in who was a well-known scholar. Now, this person had once been caught in adultery in Rome, [2] and Epictetus went on, "But if we renounce this trustworthiness, which is our birthright, and set out to seduce our neighbor's wife, what kind of act is that? A destructive and ruinous one, surely, isn't it? What does it destroy? The man that he was: trustworthy, self-respecting, and pious. [3] Is that all? Aren't we destroying neighborliness, friendship, the state? And where does that leave us? How am I to treat you now, man? As a neighbor, a friend? A fine neighbor you are! As a fellow citizen? How can I trust you? [4] I mean, if you were a pot that was too defective to be usable for anything, you'd be thrown out onto the waste pile and no one would retrieve you from it. [5] You're a human being, not a pot, but if you're unable to function as a human being, what shall we do with you? Given that you can't occupy the position of friend, could you be a slave? But you're utterly untrustworthy. So shouldn't you, too, be thrown out onto the waste pile like a useless pot, like a turd? [6] And won't your complaint then be 'No one cares for me, and I'm a man of learning'? Yes, because you're a bad man and a useless human being. Your complaining is like wasps being irritated by the fact that no one cares for them and that instead everyone tries to avoid them and swats them dead if they can. [7] Your prick is such that you cause trouble and pain for anyone you use it on. What should we do with you? You don't belong anywhere."

[8] "But aren't women naturally common property?"*

"I agree. I mean, a piglet, too, is shared among the guests at a dinner party. But once everyone has his portion, go and grab your neighbor's, if you feel like it. Surreptitiously steal it from him or reach out your hand and indulge your greed. If you can't tear off a chunk of meat, get grease on your fingers and lick it off. A fine table companion you make, a Socratic kind of guest!"*

[9] "All right, but a theater is shared by all the citizens of a state, isn't it?"

"So once they're seated, go, if you feel like it, and throw someone off his spot. Women are naturally common property, too, [10] but once the legislator has distributed them among the men, like a host at a dinner party, shouldn't you look for your own portion rather than snatching someone else's and indulging your greed? 'But I'm a scholar and an expert in Archedemus.'* [11] Well, you can be an expert in Archedemus and still be an untrustworthy adulterer—a wolf or an ape instead of a human being. What's to stop you?"

2.5
How are greatness of mind and carefulness compatible?

[1] "Material things are indifferent, but the use one makes of them isn't. [2] How, then, is one to retain one's self-possession and peace of mind, and at the same time be careful rather than purposeless or negligent? If one imitates people playing a board game. [3] The counters are indifferent and the dice are indifferent: how do I know which way they'll fall? But to use the throw carefully and skillfully, that's my job. [4] By the same token, then, my principal task in life as well is to divide things up, see their differences, and say, 'Externals are not up to me; will is up to me. [5] Where shall I look for good and bad? Inside myself, among the things that are mine.' But never call anything that isn't yours either good or bad, or employ in their case terms such as 'benefit' or 'harm.'"

[6] "So are you saying that external things should be treated carelessly?"

"Certainly not, because that's bad for the will and hence contrary to nature. [7] No, they should be treated with care, because the use to which we put them isn't a matter of indifference, and at the same time with self-possession, because material things are indifferent. [8] The point is that, where everything important is concerned, no one can impede or constrain me. The getting of things in the realm where I can be impeded and constrained is not up to me and is neither good nor bad, but the use I make of them is good or bad, and that is up to me.

[9] "It's not easy to blend and combine these things—the care typical of someone who's devoted to material things and the self-possession typical of someone who treats them as unimportant. It's not impossible, however. Otherwise, it would be impossible for us to be happy. [10] Suppose we were on a voyage. What is it within my power to do? To choose the captain and the crew, and the day and time of departure. [11] Then a storm falls on us. Why should that be any concern of mine? I've done all I can. Coping with the storm is someone else's business, the captain's. But now the ship is starting to sink. [12] What can I do? All I can do is do what I can. So I drown without being frightened, without screaming, without cursing God, knowing that everything that's born is bound to die. [13] I'm not a form of everlasting life but a human being, a part of the universe as an hour is part of a day. Like an hour, I'm present and then I pass. [14] So what difference does it make to me how I pass, whether by drowning or fever? Some such thing is going to see to my passing anyway.

[15] "You see skilled ballplayers doing the same thing. None of them is concerned about the ball, as though it were good or bad, but they are concerned about how they throw and catch. [16] It's in throwing and catching that their deftness, skill, speed, and responsiveness are manifest, with the result that while *I* may not be able to catch the ball even if I make a pouch out of my toga, an expert ballplayer can catch any ball I throw.* [17] But if we're anxious and frightened as we catch or throw the ball, what becomes of the game? How can one have the required composure? How will one see what the next move in the game is supposed to be? One player will be saying 'Throw!', another 'Don't throw!', and another 'Don't hold onto it!' This is no game, but a brawl.

[18] "In fact, Socrates was an expert ballplayer. What do I mean? He knew how to play in the law court.* 'Tell me, Anytus,' he said, 'how can you say that I don't believe in God? What do you think superhuman beings are? Aren't they either the offspring of gods or, in some cases, of both gods and men?' [19] And, after securing his agreement on this, he went on, 'So do you think it's possible for someone to think that mules exist, but not donkeys?'* It was as though he were a player in a ballgame. And in the law court, what was the ball that

FIGURE 3. A marble base for a funerary *kouros*. Pentelic marble, ca. 510 BCE, Kerameikos, built into the Themistoclean wall of Athens. The base depicts young men playing a ball game called *episkyros*. The rules are unclear, but the game seems to involve catching, as Epictetus describes, since the athlete on the far left is about to throw a ball forward through the air. Athens, National Archaeological Museum of Athens, inv. no. 3476.

Photo by Zde, Wikimedia Commons (CC BY-SA 3.0 [https://creativecommons .org/licenses/by-sa/3.0/deed.en])

was in play? Life, imprisonment, banishment, a dose of hemlock, losing a wife, leaving children fatherless. [20] That was what was at stake, but he still played and he handled the ball deftly.

"So we too need both the care of an expert ballplayer and indifference, as if what was at stake were only a ball. [21] That is, we should do our absolute best to deal skillfully with any external material object, and rather than thinking it important, we should display our skill in handling it, whatever it may be. In the same way, a tailor doesn't make wool but works with skill on whatever wool he's given. [22] Your food and possessions are gifts from someone else, and he can take them away again, and your body itself as well. You should just work with the material you've been given. [23] And then, if at the end you've suffered no harm, all your other acquaintances will congratulate you on your escape, but a perceptive man will praise you and be pleased for you only if he sees that you behaved throughout in a dignified manner. If he sees that you engineered your escape by behaving with a certain lack of decorum, however, he'll do the opposite, since it's only when being pleased is a reasonable response that congratulating someone is too.

[24] "What's the meaning of the saying that external things may be either in accord with nature or contrary to nature?* It depends on whether or not we see ourselves as isolated entities. Consider a foot, for instance. I may think that it's natural for a foot to be clean, but if you take it as a foot, and not in isolation, it will also be appropriate for it to step in mud or on thorns, and sometimes to be amputated for the sake of the whole. Otherwise, it isn't a foot.* [25] We should think similarly of ourselves as well. What are you? A human being. If you look at yourself in isolation, it's natural for you to live to an old age, to be rich, to be healthy. But if you look at yourself as a human being and as a part of some whole, for the sake of that whole it may be appropriate for you to be ill, or risk your life at sea, or be poor, or die young. [26] Why get angry, then? Don't you realize that, just as a foot taken in isolation isn't a foot, the same goes for you as a human being? After all, what is a human being? A part of a city—in the first place, a part of the city made up of gods and human beings, and then a part of the city that is supposed to be our nearest and dearest, which is a small copy of the universal city."*

[27] "So must I be put on trial now?"

"Must someone else be ill now, or travel by sea, or die, or be condemned in the courts? Yes, because as long as we're in a body like this one, in this world, and among people like these, it's impossible for us not to have all sorts of different experiences. [28] It's your job, then, to go and say what you must and to manage this business properly. [29] And then, if the judge pronounces you guilty, you say, 'Much good may it do you! I have done my part, and it's for you to decide whether you did the same.' After all, there's risk involved in being a judge as well. Don't forget that."*

2.6
On indifference*

[1] "A conditional* is an indifferent; how we judge it isn't indifferent, but is either knowledge, belief, or delusion. Likewise, life is an indif-

ferent, but what we make of life isn't indifferent. [2] So, when you're told that even these things are indifferents, that's not a reason for carelessness; and when you're urged to take care, that's not a reason for debasing yourselves and placing value on material things."

[3] "It's also good to be aware of one's aptitude and abilities, so that, in matters where you lack competence, you keep quiet and don't take it amiss if others do better at them than you. [4] I mean, suppose you consider yourself to be better at syllogisms: if that annoys other people, you can soothe them by saying, 'I've studied them, you haven't.' [5] In the same way, in areas where expertise requires practice, you shouldn't expect to have the advantage over others that only practice delivers. Instead, you should acknowledge the advantage that old hands have, and be content to retain your self-possession."

[6] "Go and pay your respects to that man."†
  "How?"
  "Without debasing yourself, even though previously you weren't allowed into his house."
  "That's because I don't know how to get in through a window, and when I find the door closed, my only options are to retreat or get in through a window."
  [7] "Anyway, go and speak to him."
  "All right. How?"
  "Without debasing yourself. [8] But the reason you were unsuccessful was because success in this case was up to him, not you. Right? There's never any point in laying claim to what isn't yours. Always bear in mind what is and isn't yours, and then you'll be impervious to anxiety. [9] That's why Chrysippus was right to say, 'As long as the future is opaque to me, I always hold fast to whatever is most apt for securing things that are in accord with nature. For God himself gave me the capacity to select them. [10] Indeed, if I knew that it was fated for me to fall ill today, I would incline toward it. After all, if a foot had intelligence, it would incline toward being muddied.'"*

[11] "I mean, look, why do ears of wheat grow? It's so that they can become dry, isn't it? And they become dry so that they can be harvested, don't they? Because they don't exist in isolation. [12] So if they were

conscious, they'd be bound to pray never to be harvested, wouldn't they? But it's a curse for ears of wheat not to be harvested. [13] By the same token, I assure you, it's a curse for people not to die; it's no different from wheat not ripening and not being harvested. [14] But since it is we ourselves who are bound to be harvested, and we also understand that we are the things being harvested, we get upset. This is because we don't know who we are and haven't studied human nature as thoroughly as horse experts have studied equine nature."

[15] "Chrysantas was about to strike an enemy when he heard the trumpet sound the retreat, and so he checked the blow, judging an order from his general more relevant than having his way.* [16] But none of us, even when necessity calls, is prepared to obey it unquestioningly. No, we suffer what we suffer with tears and complaints, and call it the force of circumstances. [17] What do you mean by circumstances, man? If you mean your surroundings, there's nothing that isn't 'circumstances.' You may mean that you hate your surroundings, but what is there to hate about the fact that everything that's born will die? [18] What kills you may be a knife, or torture, or the sea, or a roof tile, or a tyrant. What do you care by which road you descend to Hades?* They're all equal. [19] And to tell the truth, the shortest road is the one down which a tyrant sends you. It never took any tyrant in the world six months to kill anyone, but fever often takes up to a year. Talk of circumstances and so on is just empty noise and the clamor of meaningless words."

[20] "By being close to Caesar I risk losing my life."

"Aren't I risking my life by living in Nicopolis? Look at all the earthquakes we have here. When you sail here across the Adriatic, aren't you risking your life?"

[21] "But I'm also threatened by a belief."

"One of yours? No, that's impossible. Who can make you believe something you don't wish to believe? So you mean someone else's? But how can the danger be yours if it's others' beliefs that are false?"

[22] "Well, there's a chance I'll be sent into exile."

"What is exile? It's living somewhere other than Rome, isn't it?"

"Yes. But what if I'm sent to Gyara?"

"If that suits you, you'll go there. If not, there's somewhere else you can go other than Gyara—somewhere the person who's sending you to Gyara will go himself, without having any say in the matter. [23] So why are you treating what you'll face back in Rome as a big deal? You have more than enough aptitude to cope with it. In fact, a gifted young man might find himself saying, 'I didn't need to spend so much time attending all those lectures, writing so many exercises, and sitting for so long beside a rather worthless old man.' [24] Just bear in mind the distinction between what is and isn't yours. Don't ever lay claim to anything that isn't yours. [25] A podium and a prison are two different places, one lofty and the other low, but, in whichever of the two you find yourself, your will is unchanged if you're prepared to keep it unchanged. [26] And when we're able to compose hymns of praise in prison, *that's* when we'll be taking Socrates as our model.* [27] But the way we've been up until now, do you think we'd tolerate it if in prison someone asked us if we wanted to hear him read some hymns? 'Why are you bothering me? Don't you realize the trouble I'm in? In these circumstances, is it likely that . . . ?' 'What circumstances are those?' 'I'm about to die!' 'And is everyone else immortal?'"

2.7
*The correct way to go about divination**

[1] "Because we rely on divination on unsuitable occasions, many of us omit many appropriate actions. [2] I mean, all a diviner can see is death, danger, disease, and so on, [3] so how can it be suitable for me to consult a diviner about whether I *should* risk my life for a friend, or whether it's even appropriate for me to die for him? Don't I have an inner diviner who's told me what goodness and badness essentially are, and has explained the signs that indicate the presence of one or the other?* [4] Then why do I need entrails or birds?* Why should I let a diviner get away with saying 'It's in your best interest'? How does he know what's in my best interest? [5] Does he know what goodness is? Is he an expert in the signs that indicate goodness and badness as well as the signs revealed by entrails? I mean, if he knows the signs of goodness and badness, then he also knows the signs of right and wrong, of just and unjust. [6] Man, it's for you to tell me whether the signs indicate life or death, poverty or wealth, but are you the one to consult about what is or isn't in my best inter-

FIGURE 4. A bronze reproduction of the Liver of Piacenza, found in 1877, and currently held at the Museo Archeologico in the Musei Civici di Palazzo Farnese in Piacenza, Italy. This third-century BCE curiosity comes from Etruria in Italy. A liver (usually from a sacrificed sheep or goat) was thought to consist of a number of different areas, each relating to a different aspect of life; the diviner looked for anything unusual in a given area and made his interpretation accordingly.

est? [7] You don't address grammatical issues, do you? So why do you address this matter of expediency and inexpediency, a topic about which no one is certain and everyone disagrees? [8] That's why the reply given by the woman who was intending to send Gratilla in her exile a boatload of supplies was so admirable. Someone warned her that Domitian would confiscate them, and she said, 'His confiscating them is, in my view, preferable to my not sending them.'*

[9] "So what is it that induces us to employ divination so constantly? A cowardly fear of future outcomes. That's why we curry the diviner's favor. 'Sir,' we say, 'shall I inherit my father's estate?' 'Let's see. Let's perform a sacrifice.' 'Yes, sir, as Fortune wills.' And then if he says, 'You'll inherit,' we thank him as though he were the one from whom we were inheriting. And so they, for their part, end up treating us with scorn.

[10] "What we should do, then, is go to them unhampered by de-

sire or aversion. We should behave like a traveler who asks a passerby which of two roads leads to his destination, without desiring it to be the road to the right any more than the road to the left, because what he wanted wasn't taking this road or that, but the one that leads to his destination. [11] That's how we ought to approach God's guidance as well. We should use him as we use our eyes. We don't ask our eyes to show us some things rather than others, but we accept the impressions of everything they show us. [12] But what happens at the moment is that we approach the augur trembling with fear; we grab hold of him, appeal to him as though he were a god, and beg him: 'Lord, have mercy! Please let me have a happy outcome!' [13] Don't you just want what's best for you, slave? And isn't what's best for you just what pleases God? [14] Why are you doing your best to corrupt the judge and lead the adviser astray?"

2.8
The essence of goodness

[1] "God is a source of benefit, but goodness is also a source of benefit. It's plausible to suggest, then, that where the essence of God is to be found, there also is the essence of goodness. [2] So what is God, in his essence? Flesh? Hardly! Land? Hardly! Status? Hardly! He is mind, knowledge, right reason. [3] So there, in short, is where one should look for the essence of goodness. I mean, you wouldn't look for it in a plant, would you? No. In a non-rational animal? No. So if you're looking for it in the realm of the rational, why look anywhere else than in what differentiates rational creatures from non-rational ones?

[4] "Plants are incapable even of making use of impressions, and that's why you don't speak of goodness in talking about them. So in order for goodness to be present, there must be the use of impressions. [5] But is that all? If it were, you might think that even non-rational animals have the potential for goodness, happiness, and unhappiness. [6] But in fact you don't think that, and you're right not to, because even if they make use of impressions to the fullest possible extent, they still don't have the capacity to understand their use of impressions. This is only what you'd expect, given that they're born to serve others and aren't themselves leaders. [7] I mean, was a donkey born a leader? No, it came into existence because we needed

a back that was capable of bearing burdens. But, by Zeus, we also needed it to be able to walk, and that's why it gained the extra ability to make use of impressions, without which walking is impossible. [8] And that's as far as its capacities go. If it had also gained the ability to understand its use of impressions, it would obviously no longer be subordinate to us in terms of its ability to reason and wouldn't provide us with these services but would be our equal, no different from us. [9] So shouldn't you look for the essence of goodness in that quality the lack of which in creatures other than human beings is what makes you refuse to talk of goodness in their case?"

[10] "So are you saying that creatures other than human beings aren't works of God?"

"They certainly are, but they're not leaders, nor are they parts of gods. [11] But you are a leader and a fragment of God. You have, within yourself, a bit of him. So why are you ignorant of your relationship with him? Why don't you know where you've come from? [12] Shouldn't you remember, when you eat, who is eating and being nourished, and when you have sex, who is having sex? When you're in company, when you take exercise, when you make conversation, don't you realize that you're feeding God, exercising God? You carry God around, and yet, poor fool that you are, you don't know it. [13] Do you take me to be talking about some external god made of silver or gold? You carry him around within yourself, and you fail to realize that you defile him with impure thoughts and unclean acts. [14] If you were in the presence of a mere statue of God, you wouldn't dare to act the way you do, yet when God himself is present within you, seeing and hearing everything, aren't you ashamed to think and act this way—you who are unaware of your own nature, you target for God's wrath?

[15] "I mean, why do we worry, when we send a young man out from the school to see to various things, that he'll do something wrong? He might eat his food in the wrong way, or have sex in the wrong way, or feel wretched if his clothes are tattered or conceited if they're elegant. [16] He doesn't know that he has his own personal god; he doesn't know in whose company he's setting out. Should we let him get away with writing, 'Wish you were here'? [17] Don't you have God there with you? So why do you still want someone else when you have God? So that you can receive different advice, perhaps?

[18] "If you were one of Phidias's statues, his Athena or his Zeus, you'd remember your maker as well as yourself and—this is all assuming you were a conscious statue!—you'd try to do nothing that might bring shame on him or yourself, and you'd try never to make an unseemly spectacle of yourself in public.* [19] But in fact it was Zeus who was your creator: doesn't that make you care what sort of person you show yourself to be? And yet, what comparison is there between the one maker and the other, or between the one artifact and the other? [20] What work of human art actually contains within itself the faculties that it's designed to represent? Man-made works of art are no more than stone, bronze, gold, or ivory, aren't they? And once Phidias's Athena has stretched out her hand for the Victory to stand on, she's stuck forever in that pose, whereas God's artifacts move, breathe, make use of their impressions, form judgments. [21] Given that you're the work of this great a craftsman, will you dishonor him? When he not only made you but entrusted you to yourself alone and made you your own guardian, will you ignore this [22] and even bring your guardianship into disrepute? If God had made you responsible for an orphan, would you be so neglectful of your charge? [23] God has put you in charge of yourself, and he says, 'There was no one I could trust more than you. Look after this person for me, keep him in his natural state, with his self-respect, trustworthiness, objectivity, imperturbability, equanimity, and serenity intact.' After all that, are you going to betray his trust?

[24] "People will say, 'How did he get so hoity-toity and stuck-up?' Actually, I'm not as proud as I might be! I still lack confidence in what I've learned and agreed to; I'm still afraid of my own weakness. [25] Just let me gain that confidence, and then you'll see the right expression and the right demeanor; that's when I'll show you the statue, once it's a complete and polished piece of work. [26] What do you think the right demeanor is? Arrogance? Far from it! The Zeus in Olympia doesn't wear a haughty expression, does he? No, he has the steady gaze of one who can say 'Nothing I do shall be vain or revocable.'* [27] That's how I shall show myself to you, as a trustworthy, self-respecting, honorable, and serene person. [28] Do I mean that I shall show myself to be immortal, unaging, and immune to illness? No, but as one who is capable of dying and being ill with godlike dignity. That's within my power and capacity, but those other quali-

ties aren't. [29] The statue that is me will display the musculature of a philosopher. And what's that? Desire that is never disappointed, aversion that consistently enables me not to encounter what I don't want to encounter, appropriate inclination, scrupulous aspiration, circumspect assent. That's what you'll see."

2.9
That despite our inability to fulfill our potential as human beings, we assume the mantle of philosophy as well

[1] "It's no ordinary matter just to fulfill one's potential as a human being. After all, what is a human being?"

[2] "A rational, mortal creature."

"Which begs the question: what does our rationality set us apart from?"

"Wild beasts."

"Anything else?"

"Sheep and so on."

[3] "So make sure you never act like a wild beast; if you do, you stop being human and you're not fulfilling your potential. Make sure that you never act like a sheep, because that's another way to stop being human. [4] What is to act like sheep? When we act to satisfy our belly or our genitals, when we act without purpose, when we act grubbily or heedlessly, where have we sunk? To the level of sheep. What have we destroyed? Our rational faculty. [5] When we act aggressively, with intent to injure, passionately, and impetuously, where have we sunk? To the level of wild beasts. [6] And while some of us are large beasts, others are vicious and small, and make us long to be eaten by a lion! [7] These are all ways in which we destroy our potential as human beings.

[8] "Under what circumstances is a conjunct proposition preserved? When it fulfills its potential, which is to say that its preservation depends on its consisting of propositions that are true. What about a disjunct proposition? When it fulfills its potential.* [9] And the same goes for pipes, lyres, horses, and dogs. [10] So why should it occasion surprise if the same goes for the preservation and destruction of a human being? Every individual is strengthened and preserved by acting in keeping with himself—a builder by building,

a grammarian by doing grammar. If he gets into the habit of writing ungrammatically, his expertise is bound to lapse and be lost. [11] In the same way, moral acts preserve a self-respecting person and shameless acts destroy him; trustworthy acts preserve a person of integrity and the opposite kinds destroy him. [12] And, conversely, the opposite kinds of acts strengthen the opposite kinds of people. A person with no sense of shame is strengthened by shamelessness, an untrustworthy person by untrustworthiness, a rude person by rudeness, an angry person by anger, a miser by his surplus revenue.

[13] "That's why the philosophers require us not to be satisfied merely with studying, but to add practice and then training. [14] Over the course of many years, you see, we've become used to doing the opposite, and the beliefs that we do hold and put to use are the opposite of the correct ones. So if we don't also put the correct ones to use, all we are is interpreters of others' views. [15] I mean, is there anyone here right now who's unable to give a theoretical account of goodness and badness? 'Things are good, bad, or indifferent. The virtues and everything in which the virtues play a part are good, and their opposites are bad. Indifferents are things like wealth, health, and status.'* [16] But then, if this disquisition of ours is interrupted by a loud noise, or by someone laughing at us, we lose our composure. [17] So, philosopher, what happened to what you were just saying? Where are they coming from, these ideas that you're citing? From your lips, that's all. Why are you defiling helpful principles that you haven't made your own? Why are you cheating in matters of the utmost importance?

[18] "It's one thing to have loaves and wine stored in the larder, and another to eat them. When you eat something, it's digested and distributed around the body, and it turns into muscle, flesh, bones, blood, a good complexion, good lungs. Stored things may be available for you to bring out and show whenever you want, but they don't do you any good at all except insofar as you gain a reputation for having them. [19] What difference does it make whether you expound these teachings or those of another school? Sit down and give a theoretical account of Epicurus's teachings; you'll probably come up with a more user-friendly version than he did! Why call yourself a Stoic, then? Why mislead the public? Why pretend to be a Jew when you're Greek?* [20] Can't you see why people are called Jews or Syrians

or Egyptians, as the case may be? When we see someone wavering between two creeds, we tend to say 'He's no Jew, he's only pretending.' It's only when he engages with the actual experience of being baptized and making a commitment that we say that he really is a Jew, as well as being called one.* [21] So we too are the uninitiated,† Jews in theory but something else in fact, since we haven't engaged at an experiential level with the theory and still have a long way to go before we put the ideas we spout into practice—the ideas we're so proud of knowing. [22] And so, even though we're unable to fulfill our potential as human beings, we assume the mantle of philosophy as well, which is an enormous burden. It's as though someone who was incapable of lifting ten pounds wanted to pick up the rock of Ajax!"*

2.10
*How the names that a person bears reveal what behavior is appropriate for him**

[1] "Consider who you are. In the first place, a human being—that is, a person whose highest faculty is will, and who subordinates everything else to his will, while keeping it unenslaved and unsubordinated. [2] Consider, then, what your possession of reason sets you apart from: it sets you apart from wild beasts and from sheep. [3] Moreover, you're a citizen of the world and a part of it, and not one of the parts destined for service, but one of the leading parts, because you're capable of understanding the divine governance of the world and of working out the implications of that governance.

[4] "So what is the job of a citizen? Never to act in his own interest and never to think about any matter as if he were an isolated entity,* but to behave as a hand or foot would if it had reason and was able to understand the natural order of things: it would never have inclinations or desires except by reference to the whole. [5] Hence the philosophers are right to say that if a truly good person were to foresee the future, he wouldn't resist even illness, death, or mutilation, because he'd realize that this is what he's been allotted at the behest of the universe, and that the whole is more important than the part, the city than the citizen. [6] But as things are, since we lack such foreknowledge, what is appropriate is to stick with the things

that naturally present themselves for our selection, because that's what we were born for.*

[7] "The next thing is to bear in mind that you're a son. What is someone in this role supposed to do? To regard everything that's yours as belonging to your father, always to obey him, never to speak critically of him to anyone, never to say or do anything that would injure him, to defer and yield to him in everything, while helping him as best you can. [8] And the next thing of which you should be aware is that you're a brother. For this role, too, you're obliged to be deferential, obedient, and polite, and never to compete with your brother over anything that isn't subject to will but cheerfully to give up your claim to it, so that you're better off in the realm of things that are subject to will. [9] Just think what a bargain it would be to win his gratitude in exchange for a head of lettuce, perhaps, or a seat in the theater!

[10] "The next thing to bear in mind, if you sit on the council of some town, is that you're a councillor; if you're young, that you're young; if you're old, that you're old; if you're a father, that you're a father. [11] For it's always the case that reflection on names like these reveals the acts that are appropriate to each of them. [12] But if you go and criticize your brother, I tell you that you're not bearing in mind who you are and what your name is. [13] Besides, if you were a smith and you began to make poor use of your hammer, you'd have lost sight of the smith you used to be. So if you lose sight of the fact that you're a brother and become an enemy instead of a brother, will it seem to you that you've exchanged nothing for nothing? [14] And if you exchange being a human being, a gentle and sociable creature, for being a wild beast, a dangerous, cunning, biting creature, have you lost nothing? Is it only financial loss that you consider detrimental? Do you think there's no other kind of loss that damages a person? [15] If you lost your ability to read or sing, you'd regard the loss as detrimental, but do you then consider the loss of your self-respect, dignity, and kindness a matter of no importance? [16] And yet the loss of the former is due to some external cause which isn't subject to will, whereas the loss of the latter is our own doing. Moreover, possessing the former isn't an honorable thing, nor is losing them dishonorable, whereas not having the latter, or losing them, is not merely dishonorable but a reprehensible disaster.

[17] "If a deviant lets himself be sexually penetrated by another man, what does he lose? The man that he was. And the person who makes use of him? In addition to a great many other things, he too loses his manhood, just as much as the deviant does. [18] What does an adulterer lose? The self-respecting, self-disciplined, self-controlled man that he was, the citizen, the neighbor. What does an angry person lose? Something else. A fearful person? Something else. [19] It's impossible to be a bad person without losing something and being damaged. It's true that, if you count only financial loss as detrimental, all the people I've just mentioned come to no harm and suffer no loss; in fact, they might even do well out of it and come out ahead, if they earn any money from what they do. [20] But beware: if you calculate everything in financial terms, you have to say that even someone who loses his nose hasn't been harmed."

"Of course he has," someone said. "His body's been mutilated."

[21] "All right, but suppose he's lost just his sense of smell. Is that losing nothing? So is there no mental faculty that it's beneficial to have and harmful to lose?"

[22] "What faculty do you mean?"

"Aren't we endowed by nature with self-respect?"

"Yes."

"If someone loses this faculty doesn't he suffer loss? Isn't he deprived of something? Doesn't he lose something that was his? [23] Aren't we endowed by nature with trustworthiness, affection, benevolence, and the ability to tolerate others? If someone allows himself to suffer loss in these respects, does he remain unharmed and unimpaired?"

[24] "Are you saying that I shouldn't injure someone who's injured me?"*

"First you need to consider what injury is, and bear in mind what you've been told by the philosophers. [25] After all, if it's true that goodness, and badness too, have to do with will, it seems possible that what you've just said amounts to: [26] 'Well, since he's harmed himself by having wronged me, shouldn't I harm myself by wronging him?' [27] Why don't we conceptualize the matter like that, instead of thinking that we're harmed only when we suffer some loss that affects our body or our possessions, and that if it's our will that's affected, we come to no harm? [28] It's because holding false beliefs or doing wrong doesn't make a person's head hurt, or his eye or his hip, nor does it make him lose any land, [29] and these are the only things that matter to us. The only time we concern ourselves with whether our will remains self-respecting and trustworthy, or becomes shameless and untrustworthy, is when it's a topic for discussion in the classroom. [30] And so we become better at arguing, but otherwise we make not the slightest progress."

2.11
The starting point of philosophy

[1] "The starting point of philosophy, at any rate for those who go about it in the right way and enter by its front door, is an awareness of one's own weakness and impotence in matters of supreme importance.* [2] We come into the world with no innate conception of a right-angled triangle or of a quarter tone or halftone. It takes technical instruction for us to learn about these things, which is why people who don't know them also don't think they do. [3] But everyone who comes into the world has an innate conception of good and bad, right and wrong, seemly and unseemly, and of happiness, of propriety and duty, and of what they ought to do and avoid doing. [4] That's what makes it possible for all of us to use these terms—that is, to try to apply our preconceptions about them to particular instances. [5] 'He's done well; that was the right (or wrong) thing for him to do; he's unhappy or happy; he's unjust or just.' Is there anyone who refrains from employing these terms? Is there anyone who postpones using them until he's received instruction, as people do when it's a geometrical or musical subject of which they're ignorant? [6] And the reason is that we come into the world after having already been relevantly instructed, so to speak, by nature in certain matters, and this instruction serves as a foundation onto which we add our own particular views."*

[7] "But *I* don't know what's right and what's wrong. Why is that? Don't I have a relevant preconception?"

"You do."

"Am I failing to apply it to particular instances?"

"No, you do that."

"Am I failing to apply it properly, then?"

[8] "That's the nub of the problem; that's where subjective opinion comes in. People start with these noncontroversial concepts and get into disputes by misapplying them to particular instances. [9] If, in addition to having preconceptions, people also had the ability to apply them correctly, they would, of course, be perfect. [10] But now, since you think you're applying your preconceptions correctly to particular instances, tell me what led you to this conclusion."

"Because I believe I'm right."

"But someone else may disagree about that, and he too thinks he's applying preconceptions correctly, doesn't he?"

"Yes."

[11] "So is it possible that both of you are applying your preconceptions correctly when there's a clash between your beliefs?"

"No, that's impossible."

[12] "Well, do you have anything to say, apart from 'I believe I'm right,' to convince us that you're the one who's applying them better? All a madman ever does is what he thinks it right for him to do. Would that serve as a criterion of truth in his case too?"

"No, it wouldn't."

"So look for something over and above belief. What is it? [13] And there you have the starting point of philosophy: recognizing that people hold conflicting opinions, looking into why the conflict occurs, condemning belief as inherently untrustworthy, investigating whether a given belief is correct, and discovering a standard, such as the scale that was devised to measure weights, or the rule that allows us to decide whether something is straight or bent.

[14] "This is how we make a start in philosophy: Are all opinions sound? But how can conflicting opinions be sound? Not all opinions are sound, therefore. But ours might be, mightn't they? [15] Why ours rather than those held by Syrians or Egyptians? Why mine rather than anyone else's? There's no good reason to prefer one over the other. So what someone believes isn't a sufficient criterion for determining the truth. After all, when it comes to weights and measures, we aren't satisfied with mere appearances but have devised standards to determine the truth. [16] So is there no standard higher than belief in the present case? But surely it's impossible for the most crucial matters in the world to be undeterminable and undiscoverable. So there must be a standard.* [17] So why don't we look

for it and discover it, and then in the future unfailingly make use of it and never even extend a finger without it? [18] This is something, I'm sure, the discovery of which will cure the madness of those who currently assess everything only by means of belief, because from then on, on the basis of known and clearly defined criteria, we'll be in a position to apply our various preconceptions to particular cases. [19] What subject for investigation do we have at hand?"

"Pleasure."

"Submit it to the standard, put it on the scales. [20] For something to be good, it has to be something that merits our confidence and trust, doesn't it?"

"Yes."

"So does anything changeable deserve our confidence?"

[21] "No."

"Well, pleasure is scarcely unchanging,* is it?"

"No."

"Remove it from the scales, then, and throw it away. Banish it far from the country of good things. [22] But if your eyesight is weak and one balance isn't enough for you, bring another. Would it be wrong for something good to make you feel proud?"

"No."

"So would it be wrong for a passing pleasure to make you feel proud? Make sure you don't say 'No,' because if you do I'll consider you unworthy of even the scales.* [23] So that's how things are assessed and weighed when we have standards ready for use. [24] And philosophy is the work of examining and establishing the standards. [25] But it takes a truly good person to become so familiar with them that he can put them to use."

2.12
On argument

[1] "What a person needs to have learned to become expert at conducting an argument has been precisely laid down by the philosophers of our school, but we have absolutely no training at all in the practical application of these instructions. [2] At any rate, give any one of us a non-philosopher to talk to, and he'll be useless. He might get the man to shift his ground a little, but he's unable to cope with

any stubbornness from him and ends up either abusing or mocking him. 'He's no philosopher,' he says. 'It's impossible to do anything with him.' [3] But when a guide comes across someone who's lost his way, he takes him to the right road; he doesn't mock him or abuse him and then abandon him. [4] You, too, should show your interlocutor the truth, and then you'll see him follow you. But as long as you're not showing him the truth, don't mock him, but rather recognize your own limitations.

[5] "What was Socrates's practice? He used to make his interlocutor his witness, and he needed no other witness. That's why he was able to say,* 'I dispense with everyone else; it's always enough for me to have my disputant as my witness. I don't ask for anyone else's vote, but only my interlocutor's.' [6] He used to clarify the consequences of ideas so well, you see, that every one of his interlocutors, no matter who he was, recognized the inconsistency in his belief-set and retreated from it. [7] 'Does envy make an envious person happy?' 'No, he's more likely to be in pain.' Here it was his proposing the contrary that moved his companion to say what he did. 'All right. Now, do you see envy as a painful experience brought on by seeing things that are bad? But how could anyone be envious of bad things?'* [8] So he's got him to say that envy is a painful experience brought on by seeing good things. 'All right. Now, can anyone envy things that are of no importance to him?' 'Of course not.'

[9] "So it's only once he's spelled out and elucidated the concept that he finishes with it. He doesn't say, 'Define envy for me,' and then, after hearing the definition, 'Your definition's no good, because the *definiens* is not extensionally equivalent to the *definiendum*.'* [10] These are technical terms, and therefore tiresome for non-philosophers and hard for them to follow, even if *we* can't do without them. [11] But we haven't the slightest ability to get our non-philosopher to change his mind by using terms that he can follow by himself, so that he's able to draw on his own impressions to accept or reject a proposition. [12] What happens next is that, as you'd expect, those of us who are aware of our limitations call a halt to the proceedings, or at least we do if we're cautious. [13] But most people aren't cautious, and when they get involved in this kind of discussion, their confusion sows confusion, and in the end, after hurling abuse and having abuse hurled at them, they walk away.

[14] "The primary and most distinctive characteristic of Socrates was that he never got irritated during an argument and never said anything rude or insulting but put up with rudeness from others and defused the conflict. [15] If you want to know how good he was at this, read Xenophon's *Symposium* and you'll see how many conflicts he resolved. [16] It's not surprising that this is therefore a quality that comes in for the highest praise from poets as well: 'Expertly he makes a quick end of even a great dispute.'*

[17] "Well, but these days it's not a particularly safe activity, especially in Rome. The reason is that, obviously, it's not the kind of activity that can be carried on discreetly. You have to approach a rich man, probably of consular rank, and ask him your questions. [18] 'Hey there! Can you tell me to whom you've entrusted the care of your horses?' 'I can.' 'Well, is he just some random person with no knowledge of horses?' 'Of course not.' 'And to whom have your entrusted your gold or silver or clothing?' 'Again, not to a non-expert.' [19] 'What about your body? Have you ever thought of entrusting that to someone's care?' 'Of course.' 'And obviously this man, too, is an expert, who knows about physical fitness and medicine?' 'Certainly.' [20] 'Are these your best possessions, or do you have something better than them?' 'What are you getting at?' 'The faculty, by Zeus, that makes use of all these things, and assesses and ponders their worth.' [21] 'Do you mean the soul?'* 'You've understood me perfectly. That's exactly what I'm getting at.' 'By Zeus, I regard this as a far better thing to have than the other things.' [22] 'So can you tell me what provisions you've made for the care of your soul? I mean, I imagine that someone as clever as you, and as highly regarded in the city, isn't casually and haphazardly letting his best possession suffer neglect and ruin.' 'Of course not.' [23] 'But have you been taking care of it yourself? Did you learn how to do so from someone else, or are you self-taught?'[24] So this is where it gets dangerous, because he might say, 'Is that any concern of yours, sir? It's none of your business.' And then, if you persist in bothering him, he may put up his fists and punch you. [25] I was very keen on this activity myself, before I ended up where I am today."*

2.13
On anxiety

[1] "Whenever I see someone in a state of anxiety, I ask myself, 'What is it that he wants?' Unless he wanted something that wasn't up to him, why would he be anxious? [2] The reason why a minstrel feels no anxiety when he's singing by himself at home but does when he enters the theater, even if he's an excellent singer and a talented player of the lyre, is that he doesn't just want to sing well but also to go down well with the audience, and that isn't up to him. [3] It's a matter of knowledge: he's confident in any field where he has knowledge—set him down before any ordinary member of the public and he won't be concerned—but when it's a field with which he's unfamiliar and to which he hasn't paid attention, he gets anxious. [4] What do I mean? He doesn't know about crowds or their approval. He's learned how to strike the strings of his instrument, but he's never thought about the approval of the masses. He doesn't know what it is or how powerful a force it is in life. [5] So he's bound to tremble and turn pale.

"So when I see a frightened man, I can't say that he's no minstrel, but I will make another point. In fact, there are a number of things I could say about him, not just one. [6] Above all, though, I think of him as a stranger. I say, 'This man doesn't know where in the world he is. Although he's been living here for a long time, he's ignorant of the city's laws and customs; he doesn't know what is and what isn't permitted. In fact, he's never consulted an expert who could tell him what the customs of the city are and could explain them to him. [7] He doesn't write a will without knowing how to write one or consulting an expert, nor does he casually go about affixing his seal to a pledge or signing a guarantee, but when it comes to his desires and aversions, and his inclinations, objectives, and intentions, he acts without consulting an expert in the customs of the city.' [8] In what sense does he lack expert advice? He doesn't know that he's wanting things that are not available to him and trying to avoid things that are unavoidable; he doesn't know what is and what isn't his. If he did know this, he'd never be obstructed or impeded, and he'd never feel anxious. [9] How could he? Does anyone worry about things unless they're bad? No. Well, does anyone worry about things that are bad when it's up to him to see that they don't happen? Of course not.

[10] "So if things that aren't subject to will are neither good nor bad, and everything that is subject to will is up to us, and no one can either take them away from us or impose them on us unless we accept them, how can anxiety take hold? [11] It's our body that causes us anxiety, and our possessions, and what Caesar will decide—externals, not things that are internal to us. Is having a false belief something that causes anxiety? No, because it's up to me. What about having an inclination that's contrary to nature? No, the same goes for that too. [12] So when you see someone turning pale, just as a doctor draws inferences from a patient's complexion and says, 'There's something wrong with this person's spleen, or with that person's liver,' so you should say, 'There's something wrong with this person's faculty of desire and aversion. He's not well, he's feverish.' [13] That's the only thing that causes pallor, trembling, chattering teeth; that's the only thing that makes a person 'shift his weight from one foot to the other, then settle firmly on both feet.'*

[14] "That's why Zeno felt no anxiety at the prospect of meeting Antigonus: the king had no power over the things the philosopher valued, and the things over which Antigonus did have power were of no concern to him. [15] But Antigonus was anxious at the prospect of meeting Zeno, and with good reason, because he wanted Zeno to like him, and that wasn't up to him. But Zeno didn't need Antigonus to like *him*, just as no expert needs the approval of a non-expert.*

[16] "Do I want to be liked by you? What's in it for me? Do you know the standards by reference to which one person judges another? Have you made an effort to find out what a good person is, what a bad person is, and what makes people good or bad? If so, why aren't you a good person yourself?"

[17] "What makes you think I'm not?"

"Because no one who's good grieves or complains or moans, nor does he turn pale, nor does he tremble and say, 'How will he receive me? What will he think of what I'm going to say?' [18] He'll receive you, slave, as he sees fit to receive you. Why should you worry about something that isn't up to you? Isn't it† his fault if what you say doesn't go down well with him?"

"Of course."

"Is it possible for one person to be at fault and another to be harmed by it?"

"No."

"So why is someone else's business making you anxious?"

[19] "All right, but I worry about how I'm going to talk to him."

"Do you mean that you can't talk to him as you wish?"

"But I'm afraid of being knocked off course."

[20] "But surely you're not afraid of being knocked off course when you're about to write the name 'Dion,' are you?"

"Of course not."

"Why is that? Isn't it because you've studied writing?"

"Of course."

"And won't you be similarly confident when you're about to read something?"

"Yes."

"Why is that? It's because expertise always brings strength and confidence in its field. [21] So haven't you studied rhetoric? And what else did you study as a student? Syllogisms and changing arguments. What was the point of that? Wasn't it so that you could argue skillfully? And isn't arguing skillfully arguing pertinently, unassailably, intelligently, flawlessly, and irrefutably—and, in addition to all this, confidently?"

"Yes."

[22] "Well, suppose you're a cavalryman and you've ridden down to level ground to take on a man who's on foot. Assuming that you're in practice and he isn't, do you feel anxious?"

"Yes, you're right, but he has the power of life and death over me."

[23] "Then speak the truth, you pitiful creature. Don't make yourself out to be more than you are, don't claim to be a philosopher—and be sure to recognize who your masters are. As long as your attachment to life gives them a hold over you, comply with everyone who's stronger than you. [24] Socrates used to practice how to speak, and hence he spoke as he did to the tyrants,* to the jurors, to his jailer. Diogenes was in practice as a speaker, and hence he spoke as he did to Alexander, to Philip, to the pirates, to the man who bought him as a slave.* [25] <Leave speaking as a philosopher>* to those who are in practice and do it with confidence. [26] As for you, go to what's yours and stick with it. Go and sit in your corner, compose syllogisms, get them published. 'We shan't look to you for someone to lead the state.'"*

2.14

To Naso

[1] Once, when a certain Roman* had come in with his son and was listening to one of his readings, Epictetus remarked that this was his teaching method, and then fell silent. [2] When the man urged him to continue, he said, "Instruction in any art is tedious for a layman who has no knowledge of it, [3] even though the products of the arts immediately display what use they are with regard to the end for which they've been produced and are for the most part rather attractive and delightful. [4] Take a cobbler, for example: there's nothing enjoyable about standing by and watching him learn his craft, but the shoe he makes is useful and, moreover, not unpleasant to look at. [5] Or again, it's no fun at all for a layman to be present as a carpenter is being instructed, but his product shows just how useful this skill of his is. [6] Music is an even clearer example: if you're there when someone's being taught, you'll think there could be no more unpleasant learning process, but the products of music are pleasant and enjoyable for non-musicians to hear.

[7] "The same goes for our case too. We imagine the product of philosophy to be somewhat as follows: a philosopher should adapt his wishes to events, so that nothing happens contrary to our wishes and nothing fails to happen when we want it to happen. [8] The outcome for accomplished philosophers is that, where desire is concerned, they are never disappointed and, where aversion is concerned, they never encounter what they seek to avoid. A philosopher on his own spends his life without grief, fear, or mental turmoil, and when he's with other people, he preserves both his natural and his acquired relationships as a son, father, brother, citizen, man, woman, neighbor, travel companion, ruler, and subject.*

[9] "Something like that is what we imagine the product of philosophy to be, and so next we want to find out how to make it happen. [10] Well, we see that a carpenter becomes a carpenter by learning certain things, and that a navigator becomes a navigator by learning certain things. Might it not be the case, then, that the same goes for philosophy, too, and it's not enough just to want to be a truly good person, but one also needs to learn certain things? So what we want to find out is what these things are. [11] The philosophers say that

the first thing we need to understand is that God exists, that he cares providentially for the universe, and that it's impossible for us to conceal from him not just our actions but our intentions and thoughts as well. [12] Then we want to find out what kind of beings the gods are, because, whatever the answer, the only effective way to win their approval and carry out their wishes is for a person to make himself like them to the best of his ability. [13] If the gods are trustworthy, he must be trustworthy too; if free, he must be free too; if benevolent, he must be benevolent too; if magnanimous, he must be magnanimous too. And so, from then on, he must emulate God in everything he does and says."

[14] "Where does one start, then?"

"I don't know whether you'll dispute this, but I'm going to say that you first have to understand the meanings of terms."

[15] "You're implying that at the moment I don't understand them?"

"That's right, you don't."

"Then how is it that I use them?"

"You use them as illiterate people use the written word and as cattle use impressions. Use, you see, is one thing, and understanding another. [16] If you think you have the required understanding, bring up any term you like and let's test ourselves to see if we understand it."

[17] "But it's galling to be tested when one is already a senior member of society and when, it so happens, one has fought in three wars."*

[18] "I'm sure you're right. I mean, you didn't come to me today because you need anything from me. It's hard to imagine what you might be in need of. You have money, probably more than one child, a wife, and an extensive household; Caesar knows you, you have plenty of friends in Rome, you do your duty, and when someone has done you good or harm, you know how to repay them in kind. [19] What could possibly be missing in your life? So if I show you that you lack everything that makes the most essential and important contribution to happiness, that up until now you've concerned yourself with everything except what should have been your concern, that, to cap it all, you don't know what God is, or what a human being is, or what is good or bad, [20] well, you may let me get away with that, but if I say that you don't know yourself, can you tolerate that and submit to the test without leaving? [21] Of course not. You'd just get cross and

leave. And yet, have I wronged you in any way? No—unless a mirror wrongs an ugly man by showing him what he looks like. Or unless a doctor wrongs an invalid by saying, 'You think you're doing fine, man, but you have a fever. Go without food today, and drink only water.' No one responds by saying, 'What a terrible insult!' [22] But if you tell someone, 'Your desires are feverish, your aversions are humiliating, your purposes are inconsistent, your inclinations are out of harmony with nature, your beliefs are random and wrong,' he ups and leaves, saying, 'You've insulted me!'

[23] "Our situation is like what you find at a festival. Cattle and oxen are driven there to be sold, and while most people are there to buy or sell, there are a few who go as spectators, to see how the festival is conducted and why, and to find out who the organizers are and what their intention was.* [24] The same goes for this festival that is life. Some people, like cattle, are interested in nothing but food. I'm talking about all those of you who care about possessions, land, slaves, and political power—things that are just fodder. [25] But there are a few who attend the festival as people who just love to observe. 'What in fact is the world? Who is directing it? No one? [26] But seeing that a state or a household is unable to last for even the shortest time without someone to direct and take care of it, is it likely that such a great and beautiful construct is maintained in good order by sheer accident and chance? So there must be someone directing it. [27] What sort of a being is this director? How does he direct it? And we who are his creatures—who are we and for what purpose did he create us? Do we have some connection and relationship with our creator or not?'

[28] "That's how these few people are affected, and from then on they devote their time exclusively to investigating the festival, before they have to leave. [29] So they attract the scorn of the mass of ordinary people, just as at the literal festival the spectators attract the scorn of those who are there to buy and sell. And if the cattle had awareness, they'd laugh at those who value anything but fodder."

2.15

To those who cling obstinately to certain of their decisions

[1] "When they hear the claims that it's good to be steadfast and that will is naturally free and unconstrained, while everything else is sub-

ject to impediment and constraint, and is under the control and in the power of others, some people's response is to imagine that none of their decisions must ever change. [2] But, in the first place, the decision must be sound. I wish to have a vigorous body, but it must be that of a healthy person, an athlete. [3] If you display the vigor of someone with brain fever and boast about it, I'll say, 'Man, go and find someone to make you better. This isn't real vigor, but infirmity in a different guise.'

[4] "That's the kind of mental stubbornness that people experience if they don't really understand what these claims mean. A friend of mine, for example, decided to starve himself to death, for no good reason. [5] By the time I heard about it, he was already over two days into his fast. I went and asked him what had happened. [6] 'I've made up my mind,' he said. 'But still, what was it that persuaded you to do it? If it was a good decision, look, here we are, by your side, and we'll help you on your way. But if it was an irrational decision, change it.' [7] 'But it's important to stick with one's decisions.' 'How can you say such a thing, man? Not every decision, but only good ones. I mean, suppose you're currently convinced that it's night; if that's your opinion, don't change it, but stick with it and insist on the importance of abiding by one's decisions. [8] Shouldn't you begin with the solid foundation of a thorough inquiry into whether or not your decision is sound, and then use that to support the edifice of your firmness, your certainty? [9] But if your foundation is rotten and crumbling, you shouldn't build on it; in fact, the bigger and stronger your superstructure, the quicker it will come tumbling down. [10] For no reason at all, you're removing from the world a person who's a dear friend of ours, and a fellow citizen of both cities, the great and the small.* [11] Moreover, you're murdering and destroying someone who's totally innocent, while saying that one must abide by one's decisions. [12] If for some reason it ever occurred to you to kill me, would you have to abide by your decision?'

[13] "Well, this friend of mine was eventually persuaded to change his mind, but it's impossible to get some people nowadays to change. So I think I now understand, as I didn't before, the meaning of the proverb 'A fool can be neither swayed nor broken.' [14] God forbid that I should ever have a clever fool for a friend! There's no one harder to deal with. 'I've reached a decision.' So do mad people,

but the more firmly they cling to their delusions, the more hellebore they need.* [15] Shouldn't you do what sick people do and call for a doctor? 'I'm ill, sir. Help me. Tell me what you prescribe. I'll do whatever you say.'

[16] "The same goes for what we're talking about at the moment. 'I have no idea what I ought to do, but I've come to find out.' No, what he says instead is: 'Talk to me about something else. I've made up my mind about this.' [17] How can we talk about something else? What could be more critical or relevant than your being persuaded that there are things that are more important than persisting in a decision? That's the vigor of a mad person, not a healthy one.

[18] "'I don't mind dying, even though I'm not being forced to.'† Why, man? What happened? 'I've made up my mind.' So I'm alive only because you never decided to kill me. [19] 'I'm refusing to accept any payment.' Why? 'I've made up my mind.' Believe me, there's nothing to stop you later from being disposed to accept payment with just as much vigor as you're now displaying in refusing to accept it—nothing to stop you saying once again 'I've made up my mind.' [20] In an unhealthy body, one that's suffering from a flux, the humor tends now in this direction and now in that,* and the same goes for a weak mind: it's not easy to be sure in which direction it's tending. But, whatever its penchant and bent, the addition of vigor makes the evil uncorrectable and incurable."

2.16
That in practice we fail to apply our judgments about what is good and bad

[1] "Where should we look for what is good? In will. And for what is bad? In will. And for what is neither good nor bad? In things that aren't subject to will. [2] All right, but do any of us remember this except when we're discussing it as we are now? Do any of us, when we're by ourselves, train ourselves in how to respond to facts the way we do in school to our questions: 'It's day, isn't it?' 'Yes.' 'Is it night?' 'No.' 'Is there an even number of stars?' 'Impossible to say.'

[3] "When you're shown some money, have you trained yourself to make the necessary response: 'Not good'? Have you trained yourself in these responses, or only in responding to tricky arguments? [4] Is

it any surprise, then, if you excel in areas where you've put in the work, and make no progress in areas you've neglected? [5] I mean, what is it that makes an orator remain anxious, when he knows that he's composed a good speech and has it off by heart, and when he comes equipped with a pleasant speaking voice? [6] It's because it's not enough for him to just practice his art. What else does he want? To win the praise of the audience. Now, the point of his training was to be able to practice oratory; it never touched on praise and blame. [7] Has he ever been told by anyone what praise and blame are—what the nature of each of them is? Does he know what kinds of praise to seek and what kinds of blame to avoid? Has he ever taken up *this* training—the training that's required by these concepts? [8] So why are you surprised to find him doing better than others in areas where he's put in the work, and being no different from ordinary people in areas where he hasn't? [9] He's like a minstrel who knows how to play the lyre, sings well, and has a fine stage costume, but who still trembles with fear when he enters the theater. He knows *these* things, you see, but he doesn't understand crowds and doesn't know about their cheers and jeers.* [10] In fact, he doesn't even know what anxiety is— whether we ourselves are responsible for it or whether it's out of our hands, whether or not it's possible to stop it. That's why, if his performance meets with approval, he leaves the stage all puffed up with pride, whereas the prick of jeers deflates that bubble of conceit.

[11] "We experience something similar as well. What do we think important? Externals. What do we take an interest in? Externals. And then we're puzzled as to why we feel fear or anxiety? [12] But that's the only possibility, as long as we regard impending events as bad. We cannot not be afraid or anxious. [13] And then we say, 'Lord God, what does it take for me not to feel anxiety?' You fool, have you no hands? Didn't God make them for you? Then you'd better sit down now and pray that your nose doesn't run. Or, better, wipe your nose and stop carping.

[14] "So has God given you nothing to help you in this regard? Hasn't he endowed you with fortitude, greatness of soul, and courage? Although you have these wonderful hands, are you still looking for someone else to wipe your nose? [15] But we don't even think about these things or pay them any attention. I mean, can you name even one person who cares about *how* he acts, who's concerned not

just with getting something, but with what he's doing? Is there anyone who, while walking, pays attention to the act of walking? Is there
anyone who, while forming a plan, pays attention to his planning,
rather than to getting the result he's planning for? [16] If he does get
it, he's delighted. 'See what good planners we are,' he says. 'Didn't I
tell you, brother, that it was impossible for things not to turn out the
way they have if we put our minds to it?' But if things don't work out
for him, the poor fool gets depressed and can find no way to explain
what happened. Is there anyone here who hasn't called in a diviner
under these circumstances? [17] Is there anyone here who hasn't
slept in a temple to find out what to do?* Please, bring me one such
person, that's all! I want to see him. I've been looking for him for so
long, this paragon, this prodigy! Whether he's young or old, please
bring him to me!

[18] "So how can it be surprising to find that, because of our pre-
occupation with material things, in our actions we're ignoble, unseemly, worthless, fainthearted, incapable of tolerating hardship—
just utter disasters! It's hardly surprising, seeing that we've been so
careless and negligent in this regard. [19] If it wasn't death or exile of
which we were afraid, but fear itself, we'd have trained ourselves not
to experience what we judge to be bad. [20] But, as it is, we're reso-
lute and fluent in the classroom, and capable of working out the consequences of any little theoretical question that comes up about any
of these matters, but if we're forced to turn to their practical application, you'll see us flounder like shipwrecked sailors. All it takes is
a troubling impression, and you'll see where we've been putting our
attention and what we've been training for!

[21] "And then, because of our lack of training, we're constantly
compounding our problems and making them out to be greater than
they really are. [22] For instance, when I'm on board a ship, I peer
down into the depths, or I look at the sea all around me, with no land
in sight, and I become unsettled and imagine myself swallowing all
that water if the ship goes down. It doesn't occur to me that three
pints is all it takes. What is it that's disturbing me? The sea? No, my
judgment. [23] Or again, when there's an earthquake, I imagine that
the whole town is going to fall on me, which is silly because a mere
stone is enough to knock my brains out, isn't it?

[24] "What is it, then, that oppresses and alarms us? It must be our

judgments, mustn't it? When someone leaves home and loses family and friends, and all his familiar haunts and affiliations, it's only a judgment that oppresses him, isn't it? [25] At any rate, a child's tears, triggered by its nurse's moving a little way off, are forgotten as soon as it's given a rusk. [26] Should we, too, be like little children? By Zeus, no! It's not a rusk I want to see having this effect on us, but correct judgments. [27] And what are they? Those that people should put into practice all day long, so that, by being attached to nothing that is not their own—friends, places, gymnasia, even their own bodies—they remember the law and keep it in mind. [28] What law? God's law: to keep to what's yours and to claim nothing that isn't yours, but to use what you're given and not long for what you haven't been given. And if something is taken from you, to let it go without hesitation or delay, grateful for the time when you had the use of it— that is, if you'd rather not cry for your nurse and your mommy! [29] After all, what difference does it make what it is that a person is subject to and dependent on? If you mourn the loss of a gymnasium or some such haunt, with its shady colonnades and youthful companions, are you any better than a man who sheds tears over a girlfriend? [30] Someone else is upset because he won't in the future be drinking water from Dirce's Spring—but is the water of the Marcian aqueduct worse than Dirce's?*

"'But I was used to it.' [31] And later you'll become used to Marcian water as well. So, if you become attached to Marcian water, mourn its loss, too, when the time comes, and try to find a way to make up a Euripidean kind of verse: 'The Baths of Nero and the Marcian water.'* Behold the birth of tragedy in the reaction of foolish people to ordinary events! [32] 'When shall I see Athens again and the Acropolis?' You poor thing, aren't you content with what you see every day? Is there anything better or greater for you to see than the sun, the moon, the stars, the whole earth, the sea? [33] If you understand the governor of the universe and carry him around with you, why do you still long for blocks of stone and a prettified rock? What will you do when you're about to leave even the sun and the moon? Will you sit and blubber like a little child?

[34] "So what did you do in school? What did you hear? What did you learn? Why style yourself a philosopher when you could tell the truth? 'I've studied a few introductions to philosophy and I've read

some Chrysippus, but I haven't crossed the threshold of philosophy. [35] How could I engage in the same occupation as Socrates, seeing how he died and how he lived? Or as Diogenes?' [36] Is it conceivable that either of them would shed tears or get upset at the prospect of their no longer seeing this man or that woman, or at the prospect of their no longer being in Athens or Corinth, but in Susa, perhaps, or Ecbatana?* [37] When someone is at liberty to leave the party whenever he chooses and to stop playing the game, why would it upset him to stay? He'll behave as one does in a game, and stay as long as he's being entertained, won't he? [38] Anyone with this attitude would easily be able to endure lifelong exile, or death if he was sentenced to death.

[39] "Shouldn't you be weaned by now, as children are, and start taking more solid food, without crying for your mommies and your nurses?† [40] 'But if I leave, it'll upset them.' *You* upset them? Hardly. It'll be the same thing that upsets you—a judgment. So what can you do? Eliminate that judgment of yours, and they'd be well advised to eliminate theirs themselves. Otherwise, they'll have no one to blame but themselves if they feel grief at your loss. [41] Man, you must be prepared right now to lose your mind, as the saying goes, in order to gain contentment, freedom, and greatness of soul. Raise your head as one who's been delivered from slavery. [42] Dare to look up at God and say, 'From now on, use me as you wish. I am of one mind with you; I am yours. Whatever you decide is fine with me. Take me where you will. Dress me how you will. Do you want me to hold public office or steer clear of politics? Do you want me to stay here or go elsewhere, to be poor or rich? Everything you do I shall justify to people. [43] I'll show them the true nature of everything that happens.'

[44] "No, you won't. You'll sit like a cow in a shed and wait for your mommy to come and feed you. If Heracles had sat around at home, what would he have amounted to? He'd have been Eurystheus rather than Heracles.* Look at all the friends and loved ones Heracles gained as he traveled around the world—but none was dearer to him than God. That's why he was believed to be a son of God, as in fact he was. So he was obeying God's will as he went from place to place, purging the world of injustice and lawlessness. [45] All right, you're no Heracles, and you can't cleanse the world of the wickedness of others, nor are you even Theseus, capable of cleansing just Attica.

So purge yourself of your own troubles. From now on, cast out of your mind not Procrustes and Sciron,* but grief, fear, craving, envy, spite, avarice, timidity, and self-indulgence. [46] The only way you can get rid of these is by making God the sole object of your attention, by being devoted only to him, by dedicating yourself to carrying out his commandments. [47] If you want anything other than this, however, you'll be pulled along, moaning and groaning, in the wake of everything that's stronger than you, because you'll always be looking for contentment outside yourself. And you'll never be able to find it, because you're not looking for it where it is, but where it isn't."

2.17
How to apply preconceptions to particular cases

[1] "What is the first work for a would-be philosopher to undertake? Eliminating presumption, because it's impossible for anyone to go about learning what he thinks he already knows. [2] On our visits to philosophers, we all argue back and forth about what we should and shouldn't do, what's good and bad, what's right and wrong, and end up by assigning praise and blame, censure and reproach, judging certain acts as right or wrong, and noting what distinguishes them. [3] But why do we go to philosophers? Because we want to learn things we *don't* think we know. And what are these things? Theories. We want to understand what the theories are that the philosophers talk about, which seem so subtle and incisive—though some are more interested in what these theories can gain them.

[4] "Now, it's ridiculous to suppose that anyone will learn anything other than what he wants to learn, and equally ridiculous to think that anyone will make progress in any subject he isn't studying. [5] But ordinary people make the same mistake as the orator Theopompus, who once took Plato to task for being obsessed with definitions.* [6] What did Theopompus say? 'Before you came along, did none of us use the terms "good" or "just"? Were we just making meaningless, empty noises, without understanding what the words signify?' [7] Look, Theopompus, no one's suggesting that we have no innate concepts and preconceptions of each of these things. But the point is that it's impossible for us to apply our preconceptions to the corresponding realities until we've elucidated each of them

and considered what kinds of instances are to be assigned to each of them.*

[8] "I mean, we could say much the same to doctors too. 'Before Hippocrates came along, did none of us use the terms "healthy" and "unhealthy"? Were these just empty noises we were making?'* [9] But the point is that, although health is another thing of which we have a certain preconception, we're no good at applying the preconception. That's why one doctor says, 'Carry on with the diet,' while another says, 'Give him food,' and why one says, 'Open a vein,' while another says, 'This calls for a cupping glass.' How do we explain this? It must be due to an inability to apply the preconception of health properly to particular instances.

[10] "The same goes here too, in our lives. We all talk about 'good' and 'bad,' 'beneficial' and 'harmful,' because we have preconceptions covering each of these terms. So the question is: have we elucidated our preconceptions? Is each of them perfectly understood? Prove it. [11] How? By applying it properly to particular instances. According to Plato's preconception, definitions are useful, while according to yours, they're useless. [12] Can you both be right? Of course not. Or consider wealth: isn't it the case that according to some people's preconception it's good, while for others it isn't? And doesn't the same go for pleasure and health? [13] What I'm getting at is the general point that if, in employing these terms, all of us have sufficient† knowledge of each of them and there's no need for us to take care to elucidate them, why are there disagreements between us? Why is there conflict? Why do we criticize one another?

[14] "And yet, why should I cite and mention this interpersonal conflict? You on your own prove the point. If you're applying your preconceptions well, why are you discontented and obstructed? [15] For the time being, let's leave aside the second domain, to do with inclinations and the skill required in their case to see that our behavior is appropriate. Let's also leave aside the third domain, to do with assent. [16] I'll let you off all that. Let's confine our attention to the first domain,* which will provide us with almost tangible evidence that you're not applying your preconceptions well. [17] Are you in fact wanting what's possible and in particular what's possible for you? If so, why are you obstructed? Why are you discontented? Are you in fact avoiding what's unavoidable? If so, why do you en-

counter difficulties of any kind? Why do you meet with misfortune? Why do things that you want to happen not happen, while things you don't want to happen do happen? [18] That's unmistakable evidence of a discontented and unhappy existence. 'I want something and it doesn't happen: am I not the most wretched creature in the world? I don't want something and it does happen: am I not the most wretched creature in the world?'

[19] "Medea couldn't endure this situation, either, and it drove her to the point of killing her children. In this respect, at any rate, she displayed a kind of greatness: she had the right impression of how awful it is for a person's wishes to be frustrated. [20] 'So I shall take my revenge on the man who wronged and insulted me. What use is a man with such an evil disposition? What form should my revenge take, then? I shall kill my children. That will hurt me, too, but what do I care?'* [21] Here we have a strong-minded woman who has gone wrong. She didn't know how we get to do what we want. She didn't know that this isn't something that comes to us from outside ourselves or from changing and rearranging our circumstances. [22] Stop wishing for your husband, and all your wishes will come true. Don't unconditionally want him to live with you; don't want to remain in Corinth, and, in short, align what you want with what God wants. Who will impede you then? Who will constrain you? No one, any more than they could impede or constrain Zeus.

[23] "When you have Zeus as your commander and align your wishes and desires with his, can you still be afraid of failing to get what you want? [24] Give your desire and aversion over to poverty and wealth, and you'll fail to get what you desire and meet with what you want to avoid. Give them over to health, and you'll be miserable. Give them over to political power, honors, country, friends, children—in short, to anything that isn't subject to will—and the same goes. [25] But give them over to Zeus and the gods—hand them over to them, put them in their charge, enroll them in their command—and how could you still be discontented? [26] However, if, pathetic creature that you are,† you're subject to envy, pity, jealousy, and fear, and if not a day goes by when you don't complain to yourself and the gods, how can you say that you've received an education? [27] In what sense are you educated, man? Because you've worked on syllogisms and changing arguments? If it were possible, shouldn't you unlearn

all that and make a fresh start, recognizing that up until now you've not embarked on the enterprise of philosophy at all? [28] From now on, shouldn't you make this your starting point, the foundation on which, step by step, you construct your edifice, and learn how to ensure that nothing happens except what you want to happen, and that nothing that you want to happen fails to happen?

[29] "Give me just one young man who has come to the school with this purpose, who masters the theory and then says, 'Speaking for myself, I can do without everything else. It will be enough for me if I can live my life without obstruction or grief, hold my head up high in the world as a free man, and look up to heaven as a friend of God, with no fear of anything that might happen.' [30] Let one of you show himself to be this kind of person and then I'll say, 'Come in, young man. You're home now. For you are destined to become an ornament to philosophy, and so all this property is yours, all these books, all these discourses.' [31] And then, once he's completed the first domain and mastered it, have him come to me again and say, 'I do indeed want to have both equanimity and serenity, but, as a respectful, thoughtful, and punctilious person, I also want to know how to behave appropriately toward gods, parents, brothers, country, and strangers.' [32] Move on now to the second domain; it, too, is made for you. [33] 'All right, I've now completed my training in the second domain as well. But I'd like what I've learned to be securely and unassailably available to me,† not only when I'm awake but also when I'm asleep, drunk, and in a black mood.' Man, these lofty ambitions make you a god!*

[34] "But no, what we hear instead is: 'I want to know what Chrysippus means in his treatise *On the Liar*.'* If that's your objective, you poor fool, why don't you go and hang yourself? What will you gain? Reading the entire book won't cure your despondency, nor will talking to others about the book put an end to your fearfulness. [35] That's how the rest of you are as well. 'Shall I read to you, brother, and you to me?' 'Man! You write amazingly well.' 'And so do you. You've really got the hang of Xenophon's style.' 'As you have that of Plato.' 'As you have that of Antisthenes.' [36] In any case, after describing your dreams to one another, you find yourselves no farther on than when you started. You have the same desires and aversions as before, the same inclinations, the same objectives and intentions; you pray for the same things and you take an interest in the same things. And

yet, instead of looking for someone who could give you a nudge, it irritates you to be told what I'm telling you now. [37] And then you say, 'What an uncaring old man! He didn't shed a tear when I left. He didn't say, "Son, things are going to be pretty tough for you out there, I can tell you. If you come through safe and sound, I'll light lamps for you." Is that the behavior of a caring person?' [38] It will indeed be truly excellent for someone like you to come through safe and sound; you'll deserve to have lamps lighted for you. You ought to be beyond the reach of death and illness.

[39] "So, as I say, before embarking on philosophical theory, we should lose the presumption of thinking that we know anything worthwhile. After all, this is what we do when we take up geometry or music. [40] Otherwise, progress will remain a distant goal, even if we work our way through all the introductory books and Chrysippus's treatises, not to mention those of Antipater and Archedemus."*

2.18
How to combat impressions

[1] "Every habit and ability is confirmed and strengthened by the relevant actions—the ability to walk by walking, the ability to run by running. [2] If you want to be a good reader, read; if you want to be a good writer, write. But just see what happens if you let thirty days go by without reading, while doing something else instead. [3] So also, if you're bedridden for ten days, when you get up and try to walk any distance, you'll see how weak your legs are. [4] In short, if you wish to do something, make it habitual, and if you don't wish to do something, don't do it, but make a habit of doing something else instead.

[5] "The same also goes for states of mind. Every time you get angry, it's not just that something bad has happened to you, believe me, but you've also strengthened the condition; it's as though you'd added fresh fuel to a fire. [6] When you've succumbed to sexual desire, you shouldn't think of that as just a single defeat, but appreciate that you've fed and strengthened your self-indulgence. [7] In other words, it's inevitable that the relevant actions won't just implant habits and capacities which didn't exist before but will intensify and strengthen those that already exist.

[8] "This, of course, is how moral infirmities take root, according

to the philosophers. As soon as you've conceived a desire for money,* if reason is brought to bear to make you aware of the danger, the desire ceases and the command center is restored to its original state. [9] But if you bring nothing to bear by way of a remedy, the command center won't return to the same state, and the next time it's aroused by a relevant impression, the flame of desire will be ignited in it more quickly than before. And, if this happens time after time, a callus is eventually formed, a condition that fixes the avarice in place. [10] A person who had a fever, for instance, and then got better isn't in the same condition as he was before the fever, unless he's completely cured. [11] The same goes also for the passions that afflict the soul. It retains certain traces and weals, and if they're not thoroughly erased,* the next thrashing in the same place will cause wounds, not just weals. [12] So if you don't wish to be short-tempered, don't feed the habit, don't add anything that will strengthen it. The first thing to do is quell your anger and count up the days when you didn't lose your temper. [13] 'I used to get angry every day, then every other day, then every two days, then every three days.' And if you go for thirty days without losing your temper, make a sacrifice to God. For a habit is first weakened and then utterly destroyed. [14] 'Today, tomorrow, and then for two or three months in succession, I didn't feel distress, but then I was on the lookout for anything that might distress me.' Believe me when I say that you're doing fine.

[15] "Today I saw a beautiful boy or girl, and I didn't say to myself, 'I wish I could have sex with her' or 'Her husband's a lucky man.' After all, anyone who calls her husband lucky is thinking that the same goes also for a man who's not her husband and who has sex with her. [16] Nor do I form a mental image of what comes next—her being with me, getting undressed, lying next to me. [17] I pat myself on the back and say, 'Well done, Epictetus! You've solved a tricky problem, much trickier than the Master Argument.'* [18] But suppose the girl is willing, gives me the nod, and beckons me over, and suppose she also touches me and presses up against me: if I resist and don't give in, I'd have solved a puzzle trickier than the Liar Paradox or the Silent Man.* *That*'s an achievement in which one might legitimately take pride—better than posing the Master Argument.

[19] "How is this to happen? You must want to win your own approval; you must want to be beautiful in the eyes of God. Desire to

become pure with the help of your pure self and God. [20] And then, when some such impression tempts you, Plato recommends that you turn to expiatory sacrifices, and go as a suppliant to the temples of the gods who ward off evil; [21] even retreating to the company of truly good people, and assessing yourself by this standard of comparison, is good enough, whether the person you take as your model is alive or dead.* [22] Go to Socrates and see him lying down with Alcibiades and making light of his allure.* Consider what a victory he knew himself to have won, a truly Olympic victory, enrolling him among the heirs of Heracles.* In fact, by the gods, one would be more justified in greeting *him* with the words 'Hail, man of wonder!' than those rotten boxers and pancratiasts* and their like—gladiators, I mean. [23] If you counter the impression with these reminders, you'll overpower it and it won't make off with you. [24] But the first thing is not to be carried away by its intensity. You should say, 'Wait a moment, impression. Let me see what you are and what you're an impression of. Let me put you to the test.' [25] And then don't let it lead you on by creating an image in your mind of what comes next; otherwise, off it goes, taking you wherever it wants. Instead, introduce an alternative impression, a fine and honorable one, and dismiss this impure one. [26] And if you make this exercise your regular practice, you'll see how your shoulders develop, and your muscles and sinews. But at the moment there's nothing more to you than theoretical quibbles.

[27] "That is the true trainee, the person who's in training to combat these kinds of impressions. [28] Be strong, poor man! Don't let yourself be carried away! Great is the struggle and divine is the work, to win a kingdom,* freedom, contentment, serenity. [29] Remember God and call on him for help and support, as sailors in a storm call on the Dioscuri.* After all, what greater storm could there be than one that's stirred up by powerful impressions and has the ability to blow reason off course? Indeed, what else is an actual storm but an impression? [30] I mean, take away the fear of death, and bring on all the thunder and lightning you like, and you'll find out how much calm and stillness there is in your command center. [31] But if you're defeated once and, despite your promise that you'll win next time, the same thing continues to happen, you can be sure that at some point you'll find yourself in such an appalling and enfeebled condition that eventually you won't even be aware of your mistakes and

you'll start to come up with reasons to justify your behavior. [32] And at that point you'll be confirming the truth of Hesiod's words: 'A postponer of labor is constantly wrestling with blights.'"*

2.19
To those who take up philosophy just to enhance their conversation

[1] "The Master Argument seems originally to have been formulated on the basis of the following principles. Since these three propositions are mutually incompatible—that everything that has happened in the past is necessarily the case; that an impossibility cannot follow from a possibility; and that something is possible even if it is not true now and never will be—Diodorus, recognizing this incompatibility, used the plausibility of the first two propositions to prove that nothing is possible unless it is or will at some point be the case.*

[2] "Now, some people keep these two propositions—that something is possible even if it is not true now and never will be, and that an impossibility cannot follow from a possibility—but not the proposition that everything that has happened in the past is necessarily the case. This seems to have been Cleanthes's position, and Antipater was largely in agreement with him.* [3] Others, however, keep a different pair of propositions—that something is possible even if it is not true now and never will be, and that everything that has happened in the past is necessarily the case—and argue that an impossibility *can* follow from a possibility. [4] But there's no way for all three propositions to be kept at the same time, because of their mutual incompatibility.

[5] "So if someone asks me which of the propositions *I* would keep, I'll tell him that I don't know, but that, according to the account that's come down to me, Diodorus kept one pair, Panthoides* (I think) and Cleanthes another, and Chrysippus a different pair again. [6] 'Yes, but what about you?' It's not my role in life to test my own impression—to compare others' views and reach my own conclusion on the matter. I'm no different in this respect from a Homeric scholar: [7] 'Who was Hector's father?' 'Priam.' 'Who were his brothers?' 'Paris and Deiphobus.' 'And their mother?' 'Hecuba. That's the account I've received.' 'From whom?' 'From Homer. But I think Hellanicus and one or two others like him have also written on the subject.'*

[8] "That's my position on the Master Argument as well: what more do I have to contribute? If I were a vain man, I could astound my companions, especially at a dinner party, by listing those who've written on it:* [9] 'Chrysippus has given a wonderful account in the first book of his *On Possibles*. And Cleanthes devoted a treatise to the subject, as did Archedemus. Antipater has written about it as well, not only in his *On Possibles*, but also in his dedicated treatise *On the Master Argument*. [10] Haven't you read it?' 'No.' 'Do so.' But what good will it do him? It'll just give him more nonsense to spout, and he'll be even more objectionable than he already is. I mean, what did *you* gain from reading it? What judgment have you formed on the matter? No, you'll only tell us about Helen and Priam and the island of Calypso, which never had any reality and never will.

[11] "Now, in the field of literature, it doesn't really matter if all we do is master the received account without forming a judgment of our own. But the trouble is that we do the same thing in ethics, and to a far greater degree. [12] 'Explain goodness and badness to me.' 'Listen: "A wind bore me from Troy to the Cicyonians."* [13] Things are good, bad, or indifferent. The virtues and everything in which the virtues play a part are good, the vices and everything in which vice plays a part are bad, and everything between these two poles of goodness and badness is indifferent—things like wealth, health, life, death, pleasure, and pain.' [14] 'How do you know?' 'Hellanicus says so in *On Egypt*.'

"The point is, what difference does it make whether you answer like this or refer to Diogenes's account in his *Ethics*,* or to Chrysippus or Cleanthes? Have you investigated these ideas at all and come to your own conclusion? [15] Show me how you typically behave on a ship in a storm. Do you remember these distinctions when the sail is cracking in the wind and some tease nearby who's heard you screaming says, 'Remind me, by the gods: what was it you were saying the other day? Being shipwrecked isn't a vice or something in which vice plays a part, is it?' [16] You'll pick up a piece of wood and lay into him, won't you? 'Damn you, man! We're dying and you come and make jokes?'

[17] "What if Caesar sends for you to answer a charge? Do you remember these distinctions? And suppose someone comes up to you as you enter the palace, all pale and trembling with fear, and says,

'Why are you afraid, man? What's at stake here for you? Here in the palace Caesar isn't dispensing virtue and vice to his visitors, is he?' [18] 'Why are you mocking me? Who are you to add to my troubles?' 'No, but seriously, philosopher, tell me why you're afraid. It's death you're threatened with, isn't it, or imprisonment, physical pain, exile, or disfavor? What else could it be? But none of these is vice or something in which vice plays a part, is it? How was it that you used to characterize these things?' [19] 'Damn you, man! I've got quite enough troubles as it is.' That's well said, because you certainly do have enough troubles—the meanness of your spirit, your cowardice, your pretentiousness here at school. Why did you pride yourself on qualities that you don't possess? Why did you call yourself a Stoic?

[20] "Observe yourselves like this as you go about your daily business and you'll discover to which school you belong. Most of you will find yourselves to be Epicureans, and a few will find themselves to be Peripatetics, albeit in a loose sense.* [21] I mean, can you show me where, in actual fact, you've taken on board the notion that virtue is as important as everything else combined, or even more important? Show me a Stoic, if there's one among you. [22] Where is he? How would you prove his credentials? There are countless people who recite Stoic doctrine, but the question is whether they're any worse at reciting Epicurean ideas. And don't they give just as accurate an account of Peripatetic views as well? [23] So who actually is a Stoic? Just as we call a statue 'Phidian' if it's been fashioned in conformity with Phidias's technique, show me someone who's been fashioned in conformity with the principles that he spouts. [24] Show me someone who's sick and happy, who's in danger and happy, who's dying and happy, who's in exile and happy, who's out of favor and happy. Show me him. By the gods, I'd love to see a Stoic. [25] But you can't show me anyone who's been fashioned in this way. Show me, at least, someone who's in the process of being fashioned in this way, who's tending in that direction. Do me that favor. Don't begrudge an old man the sight of something special he's never seen before. [26] Do you think you'll be showing me Phidias's Zeus or Athena, a construct of ivory and gold?* Let one of you show me a human soul that's willing to be of one mind with God, to never again find fault with God or man, to never fail to get what he desires, to never meet with anything he wants to avoid, to never be angry or envious or jealous, a soul—why

should I beat around the bush?—[27] a soul that aspires to become a god rather than a human being, and, although confined within this carcass of a body, plans to achieve communion with God. Show me such a soul. But you can't. [28] So why do you delude yourselves and cheat everyone else? Why do you walk around dressed in clothes that aren't yours, as thieves and robbers of titles and concerns that in no way belong to you?

[29] "Anyway, the fact of the matter is that I'm your teacher and you're here as my students. I intend to make you unimpeded, unconstrained, unobstructed, free, content, and happy, and have you look to God in everything great and small, and you're here to learn how to do this and put it into practice. [30] So why is the work unfinished, if you have the right intention and I have the right aptitude to go with my intention? What's missing? [31] When I see a carpenter who has his materials at hand, I expect to see the finished product. In our case, here's the carpenter, here are the materials:* what are we missing? Is the matter not something that can be taught? No, it can be taught. [32] Is it, then, not up to us? No, it's the one thing in the world that's up to us. Wealth, health, status—these things aren't up to us, nor, in short, is anything except the right use of impressions. It's the only thing that's naturally unimpeded and unobstructed. [33] So why don't you complete the work? Explain this to me. It must be due either to me, or to you, or to the nature of the undertaking. The undertaking itself is doable and is the only thing that's up to us. It follows, then, that it must be due either to you or to me, or, more accurately, to us together. [34] Well, then, shall we at last make a start, here and now, on salvaging the project? Forget everything we've done up until now. Let's just make a start and, trust me, you'll see."

2.20

Against the Epicureans and Academics

[1] "When a proposition is sound and self-evident, even people who contradict it necessarily make use of it. Indeed, the fact that even those who contradict it inevitably find themselves making use of a proposition is just about the most compelling evidence there could be that it's a self-evident proposition. [2] For example, anyone who denied the proposition 'There are such things as universal truths'

would clearly be obliged to affirm the contrary: 'Nothing is universally true.' [3] That can't be true either, slave! I mean, what your assertion amounts to is 'If any proposition is universal, it is false.'* [4]
Or again, suppose someone comes up and says, 'Believe me when I say
that nothing is knowable and everything is uncertain.' Or here's another example, someone who says, 'Trust me—you won't regret it—
when I say that no one is to be trusted.' Or here's yet another, someone
who says, 'Learn from me, man, that nothing can be learned. This is
a true statement, and I'll prove it to you if you like.' [5] So is there any
difference between these people and, say, those who call themselves
Academics? After all, they say, 'People, give your assent to the proposition that no one assents. Trust us: no one assents to anything.'

[6] "Epicurus does the same as well. When he sets out to abolish
the natural sociability that binds people together, he makes use of
the very thing that he's trying to destroy. [7] Listen to what he says.
'Don't be deceived, people, don't err and stray. It's not the case that
rational beings have a natural sense of community with one another.
Trust me. Anyone who says anything different is tricking you with
invalid arguments.' [8] But, then, why do you care?* Leave us to our
error. Will you be at all worse off if the rest of us believe that we have
a natural sense of community with one another, and that we should
do all we can to preserve it? In fact, your position will be much better
and more secure.

[9] "Why do you worry about us, man? Why do you go without sleep
for our sakes? Why do you burn midnight oil? Why do you forsake
your bed? Why do you write such long books? Is it to save us from
the error of thinking that the gods care for people, or in case we hold
anything to be essentially good other than pleasure?* [10] If that's
the case, lie down and go to sleep. Lead the life of a worm, which is all
you've judged yourself worthy of: eat, drink, have sex, defecate, and
snore. [11] Why do you care whether others' opinions about these
matters are sound or unsound? What are we to you? I mean, you take
an interest in sheep because they let themselves be fleeced, milked,
and eventually slaughtered by us. [12] Wouldn't it be the answer to
your prayers if people could be charmed and bewitched by the Stoics until they dozily let themselves be fleeced and milked by you and
others like you? [13] I mean, shouldn't you reserve these teachings
for your fellow Epicureans and keep them hidden from rest of the

world? Shouldn't you do your best to persuade other people above all that humans are by nature social beings and that self-control is good, so that you can keep everything for yourself? [14] Or are we to maintain this fellowship with some people, but not others. If so, who are to be included? Those who maintain it in return, or those who infringe it? And who are more likely to infringe it than you Epicureans, with these ideas of yours?

[15] "So what was it that roused Epicurus from his sleep and made him write what he wrote? It must have been what is, after all, the strongest force in human life, nature, which compels people to do its bidding, reluctant and complaining though they may be.* [16] 'Write down these antisocial ideas of yours and leave them for others to read. Lose sleep over them—and in so doing become the denouncer of your own views.' [17] So why should we bring up how Orestes was hounded by the Furies and kept from sleeping* when the savagery of the Furies and Vengeful Spirits that troubled Epicurus was worse? They roused him from his sleep, denied him rest, forced him to divulge his own ills—the same effect that madness and wine have on the Galli.* [18] That's how invincibly strong human nature is. I mean, can a vine be affected like an olive tree, not a vine? Or, conversely, can an olive tree be affected like a vine, not an olive tree? Impossible, inconceivable. [19] Nor can a human being altogether lose his human drives. Even men who've castrated themselves can't cut off their masculine appetites. [20] The same goes for Epicurus too. He cut off everything that makes a man a man—being head of a household, a citizen, a friend—but he didn't cut off his natural human appetites. He couldn't do that, any more than the lazy Academics can lose their sense organs or blind themselves, although they're more intent on that than anything else. [21] It's a real affliction, when nature has supplied someone with measures and standards to enable him to discover the truth, if he fails to apply his ingenuity to them by taking on and completing the work that remains to be done, but does the opposite. That is, if he actually has a faculty that would enable him to discover the truth, but tries to eradicate and destroy it.

[22] "What do you say, philosopher?* What are your thoughts about piety and religiosity? 'If you like, I shall prove that it's a good thing.' Yes, please do. Then, once our citizens have been converted,

they'll honor the divine and stop being so perfunctory about matters of supreme importance. 'Oh, I see. You already have the proofs.' Yes, I do, thankfully. [23] 'So, since you're perfectly content with them, I'll give you the contrary position. The gods don't exist and, even if they do, they pay no attention to people, nor do we have anything in common with them. This "piety and religiosity" that the common run of people talk about is a fiction made up by charlatans and sophists—or by lawmakers, by Zeus, to frighten people and deter wrongdoing.'* [24] Bravo, philosopher! You've served our citizens well. That's the way to recall our young men from their tendency to despise the concept of divinity! [25] 'You mean you don't like what I'm saying? Next I'll argue that there's no such thing as justice, that morality is foolishness, and that there's no such thing as a father or a son.' [26] Bravo, philosopher! Carry on, please. Win our young men over. Let's have even more of them who feel and think as you do.

"Are these the ideas that enabled our well-governed states to grow great? Do these teachings account for the greatness of Sparta? Were these the convictions that Lycurgus* instilled in the Spartans by means of his laws and his educational system—that slavery is no more bad than good, and freedom no more good than bad? Was it because they held these views that the Thermopylae dead died? I suppose it must have been these views that led the Athenians to abandon their city.* [27] In any case, the propounders of these views marry, have children, take part in the public lives of their states, and get themselves appointed as priests and spokesmen of the gods! What gods? The non-existent ones! They even personally consult the Pythia* to hear her 'lies' and interpret them for others. What monumental effrontery and fraudulence!

[28] "What are you doing, man? You refute yourself on a daily basis, so shouldn't you abandon these pointless endeavors? When you eat, where do you move your hand to: your mouth or your eye?* When you bathe, what do you step into? Do you ever call a pot a plate or a ladle a spit? [29] If I were a slave and one of these men was my master, I'd torment him, even if it earned me a thrashing a day. 'Boy, pour some oil into my bath.' I'd get some fish sauce and pour it on his head. 'What's this?' 'The impression I received was indistinguishable from an impression of oil. I couldn't tell the difference, I swear on your

life.' [30] 'Give me my porridge.' I'd fill a bowl with vinegared fish and bring him that. 'Didn't I ask for porridge?' 'Yes, master. This is porridge.' 'Isn't this vinegared fish?' 'Why is it vinegared fish any more than it's porridge?'* 'Take some and smell it; take some and taste it.' 'But if our senses deceive us, how will that help you to know?' [31] Given three or four fellow slaves who were in on the scheme, I'd get him to hang himself in exasperation, or make him change his mind. But at the moment these people are mocking us by making use of all the faculties they've been granted by nature while abolishing them in theory.

[32] "What gratitude and respect they display for these gifts! At the very least, while eating bread every day, they have the cheek to say, 'We don't know if there's a Demeter, a Maiden, a Pluto.'* [33] I hardly need to add that, although they enjoy night, day, the changing seasons, the heavenly bodies, the sea, the earth, and the help they receive from others, none of these things makes them reconsider their views in the slightest. They just look for an opportunity to spew up their stupid little argument, and after having exercised their stomachs, they go and bathe. [34] But they've never stopped to think for even a moment about the significance of what they're about to say, or what they should talk about, or whom they should talk to, or what impact their arguments will have on those who hear them. I worry that a noble-spirited young man who listens to them might be influenced by them and, as a result of that influence, might lose the seeds of his nobility. [35] I worry that we may be providing an adulterer with ways to excuse the immorality of his acts, that an embezzler of public funds might draw on their arguments to get hold of some specious justification for his theft, that someone who's neglecting his parents might also draw on the arguments to increase his insolence toward them.*

"So what, according to you, is good or bad, right or wrong? This behavior? That behavior? [36] Is there any point, then, in arguing against any of these people, in engaging them in the back-and-forth of discussion, or in trying to change their minds? [37] By Zeus, one has a much better chance of getting a sex addict to change his ways than people who've become so completely deaf and blind."

2.21
On inconsistency

[1] "Some of their faults people readily admit, others not so readily. No one will admit that he's stupid or unintelligent. Quite the opposite, in fact: one constantly hears people saying, 'I wish my luck was as good as my brain.' [2] They readily admit to timidity: 'I'm rather timid, I agree,' they say, 'but in other respects you won't find me weak-minded.' [3] However, people don't readily admit to lack of self-control, under no circumstances to injustice, and never to envy or to sticking their noses in where they don't belong; but most people are ready to admit they feel pity.

[4] "How do we explain this variety? The most prevalent reason is our inconsistency and confusion in matters pertaining to good and bad; otherwise reasons vary from person to person, though by and large they never admit to anything they see as shameful. [5] People see timidity as a sign of sensitivity, and pity, too, but unintelligence as utterly slavish, and they never admit to antisocial behavior. [6] They are particularly likely to admit their faults—and this applies to a great many faults—insofar as they think there's an involuntary aspect to them, as there is in timidity and pity. [7] So if someone admits that he lacks self-control, he brings love into the equation, asking to be forgiven as though he had no choice. But they never see injustice as involuntary. Jealousy, however, they do see as having an involuntary element, and that's why it's something they admit to feeling.

[8] "Since we're surrounded by people who are so confused and so unaware of what they mean by a fault and what faults they have or don't have, or how they came to have them, or how they can rid themselves of them, it seems to me that we ought to keep a constant eye on ourselves as well. [9] 'Might I be one of those people myself? How do I see myself? How do I regard myself? Do I act prudently? Do I behave with self-control? Do I ever say what they say? Can I say that my background has equipped me to meet every eventuality? [10] Am I aware of my ignorance, as one who knows nothing ought to be? Do I go to my teacher as I would to an oracle, ready to do his bidding? Or do I, too, enter the school stuffed with snot, wanting only information and the ability to understand books I didn't understand before, so that I can interpret them for others if the occasion arises?'

[11] "Man, at home you've been sparring with your slave, turning the household upside down, disturbing the neighbors. And then you come here, standing on your dignity as though you were a philosopher, and sit and pass judgment on my interpretation of texts, deciding— what might it be?—that I spout any old nonsense that occurs to me? [12] You've come here filled with envy, in reduced circumstances because you're not being supplied from home, and you sit through the lectures thinking only about your father's or your brother's opinion of you. [13] 'What are people back home saying about me? Right now, they're imagining that I'm making progress. "He'll come back stuffed with knowledge," they say. [14] I'd really like to go back home eventually having learned all there is to know, but that requires a lot of hard work, and no one's sending me any supplies, and you can't get properly clean in Nicopolis bathhouses, and my lodgings are awful, and here at school it's awful too.'

[15] "And then people say that going to school never does anyone any good. But that's because no one goes to school to be cured, or to make their judgments available for purging, or to become aware of their failings. [16] So it's hardly surprising, is it, if you take away from school exactly what you bring to it? I mean, you didn't come in order to set any of your judgments aside or correct them or exchange them for others. No way. Far from it. [17] But what about what you *do* come for? You'd better check to see whether you're at least getting that. You want to incorporate philosophical theories into your conversations. All right, then. Aren't you becoming better at talking drivel? And don't these theories furnish you with material for showing off? Aren't you analyzing syllogisms and changing arguments? Aren't you investigating the assumptions of the Liar Paradox and of hypothetical arguments? In that case, why are you cross if you're getting what you came for?"

[18] "Yes, but if a child of mine dies, or my brother, or if I myself am facing death or torture, what use will these things be to me?"

[19] "But that's not what you came for, is it? That's not why you attend my talks. Has that ever led you to light a lamp or go without sleep? When you're out in the covered walk, have you ever set an impression before your mind instead of a syllogism, and investigated that along with your companions? When did you ever do that? [20] And then you say, 'Philosophical theories are useless.' To whom? To

those who don't use them right. Eye salves aren't useless to people who use them when and as they should, nor are poultices, nor are weights. It's just that they're useless to some people, but useful, despite that, to others. [21] If your question for me today is 'Are syllogisms any practical use?', I'll tell you that they are, and I'll prove it to you, if you like."

"So what use have they been to me?"

"Man, your question wasn't whether they're useful to *you*, but whether they're useful in general, wasn't it? [22] If someone with dysentery asks me whether vinegar is useful, I'll say that it is. 'So is it useful to me?' To that, I'll say no. First find a way to stop the flux and heal the ulcers.* The same goes for you, gentlemen. First heal your ulcers, stop your fluxes, calm your minds, and bring them untroubled into the school. Then you'll find out how powerful reason is."

2.22
On friendship*

[1] "A person is most likely to love something if he prizes it. Do people prize things that are bad? No. Do they prize things about which they're indifferent? Again, no. [2] So, by a process of elimination, people prize only good things; and if they prize them, they also love them. [3] So anyone who knows what's good would also know how to love. But anyone who's incapable of telling good and bad things apart, and unable to distinguish things that are indifferent from things that are good or bad, must be incapable of loving. The ability to love therefore belongs exclusively to a wise person."

[4] "What do you mean?" someone said. "I'm not wise, but I love my child."

[5] "I can hardly believe my ears, by the gods! Right from the start, you've admitted that you lack wisdom. What is it that makes you fall short? Don't you have the use of your senses and the ability to tell impressions apart? Don't you provide your body with suitable nourishment, covering, and housing? So what's making you admit your lack of wisdom? [6] It's this, by Zeus—that you're often confused and disturbed by impressions, and their appearance of truth gets the better of you. You take certain things to be good for a while, and then you think of them as bad, and later again as neither good nor bad. In

short, you're subject to distress, fear, envy, turmoil, and change, and that's why you admit that you lack wisdom. And aren't you fickle when it comes to friendship? [7] It's not just that you sometimes think of wealth, pleasure—*things*, in other words—as good, and sometimes as bad, but you also veer between judging the same people good and bad, and you vary between liking them and disliking them, between praising them and finding fault with them."

"Yes, that's exactly what happens."

[8] "Well, do you think a person can be someone's friend if he has been deceived about him?"

"Certainly not."

"And can a person be a loyal friend if he's changeable with regard to what he looks for in a friend?"

"Again, no."

"What about a person who alternates between reviling someone and admiring him?"

"And again, no."

[9] "Now, I'm sure that at some point the sight of puppies frolicking and playing together has moved you to say, 'What a perfect example of friendship!' But if you want insight into friendship, toss a scrap of meat between them, and then you'll see! [10] Toss a plot of land between you and your son and you'll realize how impatient he is to see you buried, and how intensely you long for him to die. And then it will be your turn to say, 'What a child I've raised! He's been planning my funeral for ages!' [11] Toss a pretty girl between you, and both of you want her, old and young. Toss some distinction or other between you and see what happens. Insofar as your life is bound to be at risk, you'll echo the words of Admetus's father: 'So you want to see the light. Do you think your father doesn't?'*

[12] "Do you suppose that this man didn't love his son when he was a child—that he wasn't in agony when he had a fever and didn't keep saying, 'I wish it was I who was ill instead'? But then just see what sentiments he utters when things come to a head and the crunch point is near! [13] Didn't Eteocles and Polynices have the same mother and father?* Hadn't they been brought up together, lived together, dined together, shared a bedroom, exchanged many a kiss? I'm sure that anyone who saw them would have laughed at the philosophers for their weird ideas about friendship. [14] But then, when the throne

was tossed between them like a scrap of meat, look at what they said:*
'Where will you take your stand in defense of the fortress?' 'Why do
you want to know?' 'Because I shall position myself opposite you, to
kill you.' 'Which is exactly what I long to do also.' That's the kind of
thing they pray for.

[15] "The point is that it's a universal fact—and you should have no
illusions on this score—that every creature is appropriated above all
to its own interest.* So if it judges something to be an impediment to
that interest, whether this impediment is a brother, father, child, beloved, or lover,* it loathes, attacks, and curses it, [16] because its nature is to love its own interest first and foremost. Self-interest is, for
it, father, brother, family, homeland, and god. [17] At any rate, whenever we judge that the gods are getting in the way of our interest, we
denounce even them, topple their statues, and set fire to their temples, as Alexander ordered the temple of Asclepius to be burned because of the death of his beloved.* [18] That's why, if a person places
his interest on the same side of the scales as piety, honor, homeland,
parents, and friends, all these things are safe, whereas if he puts his
interest on one side, and friends, family, homeland, and justice itself
on the other, they are all lost, outweighed by his interest. [19] Wherever 'I' and 'mine' are placed, you see, the creature is bound to tend in
that direction. If one identifies with the body, the body is dominant;
if one identifies with will, will is dominant; and if one identifies with
externals, externals are dominant. [20] It follows that it's only if I'm
identified with my will that I'll be the kind of friend, son, and father
that I should be, because then it will be in my interest to preserve my
trustworthiness, self-respect, patience, self-control, and amenability, and to maintain my various family relationships.* [21] But if I
place myself on one scale and honor on the other, then what Epicurus
said becomes valid, when he declared that what is honorable is either
nothing at all or no more than a conventional idea.*

[22] "It was ignorance of this that led the Athenians and Spartans
to fall out with one another, and the Thebans to fall out with both the
Athenians and Spartans, and the Persian king to fall out with the
Greeks, and the Macedonians to fall out with both the Persians and
the Greeks; it is currently the cause of the Romans' conflict with the
Getae and, way back in time, it was the cause of the Trojan War.* [23]
Paris was a guest of Menelaus, and seeing the warmth with which

they behaved toward each other, you'd never have believed anyone who doubted their friendship. But a tasty morsel was tossed between them, a pretty young woman, and war broke out over her.

[24] "So now, when you see friends or brothers who seem to be getting along, don't leap to any conclusions about their friendship, not even if they swear to it and say that they can't bear to be apart from each other. [25] The command center of a bad person isn't to be trusted; it's unstable and undecided, won over by one impression after another. [26] Don't inquire, as everyone else does, whether they had the same parents and had been brought up together, sharing the same minder.* No, the only question to ask is where they locate their interest, whether it's outside themselves or in their will. [27] If it's outside themselves, there's as little reason for calling them friends as there is for thinking of them as trustworthy, reliable, courageous, or free. In fact, the sensible course would be not even to call them human. [28] I mean, it isn't a human judgment that makes them bite each other, revile each other, or take to the agora (as brigands take to the desert or the mountains)† and make a display of their brigand-age in the law courts. Nor is it a human judgment that makes them incapable of resisting lust and turns them into adulterers and se-ducers, or makes them commit all the other crimes that people can commit against one another. All this is the outcome of just one judg-ment alone—the location of themselves and all they are in externals, things that aren't subject to will. [29] On the other hand, if you hear that these people truly believe that the good is to be found nowhere else but in will and in the right use of impressions, there's no lon-ger any need for you to try to find out whether they're son and father, or brothers, or friends who spent a long time in the same school to-gether. No, as long as you know just this one thing about them, you can confidently declare that they're friends, and by the same token that they're trustworthy and honest. [30] After all, where else might friendship be found than where there's trustworthiness and self-respect, and where the focus is on what's right and on nothing else?

[31] "'But he's been taking care of me for all these years. Did he really not love me all that time?' Slave, what makes you so sure that he hasn't been taking care of you in the same way that he cleans his shoes or looks after his mule? What makes you so sure that, once

you've exhausted your usefulness as a utensil, he won't throw you away like a broken plate?

[32] "'But she's my wife and we've been married for ages.' Well, how long was Eriphyle Amphiaraus's wife and the mother of his many children? But a necklace came between them.* [33] And what is a necklace? It's a judgment about things like a necklace. That was the brutalizing factor, that was what shattered their love, what stopped the woman from being a wife and the mother from being a mother.

[34] "So anyone here who's interested in either being a friend or making a friend should excise these judgments as repellent and banish them from his soul. [35] This will ensure, first, that he'll be free of self-hatred, inner conflict, regrets, and anguish. [36] Second, in his dealings with others, he'll be direct with anyone who's like himself, and with everyone else he'll be tolerant, indulgent, kind, and forgiving, on the grounds that he's dealing with people who are ignorant and mistaken about matters of supreme importance. He won't be hard on anyone, because he'll have fully taken on board Plato's saying that no soul is willingly deprived of the truth.* [37] But if you fail to excise these judgments, you'll behave exactly as friends do: you'll drink together, share the same berth, take trips by sea together, and you may even have the same parents—after all, even snakes do—but snakes don't make true friends and neither will you, as long as you retain these inhuman and repulsive judgments."

2.23
On rhetoric

[1] "The clearer the script in which a book has been written, the more pleasure a reader gets from it, and the easier it is for him to read. So wouldn't everyone also find it easier to listen to speeches that are characterized by elegant and attractive language? [2] One shouldn't deny the existence of a faculty of expression, then, because anyone who does that proves himself to be simultaneously impious and cowardly. He's impious because he's dishonoring gifts that come from God, which is no different from denying the usefulness of the faculty of sight or the faculty of hearing, or of speech itself.* [3] Did God give you eyes for no purpose? Was it for no purpose that he infused

eyes with a spirit that is so powerful and ingenious that it reaches far out* and takes on the imprints of the things we see? Is there any messenger that stands comparison for speed and diligence? [4] Was it also for no purpose that he made the intervening air so activated and tense that seeing can somehow extend through it thanks to its tension?* Was it for no purpose that he made light, without which the other elements of seeing would all be useless?

[5] "Don't be ungrateful, man, but at the same time don't forget that there are greater gifts than these. Give thanks to God for sight and hearing, and, by Zeus, for life itself and all that supports it—cereals, wine, olive oil—[6] but remember that he has given you something else that is greater than all of these: the faculty that makes use of them, assesses them, and calculates the worth of each of them. [7] I mean, what is it that declares, on behalf of each of these faculties, how much it's worth? It can't be the individual faculties themselves, can it? Have you ever heard the faculty of sight or the faculty of hearing saying anything about itself? No, they act as servants and slaves, with the job of ministering to the faculty that makes use of impressions. [8] And if you ask how much each of them is worth, to what are you addressing your question? What gives you an answer? So how can any other faculty be superior to this one, which treats all the others as its servants, assesses each of them, and makes known its conclusions?

[9] "Does any other faculty know what it is and what it's worth? Does any other faculty know when it should and shouldn't be used? Which of them is it that opens and closes the eyes, turning them away from what they shouldn't see and directing them toward other objects? The faculty of sight? No, the will. [10] Which of them is it that closes and opens the ears? Which of them is it that makes us inquisitive and interested, or, conversely, unmoved by what we hear? The faculty of hearing? No, it's the will. [11] And then, when it sees that all the other faculties around it are blind and deaf, incapable of being aware of anything other than precisely those acts which are the ways in which they serve and minister to it, while it alone sees clearly and surveys not only all the other faculties, to see how much each is worth, but also itself—given all this, it's hardly going to award first place to any faculty other than itself, is it? [12] All the eye does when it's open is look, but what tells us whether and how we should be look-

ing at someone's wife? The will. [13] And what tells us whether or not we should believe what we've been told, and, if so, whether or not we should be irritated by it? It's the will, isn't it?

[14] "As for the faculty in question (if it really is a distinct faculty), that enables us to express ourselves in speech and embellish our language, all it does is embellish the language with which we address any given topic, and arrange it as hairdressers arrange hair. [15] But whether it's better to speak or say nothing, whether it's better to express ourselves this way or that, whether what's said is suitable or unsuitable, and the right moment for anything we say, and its usefulness—it's only will that tells us all this, isn't it? So would you have it come forward and vote against itself?"

[16] "All right," someone said, "but what if this is how things stand? What if it is in fact possible for the servant to be superior to what it's serving—the horse to the rider, the hound to the hunter, the instrument to the lyre player, the underlings to the king?"*

[17] "But what is it that makes use of things? Will. What is it that attends to everything? Will. What is that destroys a man utterly, by starving him or hanging him or hurling him over a cliff, as the case may be? Will. [18] So is there anything stronger than will in human life? Of course not: it's impossible for things that are impeded to be stronger than something unimpeded. [19] What things are naturally capable of obstructing the faculty of sight? Both will and things that aren't subject to will. The same goes for hearing, and likewise for the faculty of expression. But what is naturally capable of obstructing will? None of the things that aren't subject to will, but only a deviant version of will itself. That's why it's only will that becomes vicious or virtuous.

[20] "So, since will is such a powerful faculty and has been set over all the others, shall we have it come forward and tell us that the body is the principal thing in the world? But even if the body itself proclaimed its superiority, no one would let it get away with it. [21] In actual fact, Epicurus, what is it that makes that assertion? What is it that wrote *On the End*, *Physics*, and *On the Canon*?* What is it that had your beard grow long?* What is that wrote, when it was dying, 'As I pass what is at once the last day of my life and a blessed day'?* Was it your body or your will? [22] So wouldn't it be crazy to recognize anything as superior to will? Are you really that blind and deaf?

[23] "Are we saying, then, that all the other faculties are unimportant? Not at all. Are we saying that there's no usefulness or gain from any faculty except will? Not at all. That would be stupid, impious, and ungrateful to God. We acknowledge the value of everything. [24] After all, even a donkey has some use, though not as much as an ox; even a dog has some use, though not as much as a slave; even a slave has some use, though not as much as one's fellow citizens; even they have some use, though not as much as the people who rule over them. [25] The fact that some things are superior to others shouldn't make one discount the usefulness of those other things.

"The faculty of expression has some value too, though not as much as the will. [26] When I say this, none of you should take me to be suggesting that you neglect the way you speak, any more than I would suggest that you neglect your eyes, ears, hands, feet, clothes, or footwear. [27] But if you ask me what the supreme thing in the world is, what am I to say? The faculty of expression? I can't say that. I can only say that it's will, when rightly applied. [28] It's will that makes use of both the faculty of expression and all the other faculties, great and small. When will is rightly applied, a person becomes good; when it's wrongly applied, a person becomes bad. [29] It's will that's responsible for our failures and successes, for our approval and disapproval of one another. In short, it's will that's responsible for unhappiness if we neglect it, and for happiness if we attend to it.

[30] "But to do away with the faculty of expression, to say that in reality there's no such thing, is not only ungrateful to those who gave it to us, but it's also cowardly.* [31] I say this because it seems to me that anyone who denies its existence is afraid that, if there is in fact some such faculty, we may not be able to think it unimportant. [32] That's how it is also for people who deny the difference between beauty and ugliness—as if seeing Thersites had the same effect as seeing Achilles, or seeing Helen the same effect as seeing an ordinary woman.* [33] But this position is taken up by foolish, uncouth people, who are ignorant of the individual natures of things, but are still afraid that, if the difference is recognized, they'll immediately be overcome and swept off their feet.*

[34] "No, what's important is to leave every individual thing in possession of its own faculty, and, having done so, to see the value of the faculty, to find out what the supreme thing is in the world, and

to pursue it without fail. In devoting oneself to it, one should count all other things as relatively trivial, but neglect them, too, as little as possible. [35] I mean, we have to take care of our eyes, too, not because they're especially important in themselves but for the sake of what actually is especially important. After all, the will won't be as nature intended unless it uses sight in a reasonable way and prefers some things over others.

[36] "But what happens is that people behave like someone who's on his way back to his homeland when he passes an excellent inn, and it pleases him so much that he stays there. [37] Man, you've forgotten your purpose: you weren't traveling *to* the inn, but *past* it. 'But it's really nice.' There are plenty of nice inns, and plenty of pretty meadows, too, but only as places on the way. [38] You have a different mission—to return to your homeland and put an end to your family's fear, and to fulfill your duties as a citizen by marrying, raising children, and holding the customary offices. [39] You didn't come into the world in order to go around picking out locations of the pleasanter kind, surely, but to live where you were born and where you've been enrolled as a citizen.

"Something similar happens where the faculty of expression is concerned too. [40] Since the spoken word is essential to the kind of teaching through which one progresses toward perfection, purifies one's will, and corrects the faculty that makes use of impressions, and since the teaching of philosophical principles demands a certain kind of diction, involving both a range of styles and forceful language, [41] some people are captivated by these things and stay where they are. They're captivated by style, or syllogisms, or changing arguments, or some other wayside inn, and they remain there and molder away, as if they'd been seduced by the Sirens.*

[42] "Man, you were supposed to be making yourself proficient at using the impressions you encounter in accord with nature; you were supposed to be making sure that you're never disappointed in your desires and that, where your aversions are concerned, you never encounter what you want to avoid, that you're never wretched, that you're never miserable, that you're free, unimpeded, and unconstrained; you were supposed to be attuning yourself to Zeus's governance of the world, making yourself obedient to it and perfectly content with it; you were supposed to be aiming for a state where

you blame no one, accuse no one, and can wholeheartedly recite the verses beginning 'Lead me, Zeus, both you and Destiny.'* [43] And yet, despite having this set of objectives, you make no progress at all, just because you took a liking to a nice turn of phrase or certain aspects of the theoretical work, and you prefer to stay put, forgetting everyone and everything at home, and saying 'How nice it is here!' Of course it's nice—but as a way station, as an inn. [44] I mean, what's to prevent someone having the eloquence of Demosthenes and being wretched? What's to prevent someone being as good as Chrysippus at analyzing syllogisms and feeling miserable, sad, envious—in a word, troubled and unhappy? Nothing. [45] So you can see that these are all inns, which have no value in themselves and have nothing to do with the goals you've set yourself.

[46] "Sometimes, when I say these things, people think I'm disparaging the study of speech or philosophical theories. No, it's not studying these things that I'm disparaging, but the inability to move on from them, and pinning all one's hopes on them. [47] If voicing these ideas harms people who hear them, number me among those who cause harm. But when I see that one thing is supreme and of supreme importance, I can't say that of something else just to gratify you."

2.24

*To someone who Epictetus thought did not have what it takes**

[1] Someone said to him, "My longing to hear you speak has often brought me here to you, and you've never responded to me. Today, if possible, please say something to me."

[2] "Do you think," said Epictetus, "that just as there are arts in other areas, there's also an art of speaking, which is such that anyone who possesses it will speak skillfully, and anyone who doesn't won't?"

"Yes, I do."

[3] "So isn't it the case that a skilled speaker is one who both benefits himself and has the ability to benefit others by what he says, while someone who's harmed instead, and who causes harm, is unskilled in this art of speaking? Wouldn't you find that some speakers are harmed while others are benefited? [4] And what about the audience? Are they all benefited by what they hear, or would you find that among them too some are helped and some are harmed?"

"Yes, that's true of them too," he said.

"So it's also true for listening that it takes skill to be benefited and lack of skill is harmful?"

He agreed.

[5] "So there's a skill in listening, just as there's a skill in speaking?"

"Apparently."

[6] "Well, if you like, we can approach the matter from the following angle as well. Who is it, do you think, who plays an instrument musically?"

"A musician."

< "And do you think that no skill is involved in listening to a musician?"

"No, it certainly takes skill."> *

[7] "And who is it, in your opinion, who makes a statue properly?"

"A sculptor."

"And do you think that no skill is involved in looking with an experienced eye?"

"That takes skill too."

[8] "So if it takes skill to speak properly, do you see that it also takes skill to listen with benefit? [9] Let's leave aside for the time being, if you don't mind, the question of what 'perfectly' and 'beneficially' really mean, since both of us have a long way to go before we can understand that kind of thing. [10] But here's something with which I think everyone would agree—that anyone who's going to listen to philosophers, at any rate, needs to be a very well-practiced listener. Isn't that so? [11] So what should I talk to you about? Tell me. What are you capable of hearing? About good and bad? Good and bad for what? For a horse?"

"No."

"For an ox?"

"No."

"For a human being?"

"Yes."

[12] "Do we know what a human being is, then—what human nature is, what the word 'human' means? Have our ears been open to any extent when this has been discussed? Do you have any idea what nature is? How much of what I say are you capable of understanding?

[13] Shall I use a demonstrative argument on you?* What would be the point? I mean, do you even understand what a proof is—how or by what means something is proved? Can you recognize an argument that appears to be sound but isn't? [14] Do you know what truth and falsehood are? Can you recognize a valid inference, a contradiction, an incompatibility, a discrepancy? And yet I'm to interest you in philosophy? [15] How can I get you to see that most people have contradictory ideas that lead them to disagree about what's good and bad, or what's beneficial and harmful, when you don't even know what contradiction is?

"Tell me, then, what's the point of my talking to you? Stir my desire to do so. [16] Just as the sight of the right kind of grass stirs in a sheep the desire to eat, whereas if you offer it a stone or some bread it remains unmoved, so there are certain natural desires in people that make them want to speak when there's someone there to listen to them and he arouses their enthusiasm to do so. But if he sits there like stone (or like grass!), how can he arouse any such desire in a person? [17] Does the vine *ask* the farmer to tend it? No, it shows on its own that anyone who tends it will profit from doing so, and that's how it calls on him to tend it. [18] It's impossible to resist the charm and exuberance of small children—impossible not to join in their games, crawl on the ground with them, and babble baby talk with them—but who wants to play or bray with a donkey? It may be small, but it's still a small donkey."

[19] "Why do you have nothing to say to me, then?"

"There's only one thing I can say to you and that's this. If a person doesn't know who he is, what he was born for, what kind of world this is in which he finds himself, with whom he shares it, what's good and what's bad, what's right and what's wrong, and if he can't follow an argument or a proof, doesn't understand truth and falsehood, and is incapable of telling them apart, none of his desires, aversions, inclinations, or objectives, and none of the occasions when he assents to an impression or withholds assent or suspends judgment, will be in accord with nature. In short, he'll go around deaf and blind, thinking that he's somebody when he's not.

[20] "It's not as if there's no precedent for this, is it? Isn't it the case that as long as the human race has existed, all our errors and misadventures have been due to this ignorance? [21] What caused

the rift between Agamemnon and Achilles?* Wasn't it ignorance of what's beneficial and what's harmful? Doesn't one of them say that it's best to return Chryseis to her father, while the other says the opposite? Doesn't one of them say that he should take the other's war prize from him, while the other says he shouldn't? Isn't this what led them to forget who they were and what they were there for? [22] Look, man, what did you come here to do? Was it to acquire concubines or to make war? 'To make war.' Against whom? Trojans or Greeks? 'Trojans.' Is that why you're ignoring Hector and drawing your sword against your own king? [23] And you, sirrah, are you ignoring your role as king, 'who bears responsibility for his people and many cares,'* and getting into a fistfight with the best warrior in your army over a mere girl, when you should be doing all you can to honor him and keep him safe? Are you letting a clever priest, with his display of the utmost care for your noble fighters, get the better of you?*

"Do you see what happens when people don't know what's good for them? [24] 'But I too am rich.' Not richer than Agamemnon, though, surely.* 'But I too am good-looking.' Not better-looking than Achilles, though, surely. 'But I too have attractive hair.' But wasn't Achilles's blond hair more lovely? And didn't he comb it and dress it attractively? [25] 'But I too am strong.' But you can't lift as large a rock as Hector or Ajax could,* can you? 'But I too am well-born.' But your mother isn't a goddess, is she, or your father a descendant of Zeus?* Anyway, what good did that do him, when he was sitting and weeping for his girl? 'But I'm a talented speaker.' [26] Are you saying that Achilles wasn't? What about how he dealt with Odysseus and Phoenix, the two most skilled speakers among the Greeks, and reduced them to silence?*

[27] "That's all I have to say to you, and I was reluctant to say even that. Why? [28] Because you didn't arouse my enthusiasm. What is there in you that might arouse my enthusiasm, as horsemen are excited by thoroughbred horses? What might I look at? Your body? But you make such ugly use of it. Your clothes? They're just another aspect of your self-indulgence. Your demeanor, your expression? No, there's nothing that could move me. [29] When you want to hear what a philosopher has to say, don't say, 'You never talk to me,' but just show yourself to be a skilled listener and you'll see how you move him to speak."

2.25
On the indispensability of logic

[1] Someone in the audience said, "Convince me of the usefulness of logic."

"Shall I prove it to you?"

"Yes, please."

[2] "Then I'd better use a demonstrative argument,* hadn't I?"

His interlocutor agreed, and Epictetus went on, "So how will you know if my argument is fallacious?"

[3] The man said nothing. "Do you see," Epictetus said, "that you are yourself admitting that logic is necessary, since without it you can't even find out whether or not it's necessary?"*

2.26
What is it that makes a mistake a mistake?

[1] "Every mistake involves a contradiction, because the person making the mistake doesn't want to be making a mistake. He wants to be right, so clearly he isn't doing what he wants. [2] After all, what does a thief want to achieve? Something that's good for him. So if thieving isn't good for him, he's not doing what he wants. [3] Now, every rational soul is naturally averse to contradiction, but as long as a person fails to notice that he's contradicting himself, there's nothing to keep him from inconsistency. If he does notice it, however, he'll find himself under considerable pressure to abandon and avoid the contradiction, just as he is sharply forced to withhold assent from a falsehood once he realizes that it is a falsehood, even though he continues to assent to it as true until he comes to that realization.

[4] "So a skillful arguer, an expert at both protreptic and refutational arguments,* is able to show an individual the contradiction that's causing him to make a mistake, and get him to see clearly that he's not doing what he wants but the opposite. [5] The point is that, once this has been pointed out to him, he'll back off from the contradiction of his own accord. But as long as you fail to show it to him, don't be surprised if he persists in it, because he's acting under the impression that he's right.

[6] "That's why Socrates, who relied on this ability in himself,

used to say,* 'It's not my practice to produce any other witness in support of what I say, but I'm always content with my interlocutor. It's
his vote I ask for, his testimony I call for, and just this single individual is enough for me; I don't need everyone else.' [7] The point is
that he knew what moves a rational soul, and that, willy-nilly, it will
tend like a balance one way or the other. Show the command center
a contradiction and it will renounce it, but if you fail to make it clear,
blame yourself rather than the person you're failing to convince."

Book 3

3.1
On personal adornment

[1] He was once visited by a young student of rhetoric who was stylishly dressed and who had a very elaborate hairdo. "Tell me," he said, "don't you find some dogs beautiful, and some horses too, and so on for every kind of animal?"

"I do," he said.

[2] "So the same goes for human beings too? Some are beautiful, some ugly?"

"Of course."

"Do we have the same grounds for calling each of these things beautiful specimens of their kind, or do we have different, specific grounds for doing so in each case? Look at it this way. [3] Since it's obvious that a dog's nature has designed it for one thing, a horse's for another, and a nightingale's, let's say, for another, it wouldn't be unreasonable to generalize and claim that anything is beautiful precisely insofar as it's in perfect conformity with its nature. And since each of them has a different nature, it seems to me that each of them is beautiful in a different way. Do you agree?"

"Yes."

[4] "So what makes a dog beautiful makes a horse ugly, and what makes a horse beautiful makes a dog ugly, if their natures are different. Yes?"

"I suppose so."

[5] "I think that's right, because in my view the physique that makes a pancratiast beautiful isn't right for a wrestler and would be

completely ridiculous for a runner. And someone who's beautiful as a pentathlete would make a hideous wrestler, wouldn't he?"*

"Yes," he said.

[6] "So what makes a human being beautiful is the same as what makes a dog or a horse a beautiful specimen of its kind?"

"Yes," he said.

"All right, then, what makes a dog beautiful? The presence of a dog's particular excellence. And a horse? The presence of a horse's particular excellence. What about a human being, then? It must be the presence of the particular excellence of a human being, mustn't it? [7] It follows, my young friend, that if you want to be beautiful you need to train yourself in human excellence."*

[8] "And what is that?"

"Think of the people you yourself praise, when you assign praise dispassionately. Do you commend justice or injustice in people?"

"Justice."

"Modesty or licentiousness?"

"Modesty."

"Self-discipline or self-indulgence?"

"Self-discipline."

[9] "So if you make yourself a person with those kinds of qualities, you may be sure that you'll make yourself beautiful. But as long as you neglect these virtues, you're bound to be ugly, whatever lengths you go to make yourself seem beautiful. [10] Other than this, I don't know what to tell you. I could tell you what I think, but that would hurt your feelings and you might leave and never come back. But if I don't speak my mind, would I be behaving as I ought, do you think? I mean, you came to me in the hope that you'd benefit, and I wouldn't be helping you at all. You came to consult a philosopher, and I wouldn't be speaking as a philosopher. [11] And of course† it would be an act of cruelty on my part to leave you unreformed. If at some point in the future you come to your senses, you'll think badly of me, and it would be reasonable for you to do so. [12] 'What was it Epictetus saw in me? Although when I visited him he could see what I was like, he left me in my disgraceful state without saying a single word to me. Did he judge my case to be so hopeless? [13] Wasn't I young? Wasn't I capable of listening to reason? How many other young people make

the same kinds of mistakes at that age, and just as frequently? [14] I've heard of a certain Polemo who completely changed after years of youthful debauchery.* All right, he didn't think I had the potential to be a Polemo, but he could have corrected the way I wore my hair and stripped me of my baubles. He could have stopped me tweezing my body hair, but when he saw me looking like a…'—what shall I say?— 'he didn't say a thing.' [15] It's not my job to tell you what your current style makes you look like. You'll tell yourself when you come to your senses and recognize what it is and the kind of people it's typical of.

[16] "What defense will I be able to make if sometime in the future you bring these charges against me? Yes, but suppose I speak and he doesn't listen. Did Laius listen to Apollo? Didn't he go away, get drunk, and take no notice of the oracle?* So what? Was that a reason for Apollo not to tell him the truth? [17] And yet, although I don't know whether or not you'll listen to me, Apollo knew perfectly well that Laius wouldn't, but that didn't stop him speaking. [18] But why did he speak? Well, why is he Apollo? Why does he deliver oracles? Why has he taken it on himself to be a prophet and a source of truth, and to have people come to him from all over the world? Why are the words 'Know yourself' inscribed on the front of his temple when no one pays them any mind?*

[19] "Did Socrates convince everyone he met to take care of themselves? Not even one in a thousand. Nevertheless, since, as he himself says,* he was assigned to his post by the god, he refused to abandon it. What is it, in fact, that he says to the jury? [20] 'If you acquit me on the condition that I stop acting as I do at the moment, I won't accept your offer or change my ways, but I'll continue to approach young and old—in short, everyone I ever meet—and I'll question them just as I do at present, but especially you, my fellow citizens, because you're closest to me.' [21] 'Are you that nosy and pushy, Socrates? Why do you care how we behave?' 'What are you saying? You're an associate and a relative of mine, and you're not taking care of yourself. You make a poor citizen for the city, a poor relative for your relatives, and a poor neighbor for your neighbors.'"

[22] "Well, who are you?"

"It would be bold to respond to this question by saying, 'I am one whose job it is to take care of people.' At the approach of a lion, it's no ordinary cow that dares to stand up to it, but if the bull offers resistance, you can ask it, if you want, 'Who are you, anyway?' and 'Why do you care?' [23] Man, every species produces exceptional individuals—cows, dogs, bees, horses. You don't need to ask one of these exceptional individuals 'Who are you, anyway?' But if you do, it will gain a voice from somewhere and reply, 'I'm like the purple in a toga. Don't expect me to be like everyone else, and don't find fault with nature in my case because it made me different from them.'*

[24] "So, then, am I one of these exceptional individuals? Certainly not. In any case,* are you the sort of person who's capable of hearing the truth? If only you were! Nevertheless, since for some reason I've been condemned to sport a white beard and a threadbare cloak,* and since you've come to consult me as a philosopher, I won't treat you cruelly or as though I judged your case to be hopeless. No, I'll say, 'Young man, who is it you want to make beautiful? Don't try to make yourself beautiful until you know who you are. [25] You're a human being, or in other words, a mortal animal with the ability to make rational use of his impressions. What is it to make rational use of impressions? It's using them in compliance with nature and faultlessly. What do you have that's exceptional? Is it the animal part of you? No. Is it the mortal part of you? No. Is it your ability to make use of impressions? No. [26] What you have that's exceptional is your rationality. That's what you should adorn and beautify. Leave your hair to the one who fashioned it as he wished.'

[27] "All right, then. What other labels do you bear? Are you a man or a woman?"

"A man."

"So adorn yourself as a man, not as a woman. A woman's skin is naturally smooth and soft; if she's hairy, she's a freak and she's put on display in a freak show in Rome. [28] In the case of a man, this happens if he's *without* hair: if he's naturally hairless, he's a freak, so if we find a man trimming and tweezing his hair, what are we to make of him?* Where shall we exhibit him and how shall we advertise him? 'Come and see a man who'd rather be a woman!' [29] What a scandalous spectacle! No one would believe the advertisement! By Zeus, I imagine that even men who tweeze do so without appreciating what it is that they're doing.

[30] "Man, what reason do you have for finding fault with nature in your case? That it brought you into the world as a man? Are you

saying that it should bring everyone into the world as women? In that case, what good would all your primping do you? If everyone was a woman, for whom would you be beautifying yourself? [31] You don't like the way things are? Then why not go the whole hog and remove— what shall I call it?—remove the cause of your hairiness. Turn yourself into a woman in all respects, so that we're not left in doubt, rather than being half man, half woman. [32] Who are you trying to please? Women? Then please them as a man."

"Yes, but they like smooth-skinned men."

"Go hang yourself! If they liked sexual deviants, would you become a sexual deviant? [33] Is that your job, is that what you were born for, to please dissolute women? [34] Is this the kind of person we make a citizen of Corinth, and possibly city warden, or superintendent of the cadet force, or commander of the armed forces, or president of the games?* [35] Come on, are you going to carry on tweezing after you're married? Who for? What for? Once you have sons, will you introduce them to the community similarly tweezed? What a fine citizen! What a fine councillor and politician! Is this the kind of young man we should pray to see born and raised in our communities?

[36] "In the name of the gods, young man, don't let this happen to you! No, hear me out, and then, after you've left, tell yourself, 'It wasn't Epictetus who said these things to me. I mean, where would *he* have got such ideas from? It must have been some kindly god, speaking through him. It would never have occurred to Epictetus to say all this, seeing that he usually doesn't speak to anyone.* [37] Anyway, I'd better do as the god says; I don't want incur his anger.' No? But if a raven's croaking carries a message for you, it isn't the raven that's communicating with you, but the god, using the raven as a medium. And if he chooses to use the human voice as his medium, it'll be a human being that he has say these things to you, won't it? Then you can appreciate the god's power and realize that he has various ways of communicating with people, and that he uses the finest of messengers for communicating matters of supreme and essential importance.*

[38] "Isn't this exactly what the poet means when he says,* 'Since we warned him by sending clear-sighted Hermes, the giant slayer, to tell him neither to kill the man nor court his wife'? [39] Hermes came down from heaven to say this to Aegisthus, and now it's you to whom the gods are sending 'Hermes, the wayfarer, the giant slayer,'

to tell you not to pervert or interfere with things that are fine as they are, but to let a man be a man and a woman a woman, and to let a beautiful person be beautiful as a human being, and an ugly one ugly as a human being. [40] The point is that you aren't flesh or hair: you are will. You're beautiful only if your will is in a beautiful condition. [41] Up until now, I haven't dared to tell you that you're ugly, because I think that's the last thing you'd want to hear. [42] But consider what Socrates says to Alcibiades, the most beautiful and desirable man in the world: 'Try to be beautiful.'* Does he say 'Dress your hair and tweeze your legs'? Hardly! No, he says 'Make your will beautiful, get rid of your pernicious judgments.' [43] So how should you treat your body? Leave it in its natural state. Someone else has taken care of these things; entrust them to him."

[44] "Are you saying that my body shouldn't be cleaned?"

"Far from it. But the person who you are, the natural you, that's what you should keep clean—clean as a man if you're a man, as a woman if you're a woman, as a child if you're a child. [45] No? Are we to pluck the hairs from a lion's mane to stop him being unclean, and remove the tufts from a cock's head? I mean, he needs to be clean as well. But he should be clean as a cock, a lion as a lion, and a hound as a hound."

3.2
The training a person needs if he is to progress, and that we neglect what is most important

[1] "There are three domains in which a person must be trained if he's to become truly good. The first is the domain of desires and aversions, and the upshot of the training is that he never fails to get what he desires and never experiences what he wants to avoid. [2] The second is the domain of inclination and disinclination, and in general of appropriate behavior, and the upshot of the training is that he acts in an orderly and well-reasoned manner, rather than being careless. The third is the domain of immunity to error and rash judgment, and in general the domain of assent.*

[3] "The most important and urgent of these domains is the one that has to do with the passions. A passion is only ever the result of frustrated desire or ineffective aversion. This is the domain that

entails mental turmoil, confusion, wretchedness, misery, sorrow, grief, and fear,† and which makes us envious and jealous, until we can't even to listen to reason. [4] The second has to do with appropriate behavior, because I shouldn't be as unfeeling as a statue, but should maintain my natural and acquired relationships toward gods, father, brothers, children, and fellow citizens. [5] The third domain is relevant to those who are already making progress. It has to do with achieving unassailability in the other two domains, so that even when asleep, drunk, or in a black mood, no untested impression slips past one's guard."

"That's not humanly possible," someone said.

[6] "But it's the third domain that philosophers nowadays focus on; they ignore the first two, and study changing arguments, those that proceed by questioning,† hypothetical arguments, and paradoxes like the Liar."

[7] "Yes, because this is the area where one must guard against being deceived."

"Who must? A truly good man. [8] Is this where you fall short, then? Have you finished working at the other domains?* Are you immune to deception where money is concerned? If you see a pretty girl, can you resist the impression? If your neighbor receives an inheritance, doesn't it gnaw at you? In effect, then, isn't the respect in which you now fall short the fact that you haven't achieved stability? [9] You pitiful thing, even while you're studying those arguments and paradoxes, you tremble with anxiety in case someone belittles you, and you keep trying to find out whether anyone is talking about you. [10] And if someone comes up to you and says, 'We were talking about who was the best philosopher, and one of our group said that the only true philosopher was you,' your soul expands a hundredfold. But if another member of the group said about you, 'What nonsense! There's no point in listening to him. What does he know? He's got the basics, but nothing more than that,' it drives you crazy. You turn pale and blurt out, 'I'll show him who I am! I'll show him I'm a great philosopher!' [11] But that's exactly the kind of behavior that shows what a man is, so why try to prove yourself in any other way? Don't you remember how Diogenes identified a certain sophist like that, by pointing at him with his middle finger,* and then, when the man had a fit, Diogenes said, 'That's the fellow. I've shown him to you.' [12] The point is that, although you can show what a stone or a plank is with a finger, you can't do the same with a human being. No, it's when a person's judgments are revealed that he's revealed as a human being.

[13] "Let's look at your judgments too. Isn't it clear that you set no value on your will but look outside yourself at things that aren't subject to will? You're concerned with what someone or other will say, what people think of you, whether they take you to be a scholar, whether they know that you've read Chrysippus or Antipater. If they think you've read Archedemus as well, your happiness is complete. [14] So there's no need for you to worry that you're not showing us who you are. Shall I tell you what you've shown yourself to be? A pathetic little man†—debased, querulous, irascible, cowardly, impossible to satisfy, critical of everyone, never calm, and boastful. That's what you've shown yourself to be. [15] Go away now and read Archedemus—but then if a mouse makes a noise as it drops to the ground, you die of fright. That's the kind of death that lies in your future, the kind that saw to—who was it?—Crinis.* He was another one who was proud of his ability to understand Archedemus.

[16] "You poor fool, shouldn't you set these things aside? They're no concern of yours; they're suitable only for people who can study them with an untroubled mind—those who can say, 'I'm not subject to anger, distress, or envy; I'm immune to impediment and constraint. What's left for me to do? I've got plenty of time and no distractions. [17] Let's see how one should deal with changing arguments. Let's see how one can accept a hypothesis without being led on to an absurd conclusion.' [18] That's the kind of person for whom these studies are appropriate. When people are faring well, that's the time to light a fire, eat a meal, and maybe even sing and dance. But you've come to me when your ship's already sinking, and you're hoisting your topsails!"

3.3

What the material is that a good person works with, and what the primary orientation of one's training should be

[1] "The material that a truly good person works with is his own command center, as the body is the material a doctor or a trainer works with, and land is the material a farmer works with. And his

job is to use his impressions in accord with nature. [2] Just as every soul naturally assents to the truth, withholds assent from falsehood, and suspends judgment in uncertain cases, so it's natural for it to be moved by desire for what is good, by aversion toward what is bad, and in neither of these ways by what is indifferent. [3] For just as neither a banker nor a greengrocer may refuse Caesar's coinage, but is willy-nilly obliged, if you offer it, to give you in exchange for it what he has for sale, so it is in the case of the soul as well. [4] No sooner does something good appear than it attracts the soul toward itself, and anything bad that comes along repels the soul from itself. A soul never fails to accept a clear impression of something good, any more than a grocer refuses to accept Caesar's coinage. These are the conditions for every movement of every soul, human and divine.

[5] "That's why goodness takes precedence over every relationship. My father is nothing to me; I value only goodness. 'Are you so hard-hearted?' Yes, because that's my nature. That's the currency God has given me. [6] That's why, if goodness is different from honor and justice, father, brother, country, and all worldly things become irrelevant.* [7] Should I give up what's good for me so that you can have what's good for you? Should I yield to you? What's in it for me? 'I'm your father.' Yes, but not my good. 'I'm your brother.' Yes, but not my good. [8] However, if we locate goodness in correct use of will, maintaining one's relationships becomes a good, and, moreover, it's a good that one gains by giving up some externals. [9] 'My father's taking away my money.' But he's not harming you. 'My brother's going get more of the estate.' Let him have all he wants. He won't be getting your self-respect, your trustworthiness, or your brotherly love, will he? [10] Who can make you part with these possessions? Not even Zeus. He chose not to be able to; he made them up to me, and gave them to me unimpeded, unconstrained, and unobstructed, just as they were in his case.

[11] "Now, different people have different currencies, and it's by offering the appropriate coinage that a person gets what he can buy in exchange for it. [12] A rapacious proconsul has come to the province.* What's his currency? Money. Offer him some and get in exchange what you want. An adulterer's in town. What's his currency? Young women. 'Take my coin,' the buyer says, 'and sell me the mer-

chandise.' Give and buy. [13] Another man prizes young boys. Give him his coin and take what you want. Another is fond of hunting. Give him a fine horse or hound and, complaining and groaning, he'll sell you in exchange whatever it is you want. The point is that someone else, someone inside himself who has established this man's particular currency, leaves him no choice.*

[14] "The primary orientation of a person's training should be as follows. When you leave your home at daybreak, examine everyone you see or hear, and answer as though you were being questioned. What was it you saw? A good-looking man or woman? Apply the test: is physical beauty subject to will or not? It isn't subject to will. Away with it. [15] What was it you saw? Someone grieving for the death of his child. Apply the test. Death isn't subject to will. Away with it. You met a consul? Apply the test. What kind of a thing is consulship? Is it or isn't it subject to will? It isn't subject to will. Away with it too; it doesn't pass the test. Throw it out, it's nothing to you. [16] If we acted like this and oriented our training in this way every day from dawn until dark, that would be quite something, by the gods. [17] But as things are, we're stunned and caught by every passing impression, and we wake up a little, if at all, only at school. But then, when we go back outside and see someone grieving, we say, 'He's a broken man.' If we see a consul, we say, 'A happy man.' If it's someone who's in exile, 'Poor fellow!' If it's someone who's destitute, 'What a pity! He doesn't have enough money for a meal.'

[18] "These, then, are the pernicious judgments we need to eliminate;* they are what we should be focusing on. After all, what is weeping and wailing? A judgment. What is misfortune? A judgment. What are strife, discord, fault-finding, negative criticism, impiety, foolish behavior? [19] All of them are nothing more than judgments, and they judge things that aren't subject to will as good or bad. But if someone transfers his judgments to things that are subject to his will, I guarantee that he'll be self-possessed, whatever circumstances he finds himself in."

[20] "The soul is like a bowl of water, and impressions are like a ray of light that falls on the water. [21] When the water is disturbed, the ray seems to be disturbed as well, even though it isn't. [22] Likewise,

therefore, when someone has a dizzy spell, it isn't his skills and virtues that become confused, but the spirit that contains them.* When the spirit settles down, they settle down as well."

3.4
To someone who expressed immoderate support in the theater

[1] The governor of Epirus* expressed immoderate support for a certain comic actor and was widely vilified for it. Subsequently he came and told Epictetus about it. He was angry with those who had vilified him, but Epictetus said, "But how were they at fault? They were expressing a preference, and so were you."

[2] "But is that the way to express a preference?" he asked.

Epictetus said, "When they saw you, their ruler, the friend of Caesar and his governor, expressing his preference in such an immoderate fashion, weren't they bound to express theirs in the same way? [3] I mean, if it's wrong to express a preference like that, it was wrong of you to do so as well. And if it's not wrong, why are you angry with them when all they did was the same as you? Who else can they take their lead from if not you, their leaders? When they go to the theater, whose behavior are they going to observe if not yours? [4] 'Look at the way in which Caesar's governor watches the show. He's just yelled something; all right, I'll yell too. He's leaping to his feet; I'll do the same. His slaves, seated here and there throughout the auditorium, are yelling; I don't have slaves, but I'll yell as loudly as I can to match all of them!' [5] You need to know, then, that when you enter the theater, you're a model for everyone else, a paradigm of correct audience behavior.*

[6] "So why did they vilify you? Because everyone hates an obstruction. They wanted so-and-so to win the crown; you wanted someone else.* They got in your way and you got in theirs. You proved to be the stronger, so they did what they could by abusing the obstacle. [7] What do you want, then? To do what you like while they can't even say what they like? And why is what they did surprising? Don't farmers abuse Zeus when they're thwarted by him? Don't sailors do the same? Do people ever stop cursing Caesar? [8] Well, do you think Zeus is unaware of this? Doesn't Caesar receive reports about what people are saying? What does he do, then? He knows that if he were

to punish everyone who spoke badly of him, there'd be no one left for him to rule. [9] Well, then, when you enter the theater, should you think, 'All right, then. Let's make sure that Sophron gets the crown'?* No, better to think, 'All right, then. Let's make sure that I keep my will in accord with nature in this matter. [10] There's no one I care for more than myself, so it would be absurd for me to come to harm just so that someone else can win the comic actor's prize. [11] So whom do I want to win? The winner. And in that way the person I want to win will always win.'"

"But I want Sophron to win the crown."

"Then put on as many contests as you like in your home and proclaim him the winner.† But in public don't demand more than your due and don't seize for yourself a right that belongs to everyone. [12] Otherwise, you must put up with being abused, because when you behave as ordinary people do, you reduce yourself to their level."

3.5
To those who quit school because of illness

[1] "I'm ill here," someone said, "and I want to go back home."

[2] "So were you never ill at home? Check to see whether any of the things you're doing here that affect your will is enabling you to improve it. If you're not making any progress, there was no point in your coming here in the first place. Go back and tend to your affairs at home. [3] If your command center can't be brought into accord with nature, at least your land will prosper.† You will at least be making money, looking after your father in his old age, going about your business in the forum, holding public office. Of course, as a bad man you'll make a bad job of everything you do from now on.

[4] "But if you find that you're getting rid of certain pernicious judgments and replacing them with better ones, that you've transferred your attention from things that aren't subject to will to those that are, and that if you ever say 'Poor me!' it isn't because of your father or your brother, but because of 'me'—if that's the case why take account of illness? [5] Don't you know that we're liable to illness and death whatever we do? They come to the farmer as he works his land and the sailor at sea. [6] As for you, what would you like to be doing when death comes, seeing that no matter what you do, its com-

ing is inevitable? If you've got something better to be doing when it comes than what you're doing here, go ahead and do it.

[7] "Speaking for myself, I hope to be overtaken by death at a time when my attention is focused exclusively on my will—when I'm trying to make it undisturbed by passion, unimpeded, unconstrained, and free. [8] That's what I'd like to be occupied with, because then I can say to God, 'Have I ever contravened your orders? Have I ever used the resources you gave me for extraneous purposes? Have I ever misused my senses or my preconceptions? Have I ever accused you of wrongdoing? Have I ever found fault with your governance? [9] I fell ill when you wanted me to—as did others, but I did so willingly. I became impoverished because you wanted me to, but I did so gladly. I didn't hold any public office, because you didn't want me to, and I never missed it. Did you ever see me downcast because of that? Didn't I always come before you with a joyful countenance, ready for whatever you might command or ordain? [10] Now you want me to leave the festival, and I do so full of gratitude for the fact that you found me worthy to share the celebration with you, see your works, and understand your governance.' [11] May my thoughts, my writing, and my reading be along these lines when death overtakes me!"

[12] "But my mother won't be around to hold my head while I'm ill."

"So go home to your mother. You're just the kind of person who needs his head held when he's ill."

[13] "But at home I used to have a nice bed to lie on."

"Off you go, then, to your precious little bed. Even when you're not ill, lying on a nice bed is just right for the kind of person you are. So don't waste the opportunity to do what you're qualified to do.

[14] "But what does Socrates say? 'As one man enjoys improving his farm and another his horse, so day by day I enjoy understanding that I'm becoming a better person.'* [15] 'Better in what respect? At coining fine phrases?' 'Hold your tongue, man!' 'At theory?' 'How can you say such a thing?' [16] 'But that's all I see philosophers spending their time over.'

"Does never finding fault with anyone, neither god nor man, seem nothing to you? Or never blaming anyone? Or always playing the same role at home and abroad? [17] These were Socrates's areas of expertise, despite his constant denial that he knew anything or taught anything.* If someone wanted to hear fine phrases or theo-

ries, Socrates took him to meet Protagoras or Hippias,* and if someone had come to him in search of vegetables, he'd have taken him to a
market gardener. [18] Do any of you have this aim? Because I assure
you, if you did, you'd have no problem with illness, hunger, and death.
[19] Any of you who's been infatuated with a pretty girl knows that
I'm telling the truth."

3.6
A miscellany

[1] Someone asked him to explain why, although more effort has
been put into cultivating reason nowadays, more significant progress was made in the past. [2] "In what respect," he said, "has reason
been worked on in our time, and in what respect was progress greater
in those days? You'll find that progress has been made in our time too,
insofar as work has gone on in our time. [3] These days, it's the analysis of syllogisms that has been worked on, and that's where you can
see progress. But in times past, people worked with the aim of keeping their command centers in accord with nature and made progress
in that respect. [4] So keep these two aims separate, and don't expect
to make progress in any field other than the one where you focus your
efforts. But see if there's anyone here who's committed to being and
living his whole life in accord with nature and who fails to make progress. You won't find a single one."

[5] "A good person is invincible, because he doesn't enter any contest
where he doesn't have an advantage. [6] 'If you want my land, you can
have it. You can have my slaves, my public offices, my body. But you
won't make me fail to attain what I desire or, where aversion is concerned, meet with what I want to avoid.' [7] This is the only contest
he engages in, that has to do with things that are subject to will. So, of
course, he's bound to be invincible."

[8] When someone asked him what common sense was, he said,
"Just as you might use the term 'common hearing' for the faculty that
merely tells sounds apart (as distinct from the ability to tell musical sounds apart, which is not common, but specialist), so there are
some things that people whose minds retain at least some degree of

normality can see by means of the resources that are common to everyone.* This condition is what we call 'common sense.'"

[9] "It isn't easy to turn soft young men on to philosophy, just as it isn't easy to pick up soft† cheese with a fishhook.* This isn't the case for gifted young men, however: even if you discourage them, they cherish reason. [10] That's why Rufus invariably used to discourage people, as a way of distinguishing those who were gifted from those who weren't. He used to say, 'Just as it's natural for a stone to fall to earth even if you throw it into the air, so it is with someone who's gifted: the more one puts him off, the more he inclines in the direction his nature takes him.'"

3.7
To the Corrector responsible for the free Greek cities,
who was an Epicurean

[1] When the Corrector,* who was an Epicurean, visited him, Epictetus said, "A good question for us non-philosophers to ask you philosophers is what the best thing in the world is, just as people arriving in an unfamiliar town question the local inhabitants, who know the place. Then, as a result of our inquiry, we too can find it for ourselves and see it, just as those visitors go and find what the town has to offer. [2] Now, almost everyone would accept that there are three relevant factors in the case of a human being: soul, body, and externals. So it's your job to tell us which of these is best. [3] What shall we tell people? That it's the body? And that it was for bodily reasons that Maximus sailed all the way to Cassiope in winter with his son, to see him on his way?* Was it for bodily pleasure?"

[4] "No," said the Corrector. "Hardly."

"Isn't it right to focus on what's best?"

"Absolutely."

"So what do we have that's better than the body?"

"The soul," he said.

[5] "Are the goods of the best part to be preferred, or those of the inferior part?"

"Those of the best part."

"And are the goods of the soul subject to will or not?"

"They are."

"So is the soul's pleasure something that's subject to will?"

"Yes."

[6] "And what is the soul's pleasure a response to? Is it responding to itself? But that's inconceivable, because there must subsist some antecedent good thing that causes us pleasure in our souls when we meet with it."

He conceded this as well.

[7] "So what is this soul pleasure a response to? If it's a response to the goods of the soul, we've discovered the essence of goodness.* After all, it's impossible for the good to be different from that which we reasonably enjoy, and it's also impossible for an antecedent cause that isn't good to have an effect that's good. I mean, in order for the effect to be reasonable, the antecedent must be good. [8] But there's no way you Epicureans can say this, if you have any sense, because you'd be disagreeing with Epicurus and saying something that doesn't fit in with the rest of your views. [9] The only thing left for you to say, then, is that pleasure in the soul is a response to bodily events, and then bodily events turn out to be the antecedent cause of pleasure in the soul and constitute the essence of goodness.

[10] "Hence Maximus acted foolishly if he undertook his voyage for anything other than bodily reasons, or in other words, for what is best. [11] And it would be foolish for an official, if he has the opportunity to take someone else's property, to refrain from doing so.* If you like, let's restrict the scenario to one where the theft is carried out in secret, safely, and without anyone knowing about it, [12] because even Epicurus himself doesn't declare stealing to be bad, but only getting caught. It's only because one can't be sure of getting away with it that he says, 'Don't steal.'* [13] But I'm telling you that if the theft is carried out cleverly and covertly, we'll get away with it. In any case, we have influential friends in Rome, both men and women, and the Greeks are weak. None of them will dare to go to Rome to pursue the matter.

[14] "So why hold back from what's good for you? That's foolish behavior, senseless. I won't believe you even if you tell me you do hold back. [15] Just as it's impossible to assent to something that seems false and to withhold assent from something that seems true, so it's impossible to forgo something good. Now, wealth is a good thing, and

in fact one would be hard put to find anything that's more productive of pleasures. [16] So why not make yourself rich? Why don't we seduce our neighbor's wife, if we can get away with it? And if her husband kicks up a fuss, let's corrupt him as well. [17] That's what you should do if you want to be a proper, complete philosopher and act in conformity with your views. Otherwise, you're no different from those of us who are called Stoics. We too say one thing and do another. [18] We talk of honor, but act dishonorably, while you're perverse in the opposite way, since your views are immoral, but you act honorably.

[19] "Good heavens! Can you imagine a city of Epicureans? 'I'm not going to marry.' 'Me neither. Marriage is wrong.' 'So is having children and taking part in public life.'* What will happen, then? Where will the next generation of citizens come from? Who will educate them? Who will act as superintendent of the cadet force or gymnasiarch?* And then, what will they be taught? Will it be the same education that young Spartans or Athenians used to receive?* [20] Take a young man and bring him up in accordance with your principles. Your principles are pernicious, subversive of the state, destructive of households, and unsuitable even for women. Give them up, man. [21] You live in an administrative center. It's your duty to hold office, to judge cases fairly, to keep your hands off others' possessions, and to regard as beautiful no woman except your wife, no boy, and no items of silver or gold. [22] Try to find principles that are in harmony with these duties of yours—principles that will make it possible for you to refrain, and refrain gladly, from things that have such a strong tendency to attract and overcome people.* [23] These things are seductive enough as it is; if we've also invented a philosophy like Epicureanism that positively pushes us toward them and increases their strength, what will the outcome be?*

[24] "Which is the best aspect of an embossed plate, the silver or the workmanship? The substance of a hand may be flesh, but of principal importance are its actions. [25] The same goes for a human being as well: it's not his matter that we should value, his corporeality, but what he does that is of principal importance. Now, appropriate actions are of three kinds:*† there are those that have to do with existence, those that have to do with a particular kind of existence, and those that are inherently valuable. [26] And what are these? Citi-

zenship, marriage, having children, honoring God, looking after parents—or, to put it succinctly, exercising desire and aversion, inclination and disinclination, as we ought in each case, which is to say, in accord with our natures. [27] And what are we by nature? We are free, honorable, and self-respecting. After all, does any other animal blush or feel shame? [28] Pleasure should be subordinated to acting appropriately; it should be the servant and attendant of appropriate actions, with the job of arousing our enthusiasm and helping us achieve constancy in acting in accord with nature."

[29] "But I'm rich and in need of nothing."

"Then why are you still pretending to be a philosopher? Aren't your gold and silver trinkets enough for you? Why do you need philosophical doctrines?"

[30] "But I'm the appointed judge of the Greeks."

"Do you know how to judge? Where did you get this skill from?"

"Caesar signed my diploma."

[31] "Let him sign one making you a judge of musicians. Would that do you any good? No, I was asking how you became a judge. Was it Symphorus's or Numenius's hand you kissed? Whose antechamber did you sleep in?* Whom did you bribe? And yet, don't you see that your being a judge is worth exactly what Numenius is worth?"

[32] "But I can have anyone I want thrown into prison."

"And you can throw stones too."

"But I can have anyone I want beaten with a cudgel."

[33] "You can do that to a donkey too. That's not the way to govern people. Govern us as rational creatures by showing us what's in our best interests, and we'll follow you. Show us what isn't in our best interests, and we'll turn away from it. [34] Make us want to be like you, as Socrates did. He was a true ruler of people, because he got people to look up to him to see how to manage their desires, aversions, inclinations, and disinclinations. [35] 'Do this and don't do that, or I shall throw you into prison.' This isn't the way to govern rational creatures. [36] No: 'Do as Zeus has ordained, otherwise you'll be damaged and harmed.' What kind of harm? Not acting as you should—*that* kind of harm. You'll destroy the trustworthy person in you, the self-respecting person, the modest person. There's no point in looking for any greater damage than that."

3.8

How we should train ourselves to deal with impressions

[1] "As we train ourselves to cope with sophistic questions, so we should also make it our daily practice to train ourselves to deal with impressions, because they too pose questions for us. [2] 'So-and-so's son died.' Answer: not subject to will; not a bad thing. 'So-and-so's father cut him out of his will. What do you think of that?' Not subject to will; not a bad thing. 'Caesar condemned him to death.' Not subject to will; not a bad thing. [3] 'He's upset about all this.' Subject to will; a bad thing. 'He endured it nobly.' Subject to will, a good thing.

[4] "If we get into the habit of doing this, we'll make progress, because we'll never assent to anything unless we have a cognitive impression of it.* [5] 'So-and-so's son died.' What actually happened? His son died. 'No more than that?' No. 'His ship was lost at sea.' What actually happened? The ship was lost. 'He was taken off to prison.' What actually happened? He was taken off to prison. But to say that this has been bad for him is an additional judgment that each individual makes for himself. [6] 'But it's not right for Zeus to do these things.' Why isn't it? I mean, he's made you capable of enduring hardship and given you greatness of soul; he's removed the label 'bad' from these things; he's made it possible for you to be happy even under these circumstances; he's opened the door for you, when you've reached your limit. Take that way out, man, and don't complain."

[7] "If you want to know how the Romans feel about philosophers, listen to this.* Italicus, who in their opinion was a philosopher par excellence, once lost his temper with his friends—I happened to be present—as though the way they were treating him was insupportable. 'I can't stand it,' he said. 'You're killing me. You'll make me just like him'—and he pointed at me!"*

3.9

*To an orator who was on his way to Rome for a lawsuit**

[1] He was once visited by a man who was on his way to Rome because he had a lawsuit pending about an honor that he claimed. Once Epic-

tetus had learned what the purpose was of his trip, the visitor asked him his opinion of the matter.

[2] "If," he said, "you're asking me what will happen to you in Rome, whether you'll succeed or fail, I have no position on that. But if you're asking me how you'll fare, what I have to say to you is that you'll do well if your judgments are sound and badly if they're not. Because every action that we take is always caused by a judgment. [3] What is it, for instance, that made you want to be voted patron of the Cnossians?* A judgment of yours. What is it that's currently making you travel to Rome? A judgment of yours. And you're doing so in winter as well, with all that means in terms of danger and expense."

"Yes, because I have no choice."

[4] "Who says you have no choice? A judgment. So if judgments cause everything we do, then if someone has unsound judgments, the outcome will be the same. [5] Now, do we all have sound judgments? Is both your view sound and that of your opponent in the case? But if so, how come you disagree? Is your view sound while his isn't? Why? Because you think it so. But so does he, and so do mad people. That doesn't give us a way to tell you apart.

[6] "Instead, show me that you've thought about your judgments and paid attention to them. Here you are now, sailing to Rome in order to become the patron of the Cnossians. You're not satisfied to stay at home with the honors you already have, but you crave something greater and more glorious. But have you ever undertaken a hazardous voyage for the purpose of examining your judgments and throwing out any unsound ones? [7] Have you ever consulted anyone on this? Did you ever set time aside for yourself? At what stage of your life did you do so? Go through all the phases of your life—to yourself if you're embarrassed to do so in front of me. [8] When you were a boy, did you examine your judgments? Isn't it the case that you acted no differently from the way you always do now? When you were a teenager, and you listened to the orators and started practicing oratory yourself, did it occur to you that you were deficient in any respect? [9] When you were a young man and you were beginning to play a part in public life, to plead cases by yourself, and to acquire a reputation, was there anyone you still took to be your equal?* Would you under any circumstances have put up with an examination by some-

one that showed how unsound your judgments are? [10] So what shall I tell you?"

"You could give me some advice that would help me in the matter."

" I don't have any suggestions to make about that. In fact, if that's what you came to me for, you aren't treating me as a philosopher, but as a greengrocer or a cobbler."

[11] "What are philosophers' suggestions designed to do, then?"

"To ensure that, whatever happens, our command center is and remains in accord with nature. Does that strike you as trivial?"

"No, there's nothing more important."

"And do you think that only a little time is needed for this? Do you think it's a faculty you can acquire in passing? If you can, please do. [12] And then you'll say, 'I met with Epictetus, and it was like meeting stone or a statue.' That's right, because all you did was see me, nothing more. You meet a man as a man when you get to know his judgments and reveal yours in your turn. [13] Get to know my judgments, show me yours, and then say that you've met me. Let's test each other: if I have a bad judgment, remove it, and if you have one, expose it for what it is. That's what it is to meet a philosopher. [14] But no, you say, 'It's not out of our way. While we're in the process of hiring the boat, we can visit Epictetus as well. Let's see what he has to say.' And then, after you've left: 'Epictetus was useless. His language was littered with mistakes and barbarisms.' Because that's the only conclusion you could have reached, since you came with that attitude."

[15] "But if I make my judgments my primary concern, I'll be just like you, with no land to my name, no silver goblets, no fine livestock."

[16] "I think all I need to say in response to this is that I don't need these things. As for you, however, the more you have, the more you'll need, so that, willy-nilly, you'll be poorer than I am."*

[17] "So what *do* I need?"

"What you don't have: self-possession, a mind that's in accord with nature, tranquility. [18] It makes no difference to me whether or not I'm a patron,* but it does to you. I'm richer than you. I don't worry about what Caesar will think of me, and I flatter no one for that purpose. That's what I have instead of silver and gold vessels. You may have golden tableware, but your reason, judgments, assents, inclinations, and desires are made of clay. [19] But when mine are in a state of conformity with nature, why shouldn't I also exercise my ingenuity on reason? I have the time to do so: my mind isn't constantly distracted. What shall I do with my undistracted mind? Is there anything more suitable for a human being than this? [20] When *you* have nothing to do, you get agitated, and you go to the theater or roam around.† Why shouldn't a philosopher cultivate his reason? [21] You have crystal ware, I have the Liar. You have murrhine ware, I have the Denier.* All your possessions seem small to you, but all mine seem great to me. Your desire is unfulfilled, mine has already been fulfilled. [22] When a child puts his hand inside a narrow-necked jar and tries to extract some tidbits, what happens? If he fills his hand, he can't get them out, and then he starts to cry. Let a few of them go and you'll get the rest out. The same goes for you too: let your desire go. If you don't want many things, you'll get what you want."

3.10
How to bear illness

[1] "When there's a need of a particular judgment, we should have it at hand: when we're eating, we should have at hand judgments relevant to eating; when we're at the bathhouse, those that are relevant to the bathhouse; when we're in bed, those that are relevant to bed.*

[2] Let not slumber approach your weary eyes
Before reviewing all that you did during the day.
[3] 'Where did I go wrong? What did I do? What duty did I leave
   undone?'
After this beginning, run back over your actions, and then
Reproach yourself for things done badly and rejoice for things
   done well.

[4] We should also have these verses available for use, not merely as a way to exercise our voices, as 'Paean Apollo!' is.'* [5] And again, when we have a fever, we should have the relevant judgments available. We need to beware in case the illness makes us abandon and forget everything we've learned: 'It's out of my hands now whether I'll continue with philosophy.' But is there anywhere you could go and take care of your body that's out of the reach of fever?†

[6] "What is it to do philosophy? Isn't it to prepare oneself for whatever happens? Don't you see, then, that what you're saying amounts to: 'It's out of my hands whether or not I ever again prepare myself to calmly accept whatever happens'? This is no different from someone giving up the pancratium because he keeps being hit!* [7] In the pancratium, it's possible to retire and avoid being pummeled, but in the case we're talking about, what will we gain if we retire from philosophy?

"So what should a philosopher say in the face of any harsh experience? 'This is what I've been training for. This is what I've been practicing for.' [8] God is saying to you, 'Prove to me that you've not infringed the rules of the contest, that you've kept to your diet, carried out your exercises, obeyed your trainer.'* And then you shy away when it comes to actually doing something? Now is the time for fever: be ill in the right way. For thirst: be thirsty in the right way. For hunger: be hungry in the right way. [9] Isn't that up to you? Who can stop you? All right, a doctor can forbid you to drink, but he can't stop you being thirsty in the right way. He may not let you eat, but he can't stop you being hungry in the right way."

[10] "But I'm not getting any studying done."†

"But what do you study *for*? Slave, isn't it to find contentment? And self-possession? Isn't so that you may be in accord with nature and remain so? [11] What's stopping you from having your command center in accord with nature when you have a fever? Just here is the proof of the matter, the test of a philosopher. I mean, illness is a feature of life, just like going for a walk, making a voyage, or journeying overland. A fever is no different. [12] You don't read while you're walking, do you? No. Nor do you read when you've got a fever. But if you go for a walk in the right way, you're fulfilling your role as a walker. If you're ill in the right way, you're fulfilling your role as someone with a fever. [13] What is it to have a fever in the right way? To have it without blaming God or man and without being negative about the experience; to await death well and in the right way,* and to do what you're told.

"When the doctor pays you a visit, don't be afraid of what he might say, and don't be overjoyed if he says, 'You're doing splendidly!' After all, is there anything good for you in his saying that? [14] And don't be depressed if he says, 'You're doing badly.' After all, what is it to be in a bad way? It means that you're close to the separation of the soul from the body. What is there to fear in that? If you're not close now, you're going to be close later, aren't you? Is the world going to come to an end when you die? [15] Why do you flatter your doctor, then? Why do you say, 'My recovery is in your hands, sir'? Why do you give him a chance to preen? Why not just pay him as he deserves? Just as you pay a shoemaker as he deserves for tending to your foot, and a builder as he deserves for tending to your house, why not also pay the doctor as he deserves for tending to your body—which isn't 'mine,' which is essentially a corpse? This is the opportunity that someone with a fever has. If he seizes it, he's doing what he's supposed to do.

[16] "The point is that it isn't a philosopher's job to keep externals safe†—not his little stock of wine or oil, and not his body either. What, then? His command center. What should his attitude be toward other things? Merely to make sure that he doesn't act thoughtlessly where they're concerned. [17] In that case, is there any occasion for fear? Or anger? Can there be any occasion for fear with regard to things that are of no concern to you, things that are worthless? [18] So there are two principles that we should have at hand: that apart from will, nothing is either good or bad, and that we ought not to try to steer events, but follow their lead.

[19] "My brother shouldn't have treated me as he did."

"No, he shouldn't, but that's his concern. My job, however he treats me, is to behave toward him as I ought. [20] That's up to me, and the rest is no concern of mine. No one can stop me from doing this, but everything else is liable to impediment."

3.11
A miscellany

[1] "Certain punishments have been ordained, as it were by law, for those who refuse to accept the divine dispensation. [2] 'Whoever shall regard as good anything other than what is subject to will shall suffer from envy and unfulfilled longing, be a flatterer, and have no peace of mind. Whoever shall regard as bad anything other than

what is subject to will shall feel distress, grief, sorrow, and misery.'
[3] And yet, despite the harshness of these punishments, we're incapable of desisting!"

[4] "Remember the poet's words concerning strangers:*

> Stranger, it isn't right for me to dishonor any stranger,
> Even if one more despicable than you should arrive.
> For all strangers and beggars come from Zeus.

[5] We should have this thought at hand for application to fathers as
well: 'It isn't right for me to dishonor a father, even one more despicable than you, for all fathers come from Zeus, the protector of parents.' The same goes for a brother too: 'For all come from Zeus, the
protector of families.' And the same goes for all our other relationships as well: we'll find that Zeus is their custodian."

3.12
On training

[1] "The training exercises that we undertake shouldn't involve anything unnatural or out of the ordinary, otherwise those of us who
claim to be philosophers will be no better than showmen. [2] I mean,
tightrope walking is difficult as well—and not just difficult but dangerous too—but does this mean that we should also train ourselves
to walk a tightrope, set up a palm tree, or hug statues?* Of course
not. [3] Not everything that's difficult and dangerous makes a suitable training exercise, but only what helps us achieve the goal we've
set ourselves to work for. [4] And what is this goal? To be unimpeded
in our desires and aversions. But what does that mean? That we
should neither fail to get what we desire nor encounter what we don't
want to encounter. That, then, is the end toward which our training
should tend.

[5] "The point is that, since it takes considerable and continuous
training to ensure that our desires aren't disappointed and, where
aversion is concerned, that we never encounter what we don't want
to encounter, you can be sure that if you allow your training to be directed outward, toward things that aren't subject to will, your desires

will be disappointed and your aversions will fail to prevent the occurrence of what you wanted to avoid. [6] And since we follow the lead of habit, a powerful influence, then given that we've become accustomed to feel desire and aversion only for externals, we must set a contrary habit to counteract this habit, and where impressions are especially slippery, we must set our training to counteract this slipperiness.

[7] "I have a propensity for pleasure; for the sake of my training, I'll correct the list by going over to the opposite extreme. I have an aversion to work; I'll train and exercise my impressions with a view to detaching my aversion from everything of that kind. [8] After all, what is it to be in training? It is to practice abstaining from desire and feeling aversion only for things that are subject to will, and it is to pay particular attention to things that are difficult to achieve. This means that different people should focus their training on different things. [9] Here at school, then, what would be the point in setting up a palm tree or carrying around a tent and a mortar and pestle?* [10] Man, if you have the grit, train yourself to put up with abuse and not get angry if you're insulted. And then you'll make such progress that, even if someone punches you, you'll tell yourself to imagine that you're hugging a statue. [11] And train yourself also to use wine with discretion, not because you plan to drink a lot (I mean, there are vulgar people who train for that), but because you plan to abstain from wine, in the first place, but then also from girls and cakes. And then one day, by way of a test, if the opportunity arises, you'll enter the fray favorably placed to find out whether impressions still get the better of you, as they used to. [12] But the first step is to keep well away from things that are too strong for you. It's not a fair fight to pit a pretty girl against a young man who's just starting on philosophy. As the saying goes, 'A pot and a stone don't go together.'

[13] "After desire and aversion, the second domain is that of inclination and disinclination.* The aim here is to get them to be obedient to reason, to operate at suitable times and places, and to be commensurate in all other such respects. [14] The third domain is that of assent, and so has to do with things that are speciously attractive. [15] Just as Socrates used to say that we shouldn't live an unexamined life,* so we shouldn't accept an unexamined impression. As sentries at night say, 'Show me your pass,' we should say, 'Wait. Let me

see what you are and what you're an impression of. Do you have the credentials from nature that every impression should have if it's to be accepted?'*

[16] "So all the exercises that physical trainers use for the body might be applicable to our training as well, if here at school they're directed toward desire and aversion. But if their point is display, that's the sign of a person who's focused on the outside world and has other goals in mind. He wants to be seen by people and to hear them exclaim, 'What a great man!' [17] That's why Apollonius's recommendation was good: 'If you want to train for your own sake, take a drink of cold water, when it's hot and you're thirsty, and then spit it out, without telling anyone.'"*

3.13
What loneliness is and the kind of person who is lonely

[1] "Loneliness is the condition of someone who's helpless. Just being alone doesn't necessarily make a person lonely as well, any more than being in a crowd means that a person isn't lonely. [2] At any rate, when we lose a brother or a son or a friend on whom we relied, we say that we've been left all alone, even if much of the time we're in Rome, where we constantly come across masses of people, share our homes with plenty of others, and may have a great many slaves. [3] It's fundamental to the concept of loneliness that a lonely person has no one to help him and is at the mercy of those who wish to harm him. That's why a prime case when we think of ourselves as lonely is when we encounter robbers on the road. After all, it isn't the mere sight of another person that relieves us of loneliness, but the sight of someone trustworthy and self-respecting, who's prepared to lend a helping hand. [4] If the bare fact of being alone were enough to make one lonely, we'd have to say that even Zeus is lonely during the conflagration,* and moans to himself, 'Poor me! I have no Hera, no Athena or Apollo—in short, no brother, son, grandson, or any other family member.'

[5] "In fact, some do attribute this behavior to him when he's all alone during the conflagration, because they have no concept of a life lived on one's own, since their premise is the fact of nature that people are gregarious and sociable, and enjoy one another's com-

pany.* [6] Nevertheless, one's skill set should also include this—the ability to be self-sufficient, to live with oneself. [7] Just as Zeus lives peaceably with and by himself, reflecting on the quality of his governance and occupying himself with thoughts that are proper to himself, so we should have the ability to converse with ourselves, to be self-reliant, and not to be helpless. [8] We should reflect on the divine dispensation and the nature of our relationships with all other objects. We should consider what our attitude used to be toward our experiences and what it is now. What are the things that still oppress us? How can they too be remedied or eliminated? If we need to work on any of them, we should do so as prescribed by our reason.

[9] "You can see that we seem to have profound peace, thanks to Caesar. There are no wars anymore,* no fighting, and no extensive brigandage or piracy. We can make overland journeys at any time of year, or travel by boat from sunrise to sunset. [10] But can Caesar provide us with peace from fever as well, or from shipwreck, fire, earthquakes, or bolts of lightning? And what about lust? No, he can't. From grief? No. From envy? No. In short, he can't give us peace from any of these things. [11] But philosophical teachings promise to provide us with peace even from these things. What do they say? 'If you pay attention to me, people, then wherever you are and whatever you're doing, you won't get distressed or angry, you'll be unconstrained and unimpeded, you won't be disturbed by passion, and you'll live a completely trouble-free life.'

[12] "When this is the kind of peace that has been proclaimed to someone, not by Caesar—this is not a proclamation he could make—but by God via reason, isn't that enough for him when he's alone? After all, he can ponder and reflect as follows: [13] 'Nothing bad can happen to me now. In my world, there are no robbers and no earthquakes. Everywhere, there's nothing but peace and serenity. No journey, state, fellow traveler, neighbor, or associate can harm me. Someone else supplies my food and clothing; someone else has given me senses and preconceptions.* [14] When he stops supplying what is necessary for life, he sounds the retreat. He has left the door open, and he says, "Go." Where? Not to anything that need cause you fear, but to your origins—that is, to things that aren't hostile or alien to you—the elements.* [15] The fire in you will return to fire, the earth to earth, the air to air, and the water to water. There's no Hades, no

Acheron, no Cocytus, no Pyriphlegethon;* there's nothing anywhere except gods and divine beings.' [16] When a person is in a position to think such thoughts, when he sees the sun, moon, and stars, and enjoys the products of land and sea, he's not helpless, and by the same token isn't lonely.

[17] "'But what if someone assaults me when I'm alone and murders me?' Fool, that's not you, but your body. [18] So does any trace of loneliness or helplessness remain? Why do we make ourselves worse than little children? When they're left on their own, what do they do? They pick up bits of broken pottery and dirt and build something for a while, and then they knock it down and build something else instead. And so they're never helpless. [19] If you all sail away from here, am I to sit and weep because I've been left alone and lonely? Won't I have my bits of broken pottery and dirt? When the unsophisticated minds of children prompt them to act as they do, are we to be made miserable by our wisdom?"

[20] "Great power of any kind is dangerous for a beginner, so we must put up with such things as best we can*—but in accordance with our natures. <Physical exercise is good for a healthy person,> but not for a consumptive.† [21] Practice at one time living like an invalid, so that at another time you can live like a healthy person. Go without food, drink nothing but water, completely abstain at one time from satisfying your appetites, so that at a later time you can satisfy them according to the dictates of reason. If you do that, then when the time comes that you have some good in you, your appetites will be good. [22] But no, that's not what we do. We want to live as wise men straightaway, and to help others. But what kind of help could we provide? What are you up to? Can you help yourself? You want to advise others, but who are you to offer advice? [23] If you want to help others, show them by your own example what kind of people philosophy produces, without relying on empty words. As you eat, help your fellow diners; as you drink, help your fellow drinkers. Yield to others always, give way to them, tolerate them. Help them in this way, not by spattering them with your spit."

3.14
A miscellany

[1] "Just as a bad singer can't sing on his own, but must be accompanied by many others, so some people are incapable of going for a stroll without company. [2] Man (if you are a man), walk by yourself, converse with yourself, and don't hide in a choir. [3] Let yourself be mocked once in a while, take stock of your life, shake yourself up. It will help you to know yourself."

[4] "When a person drinks nothing but water or adopts some other ascetic practice, he seizes every opportunity to tell everyone about it. [5] 'I drink nothing but water.' What? Is that why you drink only water?† Man, if drinking only water does you good, do it. If you do it for any other reason, you're making a fool of yourself. [6] But if it does you good and you do it, don't talk about it to people who are irritated by teetotalers. Are these really the people you want to please?"

[7] "Some actions are performed for their inherent value, while others are prompted by circumstances or business, or are done out of consideration for others or because they fit in with one's way of life."

[8] "Two characteristics that should be eliminated from people are presumption and diffidence. Presumption is thinking that there's nothing you lack, and diffidence is believing that contentment is impossible given all the adverse circumstances with which one contends. [9] Presumption is removed by challenging cross-examination, which originated with Socrates. <...>* But you need to consider and try to prove to yourself that the matter is doable. [10] This investigation will do you no harm, and in fact that's pretty much what philosophy is, trying to find how it's possible to exercise desire and aversion without being obstructed."

[11] "'I'm better than you because my father has consular rank,' says one. [12] 'I've been a tribune and you haven't,' says another. But if we were horses, would you say, 'My father runs faster than you'? Would you say, 'I've got plenty of barley and grass,' or 'I've got a lovely hal-

ter'? What if I responded to your talking like this by saying, 'All right, so let's run a race'? [13] Tell me, is there nothing in the human realm that corresponds to horses' running a race, in that it enables us to distinguish better from worse? Are there no such things as a sense of self-respect, trustworthiness, and justice? [14] Prove yourself better in these respects and then you'll be better as a human being. But if you tell me that you've got a powerful kick, I for my part will tell you that you're proud of something a donkey does."

3.15*
That we should approach everything with circumspection

[1] "In every project you undertake, consider what preliminaries are required and the consequences before proceeding to act. Otherwise, you'll make an enthusiastic start, because you won't have given any thought to what comes next, and then later you'll shamefully abandon the project when faced with some of the consequences. [2] 'I want to be a victor at the Olympic Games.' But consider the project from start to finish and then, if you find it in your best interests, set about it. [3] You have to be disciplined, maintain a strict diet, give up sweet pastries, undergo a strict training regime, exercise regularly every day however hot or cold it may be, refrain from cold drinks, drink no wine except when prescribed. In short, you have to submit to a trainer as you would to a doctor. [4] Then, during the contest, you have to wield a spade,* risk dislocating a wrist or spraining an ankle, swallow a lot of sand, be flogged,* and, as if all that wasn't enough, possibly suffer defeat as well.

[5] "Once you've taken all this into consideration, go and compete if you still want to. Otherwise, recognize that your behavior will be comparable to that of children, who at one moment pretend they're athletes and at another gladiators, then they're blowing trumpets, and then they're actors in a play. [6] That's what you're like as well: at one moment an athlete, at the next a gladiator, then a philosopher, then an orator—without committing yourself wholeheartedly to anything. Like an ape, you imitate every passing thing you see, and one thing after another attracts you. [7] You don't think through any of your projects, look at them in the round, or appraise them; you act without purpose and without really wanting anything.

[8] "This is no different from how some people, after seeing a philosopher and hearing one of them speaking as persuasively as Euphrates* (not that anyone can really speak like him), want to take up philosophy themselves. [9] Man, first consider what kind of venture it is. Then you should take a long, hard look at your own nature, to see if you've got what it takes. If you want to be a wrestler, look at your arms, your thighs, your loins. Different people are naturally suited for different things. [10] Do you think that, doing what you do now, you can be a philosopher? Do you think you can eat and drink as you do now, or get angry or irritated as you do now? [11] As a philosopher, you have to go without sleep, work hard, master your appetites, withdraw from friends and family; you'll find yourself sneered at by slaves, mocked by everyone you meet, and inferior in everything—in honor, in political power, and in the courts. [12] Once you've taken all this into consideration, take up philosophy if you think it's right for you—if you want to exchange these external things for equanimity, freedom, and peace of mind. And if you don't, steer clear of philosophy. Don't act as children do and be a philosopher today, a tax collector tomorrow, then an orator, and then an imperial procurator. [13] These things don't fit well together. You must be one person, whether good or bad. You have to choose between cultivating your command center or the outside world—between working at inner things or outer things, or in other words, between taking a stance as a philosopher or as a man of the world."

[14] "After Galba was assassinated,* someone said to Rufus, 'So is the world now governed by providence?'* And he replied, 'Did I ever, even in passing, make Galba the basis for an argument that the world is governed by providence?'"

3.16
That venturing into company requires caution

[1] "Anyone who often associates with others for conversation or dinner parties, or simply for companionship, is bound either to become like them himself or to change them until they resemble him. [2] After all, if you put a dead coal next to a live one, it will either extinguish the live one or be set alight by it. [3] Since the risk is so

great, then, we should exercise caution when we fraternize with non-philosophers. We need to bear in mind that it's impossible to brush against someone covered in soot without getting sooty oneself. [4] I mean, what will you do if he starts talking about gladiators, horses, athletes, or, even worse, about people? 'So-and-so is a bad man, so-and-so is a good man. This one did well, that one badly.' And what will you do if he mocks others or ridicules them, and sees the worst in everyone? [5] Do any of you have a skill comparable with that of a musician, that enables him, when he handles a lyre, to know which strings are out of tune, as soon as he's touched them, and to tune them? Or do you have Socrates's ability to win those who were with him over to his point of view, whatever company he was in? [6] Of course not. No, you're bound to be won over by the non-philosophers.

[7] "Why is it, then, that they're stronger than you? It's because their flawed assertions are based on judgments, whereas your clever ones come only from your lips. That's why what you say is feeble and lifeless, and it's sickening to hear you promote philosophy and to listen to you babble on about your pathetic 'virtue.' [8] And that's how non-philosophers defeat you, because always and everywhere judgment is invincibly strong. [9] So until your pleasantries become solid beliefs and you've acquired some means of keeping yourselves safe, I'd advise you to be cautious when engaging with non-philosophers. Otherwise, whatever you inscribe on your minds in the classroom will melt away, day by day, like wax in the sun. [10] Take yourselves off, then, to somewhere far from the sun, as long as your beliefs are as impermanent as wax. [11] That's why philosophers advise us even to leave our homelands, because ingrained habits lead us astray and prevent us from making a start on gaining new ones. And that's also why we feel uncomfortable when acquaintances say, 'Really? He's a philosopher? Someone like him?' [12] Doctors do the same as well when they send people with chronic illnesses off to a different place and a different climate. [13] You too should introduce other habits to replace your old ones. Firm up your beliefs; make them your training ground.

[14] "But no, you go from here to a show, to a gladiatorial contest, to a gymnasium, to a circus. Then you come back here, then you leave here and go back there again, and you never change. [15] You have no good habits. You don't care for or pay attention to yourselves. You

don't observe yourselves and ask, 'How am I using the impressions that occur to me? In accord with nature or not? How am I responding to them?† As I should or not? Do I tell things that aren't subject to will that they're nothing to me?' [16] Until you reach this point, flee from your old habits, and flee from non-philosophers, if you want to make a start on sometime being somebody rather than nobody."

3.17
*On providence**

[1] "Whenever you find fault with providence, stop and think, and you'll recognize that what happened was in accord with reason. [2] 'Yes, but now a dishonest man has an advantage over me.' In what respect? He has more money? That's because he's better than you at flattery, effrontery, and doing without sleep. So it's hardly surprising, is it? [3] But check whether he has an advantage over you with regard to trustworthiness and self-respect. You'll find that he doesn't. Where your strengths lie, you'll find that it's you who has the advantage.

[4] "I once said to someone who was angry about Philostorgus's prosperity, 'Would *you* have wanted to sleep with Sura?'* 'May that day never come!' he replied. [5] 'Then why are you angry if Philostorgus gets something for what he's selling? In any case, how can you think a person happy when he acquires his prosperity by means that you despise? Is it wrong of providence to give better things to better people? Isn't self-respect better than wealth?' He agreed. [6] 'So why are you angry, man, seeing that what you have is better than what he has? Always bear in mind, then, and have at hand the law of nature that what is superior is better off than what is inferior in the respect in which it's superior, and then you'll never get angry.'"

[7] "But my wife is horrible to me."

"Very well, if someone asks you what this amounts to, say, 'My wife is horrible to me.'"

"Nothing more than that?"

"No, just that."

[8] "My father doesn't give me a thing."

"All this amounts to is that your father doesn't give you a thing. Do you have to add the extraneous† notion that this is something bad, which is to add a falsehood? [9] That's why it's not poverty that we need to get rid of, but our judgment of poverty. Then we'll be content."

3.18
That there is no need for news to worry us

[1] "Whenever you receive some 'worrying' news, have at hand the thought that news can never be about anything that's subject to will. [2] After all, can anyone bring you news that a belief or a desire of yours is wrong? Of course not. But he can inform you of someone's death. Well, what's that to you? Or he can tell you that someone is maligning you. What's that to you? [3] Or that your father is up to something. What's the object of his scheming? Not your will, surely. That's impossible. Your body or your possessions. You are safe; his plans don't affect you.

[4] "But the judge pronounces you guilty of impiety.* Didn't the judges make the same pronouncement in the case of Socrates? The pronouncement is the judge's business, not yours, isn't it? Yes. Then why let it bother you? [5] Your father has a certain function to perform, and if he fails to do so, he destroys the father in him, the man who feels affection for his children and treats them gently. Don't try to get him to lose anything else on this account. I mean, it's never the case that someone goes wrong in one respect and is harmed in another. [6] For your part, it's your job to defend yourself without losing your self-possession and self-respect, and without getting angry. Otherwise, you in your turn destroy the son in you, the man who's self-respecting and honorable. [7] So am I saying that the judge is perfectly safe? No, in fact he runs just as great a risk.* So why are you afraid of his judgment? When something is bad for someone else, what has that to do with you? [8] What's bad for you is to mount a bad defense. That's all you need watch out for. But precisely because your being condemned or acquitted is someone else's business, it's bad for someone else, not for you. [9] 'So-and-so is threatening you.' Me? No. 'He's disparaging you.' That's his business; he'll see to it. 'He's about to condemn you unjustly.' The poor man!"

3.19

How a non-philosopher's stance differs from that of a philosopher

[1] "The primary difference between a non-philosopher and a philosopher is that the one says, 'Oh, how I'm made to suffer by my child, my brother, my father,' while the other, if he's ever compelled to say such a thing, says, 'Oh, how I'm made to suffer...', and then, after a pause, he adds, 'by myself.' [2] The point is that will can't be impeded or harmed by anything that isn't subject to will, but only by itself. [3] So if we, too, tend in that direction—that is, if we blame ourselves when the going gets tough, and remember that the only thing that ever causes disquiet and confusion is a judgment—I swear to you by all the gods that we've made progress.

[4] "As things are, however, we've taken the wrong road right from the start. While we were still very young, if we ever bumped into something because we weren't looking where we were going, our nurse didn't scold us, but hit the stone. I mean, what had the stone done? Should it have moved out of the way because of your childish silliness? [5] Or again, if after bathing we couldn't find anything to eat, our minder never curbed our appetite, but thrashed the cook. Man, we didn't give you the job of minding the cook, did we? No, you're supposed to look after our child. He's the one you should be correcting and helping. [6] And so we're childlike even when we're adults, because it's characteristic of a child not just to be uncultured and illiterate, but also uneducated in life's lessons."

3.20

That it is possible to turn every external circumstance to good account

[1] "At a theoretical level, hardly anyone disputes the fact that 'good' and 'bad' are in us, not in external things. [2] No one describes the proposition 'It is day' as good and 'It is night' as bad, or says that the acme of evil is the assertion 'Three equals four.' [3] But what do they say? That knowledge is good and error is bad, which means that something good occurs even in the realm of falsehood—the knowledge that something false is indeed false. [4] And so it should be in

life as well. Is health good and illness bad? No, man. What, then? Health managed well is good, but when badly managed it's bad."

"So it's possible to turn even being ill to good account?"

"Yes, by God! After all, it's possible to profit from death, isn't it? And from being maimed? [5] Do you think that Menoeceus benefited only a little from his death?"*

"If anyone thinks that, he deserves to be benefited the same way that Menoeceus was!"

"Come on, man! Didn't he preserve the patriot in him, the person of principle, trustworthiness, and honor? [6] If he'd remained alive, wouldn't he have lost all those aspects of himself? Wouldn't he have acquired the opposite features and assumed the characteristics of someone who's cowardly and base, who hates his country and clings to life? So do you really think he gained only a little by his death?"

"No."

[7] "Well, what about the father of Admetus?* Was it really in his best interests to continue his dishonorable and pitiful life? Didn't he die later? [8] I implore you all in the name of the gods, stop valuing material things! Stop enslaving yourselves, first to mere things, and then, because of them, to the people who are able to procure them for you or deny them to you."

[9] "So it's possible to turn these things to good account?"

"Yes, all of them."

"And being insulted too?"

"What does an athlete gain from his training partner? A very great deal. So someone who insults me is training me up. He gives me practice in tolerance, in not losing my temper, in being mild-mannered. [10] You disagree? But if it does me good to have someone grab me by the neck and for him to get my loins and shoulders into shape, and if the trainer is right to ask me for a two-handed lift of the pestle, and the heavier the pestle, the more I'm benefited,* then doesn't someone do me good if he trains me in not losing my temper? [11] You seem not to know how to turn other people to good account. Do I have a bad neighbor? Bad for himself, but good for me, because he enables me to practice being courteous and fair. Do I have a bad father? Bad for himself, but good for me. [12] Here's what the magic wand of Hermes promises:* 'Touch what you want and it will turn to gold.' Well, I can't promise that exactly, but whatever you present me with, I'll turn to good account. Bring illness, death, poverty, insults, a trial on a capital charge: at a touch from the magic wand, all these will turn into things that do one good."

[13] "What will you make of death?"

"I'll make it a way to acquire honor, of course, or a way to show by example what it is for someone to follow the will of nature."

[14] "And what will you make of illness?"

"I'll show what it's like, I'll be an exemplary invalid, I'll retain my self-possession, I'll be content, I won't flatter my doctor, I won't pray for death. [15] Any further questions? I'll turn whatever you submit into a blessing, a source of happiness, something grand and enviable. [16] But no, instead you say, 'Take care not to get ill; it's a bad thing.' Which is no different from saying, 'Take care not to accept the impression that three equals four; it's a bad thing.' Man, how is it bad? If my view of it is correct, how can it harm me? Won't it actually do me good, rather? [17] If my view of poverty, illness, and political obscurity is correct, what more can I want? Won't they be things I can turn to good account? So what sense would it make for me to look to externals for things that are good and bad for me? [18] But what actually happens? These ideas go no farther than the classroom; no one takes them back home with him. As soon as you get home, you're at war with your slave, your neighbors, your detractors, those who mock you. [19] I wish Lesbius nothing but good, for proving to me every day that I know nothing!"*

3.21
To people who too readily set out to become lecturers

[1] "Some people no sooner ingest abstract theories than they want to spew them out, just as those with weak stomachs do their food. [2] Digest them first, and then you won't throw up. Otherwise, something that was wholesome really does become inedible vomit. [3] But show us the changes your absorption of these ideas have made to your command center, just as athletes show how their shoulders have changed as a result of their exercises and diet, and as people who've mastered an art show the results of their training. [4] A builder doesn't come and say, 'Listen to me lecture on building,' but he accepts payment, builds this house, and thereby shows his expertise as

a builder. [5] You should do likewise as well. Eat and drink as a member of the human race, dress, marry, have children, play your part as a citizen of your community; tolerate insults, put up with a hard-hearted brother, put up with father, son, neighbor, travel companion. [6] Show us this and then we'll see that you really have learned something from the philosophers.

"But no, what we get from you is: 'Come and listen to me reading from my commentaries.' Be off with you! Find others to throw up on! [7] 'But I'll give you a better interpretation of Chrysippus than you've ever heard before. I'll disentangle his language to make it perfectly comprehensible, and I'll add some of what I've gleaned from Antipater and Archedemus as well.' [8] Is it for this, then, that young men should leave their homelands and their parents, to come and hear you interpreting mere words? [9] When they get back home, shouldn't they be people who are tolerant, helpful, imperturbable, serene? Shouldn't they be furnished with the kinds of provisions for their journey through life that will enable them to endure everything that happens to them, and to endure it well and in a way that redounds to their credit? [10] But how can you impart these qualities to others when you don't have them yourself? I mean, all you've done right from the start is devote your time to the analysis of syllogisms, changing arguments, and arguments that proceed by questioning."

[11] "But so-and-so has a school. Why shouldn't I?"

"This isn't something that happens by chance or accident, slave; there are conditions to be met, in respect of age, mode of life, and obedience to God. [12] No? But no one sails out from a harbor without having sacrificed to the gods and asked for their help, nor do people sow their fields at random without first invoking the aid of Demeter. So can anyone who sets about work as important as the teaching of philosophy do so safely without the help of the gods, and will good fortune otherwise attend those who come to him?

[13] "There's no other way to describe what you're doing, man, than to say you're scorning the mysteries.* You're saying, 'Eleusis isn't the only place with a shrine: look, there's one here too. They have a hierophant, and I'll create the position here too. They have a herald, but I'll appoint one too. They have a torchbearer; I'll have a torchbearer. There are torches here no less than there. The promises are the same.* What's the difference between what they do there

and what we do here?' [14] It's the height of impiety, man, to suggest that there's no difference. Is the process beneficial if it happens in the wrong place and at the wrong time? Shouldn't there be sacrifices and prayers from a person who's first been purified and mentally prepared by the thought that he'll be approaching sacred rites of great antiquity? [15] These are the conditions under which the mysteries do us good and we come to appreciate that all these things were established by men of old for educational and correctional purposes. [16] But you're broadcasting the secrets and mocking them by performing them at the wrong time, in the wrong place, without sacrifices, and without purification. You don't have the hierophant's proper clothes, hair, headband, voice, or age. You're haven't purified yourself as he has, but you merely appropriate his words and repeat them. Are the words sacred all by themselves?

[17] "That's not the way to approach these matters. It's a great undertaking, a solemn mystery, and it isn't granted lightly or to just anyone. [18] It may be that even wisdom isn't a sufficient qualification for taking care of young minds. One also needs a certain propensity and aptitude for the work; by Zeus, one also needs a particular kind of physique as well. But, above all, occupation of the educational realm needs to have been urged by God, [19] as he advised Socrates to take the realm of refutational argument, Diogenes the realm of kingship and reproof, and Zeno the realm of instruction and doctrine.* [20] You're setting yourself up as a doctor when you've got nothing more than the medicines; you have no idea and you've never bothered to find out when and how they should be applied. [21] 'Look, he's got salves, and I've got the same salves.' So do you have the ability to use them properly? Have you the slightest notion of when and under what circumstances they'll do good, and to whom?

[22] "Why, then, are you cheating in matters of the utmost importance? Why are you behaving so casually? Why are you setting about an enterprise for which you're entirely unsuited? Leave it to those who are able to do it and do it well. Don't be another one of those who are responsible for bringing philosophy into disrepute; don't add to the number of those who discredit the enterprise. [23] If you find theories attractive, sit and ponder them by yourself, but don't ever call yourself a philosopher or allow anyone else to describe you that way. Say instead, 'He's wrong. My desires are no different from

before, my inclinations are for the same objects, and I give my assent to the same things. In short, there's no change at all in the way I use impressions now from how I did before.' [24] This is what you should be thinking and saying about yourself, if you care to think as you ought. Otherwise, carry on with your cheating and continue to act as you do at present. That's right for you."

3.22
On Cynicism*

[1] He was once asked by one of his students, who was evidently attracted by Cynicism, "What sort of person should a Cynic be? What's your opinion of that line of work?"

[2] "We'll take our time over considering the matter," he said.* "But I can tell you this much straightaway: anyone who undertakes something as great as this without the support of God is making himself a target for God's wrath, and is in effect wanting to make a public disgrace of himself. [3] After all, in a well-managed household, no one comes along and says, 'I ought to be in charge here.' Or if he does, when the master of the house returns and sees him haughtily giving orders, he'll drag him outside and cut him down to size.

[4] "That's how it is in this great city too.* Here too there's a master of the household who gives the orders. [5] 'You are the sun. As you circle the heavens, you have the power to create the year and its seasons, to make crops grow and to nourish them, to raise and calm the winds, and to warm the bodies of human beings in due measure. Go, circle the heavens, and thus start everything into motion from the greatest to the smallest. [6] You are a calf; when a lion appears, play your proper part, or you'll regret it. You are a bull; go out and fight, because that's your purpose and your duty, and you're capable of doing it. [7] You have what it takes to lead an army against Troy; be Agamemnon. You are capable of meeting Hector in single combat; be Achilles.' [8] But if Thersites had come forward and claimed the command for himself, either he wouldn't have obtained it, or, if he had, he'd have brought shame on himself before a great many witnesses.*

[9] "You, too, should think carefully about what you're getting into. It isn't what you take it to be. [10] 'I wear a threadbare cloak

these days,* and I'll still be wearing one then. I sleep on a hard bed nowadays, and I'll do so then. I'll get hold of a satchel and a staff, and embark on a life of going around begging from and abusing people I meet. If I see anyone waxing his body hair, or with a fancy hairstyle, or walking around in a purple-bordered toga, I'll tear into him.' [11] If you imagine Cynicism to be like this, steer well clear of it. Stay away; it's not for you. [12] But if you have the right idea of it and think you can handle it, consider the magnitude of the enterprise you're taking in hand.

[13] "First, with regard to yourself, you must change your current behavior in every respect and be seen to do so. You must never blame either God or man. You must eliminate desire altogether* and transfer aversion exclusively onto things that are subject to will. There must be no trace of anger in you, or injured pride, or envy, or pity. You mustn't be attracted to any girl, distinction, slave, or cake. [14] You need to appreciate that other people have the protection of walls, houses, and darkness (when they do something that requires the cover of darkness); they have many ways to conceal what they're doing. A man shuts his door and stations someone at the entrance to his bedroom: 'Tell any visitors that I'm out and don't have time to see them.' [15] But a Cynic has none of these things and is obliged to protect himself with his self-respect. If he doesn't, he'll cut a disgraceful figure, since he's defenseless and out in the open.* His self-respect is his house, his closed door, his doorkeepers, his darkness. [16] There must be no aspect of his life that he feels the need to hide, otherwise he's lost: he'll have destroyed the Cynic in him, the man who lives in the open, the man who's free; he'll have begun to fear something external to himself, he'll have begun to need a place to hide. But he is unable to hide even if he wants to. I mean, where and how will he hide himself? [17] And if by chance he should slip—this public educator, this minder of our morals—think what he's bound to suffer. [18] So can someone who's consumed by these fears still confidently and wholeheartedly supervise other people's conduct? No way; it's impossible.

[19] "The first step, then, is for you to purify your command center and to adopt the following rule of life: [20] 'Now my own mind is the material I work with, as a carpenter works with wood and a shoemaker with leather, and my job is to make correct use of my im-

pressions. [21] My body is nothing to me; its parts are nothing to me. Death? Let it come when it likes, whether it's the death of the whole or of a part. [22] Exile? Where can anyone banish me? He can't send me beyond the universe, and wherever I go the sun will still be there, the moon and the stars will still be there, and I'll still have dreams, portents, and my converse with the gods.'

[23] "The next step for the true Cynic,* once he's prepared himself in this way, is not to be satisfied with what he's gained so far, but to understand that he's a messenger who's been sent to humankind by Zeus to show us that our notions of good and bad are wrong, that we're looking for the essence of goodness and badness in the wrong place, where they aren't to be found, and that we have no idea where they are to be found. [24] He also has to understand that he's a spy, just as Diogenes was when he was taken off to Philip after the battle of Chaeronea.* A Cynic is a true spy, you see, because his mission is to find out what friends and enemies humankind has. [25] And on his return, once he's thoroughly scouted the terrain, he has to report the truth, without being cowed by fear into designating as enemies those who aren't, and without being disconcerted or confused in any other way by his impressions. [26] He must, then, if the opportunity comes his way, be able to raise his voice, mount the tragic stage, and echo Socrates's words:* 'O people, where are you off to? What are you doing, you poor fools? The way you weave all over the place, it's as though you were blind. You've left the true path and are setting off on another one. You're looking for contentment and happiness in the wrong place, where they aren't to be found, and when someone shows you the way you react with disbelief.'

[27] "Why do you all look for happiness in externals? It's not to be found in the body. If you don't believe me, look at Myron or Ophellius.* It's not to be found in possessions. If you don't believe me, look at Croesus, or at today's superrich, and see how their lives are filled with lamentation. It's not to be found in holding high office. If it were, men who've been consuls two or three times would be happy, but they aren't. [28] Whom shall we believe on this? You, who view their situation from the outside and are dazzled by the impressions they give, or the men themselves? [29] And what do they say? Listen to them as they complain and moan, regarding their situation as more pitiable and more dangerous precisely because of their consulships,

their high standing in society, their glory. [30] It's not to be found in kingship. If it were, Nero would have been happy, and so would Sardanapallus.* In fact, even Agamemnon wasn't happy, though he was a better man than either Sardanapallus or Nero, but, while everyone else is fast asleep, what's he up to? 'He was pulling hair by the handful from his head by the roots.' And, in his own words: 'I'm lost,' and 'I'm in agony, my heart is pounding in my chest.'*

[31] "Poor man, what is it of yours that's in a bad way? Your possessions? No. Your body? No. In fact, you're 'rich in gold and bronze.' So what's wrong with you? It's this, that you've neglected and corrupted your faculties of desire, aversion, inclination, and disinclination. [32] How have they been neglected? He has no notion of the essence of goodness, which is his birthright, or of the essence of badness, or of what is and isn't his. And when something that isn't his is in a bad way, he says, 'Woe is me! The Greeks are in danger.' [33] Pity his command center! It's the only thing he's neglected and disregarded. 'They're going to die, slain by the Trojans!' But if the Trojans don't kill them, they're going to die anyway, aren't they? 'Yes, but not all at once.' What difference does that make? If dying is bad, it's just as bad whether they die all at once or one by one. All that's going to happen is the separation of the body and the soul, isn't it? 'Yes.' [34] And if the Greeks die, is the door closed for you? It's still possible for you to die, isn't it? 'Yes.' Then why are you dejected? 'Woe is me, a king, a holder of the scepter of Zeus!' There's no such thing as an ill-starred king, any more than there's an ill-starred god. [35] What are you, then? The designation 'shepherd' is perfect for you.* You're shedding tears as shepherds do when a wolf seizes one of their sheep. And your subjects are sheep. [36] Why did you even come here in the first place? Your desire wasn't threatened at all, was it, or your aversion, or your inclination, or your disinclination? 'No, but my brother's wife was abducted.' [37] Well, isn't he much better off without an adulterous wife? 'So are we to let the Trojans think us cowards?' What kind of people are they? Are they wise or foolish? If they're wise, why are you fighting them? If they're foolish, why do you care what they think of you?

[38] "So where is the good to be found, since it isn't to be found in these things? Tell us, sir, our messenger and spy.* 'Where you don't expect to find it; where you're not even prepared to look for it. If you

were, you'd have found it within yourselves and you wouldn't be wandering among things external to yourselves, or looking for what's yours among things that aren't yours. [39] Focus on yourselves, recognize your preconceptions. How do you conceive of the good?'

"'As contentment, happiness, and freedom from obstruction.'

"'All right, but don't you see it something inherently great? Don't you think of it as important? As incapable of causing harm? [40] So where, in what kind of thing, should we look for what brings contentment and is immune to obstruction? Should it be enslaved or free?'

"'Free.'

"'Well, is your body free or enslaved?'

"'We don't know.'

"'Don't you know that it's subject to fever, gout, eye disease, dysentery, tyrants, fire, weaponry, and everything that's stronger than it?'

"'All right, it's enslaved.'

[41] "'So if that's the case, how can anything bodily be unobstructed? How can something be great or important when in itself it's no more than a corpse, a piece of earth, a lump of clay? Do you have nothing that's free, then?'

"'Perhaps not.'

[42] "'Well, can you be compelled by anyone to assent to something that seems to you to be false?'

"'No.'

"'Or to refuse to assent to something that seems to be true?'

"'No.'

"'So you can see that there *is* something in you that's naturally free. [43] Now, is there anyone here who's capable of feeling desire or aversion, or an inclination or disinclination, or of preparing himself or devising projects, without first forming an impression of what is expedient or inappropriate for him?'

"'No.'

"'So here too you have something that's unimpeded and free. [44] You poor fools, that's what you should cultivate, that's what you should be taking care of, that's where to look for what's good for you. [45] Now, how is it possible for someone who lives without possessions, clothing, house, hearth, cleanliness, slaves, or state, to live a contented life? [46] Look! God has sent you someone to show you by his example that it's possible. [47] Look at me! I have no house, I'm stateless, I have no possessions or slaves. I sleep on the ground. I have no wife, no children, no household staff, but only the earth and sky and a single threadbare cloak. [48] And yet, is there anything I lack? Am I not impervious to distress and fear? Am I not free? Has any of you ever seen me fail to attain what I desire or, where my aversions are concerned, experience what I want to avoid? Have I ever found fault with God or man? Have I ever blamed anyone? You've never seen me downcast, have you? [49] When I come across the kinds of people you fear and admire, what's my behavior like? I treat them as slaves, don't I? Is there anyone who catches sight of me and doesn't think that he's seeing his king and master?"*

[50] "There you have it. That's what a Cynic says, that's what his character is like, and that's how he intends to live. But instead you focus on his satchel, his staff, and his mighty jaws—his habit of devouring or hoarding everything you give him*†—or his outrageous reviling of passersby, or his displaying a fine shoulder.* [51] What about you? Are you ready to embark on such a great enterprise? First get hold of a mirror, look at your shoulders, examine your loins and thighs. You're going to register for the Olympic Games, man, not for some pointless, inferior contest. [52] At the Olympic Games, you can't just be defeated and leave. In the first place, your disgrace is bound to be witnessed by the entire world, not just Athenians or Spartans or Nicopolitans.* In the second place, if you enter the contest trusting to chance, you're bound to be flogged as well, and before being flogged, you're going to be parched with thirst and scorched by heat, and you'll find yourself swallowing a lot of sand.*

[53] "Think more carefully about what you're getting into. Know yourself. Consult divinity and don't embark on the undertaking without God's confirmation. If he advises you to go ahead, you can be sure that he wants you to become great—or thoroughly beaten. [54] Because another truly delightful strand in a Cynic's life is that he's certain to be lashed like a donkey,* and that while being lashed he must love those who are doing it to him, as though he were the father or brother of them all. [55] But no, if that happens to you, go and stand in a public place and cry out, 'Caesar, you may have brought peace to the world, but see what I have to put up with! Let's haul them off to the proconsul.'* [56] But to a Cynic, what is Caesar or a proconsul, or anyone except Zeus, who commissioned him and whom

he serves? Does he call on anyone other than Zeus? Isn't he certain that, if he suffers in any of these ways, it's Zeus's way of training him? [57] When Heracles was being trained by Eurystheus,* he didn't think of himself as pitiable but unhesitatingly carried out all his orders. But is our Cynic going to cry out and complain when it's Zeus who's putting him through his paces and training him? Not if he deserves to take Diogenes's staff in his hands. [58] Listen to what Diogenes said to passersby when he had a fever: 'You vile wretches! Why don't you stop? You'll make the arduous journey to Olympia to see athletes fight and kill one another,* but don't you want to see a fight between man and fever?'

[59] "A man like this—a man who used to flaunt his difficult circumstances and chose to be a spectacle for passersby—is hardly likely to have castigated the god who commissioned him for treating him unfairly. Why would he have castigated him? Because of the seemliness of his life? Why would he denounce him? Because he's making too glorious a display of his virtue? [60] Come now, what does he say about poverty, death, pain?* How did he compare his happiness with that of the Great King?* In fact, he thought there was really no comparison between them, [61] because there can be no room for happiness where there's disquiet, distress, fear, unsatisfied desires, ineffective aversions , envy, and jealousy. And all these qualities are necessarily present wherever there are unsound judgments."

[62] The young man had another question. "Suppose I'm ill," he said, "and a friend asks me to come to his house to be properly looked after, should I accept his invitation?"*

[63] "It's not easy to find a Cynic's friend," said Epictetus. "He must be just like him, otherwise he won't be good enough to be counted a friend of his. He must share his scepter and his kingship, and be an exemplary assistant, if he's to be thought worthy of friendship. That's how Diogenes became a friend of Antisthenes, and Crates of Diogenes.* [64] Or do you think that all it takes to become a Cynic's friend and be thought worthy to be received by him is to come up and greet him? [65] Well, if that seems likely to you, if that's what you think, you'd do better to look around for a nice pile of manure in which to nurse your fever, one that will protect you from the north wind and stop you shivering.* [66] But I get the impression that you

want to spend time in someone's house so as to be fattened up. If so, why are you even considering embarking on such a great enterprise?"

[67] "What about marriage and children?" the young man asked. "Are these duties that a Cynic will undertake as things that are valuable in themselves?"*

"In a city of sages," said Epictetus, "if you'll allow me this assumption, probably no one would bother to turn to Cynicism. After all, for whose sake would he be taking on the Cynic way of life? [68] Nevertheless, supposing he did, there'd be nothing to stop him marrying and having children, because his wife would be as wise as he is, and so would his father-in-law, and his children would be brought up to be wise as well. [69] But in the real world, as things are today, it's as if a Cynic is in the front line of a battle, so it's important that he should be undistracted, wholly devoted to the service of God, and able to go about among people without being tied down by private duties or entangled in personal relationships. Don't you agree? The point is that if he failed to do his duty by these relationships, that would be the end of his role as a person of blameless virtue, and if he did his duty by them, that would be the end of his role as the messenger, the spy, the herald of the gods.

[70] "Look at it this way. He'd be obliged to behave in certain ways toward his father-in-law, and to render certain services for his wife's other relatives and for his wife herself. In the end, he'd be cut off from his calling and driven to be a nurse and a provider for his family. [71] Not to mention everything else, he'd need to own a kettle to heat water for his baby to be washed in a basin, and wool for his wife after the baby's born, olive oil, a cot, a cup—the implements and utensils are adding up already*—and then there are all the other jobs that will take up his time and occupy his attention. [72] In the end, what will become of that king who used to devote his time to the public interest, 'the people's guardian, laden with responsibilities'?* He should be supervising everyone else, all those who are married and all those who have children, to see who's treating his wife well and who's treating her badly, who's arguing, which households are troubled and which aren't. [73] He should be like a doctor who goes around taking pulses and says, 'You've got a fever; you've got a headache; you've got gout. No food for you; food for you; no bathing for you; you need

surgery; you need cautery.' [74] Where does he find the time for this
if he's tied up with private duties? He's got to make sure that his children have clothes, hasn't he? Tell me, doesn't he have to send them
off to school with their writing tablets and styluses, and make their
beds as well? After all, they can't emerge from their mother's womb
as ready-made Cynics. If he fails to do all this for them, it would have
been better for him to have exposed them at birth than to kill them
by neglect.* [75] You can see how low we're dragging our Cynic and
how we're depriving him of his kingship."

[76] "Yes, but Crates was married."*

"That was a special case, a true love affair, and the wife in this instance was another Crates. But our inquiry concerns ordinary mar-
riages, those with no mitigating circumstances, and it's showing us
that marriage, under present conditions, is not something that a
Cynic will choose as inherently valuable."

[77] "In that case," the student said, "how will he perpetuate the
community?"

"Oh, for heaven's sake, are people benefited more by those who
bring two or three snotty children into the world to replace them, or
by those who oversee the entire population, to the extent that they
can, to see what they do, how they spend their time, what they care
for, and what they wrongly neglect? [78] Who did the Thebans more
good, those who bequeathed them children, or Epaminondas, who
died childless?* Did Priam, the father of fifty trashy children, contribute more to society than Homer? Did Danaus? Or Aeolus?* [79]
Moreover, if military command or writing a book is enough to excuse
a man from marrying or having children, without his being thought
to have given nothing in exchange for his childlessness, will a Cynic's
kingship not be adequate compensation?

[80] "Perhaps we fail to recognize the greatness of a Cynic. Perhaps our picture of Diogenes's character fails to do him justice, because all we can see are the present-day versions, those 'dogs of the
table, guards of the gate,'* who are nothing like their predecessors
and resemble them only in that they, too, fart in public. [81] If we had
a true conception of a Cynic, the points you've been raising wouldn't
disturb us, and we wouldn't be surprised that he won't marry or have
children. Man, the Cynic is the father of the entire human race—
men are his sons and women his daughters—and he relates to all

FIGURE 5. Wall painting showing the Cynic philosophers Crates and Hipparchia, ca. first century CE. From the garden of the Villa Farnesina, Museo delle Terme, Rome. Hard-core Cynics were supposed to live as vagabonds, owning no more than what they could carry. Here we see the famous Cynic couple Crates and Hipparchia with all their worldly goods.

human beings as a father and cares for them all as a father. [82] Or do you think it's officiousness that makes him insult the people he meets? No, he does so as their father, as their brother, and as the servant of Zeus, the common father of humankind.

[83] "If you want, ask me also whether a Cynic will play a part in public life. You idiot, can you imagine any form of public service greater than the kind in which he's engaged? [84] Why would you want someone to step up in Athens and talk about revenues and resources when it's his job to talk to people in general, Athenians, Corinthians, and Romans alike, not about resources and revenues, nor about peace and war, but about happiness and unhappiness, success and failure, slavery and freedom? [85] The man is engaged in public service of this importance, and you ask me whether he's to play a part in public life? Ask me also whether he'll hold high office and I'll tell you again, 'Fool, what office could be more important than the one already holds?'

[86] "What is necessary, however, is that he should have a certain kind of physique. I mean, look: if he presents as a consumptive, all thin and pale, his testimony will no longer carry the same weight.

[87] He must not only demonstrate to non-philosophers, by displaying his mental and spiritual attributes, that it's possible to be a truly good person without having the things they value, but he must also demonstrate by means of his body that a plain and simple life, lived in the open air, does no harm to the body either. [88] 'Look! My body joins me in bearing witness to the truth of what I'm saying.' That's what Diogenes did. He went around glowing with health and attracted the attention of ordinary people just by his physique.* [89] But a Cynic who arouses pity is taken to be a beggar. Everyone turns away from him and finds him offensive. Nor should he look dirty, otherwise he'll frighten people away for that reason too; his very shabbiness should be clean and attractive.

[90] "Moreover, a Cynic must have considerable natural charm and wit (without which he's no more than a prig), so that he's able to respond readily and appropriately to whatever he's confronted with. [91] So, when someone asked Diogenes, 'Are you the Diogenes who claims that there are no gods?', he said, 'Of course not, since I regard you as being hateful to the gods.' [92] Or again, when Alexander stood over him as he slept and quoted the line 'A man burdened with counsels should not sleep through the night,' he replied, still half asleep, 'The people's guardian, laden with responsibilities.'*

[93] "But above all his command center must be purer than the sun, otherwise he's bound to be a hustler and a cheat, since he'll be censuring others while being in the grip of some vice himself. [94] Here's how things stand, you see. For the kings and tyrants of this world, it's their bodyguards and weaponry that enable them† to censure others and punish wrongdoers, however wicked they are themselves; but what gives a Cynic this right isn't weaponry and guards but his conscience. [95] Knowing that he's lost sleep and toiled for the sake of others, that he's gone to sleep pure and that sleep has left him still more pure; knowing that his every thought is that of a friend and servant of the gods, and of one who is a colleague in Zeus's government; knowing that, wherever he finds himself, he has at the forefront of his mind the sayings 'Lead me, Zeus, both you and Destiny' and 'If this is what the gods want, so be it;'* [96] knowing all this, why shouldn't he have the confidence to speak candidly to his brothers, his children—to his relatives, in short?

[97] "So someone like this is no interfering, officious busybody,

because he isn't meddling in other people's affairs when he supervises human life but minding his own business. Otherwise, you'd have to say that a general is a busybody when he inspects, reviews, and observes his troops, and punishes those who are out of line. [98] So if you censure others while keeping a cake in your pocket, I'll say to you, 'Wouldn't you rather go off into a corner and eat what you've stolen? What has other people's business to do with you? [99] Who are you, anyway? Are you the bull of the herd? Are you the queen bee? Show me your leadership credentials, of the kind a queen bee has by nature. But if you're a drone who's laying claim to sovereignty over the hive, shouldn't you expect your fellow citizens to reject you, as bees reject drones?'

[100] "A Cynic must be a person of such great endurance that ordinary people take him to be as unfeeling as a stone. No one can insult him, no one can hit him, no one can humiliate him. Any way that anyone wants to treat his body is all right with him, [101] because he bears in mind that what is superior is bound to prevail over what is inferior, in the respect in which it's inferior, and that his body is necessarily inferior to the mass of ordinary people, as the weaker is to the stronger. [102] So he never gets involved in this contest, which he can only lose, but instead completely renounces everything that's external to him and claims nothing that's enslaved as his own.

[103] "However, where it's a matter of will and use of impressions, there you'll find he has so many eyes that you'd call Argus blind by comparison.* [104] Does he ever rush too quickly into assent? Are his inclinations random? Is his desire ever disappointed? Does his aversion ever encounter what it wants to avoid? Are his intentions ever unfulfilled? Is there in him any trace of fault-finding, despondency, or envy? [105] This is where he devotes his attention and his efforts, and where everything else is concerned, he's relaxed to the point of snoring, and is entirely at peace. His will isn't subject to thievery and tyranny, [106] but what about his body? Yes, it is. And his possessions? Yes. The same goes for political power and honors. So why should they be any concern of his? If anyone ever tries to use these things to frighten him, he says, 'Go and look for some children. They find masks frightening, but I know they're made of clay and are empty inside.'*

[107] "This is what the enterprise is like that you're contemplat-

264   EPICTETUS: THE COMPLETE WORKS

ing getting into. So if that's what you want to do, I beg you in the name
of the gods to hold off for a while, and first see whether you have the
aptitude for it. [108] Remember what Hector says to Andromache:
'It's better that you should go into the house and see to the weaving.
War is the concern of men—of all men, but especially me.'* [109]
This shows that he was aware not only of his own aptitude but also of
the limits of her competence."

3.23
To those who give readings and lectures just to be admired

[1] "First tell yourself what kind of person you want to be, and then
act accordingly in everything you do. After all, in almost every walk
of life that's what we see happening. [2] Athletes first decide what
kind of athletes they want to be and from then on act accordingly.
One wants to be a long-distance runner, so he establishes the appropriate regime in his diet, exercising, massage, and training. Another
wants to be a sprinter, so he adopts a different regime in all these respects. Another wants to be a pentathlete, so his regime is different
again. [3] And you'll find that the same is true of the arts. If you want
to be a carpenter, you'll have one kind of training, and if you want to
be a smith, another. In everything we do, if we refer it to no end, we'll
be acting at random, and if we refer it to an unsuitable end, we're
bound to fail.

[4] "Moreover, there are two kinds of end to refer to, one general
and the other personal. In the first place, one must act as a human
being. What does that involve? Not acting like a sheep, gently but
purposelessly,† and not acting destructively, like a wild beast. [5]
The personal end has to do with an individual's occupation and calling. A minstrel must act as a minstrel, a carpenter as a carpenter, a
philosopher as a philosopher, an orator as an orator. [6] So when you
say, 'Come and listen to my lecture!' you need to check first that lecturing is compatible with your purpose, and then, if you find that
it is, you need to check whether this end is right for you. [7] Do you
want to do good with your lecturing or to be praised for it? The answer comes straightaway: 'The praise of the masses is meaningless
to me.' That's well said, because it's meaningless to a musician, insofar as he's a musician, and to a geometer likewise. [8] So you want to

do good. To whom? Tell us, too, so that we can join the stampede to your lecture hall.

"Now, is it possible to benefit others unless one has been benefited oneself in the past? No, no more than a non-carpenter can help others in carpentry, or a non-shoemaker in shoemaking. [9] So you want to know if you've been benefited? Take a look at your judgments, philosopher. What is the prospect held out by desire? Not to be thwarted. What about aversion? Not to meet with what one wants to avoid. [10] All right, then, are these potentials being fulfilled in our case? Tell me the truth, or here's what I'll say to you: 'The other day you met with a rather cool reception from your audience, and when they failed to applaud, you left in a sulk. [11] On another occasion, when they did applaud, you went around asking everyone, "How do you think I did?" "On my life, sir, it was wonderful!" "How about that bit…?" "Which bit?" "…where I described Pan and the Nymphs." "It was extraordinarily good."'* [12] And then you tell me that where your desires and aversions are concerned, your conduct is in accord with nature? Be off with you! Try that out on someone else!

[13] "Now, the other day didn't you insincerely praise someone? And didn't you flatter that man from a senatorial family? Would you like your children to behave like that?"

"God forbid!"

[14] "Then why did you praise him and treat him with respect?"

"He's a gifted young man and enjoys listening to lectures."

"What gives you that idea?"

"He thinks I'm great."

"There we have your evidence! But next let me ask you this. Do you really think that the same people who applaud you don't secretly look down on you? [15] So when a young man who knows perfectly well that he's never done or thought anything of value comes across a philosopher who praises him for his talent, candor, and sincerity, what else do you think he can say to himself but 'This person needs me for something'? [16] Or else tell me: what has he done to prove that he's talented? Look, he's been in your circle for all this time, and he's listened to your lectures and readings. Has he put his life in order? Has he turned his attention onto himself? Has he come to recognize the terrible state he's in? Has he eliminated presumption? Is he looking for a teacher?"

"He is," he said.

[17] "Someone to teach him how to live? No, you fool! He's looking for someone to teach him how to express himself well, because that's what he admires you for. Listen to what he says: 'The person I'm talking about writes with outstanding artistry, much better than Dio.'* That's an entirely different matter. [18] He isn't saying, 'He's a person of self-respect, he's trustworthy, and he's imperturbable,' is he? And even if he was, I'd say to him, 'If he's a trustworthy person, what is it to be a trustworthy person?' And if he proved unable to answer, I'd add, 'First gain some understanding of what you're talking about, and then talk.'

[19] "So how do you intend to benefit others when you're in such a terrible state, longing for praise and counting the number of people in your audience? 'Today I had a much larger audience.' 'Yes, there were lots of people there.' 'Five hundred, I reckon.' 'Nonsense! Make it a thousand!' 'Dio never drew such a large crowd.' 'Of course not.' 'And they have a pretty good feeling for what I say.' 'Even a stone, sir, may be moved by beauty.' [20] There you have the words of a philosopher! There you have the temperament of one who wants to be of benefit to people! There you have a person who's listened to reason, and who's read the Socratic literature as Socratic, and not as though it were written by Lysias or Isocrates!* "'I have often wondered what arguments...' No, let's make it "what argument": that flows better.'*

[21] "The point is that you've been reading Socratic literature as you'd read song lyrics, haven't you? If you'd read it properly, you wouldn't have focused on these aspects, but you'd have been looking at this instead: 'Anytus and Meletus can kill me, but they cannot harm me.' Or this: 'I've always been the kind of person to pay attention to nothing of mine, but only the argument that strikes me on reflection as being the best.'* [22] And so no one ever heard Socrates saying, 'I know things and I teach them to others.' Instead, he'd send people elsewhere, to one teacher or another. In fact, people used to come to him to hear which philosophers he recommended for them, and then he'd take them off and introduce them.* [23] But no, you suppose that, as he was walking along with them, he'd say, 'Come and hear me lecturing today in Quadratus's house.'* Why should I listen to you? Do you want to show me how cleverly you string words together? You do a fine job, man—and what good does it do you?"

"Well, you could give me some praise."

[24] "What do you mean by 'give me praise'?"

"Say 'Bravo!' or 'Amazing!'"

"All right, I'll praise you. But if praise is to be reserved for things that count as good, as the philosophers say, what can I praise you for? If correct diction is a good thing, convince me of that, and I'll give you praise."

[25] "Are you saying that one should take no pleasure in listening to such things?"

"Far from it. I don't listen even to a minstrel without feeling pleasure. But that doesn't give me a reason to stand up and sing, does it? Listen to what Socrates says: 'It wouldn't be appropriate, gentlemen, for a man of my age to come before you crafting my words, as though I were a teenager.'* [26] 'As though I were a teenager,' he says, because it's really just a flashy trick, to select one's words and arrange them, and then to step up and read or recite them in a clever manner, and to interrupt one's reading by exclaiming, 'There aren't many who can understand these things, I swear!'

[27] "Does a philosopher advertise his talks? Isn't it the case that, just as the sun draws its nourishment to itself,* so a philosopher attracts people who'll be benefited by him? What kind of doctor invites people to come and be cured by him? Though actually I hear that nowadays in Rome even doctors advertise. [28] 'I invite you to come and hear that you're in a bad way, that you pay attention to everything rather than what you should be paying attention to, that you don't know what's good and what's bad, that you're unhappy and miserable.' A fine invitation that would be! And yet if a philosopher's words fail to produce that effect, they're lifeless, and the speaker's a corpse too. [29] Rufus used to say, 'If you've got nothing better to do than praise me, my speaking is a waste of time.' In fact, he used to speak in such a way that each of us sitting there would think that someone had snitched on him. That's how good he was at grasping the facts and getting each of us to see his faults.

[30] "Gentlemen, a philosopher's school is a doctor's office. You shouldn't leave after having had a pleasant time, but a painful one, because you arrive unhealthy, one with a dislocated shoulder, another with a tumor, another with an abscess, another with a headache. [31] So am I to sit here and regale you with clever ideas and bons mots

so that you can leave after praising me, one of you with his shoulder just as it was when he arrived, another with his head in the same condition, another with his abscess, another with his tumor? [32] And is it for this, then, that members of the younger generation are to leave their homes, parents, friends, relatives, and property—so that they can say 'Bravo!' when you come up with a witty expression? Was that what Socrates used to do, or Zeno, or Cleanthes?"

[33] "Are you saying that there isn't a special protreptic way of speaking?"

"That's undeniable. Just as there's a critical style† and a didactic one.* But have you ever heard anyone mention a fourth style in this context, an epideictic one?* [34] Now, what is the protreptic style? It's the ability to show people, both individuals and larger audiences, the conflict in which they're mired and that they concern themselves with everything except what they truly want. What they want are things that bring them happiness, but they look for them in the wrong place. [35] In order for this to happen, is it necessary for a thousand seats to be set up and an audience to be invited? Is it necessary for you to dress in a fancy robe or cloak, ascend a podium,† and describe how Achilles died?* In the name of the gods, stop doing all you can to bring noble names and achievements into disrepute! [36] What could be less protreptic† than a speaker showing his audience that he needs them? [37] Unless you can tell me of anyone who, on hearing you reading or talking, became worried about himself, or turned his attention onto himself, or left saying, 'The philosopher got right through to me. I must change my ways.' [38] On the contrary, if you achieve a notable success, don't people from your audience say to one another, 'He expressed himself really well in that bit about Xerxes,' and 'No, his description of the battle of Thermopylae* was better.' Is this what it is to listen to a philosopher?"

3.24

On the necessity of not being attached to things that are not up to us

[1] "If someone else is out of touch with nature, that shouldn't have a negative effect on you. You were born to share not in the debasement or misfortune of others, but in their good fortune. [2] If someone experiences misfortune, remember that it's his own doing, be-

cause God created everyone for happiness and self-possession. [3] He supplied them with the resources to achieve this by giving each individual some things that are his and others that aren't. Those that are subject to impediment, removal, and constraint aren't his, while those that aren't subject to impediment are. And, as was only right and proper for one who cares for us and protects us like a father, he included what is essentially good and bad among the things that are up to us."*

[4] "But I've parted company with him, and he's in pain."

"Yes, but why did he regard what was not his as his? Why, when he was enjoying seeing you, didn't he take account of the fact that you're mortal, that you're bound to leave for elsewhere? So he's paying the penalty for his own foolishness. [5] But what are *you* paying for? Why are you feeling sorry for yourself? Can it be that you, too, have failed to pay attention to the facts? Have you, like superficial women, been enjoying everything—places, people, lifestyle—on the assumption that they'd be there for you forever? And now you sit and weep because it's no longer the same people who pass before your eyes and you're not spending time in the same places. [6] Yes, this is what you deserve, to be more wretched than ravens and crows! They can fly wherever they want, move their nests, cross seas, and they do so without moaning or missing what they had before."

[7] "Yes, but that's the effect of their being non-rational creatures."

"So has rationality been given us by the gods for misery and unhappiness, for us to spend our lives in sorrow? [8] Or are we all to be immortal? Is none of us ever to go on a journey?† Are we to stay rooted to the spot like plants? And if one of our friends goes away, are we to sit and weep, and then dance and clap our hands like children if he returns? [9] Why don't we wean ourselves at last and remember what we heard from the philosophers—if we did in fact learn from them and weren't listening to them as though they were chanting incantations? [10] They say that this world is a single city, that the substance from which it's made is single, and that there's necessarily a cyclical replacement of things by other things—that some things are dissolved while others come into being,* and some things stay in place while others move. [11] They claim that there's no shortage of friends in the world—the gods, in the first place, and then also human beings, who have a natural affinity with one another. It's inevitable, they say, that some people are together while others are apart, and we should enjoy the company of those we're with and not regret the absence of others. [12] And they say that a human being, in addition to having greatness of mind and the ability to see the unimportance of everything that isn't subject to will, has this further attribute, that he isn't rooted or attached to the earth, but moves from time to time to different places, sometimes driven by certain needs and sometimes just to see what there is to see.

[13] "That's how it was for Odysseus too: 'Many the cities of men that he saw and learned their minds.'* And still earlier it was Heracles's lot to travel around the entire world, 'observing both the unruliness of men and their obedience to law,'* expelling and purging the world of the one, while establishing the other in its place. [14] But how many friends do you think he had in Thebes, in Argos, in Athens? And how many new friends did he make in the course of his travels, especially since he even had the habit of taking a wife if the opportunity presented itself, and having children, whom he would then abandon without regret, without a sense of loss, and without feeling that he was leaving them orphaned?* [15] He knew that no one is an orphan, but that always and forever everyone has a father who cares for them. [16] The point is that, for him, it was no mere story he'd heard, that Zeus is the father of humankind; he regarded him as his father, called him 'father,' and took him into account in all he did.* That's how it was possible for him to live happily wherever he was. [17] It's never possible for happiness and hankering after things to coexist. In order for something to be happy, it has to have everything it wants, like someone who's eaten his fill. It must feel neither thirst nor hunger."

[18] "But Odysseus missed his wife and wept as he sat on a rock."*

"So do you trust everything Homer says and believe all his tales? If Odysseus really did weep, he must have been miserable, mustn't he? But can a truly good person be miserable? [19] The universe is badly governed indeed if Zeus doesn't make sure that his fellow citizens resemble him in being happy. [20] No, it's unlawful and impious to entertain any such thought, so if Odysseus wept and mourned, he can't have been a good man. How can someone be good if he doesn't know who he is? And no one knows who he is if he's forgotten that everything that's born will die, and that no two people can be together forever. [21] So wanting the impossible is slavish, idiotic, and the mark of someone who's a stranger in the world and is fighting God with the only weapons at his command, his judgments."

[22] "But my absence makes my mother sad."

"Yes, but why hasn't she taken these principles on board? I'm not saying you shouldn't try to relieve her sadness, but I am insisting that a person shouldn't unconditionally want what isn't his. [23] Someone else's distress isn't mine; only my own distress is. So I'll go to any lengths to put an end to mine, because that's up to me, and as for what isn't mine, I'll do what I can to end it, but I won't go to any lengths, [24] because that would be to fight God—to take up a position against him, to take the opposite side from him over the universe. And the penalty for this hostility toward God, for this disobedience, won't be paid by my children's children, but by myself in person, not just by day but at night when I'm jolted awake from my dreams, when I'm troubled in my mind, when I tremble in fear at every message, when my peace of mind depends on letters written by others. [25] Someone arrives from Rome: 'Just let there be no bad news.' But how can anything bad happen to you in a place where you aren't? Someone arrives from within Greece: 'Just let there be no bad news.' This is the way to make every place in the world a source of misery for yourself. [26] Isn't it enough for you to be miserable where you actually are? Do you have to let what's happening overseas and news received by letter make you miserable as well? Is that how unassailable you are?"

[27] "But what if friends of mine in Rome die?"

"Well, that's just the death of some mortal beings. Do you really expect to reach old age without seeing the death of any of those you love along the way? [28] Don't you realize that over a long stretch of time all sorts of different things are bound to happen? A fever will get the better of one, a robber of another, a tyrant of a third. [29] That's the nature of the world we live in; that's the nature of the people who live in it alongside us. Cold, heat, malnutrition, land or sea travel, winds: there are all kinds of accidents that kill people, drive them into exile, or force them to leave on an embassy or a campaign. [30] Settle down, then, and let all these things upset you, cause you grief, and make you wretched and miserable. Be at the mercy of something other than yourself, and not just one or two things, but countless thousands.

[31] "Is that what you heard when you were being schooled in philosophy? Is that what your lessons consisted of? Don't you realize that what we're involved in is a military operation? One person has to stand guard, another go out on reconnaissance, and another even has to go out and fight. It's neither possible nor desirable for everyone to stay in the same place. [32] But you're failing to carry out the duties assigned you by your commanding officer, you protest when you're given work that's at all demanding, and you fail to appreciate the effect you're having on the army, insofar as it's something you can affect. If everyone copied you, no one would dig a trench, erect a palisade, keep awake through the night, or expose himself to danger. Everyone would prove to be useless as a soldier. [33] Or again, if you're a sailor on board a ship, occupy one position and stick to it obstinately. If you have to climb the mast, refuse; if you have to run to the bow, refuse. And is there any conceivable captain who'll put up with you? Won't he throw you overboard as he would a useless piece of equipment, and judge you to be a sheer nuisance and a bad example for the rest of the crew?

[34] "The same goes in the real world. Every individual's life is a military campaign, and a long and complex one at that. You have to keep to your role as a soldier and carry out every single one of the general's commands—even guessing what he wants you to do, if possible. [35] His strength and the superiority of his character are incomparably greater than those of an ordinary general. [36] You've been assigned to an imperial city, and you don't occupy a lowly position, but you're a senator for life. Don't you realize that such a person necessarily has little time to spend on domestic business but is bound to spend most of his time away from home, giving or receiving orders, serving in some official capacity, out on campaign, or sitting as a judge? Under these circumstances, do you really want to stick fast to a single place like a plant and take root there?"

[37] "Why not? It's pleasant."

"Of course it is. But so is a sauce or a beautiful woman. Isn't that in effect what hedonists say? [38] Don't you realize which group of people it is whose words you echoed? They're Epicureans and bum boys.* You follow their practices and you hold their views—and then you quote Zeno and Socrates to us? Won't you hurl away from yourself, as far as you can, these alien trappings with which you adorn yourself despite their unsuitability for you? [39] All these people want to do is sleep without being disturbed and get up at their leisure, and then once they're up, they want to take their ease, yawn, and wash their faces, and then read and write as the fancy takes them, and then talk some nonsense that, whatever it may be, will meet with praise from their friends, and then go out for a stroll, but not for long, and then take a bath, and then eat, and then lie down in the kind of bed in which it is likely that such people sleep. Need I say more? It's not hard to guess what it would be.

[40] "All right, then, let's also see the way of life that you long to lead, as an adherent of truth and an emulator of Socrates and Diogenes. What do you want to do in Athens? Exactly the things I've been saying? Nothing different? Then why call yourself a Stoic? [41] People who falsely claim to be citizens of Rome are severely punished: should people who falsely lay claim to such a great and distinguished calling and name get away with it scot-free? [42] But perhaps it's impossible to get away with it. Perhaps there's a law—a divine, powerful, and inescapable law—that exacts the greatest penalties from those who commit the greatest wrongs. How is this law worded? [43] 'Anyone who affects qualities that do not pertain to him shall be a charlatan, an impostor. Anyone who refuses to be compliant to the divine dispensation shall be an object of contempt, a slave; he shall feel distress, envy, pity, and in short shall be miserable and querulous.'"

[44] "So are you saying that I should curry his favor?* That I should make my way to his door?"

"If that seems the reasonable thing to do for the sake of your country, your family, or humankind in general, why not go? You're not ashamed to go to the door of a cobbler when you need shoes, or to the door of a market gardener when you need lettuce, so why be ashamed to go to the doors of rich men when you have some similar need?"

[45] "Yes, but I find nothing admirable in a cobbler."

"Don't in a rich man either."

"Nor is a gardener a person I'd flatter."

"Don't flatter a rich man either."

[46] "Then how am I to get what I need?"

"Am I suggesting you go so that you can get what you need? Aren't I just saying that you should go in order to do what's right for you?"

[47] "In that case, why would I go at all?"

"To have gone. To have performed your function as a citizen, a brother, a friend. [48] Moreover, you should remember that it's a cobbler you've come to, a seller of vegetables, who has power over nothing that's important, nothing that deserves respect, even if he asks a high price for it. You're going there for the equivalent of lettuces, and they sell for an obol, not a talent. [49] Apply this to the present case. Is the matter important enough for me to go to his door? Very well, I'll go. Is it worth discussing? Very well, I'll discuss it with him. But if I have to kiss his hand and flatter him with words of praise, forget it. That's paying a talent. Destroying the good citizen and the friend in me is no help to anyone—not to me, not to the city, not to my friends."

[50] "But if you're unsuccessful, it will look as though you didn't really try."

"You're forgetting again why you'll have gone. Don't you know that a truly good person does nothing for the sake of appearances but only for the sake of doing it right?"

[51] "But what does he gain from acting rightly?"

"What does someone gain from writing the name 'Dion' as it's supposed to be written? The writing of it."

"There's no actual reward, then?"

"Are you asking whether there's any greater reward for a good man than acting rightly and fairly? [52] At Olympia, you don't want more, but you think it enough to have received an Olympic crown.* Does it strike you as such a trivial and worthless thing, being a truly good person and a happy one? [53] This is the purpose for which you were put in this great city by the gods. Now that it's your duty to set your hand to work that is proper to a man, are you longing for nurses and the breast? Does the weeping of foolish women sway you and soften your resolve? Are you going to remain a child forever and never grow up? Don't you realize that childish behavior becomes more ridiculous the older a person gets?

[54] "In Athens, did you see no one when you went to his house?"

"No, I saw the man I wanted to see."

"The same goes in this case too: if he's the man you want to see, you'll see the man you want to see. Just do so without demeaning yourself, and without desire or aversion, and then all will be well with you. [55] But that doesn't depend on your going to his house or standing in his doorway, but on an internal factor, your judgments. [56] When you've learned not to value things that are external to you and aren't subject to your will, when you realize that none of them is yours but that the only things that are up to you are assessing things correctly and your beliefs, inclinations, desires, and aversions—under these circumstances, there's no point to flattery or obsequiousness, is there? Under these circumstances, why miss the peace and quiet you enjoyed there and your familiar haunts? [57] Wait a bit and places here will be familiar to you in their turn. And then, if you're so small-minded, weep and moan all over again when it's time for you to leave these places as well."

[58] "So how do I show affection for my family?"

"As a noble person and as one blessed with good fortune. Reason never wants anyone to be obsequious, submissive, dependent on someone else, or the kind of person who might find fault with God or another human being. [59] So show affection as one who observes these rules. But if this affection—or whatever it is that you call by that name—is going to turn you into a pathetic slave, it does you no good to be affectionate. [60] What's stopping you from loving someone knowing that he's mortal and is likely to leave for elsewhere? Didn't Socrates love his sons? He did, but as a free man and as one who bears in mind that his primary relationship should be with the gods. [61] That's why he consistently behaved as was appropriate for a good man, not just when delivering his defense speech but when proposing a counterpenalty as well,* and even before his trial, when he was serving on the Council or in the army.

[62] "But we find all sorts of excuses for debasing ourselves; for some it's a child, for others a mother or a brother. [63] But it's wrong for anyone to make us miserable; rather, everyone should make us happy, and especially God, because that's what he created us for. [64] Consider now: was there anyone Diogenes didn't love? Look at all the hardship and bodily abuse he gladly accepted for the common good of humankind. That's how kind and benevolent he was. [65] But how did he love people? As was proper for a servant of Zeus, in that he cared for people and at the same time deferred to God. [66] That's why he was the only one whose country was the whole world rather than any particular place.* When he was taken captive, he didn't miss Athens and his friends and acquaintances there but got on good

terms with the pirates themselves and tried to reform them. And later, after he'd been sold into slavery in Corinth, he lived exactly as he had earlier in Athens, and if he'd ended up in Perrhaebia, he'd have done the same there as well.*

[67] "That's how freedom is achieved. That's why he used to say, 'Slavery became a thing of the past for me after Antisthenes set me free.'* [68] How did Antisthenes set him free? Listen to what he says: 'He taught me what's mine and what isn't. Possessions aren't mine. Relatives, family, friends, fame, familiar places, familiar patterns of life—he taught me that none of these are mine.' [69] 'What is yours, then?' 'The use of impressions. He showed me that this is something I have that's unimpeded and unconstrained. No one can obstruct me and no one can compel me to use impressions except as I wish. [70] So who can have power over me? Philip? Alexander? Perdiccas? The Great King?* How could they? After all, anyone who's going to be subjugated by another person must first be subjugated for a long time by things.'*

[71] "So a person over whom pleasure, pain, reputation, and wealth have no power, and who's capable, when it seems the right thing to do, of spitting his entire body at someone and departing*—whose slave can he be, whose subject? [72] If Diogenes had succumbed to the pleasures of living in Athens, he'd have been under everyone's thumb, and anyone who was stronger than him would have had the power to cause him distress. [73] Can you imagine him wheedling the pirates into selling him to some Athenian or other, so that he could see fair Piraeus again, and the Long Walls, and the Acropolis?* [74] See the sights, slave, but what kind of person will you be? A despicable slave. What good will it do you?"

"I'm no slave, but a free man."

[75] "Are you free? Prove it. Look, someone has laid hold of you— it's the person who's currently plucking you out of your familiar way of life—and he says, 'You're my slave, because it's up to me to stop you living as you wish. It's up to me to set you free or bring you low. I can put a smile back on your face if I choose, and off you'll go to Athens in high spirits.' [76] What do you say to this man, who's made a slave of you? What kind of manumitter can you present him with?* Or perhaps you won't make eye contact at all with him and, rather than going through the whole procedure, you'll just beg him to let you

FIGURE 6. View from Philopappos Hill of the Athenian Acropolis. Epictetus refused to see anything in the famed beauty and majesty of the Athenian Acropolis except "blocks of stone and a prettified rock" (2.16.33). In his view, anything made by human hands was insignificant compared to the natural beauty of the world, made by God.

Photo by Alexander Savin, Wikimedia Commons (CC BY-SA 3.0 [https://creativecommons.org/licenses/by-sa/3.0/deed.en])

go. [77] Man, you should be happy to go off to prison! You should eagerly run ahead of those who are taking you there! And then not only are you reluctant to live in Rome, but you long for Greece? And when it's time for you to die, are you going to use that as another occasion to come to us bewailing the fact that you're never going to see Athens again or stroll in the Lyceum?*

[78] "Was it for this that you left home? Was this why you wanted to meet someone who could do you good? What good? To help you analyze syllogisms more fluently, or investigate hypothetical arguments? Was it because you wanted to return home with these abilities that you left your brother, country, friends, and family? [79] In other words, you didn't travel in search of self-possession and peace of mind, did you? It wasn't so that, once you'd become immune to injury, you could stop blaming and criticizing others; it wasn't to make it impossible for anyone to do you wrong, so that you could preserve your various relationships with others without obstruction.

[80] What excellent goods you've supplied yourself with: syllogisms, changing arguments, and hypotheticals! Why not go and sit in the marketplace, if you like, and hang out a sign, as herbalists do?

[81] "Actually, will you please deny knowing all the things you've learned, so as not to have philosophical theories maligned as useless? What harm has philosophy ever done you? What wrong has Chrysippus done you, to make you want to prove by your behavior that he labored in vain? Weren't the troubles you had at home enough for you? Look at all the pain and grief they caused you, with no traveling involved. Why have you added to their number? [82] And if you ever make new friends and acquaintances, they'll just give you more reasons to feel sorry for yourself, and so will your becoming attached to a new place. What reason do you have for living, then? Is it so that you can surround yourself with more and more ways to make yourself miserable? [83] And you call this affection? Man, what kind of affection is that? If it's a good thing, its outcome is never bad; if it's bad, it's no concern of mine. I was born for things that are good for me, not for those that are bad.

[84] "How can we train ourselves in this regard? First, the highest and principal discipline, which stands right at the entrance, so to speak, is that whenever you become attached to anything, don't treat it as something irremovable, but as though it belonged to the same category as a pot or a cup, so that when it gets broken, you remember what it was and don't get upset. [85] The same goes for what we've been talking about as well. If you kiss your child or your brother or your friend, never give the impression free rein. Don't allow it to expand as much as it wants, but hold it back: curb it in the same way that those who stand behind generals as they're celebrating a triumph remind them of their humanity.* [86] In much the same way, you, too, should remind yourself that what you love is mortal. It isn't something that belongs to you; it's been given to you for the time being, not as something irremovable or permanent. It resembles a fig or grapes, in the sense that they arrive at a particular time of the year and it would be stupid to long for them in winter. [87] So if you long for your son or your friend at a time when they aren't given to you, you're longing for a fig in winter, believe me. As winter is to a fig, so every circumstance given by the universe is to the things that are destroyed by that circumstance.

[88] "Moreover, at the very time that you're taking pleasure in something, present yourself with the opposite impressions. Can there be any harm in murmuring in an undertone as you kiss your child, 'Tomorrow you will die'? And the same goes for your friend: 'Tomorrow you'll leave the country, or I will, and we won't see each other again.'"

[89] "But these are words of ill omen."*

"Yes, and so are some incantations, but because they do good, I don't mind—just so long as they do good.* When you call a word 'ill-omened,' you mean that it portends something bad, don't you? [90] 'Cowardice' is ill-omened, 'abasement' is ill-omened, and so are 'grief,' 'distress,' and 'shamelessness.' They're all words of ill omen. But we shouldn't hesitate to speak them, either, to help us protect ourselves against the things to which the words refer. [91] Are you saying that a word is ill-omened if it indicates a natural event? Then you'd have to say that it's inauspicious for wheat to be harvested, because it indicates the destruction of the wheat, though not of the universe. You'd have to say that it's inauspicious for leaves to fall, for a fig to be replaced by a dried fig, and a grape by a raisin. [92] I mean, all these are changes of things that existed before into other things. It's not a matter of destruction but of ordered management and regulation. [93] The same goes for traveling abroad: it's a change, though just a small one. The same goes for death: it's a change, a greater one, from what is now, not to what is not, but to what is not now."*

[94] "So I'll no longer exist."

"You won't exist, but something else will, which the universe needs at that moment. After all, you too were born not at a time of your choosing but when the universe needed you. [95] That's why a truly good person, who remembers who he is, where he's come from, and by whom he was created, focuses his attention on one thing alone, how he may occupy his station in a disciplined manner and in obedience to God. [96] 'Do you still want me? I shall remain free and honorable, as you intended me to be, because you created me to be, in myself, unimpeded. [97] And now you have no further need of me? All right. No one else but you has been responsible for my being here up until now, and now in obedience to you I take my leave.' [98] 'And what is your disposition as you leave?' 'Again, as you intended me to be—as a free man, as your servant, as one who hearkens to your commands and prohibitions. [99] But as long as I linger here in your service, what do you want me to be? A senator or a private citizen? A foot soldier or a general? A teacher or the head of a household? Whatever post you entrust me with, and whatever rank, I shall die ten thousand times, as Socrates says, before abandoning it.* [100] And where would you like me to be? Rome? Athens? Thebes? Gyara? All I ask is that you are mindful of me there. [101] If you send me somewhere where a life in accord with nature is not humanly possible, I shall depart—not out of disobedience to you but on the assumption that you're giving me the signal to retreat. I'm not leaving you—as if that were possible!—but I see that you have no need of me. [102] However, if a life in accord with nature is possible for me, I shan't go looking for any place other than where I am, or people other than those I'm with.'

[103] "Keep these ideas at hand night and day. Write them down, read them, talk them over with yourself and with a friend: 'Can you help me in this regard?' Then go to someone else, and someone else again. [104] And then, if something happens that is generally held to be undesirable, the first result will be that you'll gain immediate relief because the event won't take you by surprise. [105] In every situation, you see, 'I knew my son was mortal' is an important reminder.* That's what you'll say, along with 'I knew I was mortal,' 'I knew I was likely to travel abroad,' 'I knew I was liable to banishment,' 'I knew I might be hauled off to prison.' [106] And then, if you reflect by yourself and try to find the place from where the event originated, in no time at all you'll remember that 'It's one of those things that aren't subject to will and aren't mine, so what's it to me?'

[107] "Then you come to the nub of the matter: 'Who was it who actually ordered up the event?' It was the ruler or general, the city, the city's laws. 'I welcome it, then, because I must always obey the law in everything.' [108] And then, when your imagination plagues you— which is something that isn't up to you—fight back with your reason, wrestle it down, don't let it prevail or advance to the next stage, that of envisaging everything it would like to happen happening just as it would like. [109] If you're in Gyara, don't imagine how things are in Rome and all the pleasant aspects of life there that you'd enjoy if you ever got back. No, since Gyara is where you've been posted, be strong and live in Gyara as someone living in Gyara should. And if

you're in Rome, don't imagine life in Athens, but apply yourself only to your life where you are.

[110] "Then, instead of all those other pleasures, introduce the pleasure that comes from the awareness that you're obeying God—that you are in actual fact, not just notionally, doing what a truly good person should do. [111] And what a pleasure it is to be able to say to oneself, 'I'm now putting into practice the apparently strange ideas that others solemnly talk about in the schools. It's my virtues that they sit there and expound, it's me they research, and it's me they praise. [112] Zeus wanted me to have proof of all this in my own person; he wanted to be sure that I was the right kind of soldier and citizen, and he wanted to present me to the rest of the world to testify about things that aren't subject to will: "See that your fears are groundless and your cravings futile. Don't look for what's good for you outside yourselves. Look for it inside yourselves, otherwise you won't find it." [113] It's for this that Zeus at one time brings me here and at another sends me elsewhere. He puts me on display as someone who isn't wealthy, has no political power, and isn't in good health. He packs me off to Gyara or throws me in prison. It isn't because he hates me. Perish the thought! Does anyone hate his best servant? Nor is it because he's neglecting me, seeing that he doesn't neglect even the least of his creatures. He's training me and using me to testify to everyone else. [114] When I've been assigned such an important task, how can I care anymore where I am or who I'm with or what people say about me? Am I not focused with all my being on God, on his instructions and commands?'

[115] "If you have these thoughts constantly at hand, if you rehearse them to yourself and make them readily available, you'll never need consolation or encouragement. [116] What's disgraceful isn't not having enough to eat, but not being rational enough to be free of fear and distress. [117] But once you've acquired immunity to distress and fear, will any tyrant, guardsman, or courtier of Caesar's exist for you? When you've been given such an important position by Zeus, will you be hurt by anyone else's appointment or by those who sacrifice on the Capitol to take the auspices?* [118] Just don't flaunt your position or boast about it, but demonstrate your caliber by your actions. And if no one notices, let it be enough that you're healthy and happy yourself."

3.25

To those who fail to see their projects through to completion

[1] "Consider all the things you originally intended to do: ask your-self which of them you brought to completion and which you didn't, and see how it pleases you to recall the former and distresses you to recall the latter. If you can, accept even those that you let slip, [2] be-cause shrinking back isn't an option for those who are engaged in the greatest of all contests, and they must take the blows as well. [3] The contest before us isn't equivalent to wrestling and pancratium, where, according as he succeeds or fails, a man may be thought the greatest or of little worth—and, by Zeus, to be the most blessed or the most wretched person in the world.* No, what's at stake in the contest before us is real success and happiness. [4] Moreover, in this contest, even if we fail, there's nothing to stop us from competing again, and we don't have to wait another four years for the next Olympics. As soon as a man has recovered and is back to his old self, and as soon as he can bring the same commitment to bear, he can rejoin the compe-tition. And if you fail once more, you can compete once more. And if one day you're victorious, it will be as though you'd never failed.

[5] "Just be sure not to get stuck in the habit and begin to be con-tent with the situation, or you'll end up like a bad athlete who trav-els around the circuit losing fights, as quails do when they run away.* [6] 'I'm overcome by the impression of a beautiful girl. So what? I was similarly overcome the other day, wasn't I?' 'I feel an urge to crit-icize someone. Well, I criticized someone the other day, didn't I?' [7] When you talk like this, it's as though you think you got off unscathed. You're like someone who's advised by his doctor to avoid bathing and who says, 'Well, I bathed the other day, didn't I?' To which the doc-tor would respond, 'All right, but what happened to you after you'd bathed? Didn't you get feverish? Didn't your head ache?' [8] So, in your case, when you criticized someone the other day, wasn't that the action of a malicious person? Of someone who says things that aren't worth saying? Didn't you feed this habit of yours by adding the fuel of further acts of the same kind? And when you were overcome by the girl, did you get away unscathed? [9] Why do you bring up your actions from the other day, then? It seems to me that you should have remembered them in the same way that slaves remember the beat-

ings they've received, to avoid repeating the same mistakes. [10] Not that the cases are the same: for the slaves, it's pain that prompts the memory, but where you and your faults are concerned, what pain do you feel? What penalty do you pay? When did you ever acquire the habit of avoiding bad actions?"

3.26
To those who fear destitution

[1] "Doesn't it make you ashamed to be more cowardly and base than runaway slaves? When they run off and leave their masters, how do they manage? What farms and slaves do they rely on? Don't they purloin a few supplies, enough for the first few days, and then afterward, wherever they go by land or sea, devise one ingenious way after another to keep themselves in food? [2] And what runaway slave ever died of hunger? But you're so frightened of running out of the means of sustenance that you can't sleep at night. [3] You pitiful creature, are you really that blind? Can't you see where lack of the necessaries of life leads? Where does it take you? To the same destination as a fever or a falling rock: death. Haven't you yourself often said as much to your companions? Haven't you often read or written the same sort of thing? How many times have you boasted of your composure at the prospect of death?"

[4] "Yes, but my family will go hungry as well."

"So what? Their hunger will just take them down the same road, won't it? Is their journey any different from yours? Isn't the destination the same? [5] So shouldn't you approach every lack and want without fear by focusing on the destination, where even the super-rich, the holders of the highest offices, and kings and tyrants themselves are bound to go—though you may go there hungry, and they bloated with indigestion and drunkenness? [6] It's not easy to find a beggar who's not old, is it? Have you ever seen one who's not extremely advanced in years? But even though they're cold night and day, lie on the ground, and have no more than the bare minimum to eat, they reach a state where it's almost impossible for them to die. [7] But you, who are unmutilated, with your hands and feet intact—are you so afraid of starving? Are you incapable of drawing water, working as a scribe or a child-minder, guarding someone's doorway?"*

"But it's shameful to be reduced to such straits."

"First learn what's shameful, and then call yourself a philosopher. As things are at the moment, you shouldn't even let anyone else call you one. [8] Can something be a source of shame for you when it's not your doing, you're not responsible for it, and it was only by accident that it happened to you? Things like a headache or a fever? If your parents were poor, or were rich but bequeathed their estate to others, and didn't support you at all while they were alive, is any of this a source of shame for you? [9] Is that what the philosophers taught you? Haven't you ever been told that nothing is shameful unless it's reprehensible, and that only something reprehensible deserves reproof? But who is reproached for something that wasn't his doing, something that he didn't bring about?

[10] "Well, was it your doing that your father is the kind of man he is? Is it possible for you to change him for the better? Is that one of your gifts? So should you be wishing for something that's impossible for you, or feel shame if you fail at it? [11] Is this really the habit that was instilled in you by your study of philosophy, to look to others and expect nothing from yourself? [12] In that case, moan and groan, and eat in fear of having nothing to eat tomorrow. Worry that your slaves might steal something, or run away, or die. [13] Live like that, with never-ending anxiety, because you haven't penetrated beyond the surface of philosophy. In fact, you've besmirched its principles, insofar as it's within your power to do so, by making it look as though they're useless and are no help to those who adopt them. Your goals were never self-possession, peace of mind, and equanimity. You've not attended any teacher for that reason, but you've attended many to learn about syllogisms. You've never tested any of your impressions by yourself, asking yourself, 'Can I bear this or not? What is there left for me to do?'* [14] No, as though you were completely fine and unassailable, you've been spending your time over the last of the domains,* the one that's supposed to give you stability, to make you stable—in what? In your cowardice, your baseness, your admiration of rich people, your unrealized desires, your ineffective aversions? These are the things that you've been concerned to make your unassailable possessions!

[15] "Shouldn't you first have gained something from reason, and then have made sure that you had it securely? Did you ever see any-

one putting a coping stone in place without first having a wall to put it on? What kind of doorkeeper is made to stand where there's no door? [16] From your studies you want to become proficient at proofs—but at proving what? From your studies you want to avoid having your mind unsettled by sophisms—but unsettled from what? [17] Show me first what it is you've got, what it is you're measuring and weighing. And then show me the scales and the bushel measure. Or how much more time will you spend measuring dust? [18] Isn't this what you should be proving: what it is that makes people happy, that allows their affairs to prosper according to their wishes, that enables them never to blame or find fault with anyone, and to submit to the governance of the universe? Prove all this to me."

[19] "Look, here's what I can show you," he said. "I'll analyze syllogisms for you."

"That's a measuring instrument, slave, not the thing to be measured. [20] That's why you're now being punished for your neglect. You're fearful and sleepless, you ask everyone's advice, and if your plans fail to meet with universal approval, you regard them as ill-considered. [21] And then you're frightened of hunger, or so you think. But it's not hunger you're afraid of. No, you're afraid of not having a cook, and another slave to do your shopping, and another to put on your shoes, and another to dress you, and others to massage you, and others to accompany you, [22] so that when you've undressed in the bathhouse and you're stretched out like a victim of crucifixion, you can be massaged all over, and then the trainer can stand over you and say, 'Move over. Give me room at his side. You take his head and let me have his shoulder.' And then when you leave the bathhouse and return home, you can bellow, 'Is no one bringing me food?' and later, 'Clear away the tables! Wipe them down!'

[23] "That's what you're afraid of. You're afraid of not being able to live the life of an invalid. I mean, look, if you want to know how healthy people live, see how slaves or farm laborers live. See how genuine philosophers live—how Socrates did, even though he had a wife and children, or Diogenes, or Cleanthes, even though he was attending classes and working as a drawer of water at the same time.* [24] If this is what you want, you'll have it wherever you find yourself, and you'll live without fear. What will give you this confidence? The only thing that truly inspires confidence—the only thing that's reliable,

unimpeded, and irremovable—in other words, your will. [25] But why have you made yourself so useless and ineffective that no one wants to receive you in his house or have anything to do with you? When an undamaged, usable tool is thrown out, anyone who finds it picks it up and thinks he's done well. No one thinks that about you, however; everyone thinks he's done badly. [26] And so you can't even be as useful as a hound or a cock. Why do you wish to keep on living when this is how you are?

[27] "Is anyone good afraid of running out of food? The blind don't run out of food, nor do the lame, so a good person won't either, will he? A good soldier never fails to find someone to pay him, nor does a good laborer or cobbler, so a good person won't either, will he? [28] Is God that neglectful of his prize exhibits—his servants, his witnesses, the only people he can use as examples for the uneducated, to show that he exists, that his governance of the universe is good, that he doesn't neglect human affairs, and that nothing bad happens to a good person either during his lifetime or after his death?"

[29] "But what if he cuts off the food supply?"

"What else could this mean except that, like a good general, he's given me the signal to retreat?* I obey, I comply, singing the praises of my leader and glorifying his works. [30] I came into this world when he decided I should, and now I'm taking my leave because he's decided that I should, and while I was alive it was my job to sing hymns of praise to God, both to myself and to others, one at a time or in larger numbers. [31] He doesn't give me much; I don't have an abundance, because he doesn't want me to live in luxury. After all, he didn't give much to Heracles, either, and he was his own son; someone else ruled over Argos and Mycenae, while Heracles was a subordinate and toiled away at his labors. [32] And while Eurystheus was what he was, king of neither Argos nor Mycenae, because he didn't even rule himself, Heracles was the ruler and leader of the entire world, both land and sea, because he purged it of injustice and lawlessness, and replaced them with justice and piety. And he did all this by himself, defenseless and alone. [33] And what about Odysseus? When he was shipwrecked and cast ashore, his destitution didn't discourage him or crush his spirit, did it? No, how did he approach the group of girls to ask them for sustenance, which is generally taken to be the most shameful thing one person can beg from another? 'Like a mountain lion.'*

[34] "What gave him this confidence? It wasn't fame or money or political power, but his own strength, or in other words, his judgments about what is and what isn't up to us. [35] Judgments are the only things that make us free and unimpeded; it's judgments that make it possible for a man who's been brought low to raise his head and look the rich and tyrants straight in the eyes. [36] This was the gift that your philosophy teacher was offering you, but instead of departing with confidence, will you tremble with fear for your clothes and your silverware? You pitiful creature, look how you've wasted your time so far!"

[37] "What if I fall ill?"

"You'll bear it well."

"Who'll take care of me?"

"God and your friends."

"I'll have a hard bed to lie on."

"But you'll bear it manfully."

"I won't have a suitable house."

"Then you'll be ill in an unsuitable one."

"Who'll prepare my food?"

"Those who prepare it for others as well. You'll be ill like Manes."*

"And what will be the upshot of my illness?"

[38] "Death, of course. Can't you see that this thing, the source of all human troubles and debasement and cowardice, isn't death, but rather the fear of death? [39] That is what you must train yourself to cope with, that is where all your reasoning should tend, and your exercises and your reading. Then you'll appreciate that this is the only way in which people can be free."

Book 4

4.1
On freedom*

[1] "A person is free if he lives as he wants, if he's not subject to constraint, impediment, or compulsion, if his inclinations are unobstructed, if his desires are never disappointed, and his aversions effectively prevent the occurrence of things he wants to avoid. Now, who wants to go through life in error?"

[2] "No one."

"Who wants to go through life believing things that are false, making overhasty judgments, doing wrong, and being dissolute, querulous, and obsequious?"

"No one."

[3] "So no bad person lives as he wants, and therefore no bad person is free either. [4] Now, who wants to go through life feeling grief, fear, envy, and pity, desiring things but failing to get them, and feeling aversion toward things that he experiences anyway?"

"No one."

[5] "So are there any bad people who are free from grief and fear? Who succeed in avoiding what they feel aversion toward and whose desires are never disappointed?"

"No."

"So, again, no bad person is free. [6] If a two-time consul heard you saying this, he'd forgive you—as long as you added: 'But *you* are a man of wisdom. None of this applies to *you*.' [7] But if you tell him the truth—if you say, 'There's absolutely no difference between you and someone who's been sold to three different masters. You're just as much a slave'—don't expect anything except a beating. [8] 'What do you mean by calling me a slave?' he'll say. 'My father was free, my mother was free, and no one owns me. What's more, I'm a senator and a friend of Caesar, I've served as a consul, and I own a great many slaves.' [9] Well, to begin with, senator, it may be that your father was the same kind of slave that you are, and that your mother was as well, and your grandfather, and all your ancestors in their turn. [10] In any case, even if they were as free as free can be, what's that got to do with you? You could still be a despicable person even if they were honorable, couldn't you? They could be fearless while you're fearful. They could be decent while you're dissolute. Isn't that so?"

[11] "But what's this got to do with being a slave?" he asked.

"Do you think that doing things you don't want to do, acting under compulsion, and feeling sorry for yourself have nothing to do with being a slave?"

[12] "But even so," he says, "is there anyone who can force me to do anything except Caesar, and he's everyone's master?"

[13] "So even you admit that you have one master, at least. And the fact that he's everyone's master, or so you say, shouldn't make you feel any better. It just makes you a slave in a large household, don't you see? [14] It reminds me of how people here in Nicopolis commonly exclaim, 'We're free! Thanks be to the Fortune of Caesar!'* [15] Still, if it's all right with you, let's leave Caesar out of it for now. Just tell me this: have you ever been in love with anyone—a girl or a boy, slave or free?"

[16] "How is this relevant to the issue of slavery or freedom?"

[17] "Did your beloved never tell you to do something you didn't want to do? Did you never flatter your slave? Did you never kiss his feet? And yet if you were forced to kiss *Caesar's* feet, you'd regard it as an outrage and the acme of tyranny. [18] Isn't that just what slavery is? Did you never go out at night somewhere you didn't want to go, or spend more than you wanted to? Did you never give voice to laments and complaints, and put up with being insulted and having the door shut in your face?

[19] "If it would embarrass you to confess your own experiences, consider what Thrasonides says and does—someone who served on many campaigns, possibly more even than you.* In the first place, he went out after dark, when Getas didn't dare to (and if Thrasonides had insisted on it, Getas would have expressed his resentment loudly

FIGURE 7. The city wall of Nicopolis. Epictetus spent the last thirty-five or so years of his life in Nicopolis, the capital of the Roman province of Epirus in Greece. The surviving walls give some idea of the magnificence of the place.

Photo by Robin Waterfield

and often, and bewailed his bitter slavery). [20] And then what does Thrasonides say? 'A cheap girl has enslaved me, something not a single one of my enemies ever managed to do.' [21] You pitiful creature, the slave of a girl, and a cheap one at that! Why do you call yourself free, then? And why bring up your campaigns? [22] And then he demands his sword and when, out of the goodness of his heart, Getas refuses to give it to him,* he gets cross with him. He sends gifts to the girl, who hates him, and pleads with her with tears in his eyes, and later, when he meets with a little success, he's overjoyed. [23] But even then, was he in any sense untouched by longing or fear? And so, was he free?

[24] "Think about how we employ the concept of freedom in the case of animals. [25] People rear tame lions in cages and feed them, and some people travel around with them. But would anyone call such a lion free? Isn't it the case that the softer the life it leads, the more it's enslaved? Is there any lion, supposing it had consciousness

and the ability to reason, that would want to be one of these tame lions? [26] And what about these birds? When they're caught and brought up in cages, look at what they go through in their attempts to escape. Some of them starve to death rather than live like that, [27] while those that live barely do so, they're so run-down and ailing, and they invariably escape if they find an opening. This goes to show how much they desire their natural state of freedom and long to be independent and unimpeded. [28] 'Why is it so bad for you to be caged?' 'What a question! I was made to fly wherever I want, to live in the open air, to sing when I want. You rob me of all this and then you ask why it's bad for me?'

[29] "That's why we should call free only those creatures that refuse to tolerate captivity and instead escape by dying as soon as they're caught. [30] Hence also Diogenes says somewhere that one way to procure freedom is to think little of dying, and in a letter to the Persian king he says,* 'You're as little able to enslave the Athenians are you are fish.' [31] 'What do you mean? I'll make them my captives, won't I?' 'If you do,' says Diogenes, 'they'll immediately take their leave of you, like fish. As soon as you catch a fish, it dies, and if the Athenians die, too, once they've been caught, what good will all your armament have done you?' [32] These are the words of a free man, who has taken the matter seriously enough to have looked into it, and, as one might have expected, he discovered the truth. But if you look for it where it's not to be found, it's hardly surprising if you never find it, is it?

[33] "A slave is always praying to be set free. Why? Do you think it's because he longs to enrich the collectors of the 5 percent tax?* No, it's because he believes that up until now he's lived a restricted and unhappy life because of being denied his freedom. [34] 'If I'm free,' he says, 'I shall immediately be completely happy, I won't have to take anyone else into consideration, I shall talk to everyone as their equal rather than as someone who's different, I'll go where I like, I'll travel from a place of my choosing to a destination of my choosing.' [35] But then, no sooner has he gained his freedom than he finds he has nowhere to eat, so he looks for someone to flatter, at whose house he can eat. And then he either prostitutes himself, with all the horrors that entails; he may have found a manger at which to eat, but he's fallen into a far harsher slavery than before. [36] Or even if he does

well for himself, he falls in love with a low girl, uncouth fellow that he is, and in his misery sheds tears of regret and longs to be a slave again. [37] 'How was slavery bad for me? Someone else supplied me with clothes and shoes, fed me, and looked after me when I was ill. My service to him wasn't arduous. But at the moment—poor me!— look at all I have to suffer! I'm a slave to several masters instead of just one! [38] Nevertheless, if I get the right to wear rings,'* he goes on, 'then I'll live in perfect contentment and happiness.' So first he suffers as he deserves in order to get the rings, and then once he's got them, it's the same old story. [39] 'If I serve in the army,' he says, 'I'll put an end to all my troubles.' So he joins up, suffers the kind of pain that's usually reserved for felons, but still asks to go out on a second campaign, and a third.* [40] And then, when he crowns his career by becoming a senator, that's when he becomes an assembly-attending slave, that's when his slavery is of the fairest and most splendid kind.

[41] "There's no need for such stupidity. He needs to learn, as Socrates used to say, the nature of each and every thing, and not apply his preconceptions haphazardly to particular entities.* [42] The cause of all human troubles, you see, is the inability to apply preconceptions to particular instances. [43] We differ in our opinions. One person thinks he's unwell when that's not the case at all, and he's just misapplying his preconceptions. Another person thinks he's poor, another that he has a harsh father or mother, another that Caesar doesn't think kindly of him. All this is one thing and one thing only: not knowing how to apply one's preconceptions. [44] After all, is there anyone who doesn't have a preconception of badness, to the effect that it's harmful, to be avoided, and to be eliminated in every way possible? There's no conflict between preconceptions, but conflict arises when one comes to apply them.

[45] "So what is this 'bad,' that's harmful and to be avoided? He says that it's not being on good terms with Caesar. He missed the mark; he misapplied his preconception. He's making difficulties for himself and trying to get something that's irrelevant to the case in hand, because even if he got to be Caesar's friend, he'd still have failed in his quest. [46] I mean, what is it that everyone is seeking? Self-possession, happiness, the ability to act as they want without being impeded or constrained. So when he becomes Caesar's friend, has he stopped being liable to impediment and constraint? Is he

self-possessed? Is he content? Whom shall we ask? What better witness do we have than this very person, the one who's become Caesar's friend? [47] Step up and tell us when you slept more peacefully, now or before you became Caesar's friend? The answer comes straight back: 'In the name of the gods, shut up! Don't make fun of my situation! You have no idea what I have to put up with, pitiful creature that I am. I'm denied any chance of sleep, what with people coming to tell me that Caesar's already awake, or that he's emerging from his chambers. Then there's all the stress and the worry.'

[48] "All right, but when did you enjoy your meals more, now or before? Listen to his reply on this matter too. He says that it causes him pain not to receive an invitation from Caesar, and that if he *is* invited to join him, he's like a slave at a master's table, since he's constantly worried about making a fool of himself by something he says or does. And what's he afraid of, do you think? Of being flogged like a slave? He should be so lucky! No, as befits such a great man, a friend of Caesar, he's afraid of losing his head. [49] And when did you enjoy more peaceful bathing? When did you have more time to exercise? In short, which life would you prefer, the one you have now or the one you had before? [50] I can assure you that no one is so dense or incurable† that he doesn't bewail his misfortunes more the closer he gets to Caesar.

[51] "So since neither those who are called kings nor the friends of kings live as they want, who is free? Seek and you shall find, seeing that nature has endowed you with the resources to discover the truth.* But if you're unable to use these resources on your own to infer the answer, listen to those who have completed the quest. [52] What do they say? Do you regard freedom as a good thing? 'There's no greater good.' Is it possible for anyone who's in possession of this supreme good to be unhappy or miserable? 'No.' So whenever you see people who are unhappy, discontented, or sad, you'll confidently assert that they aren't free. 'That's right.' [53] So we're no longer talking about buying and selling and so on—the acquiring of property by commercial means, that is.* I mean, if you're right to have made these concessions, then if the Great King is unhappy, he isn't free,* and the same goes for a lesser king, a man of consular rank, and a man who's twice been consul."

"Agreed."

[54] "Here's another point on which I'd like to hear your answer. Do you think that freedom is a great and noble thing, and valuable?"

"Of course."

"So is it possible for someone who's in possession of such a great, valuable, and noble thing to demean himself?"

"No, it's not."

[55] "So when you see someone groveling to another person or flattering him insincerely, you'll confidently affirm that he's not free either. And you'll do so not only if his behavior is prompted by his wanting some food, but even if it's a governorship or a consulship he's after. In fact, the former, those who behave that way for the sake of petty things, you'll call minor slaves, and you'll call the latter, as they deserve, major slaves."

"Again, agreed."

[56] "Now, do you think that freedom entails independence and self-determination?"

"Of course."

"So you'll confidently affirm that anyone who can be impeded and constrained by another person isn't free. [57] You won't be looking at his grandfathers and great-grandfathers or trying to find out if any buying and selling was involved, but if you detect him inwardly say-ing 'Master' and doing so with feeling, call him a slave even if he's preceded by twelve fasces.* And if you hear him saying, 'Poor me! How I'm suffering!' call him a slave. In short, if you see him bemoan-ing his lot, complaining, and expressing discontent, call him a slave in a purple-bordered toga. [58] And even if he does none of these things, don't call him free until you've examined his judgments to see whether they're constrained and impeded in any way and make him discontented. And if you find that to be so, call him a slave on a break for the Saturnalia.* Say that his master is away from home, but he'll soon be back, and then you'll see how the slave will suffer."

[59] "Who's the master who'll be back?"

"Anyone who has the power to procure for him or deny to him any of the things he wants."

"So we have a great many masters, do we?"

"Yes, because, before these masters, we first enslave ourselves to things, and there are a great many things. That's why people who control our access to any of these things are bound to be our masters. [60] I mean, look, it isn't actually Caesar that people fear, but death, exile, the confiscation of property, prison, loss of citizenship. Nor does anyone love Caesar, either, unless Caesar is a man of great merit, but we love wealth, the tribunate, the praetorship, the consulship. As long as we love, hate, and dread these things, those who control our access to them are bound to be our masters. [61] That's why we worship them as though they were gods, because we think of the divine in terms of its ability to confer the greatest benefits, and then we wrongly add the premise, 'This man has the power to confer the greatest benefits.' And what follows from these premises is necessarily an invalid inference.

[62] "What is it, then, that makes a person unimpeded and independent? It's not wealth, consulship, governorship, or kingship, so we need to come up with something else instead. [63] Well, what is it that makes us unimpeded or unobstructed when writing?"

"Knowing how to write."

"And when playing the lyre?"

"Knowing how to play the lyre."

[64] "So in life, then, it must be knowing how to live. Now, you've already taken this in as a general principle, but consider it also when it's applied to particular cases. Is it possible for someone to be unimpeded if he wants to have something that's up to others?"

"No."

"Is it possible for him to be unobstructed?"

"No."

[65] "So he's not free either. Now consider this. Is there nothing we have that's up to us alone, or is everything up to us alone, or are some things up to us and some things up to others?"

[66] "What do you mean?"

"Is wanting your body to have no defects up to you or not?"

"It's not."

"Wanting it to be healthy?"

"Nor is that either."

"Wanting it to be attractive?"

"Nor that either."

"Wanting it to live or die?"

"Nor that either."

"In other words, your body isn't yours but is subject to anything that's stronger than it."

"Agreed."

[67] "Now consider your land: is it up to you to have land when you want, for as long as you want, and in the condition you want?"

"No."

"What about your slaves?"

"No."

"Your clothes?"

"No."

"Your house?"

"No."

"Your horses?"

"None of these things is up to me."

"And if you want your children not to die under any circumstances, or your wife, brother, or friends, is that up to you?"

"No, that isn't either."

[68] "So is there nothing you have that's independent and exclusively up to you, or do you have something of that kind?"

"I don't know."

[69] "Well, look at it this way. Here's a question for you. Can anyone make you assent to a falsehood?"

"No."

"So in the domain of assent, you're unimpeded and unobstructed."

"Agreed."

[70] "Now, can anyone force you to have an inclination for something you don't want?"

"Yes, they can. When someone threatens me with death or imprisonment, he's forcing me to incline toward it."

"But if you regard death and imprisonment as unimportant, would you pay him any mind?"

"No."

[71] "And is regarding death as unimportant up to you or not?"

"It is."

"So, then, are your inclinations up to you or not?"

"All right, yes, they're up to me."

"And disinclination? That must be up to you as well."

[72] "What if I have an inclination to go for a walk and someone stops me?"

"What in you will he be impeding? Your faculty of assent?"

"No, my body."

"Quite, just as he'd impede a rock."

"All right, but the point is that I won't be going for a walk."

[73] "Who told you that going for a walk is up to you and not liable to impediment? What *I've* been saying is that the only unimpeded thing is inclination. As for making use of the body and having it do what you want, you've known for a long while that it's not up to you at all."

"I grant you that as well."

[74] "Can anyone force you to desire something you don't want?"

"No."

"What about having a purpose or an objective, or, to generalize, making use of the impressions that occur to you?"

[75] "No, no one can compel me in this respect either. But when I desire something, people can stop me getting it."

"If you desire something that's yours, something that isn't liable to external impediment, how can they stop you?"

[76] "So I shouldn't desire health?"

"No, nor anything else that isn't yours. [77] Anything that isn't yours to acquire or keep as and when you want isn't yours. You should keep your hands well off it, but what's far more important is to keep from desiring it. Otherwise, you'll have turned yourself into a slave. You'll have bowed your neck to the yoke if you value anything that isn't yours, if you become attached to anything that depends on someone else and is perishable."

[78] "So is my arm not mine?"

"It's part of you, but in itself it's clay, liable to impediment or constraint, a slave to everything that's stronger than it. [79] But why am I telling you just about your arm? You should treat your entire body as though it were a donkey with a load, as long as you can, as long as you have that possibility. But if it's pressed into public service and a soldier commandeers it, let it go, don't resist or complain. Otherwise, you'll get a beating and lose your donkey just the same. [80] But if this should be your attitude toward your body, consider what that implies for all those other things that are procured for the sake of the body. If your body is a donkey, they're all just donkey bridles, packsaddles, shoes, barley, and hay. Let them go, cut them loose more quickly and readily than you let go of the donkey itself. [81] Once you've prepared and trained yourself in this way, so that you're able to distinguish what isn't yours from what is, what's liable to impediment from what isn't, and once you're able to regard the latter as your concern and the former as nothing to you, and once your desire is directed toward the latter and your aversion toward the former, will there be anyone for you to fear?"

"No."

[82] "That's right, because there'll be nothing for you to be fearful about, will there? Not the things that are yours, where goodness and badness are essentially located, because they aren't subject to anyone else's control. Who can deprive you of them? Who can obstruct them? No one, any more than he could obstruct God. [83] But will you be fearful for your body and your property—for things that aren't yours, things that are no concern of yours? But isn't that exactly what you've been training yourself for right from the start, to be able to distinguish what's yours from what isn't, what's up to you from what isn't, what's liable to impediment from what isn't? Why have you been going to the philosophers? To be just as wretched and miserable as before? [84] In that case, you won't be free of fear and mental turmoil. And will distress be anything to you? I ask because fear arises when things are anticipated and distress when they're present. And will there be anything you still crave? You'll have a moderate and settled desire for things that are subject to will, inasmuch as they're both yours and present, but you'll desire nothing that isn't subject to will, and so you'll have eliminated that irrational element, with all its pushiness and immoderate urgency. [85] When this is your attitude toward things, is there anyone on earth who can make you fearful? After all, what is it about a person that might make another person fear him—the way he looks, the way he talks, the way he behaves in general toward him? No more is a horse is an object of fear to another horse, or a dog to a dog, or a bee to a bee. No, it's *things* that make us afraid, and when a person has the ability to procure them for someone else or deny them to him, that's when he becomes an object of fear.

[86] "How is a citadel destroyed? Not by iron or fire, but by judgments. We may be able to seize an actual citadel in a city, but that still

leaves us with the citadel of fever, the citadel of attractive women, and in short, the citadel within us, doesn't it? Nor have we driven out our internal tyrants, those who are set over us on a daily basis—not that they're always the same, since they change from time to time. [87] But our starting point, the point from which we set out to seize the citadel and expel the tyrants, has to be this: we must let go of our body and its parts and faculties, our possessions, reputation, public offices, honors, children, brothers, and friends, and regard all these things as not ours. [88] And if the tyrants are expelled from the citadel, is there any need for me to go on to demolish it, at any rate on my account? If it remains intact, what harm does it do me? Why should I expel the tyrants' bodyguards? They don't affect me. They wield their rods and poles and daggers against other people.* [89] I've never been prevented from doing what I want, nor have I been forced to do what I don't want. Both are impossible, because I've submitted my inclinations to God. He wants me to have a fever; that's what I want too. He wants me to have an inclination for something; that's what I want too. He wants me to desire; that's what I want too. He wants me to get something; that's what I want too. Unless he wants something, I don't want it. [90] And so I'm willing to die or be tortured. Under these circumstances, who can impede or constrain me contrary to my own judgment? No one, any more than he could impede or constrain Zeus.

[91] "This is also what the more cautious kind of traveler does. He's heard that the road is infested with robbers. He doesn't dare to set out on his own, so he waits for a travel companion—an ambassador, a quaestor, a proconsul*—and travels in safety by attaching himself to their party. [92] A sensible person does the same in life. 'There are many bands of robbers—tyrants, storms, financial setbacks, losing those that I hold most dear. [93] Where is safety to be found? How is one to travel without being set upon by robbers? What kind of companion should one wait for in order to complete a journey in safety? [94] To whom should one attach oneself? To just anyone? To a rich man? To someone of consular rank? What good will that do me? He himself is vulnerable to being stripped naked and to moaning and dejection. And what if my companion turns against me himself and is the one who robs me? [95] What shall I do? I'll become a friend of Caesar. No one will do me wrong if I'm close to him. But what a lot I

have to suffer and endure first in order to become his friend! Look at all the times I have to be robbed, and all the people who'll rob me! And then if I do become his friend—well, he's just as mortal as anyone else. [96] And if something should go wrong and turn him into my enemy? Might it not perhaps be better for me to retreat somewhere, to a desert? Hang on, though. Fever can find its way to a desert, can't it? [97] So what am I to do? Is it impossible to find a travel companion who's safe, trustworthy, and strong, and who won't intrigue against me?' [98] These are the thoughts that go through his mind, and he realizes that it's only if he attaches himself to God that he'll complete his journey in safety."

[99] "What do you mean by 'attach himself'?"

"I mean that what God wants, he wants too, and what God doesn't want, he doesn't want either."

"How does this come about?"

[100] "Just by observing God's acts and the way he governs the universe. What has he given me that belongs to me and is independent, and what has he kept for himself? He's given me the things that are subject to will, and he's made them up to me, unobstructed, and unimpeded. How could he have made my body, a thing of clay, immune to impediment? So he assigned it its place in the cosmic cycle,* along with my property, furniture, house, children, and wife. [101] So why would I fight God? Why would I want things that aren't subject to my wishes, things that weren't unconditionally given to me? How do I possess them? As conditionally as they were given and for as long as they're available to me. But the giver can take them away again. So what would be the point of resistance? Not to mention how stupid it would be of me to try to use force against one who is stronger than me—and, more importantly, how wrong it would be. [102] After all, how did I come to have these things when I came into the world? They were gifts from my father.* And who gave them to him? Who made the sun, the fruits of the earth, the seasons? Who made human society and community?

[103] "When you've been given everything, including your own self, by someone else, are you going to resent it and complain if the giver takes something from you? [104] Who are you? For what purpose were you born? Wasn't it he who brought you into the world? Wasn't it he who showed you the light? Who gave you helpmates,

senses, rationality? When he brought you into the world, what kind of being were you? A mortal one, right? One who would live here on earth along with a scrap of flesh, to witness his governance and play a small part in this procession, this gala that he's laid on. [105] So shouldn't you use your allotted time to be a spectator of the pageant and the festival? And then, when he leads you away, shouldn't you go with reverence, thanking him for all you've heard and seen? [106] 'No. I wanted to stay at the festival.' Yes, and initiates of the mysteries would like the rites to be prolonged,* and visitors to the Olympic festival would like to see more athletes. But the festival can't go on forever. Leave, depart with gratitude and respect. Make room for others. They too need to be born, just as you were, and once born they need space, somewhere to live, and all that is necessary for life. If those who went before don't make way for them, what will be left for them? Why are you so greedy? Why are you incapable of being satisfied? Why are you crowding the world?"

[107] "All right, but I want my children and wife to be with me."*

"Because they're yours? Don't they belong to him who gave them to you? To the one who created you? So won't you give up your claim to what isn't yours? Won't you yield to your superior?"

[108] "So why did he bring me into the world on these conditions?"

"If they're not to your taste, leave. He doesn't need a captious spectator. He needs people who participate in the festival and the dancing. He wants them to applaud, to see it as a holy time, to celebrate the festival with hymns of praise. [109] He won't be sorry to see faint-hearted people who are incapable of enduring hardship excluded from the celebrations, because even when they were there, they didn't behave as though they were at a festival. Instead of fulfilling their role, they deplored their circumstances and blamed others—the gods, fortune, the people around them. They were unaware of what they had and of their own faculties, which were given to them for the opposite purposes—for greatness of soul, excellence, courage, and the very freedom that's the subject of our inquiry."

[110] "What's the point, though? Why have I been given these things?"

"To make use of them."

"For how long?"

"For as long as the one who lent them to you wants you to."

"But what if they're necessary to me?"

"Don't get attached to them and they won't be. Don't tell yourself that they're necessary to you and they aren't. [111] You should make this your practice all day and every day. Start with the most trivial and easily damaged things—a pot, a cup—and then move on to a toga, a dog, a horse, a plot of land. And move on from there to yourself, your body, the parts of your body, your children, wife, brothers. [112] Look around everywhere for such things and then discard them. Purge your faculty of judgment, so that nothing that isn't yours clings to it or has been grafted onto it, which might cause you pain when it's torn off. [113] And while you exercise in this way every day, as you do there,* tell yourself that you're not doing so because you're a philosopher—which, you must admit, would be a vulgar claim to make—but because you're claiming the right to manumission.* After all, what we're talking about here is true freedom.

[114] "This was the freedom that Diogenes gained from Antisthenes, and afterward he said that he could no longer be enslaved by anyone.* [115] That's what enabled him to behave as he did when he was captured, to treat the pirates as he did. He didn't come close to calling any of them his master, did he? I don't mean just that the word never crossed his lips, because there's nothing to fear in a mere word. No, what's horrifying is the attitude of which the word is an expression. See how he told them off for not giving their captives enough food. [116] See what happened when he was sold. It wasn't a master that he was looking to get, but a slave! And after he'd been sold, how did he behave toward his owner? He immediately spoke to him and told him that his clothing and his hairstyle were inappropriate, and talked about how his sons ought to live. [117] Not that there's anything surprising in this. If the man had bought a trainer, would he have treated him, in the field of wrestling, as a servant or a master? And the same goes if he'd bought a medical expert or a master builder. Whatever the field, it's absolutely essential for the expert to have authority over the non-expert. [118] In general, then, anyone who's acquired expertise in the art of living is bound to be the master. What else could he be? I mean, who's the master on a ship?"

"The captain."

"Why? Because anyone who disobeys him is punished."

"But he can have me flogged."*

"Not without being punished for it, surely."

[119] "Well, actually, that is what I've been thinking."

"But the fact that he won't go unpunished proves that he can't go unpunished. No one can do wrong with impunity."

[120] "And what penalty does a person pay if he hog-ties a slave of his, do you think?"

"His tying him up is itself the penalty he pays. I'm sure you, too, will admit this, unless you want to make nonsense of the idea that a human being is a tame animal, not a wild beast. [121] After all, under what circumstances does a vine fare badly? When it's not acting in accord with its nature. And a cock? The same. So also for a human being. [122] So what is it natural for a human being to do? Bite and kick? Throw people in prison and cut off their heads? No. It's human nature to do good, to be helpful, to pray for others' success. So, whether you like it or not, someone hard-hearted fares badly."

[123] "So Socrates didn't fare badly?"

"No, but his judges and accusers did."

"And, to take a Roman example, Helvidius didn't either?"

"No, but the man who killed him did."*

[124] "What do you mean?"

"Well, I'm sure you wouldn't say that a cock that won its fight fared badly, even if it was all cut up; you'd say it was the uninjured one that came off worst. Nor would you think of a hound as happy if it wasn't chasing something down and making a strenuous effort, but you would if you saw it sweating, aching, and exhausted by its running.* [125] Is there anything strange, then, in our saying that for every creature, what's bad for it is what goes against its nature? Is that at all mystifying? Seeing that you say as much for all other creatures, why treat human beings as though they alone were different? [126] Now, we're saying that human nature is civilized, sociable, and trustworthy. That's not a strange thing to say, is it?"

"No, I accept that as well."

[127] "So under what circumstances does a person come to no harm if he's flogged or imprisoned or has his head cut off? Isn't it when he endures it nobly, and therefore ends up even turning it to good account and coming out ahead? On the other hand, isn't the

one who's harmed the one who suffers the most pitiful and deplorable fate—the one who turns from a human being into a wolf, a snake, or a wasp?

[128] "All right, then, let's review our findings. An unimpeded person is free and finds things at hand as he wants them. However, anyone who can be impeded, constrained, or obstructed, or who can be thrown into a situation against his wishes, is a slave. [129] What makes a person unimpeded? If he wants nothing that isn't his. What isn't ours? Anything that isn't up to us; it's not up to us whether or not we have it, and, if we have it, it's not up to us what it's like or how we come by it. [130] So the body isn't ours, body parts aren't ours, and possessions aren't ours. If you become attached to any of these things, then, as though it were your own, you'll receive the punishment that a person deserves for wanting something that isn't his. [131] The road that leads to freedom, and the only way to be delivered from slavery, is for someone to be able to say, with all their heart, 'Lead me, Zeus, both you and Destiny, wheresoe'r you have ordained for me.'*

[132] "But what do you say, philosopher? A tyrant calls on you to say something that's not worthy of you. Do you do so or not? Tell me."

"Let me think about it."

"What, *now*? What did you spend your time thinking about while you were in school? Didn't you look into what is good, bad, and indifferent?"

"Yes, I did."

[133] " And what conclusions did you come to?"

"If something is just and honorable, it's good, and if something is unjust and shameful, it's bad."

"Living isn't a good thing, is it?"

"No."

"And dying isn't bad?"

"No."

"Nor imprisonment?"

"No."

"What about saying something despicable and dishonest, betraying a friend, and flattering a tyrant? What conclusion did you reach about these things?"

"That they're bad."

[134] "So why are you still undecided? Why do you still need to

think and make up your mind about this issue? I mean, it hardly takes much thought to decide whether it's appropriate for me, when I have the ability to do so, to procure the greatest goods for myself and avoid the greatest evils, does it? 'That's a good question—essential, in fact—and it needs a lot of thought.' Why are you making fun of us, man? No one ever treats this as a matter for investigation. [135] If you really thought that disgraceful things are bad and that all other 'bad' things are indifferent, you'd never have needed to stop and think, not even for a moment, but you'd have been able to decide the issue on the spot with your mind, just as you'd decide other cases with your eyes. [136] I mean, do you ever think about whether something black is white, or whether something heavy is light? Don't you follow the clear evidence of your senses? So how come you're now talking about considering whether things that are indifferent are to be avoided more than bad things? [137] The fact of the matter is that you don't judge things that way. You don't regard these things as indifferent, but as the greatest evils, and you don't regard those other things as bad, but as no concern of ours.

[138] "The trouble is that you got into a bad habit right from the start. 'Where am I? In school. Who are these people who are listening to me talk? I'm among philosophers. But now that I've left the classroom, let's have no more of those pedantic and idiotic notions!' [139] That's how a philosopher comes to bear witness against a friend, how he becomes a parasite, how he hires himself out for money. That's how a man comes to deliver insincere speeches in the Senate. [140] Internally, his judgment is yelling at him—and this is no pointless, pathetic judgment that's kept hanging in place by the thread of futile argument, but a strong, serviceable one that has proved itself in the gymnasium of practical experience. [141] Watch yourself and see how you receive the news—I won't say that your child is dead, because that would have no meaning for you—but that your oil has been spilled, or your wine all drunk up. [142] Seeing you get all worked up, a bystander would have only this to say: 'Philosopher, you talk differently in the classroom. Why deceive us? Why claim to be a human being when you're a worm?' [143] I wish I could stand over one of them when he's having sex, so that I could see how he exerts himself and hear the noises he makes. Then I'd see whether he remembers the name he bears, and whether he's keeping in mind the arguments

he hears in the classroom, or affirms in his lectures, or reads in his books."

[144] "And what has all this got to do with freedom?"

"It's precisely and exclusively relevant to freedom, whether you rich folk like it or not."

"And what's your evidence for this?"

[145] "Just you and your kind—people with a great master who live at his beck and call. You faint at just a frown from him, you sweet-talk old women and men, and you say, 'I can't do that; I'm not allowed to.' [146] Why are you not allowed to? Weren't you insisting to me just now that you're free? 'But Aprulla won't let me.'* So tell the truth, slave. Don't forsake your masters. Don't try to disavow them, or have the effrontery to claim the right to manumission when there's so much evidence of your enslavement. [147] Now, when it's love that compels someone to act against his better judgment—when he can see the right thing to do, but lacks the moral fiber to do it—one might be somewhat inclined to think that he deserves to be forgiven, seeing that he's in the grip of a powerful force, and one that is, in a sense, divine. [148] But who could find any excuse for you, given that it's old women and men you fall in love with? You wipe their snotty noses, wash their faces, and bribe them with gifts; you tend them like a slave when they're ill, while praying for them to die and interrogating their doctors to try to find out whether they're at last on the point of death. Or again, who could forgive the way you kiss the hands of other people's slaves, with an eye on these important and majestic positions and honors, thus making yourself a slave of people who aren't even free themselves? [149] And then you walk around with your nose in the air because you're a praetor or a consul—as though I don't know how you got to be a praetor, how you acquired your consulship, who gave it to you. [150] Speaking for myself, I wouldn't even want to live if my life depended on Felicio* and I had to put up with his scorn and his slavish arrogance. After all, I do know what a slave is like when he's doing well in the eyes of the world and has become puffed up with pride."

[151] "So are *you* free?" he asked.

"I want to be, by the gods, and that's what I pray for, but I'm not yet able to look my masters in the eyes.* I still value my body. I place great store on having it whole and unmutilated, even though it isn't.*

[152] But I can show you a free man, so that you won't have to spend any more time looking for an example. Diogenes was free. How did that come about? It wasn't due to the fact that his parents were free, because they weren't.* It was because he himself was free, in that he had rejected everything that might allow slavery to get a grip on him, plus the fact that there was no way to get at him and no way that he could be seized for enslavement. [153] Everything he had was disposable; everything was just an appendage. If you seized some possession of his, he'd let it go rather than be pulled along behind it. If you grabbed his leg, he'd let that go; if you seized his whole body, he'd let that go, and likewise his family, friends, and country. He knew how he came to have these things, who gave them to him, and on what conditions he was given them.

[154] "But he would never have abandoned his true ancestors, the gods, or his true country. He'd never have allowed anyone else to surpass his obedience and submission to the gods, and no one would have given his life for his country more readily than he, [155] because, although he never sought to be known as one who acts on behalf of the universe, he bore in mind that the universe is the source of everything that happens, and that every event happens for its sake and is ordained by the director of the universe. [156] See, therefore, what he himself says and writes: 'That, Diogenes, is why you can talk as you want with the Persian king and Archidamus of Sparta.'* [157] Was this because he was freeborn? Sure, and I suppose it was because they were all slave-born that the Athenians, Spartans, and Corinthians were unable to talk to them as they wanted, but were afraid of them and flattered them. [158] 'So why is it that you can do that?' 'Because I don't consider my body to be mine, because I need nothing, because the law is everything to me* and everything else is nothing.' This is what made it possible for him to be free.

[159] "Now, I wouldn't want you to think that my exemplar has to be a solitary man, one with no wife, children, country, friends, or relatives to divert him and deflect him from his course, so take Socrates. In him, you see a man who had a wife and children but treated them as though they weren't his; who had a country to the extent that and in the way that he was obliged to; and who had friends and relatives—but who in all these cases gave primacy to law and his obedience to law. [160] Hence, whenever he was obliged to serve in the

army, he was the first to set out, and when they reached the front line, he would face danger without a thought for his own safety.* When the tyrants sent him to fetch Leon, he regarded the mission as shameful, and so he didn't give it even a moment's thought, although he knew that he would very probably be put to death.* [161] But what did that matter to him? There was something other than his body that he wanted to keep safe—the person that he was, trustworthy and self-respecting. These are qualities that are not to be tampered with or made to play a subordinate role. [162] And then, when he had to defend himself in court on a capital charge, did he behave like a man with children and a wife? No, he behaved as though he were on his own. [163] And what about when he was obliged to drink the poison, how did he behave then? He could have saved himself, and Crito was telling him to escape for the sake of his children, but what does Socrates say? Did he regard the opportunity to escape as a godsend? Of course not! He took into consideration only what it was right for him to do and didn't spare a glance or a thought for anything else. He didn't want to save his body, he said,* but only that part of himself that gains strength and is maintained by right action, and is diminished and ruined by wrong action. [164] Socrates turned down the opportunity to save his life by an unworthy act; after all, this was the man who had refused to put a vote to the Assembly, even though the Athenians were calling on him to do so,* who treated the tyrants with contempt,* and who was constantly† talking about virtue and true goodness. [165] It's out of the question for the life of such a person to be saved by shameful means; death is what saves him, not flight. Even a good actor is saved by stopping at the right time, rather than by continuing to act when it's out of place.

[166] "'What will become of the children?' 'If I'd gone to Thessaly, you'd have looked after them, so, now that Hades is my destination, will there be no one to take care of them?'* See how he glosses over death and scorns it. [167] If you or I had been in that situation, we'd immediately have become all philosophical and argued that people who do wrong should be repaid in kind, and we'd have capped our position with 'Alive, I can help a lot of people, but not if I'm dead.' We'd have squeezed through a mouse hole, if that was what it took to escape. [168] In any case, how would we have helped people? After

all, they'd still have been in Athens, wouldn't they?* Even if we were of some use, wouldn't we have done far more good to people by dying when and as we should? [169] Socrates may be dead now, but the memory of what he did and said while he was alive does people just as much good, if not even more, than his living presence.

[170] "Study these things—these notions, these arguments—and look to the examples of Diogenes and Socrates if you want to be free, if you long for it as much as it deserves. [171] It's hardly surprising, is it, if such a major undertaking demands so much from you in payment? For the sake of conventional freedom, people have hanged themselves and hurled themselves off cliffs, and sometimes whole cities have even been utterly destroyed. [172] For the sake of true freedom, which is immune to intrigue and safe from harm, won't you give up what God has given you when he asks for it back? Won't you prepare yourself by training not just, as Plato says, for death,* but for being tortured, exiled, and whipped? In short, won't you train yourself to give back things that aren't yours? [173] Otherwise, you'll be a slave among slaves, and it will make no difference even if you're a consul countless times, even if you rise as far as the palace. And you'll come to see that, as Cleanthes said, philosophical ideas may conflict with opinion, but they don't conflict with reason. [174] Your experience will teach you that these ideas are true, and that it does people no good to get the things they value and think important. Meanwhile, those who haven't yet got them imagine that everything good will be theirs once they have them, and then, when they've got them, there's no lessening of their fever, but the same old tossing and turning, the same agitation, and the same longing for what they don't have. [175] For freedom isn't a product of the satisfaction of craving, but of its suppression.

[176] "You'll come to realize the truth of what I've been saying if you transfer to this new line of work the same amount of effort you expended on the former one. Pass sleepless nights in the hope of procuring for yourself a judgment that will set you free. [177] Cultivate a philosopher instead of a rich old man; be seen standing in *his* doorway.* There's no disgrace in being seen there, and you won't leave empty-handed and with no profit if you approach him properly. Anyway, at least give it a try. There's no shame in trying."

4.2

On social intercourse

[1] "This is a topic to which you should pay attention before all others, in order to avoid being so bound up with any of your former friends and acquaintances that you sink down to his level. If you do that, you're lost. [2] 'But he'll think me rude and he won't be as warm toward me as before.' If this thought occurs to you, remember that nothing comes for free, and that a change of lifestyle is bound to make someone a different person. [3] So you need to choose between two options: either to be loved to same degree by your former friends by remaining the same as your former self, or to be better than you were and forgo being treated the same. [4] If the latter course seems better, set off in that direction at once, and don't let any other considerations deflect you.

"The point is that no one can make progress if he tries to do two things at once. If you've chosen this course over any other, if you want to focus on it alone and to devote your energy to it, you have to let go of everything else. [5] Otherwise, if you're torn between two courses, each of them will have an effect on you, and you'll neither make progress as you should nor get what you used to have. [6] Before, when your goals consisted purely of things that are of no value, your friends enjoyed your company. [7] But you can't do well in both of two courses. No, it's inevitable that, to the degree that you're involved in one of them, you'll be a failure in the other. If you don't drink with your former drinking companions, it's impossible for them to enjoy your company to the same extent. Choose, then, whether you want to drink deep and please them or to be sober and displease them. If you don't sing with your former singing companions, it's impossible for them to love you as they did. Here too you have to choose which course you prefer.

[8] "The point is that, if it's better to be a self-respecting person and to moderate your behavior than to have people say of you, 'What a nice guy!' you have to let go of everything else. Give it up, turn away from it: it's no business of yours. [9] But if that isn't to your taste, turn with your whole being in the opposite direction. Become a sexual deviant, become an adulterer. All you have to do is act accordingly and you'll get what you want. Leap to your feet and loudly acclaim the

dancer.* [10] But roles that differ so greatly don't mix. You can't play the part of both Thersites and Agamemnon. If you want to be Thersites, you must be humpbacked and bald. If you choose to be Agamemnon, you must be tall, handsome, and devoted to your subjects."

4.3
What should be exchanged for what

[1] "The question that should be in the forefront of your mind whenever you relinquish an external object is: what are you getting in exchange for it? If what you get is worth more, never think that you lost out. [2] You wouldn't think that if you got a horse in exchange for a donkey, an ox in exchange for a sheep, a favorable outcome in exchange for a bit of cash, decorous quiet instead of pointless talk, self-respect instead of lewd talk. [3] If you keep this in mind whatever your circumstances, you'll preserve your character as it ought to be. Otherwise, I think you should realize that your time is being wasted and that you're in danger of squandering and ruining all the work you're currently putting in on yourself.

[4] "It doesn't take much to spoil and ruin everything, just a slight deviation from reason. [5] It doesn't take as much aptitude for a helmsman to capsize his ship as it does for him to keep it safe; all he needs to do is turn a little into the wind and he's undone. Even if he doesn't do so deliberately, but through a lapse of attention, he's undone. [6] The same goes here too. You only have to nod off for a moment and everything you've gathered up until then vanishes. So pay attention to your impressions and keep a close watch on them. [7] It's nothing trivial that you're protecting but your self-respect, trustworthiness, equanimity, self-possession, immunity to distress, immunity to fear, serenity—in a word, your freedom. [8] What are you going to sell these qualities for? How much do you think they're worth?"

"But I won't get anything of comparable value in exchange."

"But if you are in fact compensated, see what you gain in exchange for what you lose. [9] 'I have decency, he has a tribunate; he has a praetorship, I have self-respect. But I don't raise my voice when it would be unseemly to do so; I won't get to my feet when I shouldn't. For I am free and a friend of God, so that I willingly obey him. [10] I shouldn't lay claim to anything else, neither body, nor possessions, nor political power, nor status—in a word, nothing. Because he doesn't want me to lay claim to them. After all, if he did want that, he'd have made them good for me. But, as things are, he didn't do that, and that's why it's impossible for me to disobey his commands.'

[11] "Protect your good always, and as for everything else, be content with what's been allotted to you, as long as you make rational use of it, and don't ask for anything more. Otherwise, you'll be miserable and wretched, impeded and obstructed. [12] These are the laws that have been relayed to us from above; these are God's commandments. You must become an interpreter of these laws and obedient to them, rather than those of Masurius and Cassius."*

4.4

To those who are intent on living a quiet life

[1] "Remember that it isn't just longing for political power and wealth that subjugates a person and makes him subservient to others, but also the desire for quiet, leisure, travel, and learning. To put it simply, whatever the external thing may be, if you value it, it makes you subservient to others. [2] Is there any difference, then, between longing to be a senator and longing not to be a senator? Between craving political power and craving not to have political power? Is there any difference between saying, 'It upsets me that I can't do a thing because I'm tied to my books like a corpse,' and 'It upsets me that I've no time for reading'? [3] The point is that a book, no less than salutations and public office,* belongs to the class of things that are external to us and aren't subject to will. [4] Why do you want to read? Tell me. If you take up a book in order to be entertained or to learn some point of theory, your reading is pointless and you're not making the most of yourself. But if you're reading for the right purpose—well, what can this be except contentment? And if your reading doesn't bring you contentment, what's the good of it?"

[5] "But it does," he said, "and that's why I don't like to be deprived of it."

"But what kind of contentment is it that can be obstructed by just anybody or anything? I'm not talking about Caesar or one of Caesar's friends, but a crow, a piper, a fever, and other things beyond number. But the chief characteristic of contentment is precisely that it isn't subject to interruption or obstruction.* [6] Suppose that I'm now being called away to do something. Off I go, with the purpose of paying attention to the measures I ought to observe—that is, to ensure that I act with self-respect, securely, and without either desire or aversion for externals. [7] Moreover, I also pay attention to other people, to see what they're saying and doing—not maliciously, not trying to find something to criticize or mock them for, but with my focus on myself, to see if I'm making the same mistakes.*

[8] "Come now, if you behave like this and make these your priorities, is that a worse thing to do than reading or writing a thousand lines? When you're eating, are you cross because you're not reading? Isn't it enough for you that the way you're eating—or bathing, or exercising—is consistent with the principles you've read about? [9] So why don't you act consistently whatever you're doing, whether it's Caesar you're with or just anyone? [10] If you retain your equanimity, imperturbability, and composure, if you're the observer of events rather than the observed, if you're not envious of people who've been preferred to you, if you're not fazed by the material world, what is it that you lack? Books? How could you miss them? What would be the point?"

[11] "Yes, but doesn't reading prepare one for living?"

"But there's a lot more to living than you can find in books. It's as if, on entering the stadium, an athlete were to be upset because he's not outside, in training. [12] This is what you were training for; this is what your weights were for, your sprinkled sand,* your training partners. Are you really missing these now, when it's time for action? [13] It's as if, in the domain of assent, where we're faced with both cognitive and non-cognitive impressions,* we were to refuse to distinguish between them and wanted instead to read a treatise *On Cognitive Certainty*.

[14] "What's the reason for this? It's because we've never read for the following purpose and never written for the following purpose— the purpose of making use, in conformity with nature, of the impressions that occur to us in real life. Instead we stop there, at learning what's being said and being able to interpret it for someone else, and at analyzing syllogisms and investigating hypothetical arguments. [15] That's why the area you're intent on is also where you'll find obstacles. If you're dead set on having things that aren't up to you, you're

bound to be impeded, obstructed, and unsuccessful. [16] But if we were to read a treatise *On Inclination* not to see what it says about the faculty of inclination but to manage our inclinations well; if we were to read a treatise *On Desire and Aversion* so that our desires are never disappointed and our aversions effectively prevent the occurrence of things we want to avoid; if we were to read a treatise *On Acting Appropriately* in order to be mindful of our relationships with others and to make sure that we never act irrationally or improperly [17]—then we wouldn't be annoyed if our reading is interrupted. We'd be satisfied to act accordingly, and we wouldn't reckon things up as we've been accustomed to in the past—'Today I read so many lines; today I wrote so many lines'—[18] but instead we'd say, 'Today I made use of my faculty of inclination as recommended by the philosophers. Today I made no use of my faculty of desire, and I restricted my aversion to things that are subject to will. I wasn't fazed by this person or put into a bad mood by that one, but I practiced forbearance, patience, and amenability.' And if we did that, we'd be thanking God for the things that demand our gratitude.

[19] "At present, however, we fail to appreciate that we ourselves are really no different from everyone else. It's only the variables that are different: they're anxious to hold public office, while you're anxious not to. [20] No more anxiety, man! You mock people who are anxious to obtain public office, and by the same token you should mock yourself. It makes no difference whether a person wants a drink of water because he has a fever or wants to avoid drinking water because he has hydrophobia. [21] Would you still be able to say with Socrates, 'If this is what God wants, so be it'?* Do you think that if Socrates had wanted to spend time in the Lyceum or the Academy, and to converse every day with the young men of Athens, he'd cheerfully have marched off to war as often as he did?* Wouldn't he have moaned and groaned? 'Poor me!' he'd have said. 'Here I am now in a pitiful and miserable state, when I could be basking in the sun in the Lyceum.' [22] Was this your function, to bask in sunlight? Wasn't it to be content, unimpeded, and unobstructed? How would he still have been Socrates if he'd moaned like that? How would he still have been able to compose hymns of praise in prison?* [23] In short, what you need to remember is that if you value anything that's external to your will,

you ruin your will. Not only is holding a public office external to will, but so too is not holding one; not only busyness, but leisure too."

[24] "So must I spend my days in the midst of commotion?"

"What do you mean by 'commotion'? Being surrounded by lots of people? Where's the hardship in that? Imagine you're at Olympia and think of it as a tumultuous festival. At Olympia, too, there's chaotic shouting and chaotic movement, with people bumping into one another and a crowded bathhouse. Yet is there anyone who doesn't find the festival enjoyable? Is there anyone who isn't sad to leave? [25] Don't be hard to please. Don't be fussy about things. 'The wine's bad; it's got a sharp taste.' 'The honey's bad; it upsets my stomach.' 'I don't want vegetables.' This is no different from 'I don't want leisure; it's empty space' or 'I don't like a crowd; it's pandemonium.' [26] No, if circumstances force you to live alone or with just a few others, call it peace and quiet and make proper use of the situation: talk to yourself, work on your impressions, apply yourself to your preconceptions. And if, on the other hand, you find yourself in the midst of a crowd, tell yourself it's an athletic meet, a festival, a celebration, and try to celebrate along with the rest. [27] When someone loves humankind, what sight could please him more than a crowd of people? We enjoy seeing herds of horses or cows; the sight of a large number of ships puts us in a good mood. Why should a person find the sight of large numbers of people disagreeable?"

[28] "But they deafen me with their shouting."

"So it's your hearing that's being obstructed. Why does that bother you? Your ability to make use of impressions isn't being obstructed as well, is it? Is anyone stopping you from making use of desire and aversion, and inclination and disinclination, in conformity with your nature? Is there any commotion that's capable of doing that?

[29] "All you have to do is remember your general principles: What's mine? What isn't mine? What's up to me? What does God now want me to be doing? What does he not want me to do? [30] A short while ago he wanted you to be at leisure, to talk to yourself, write about these matters, read, attend lectures, and get yourself ready. You had enough time for that. Now he's saying to you, 'It's time for you to move on to the actual contest. Show us what you've learned and how successful your training has been. For how long will

you exercise all by yourself? Now it's time for you to find out whether you're the kind of athlete who deserves victory or the kind who travels around the world getting beaten.' [31] So why are you displeased? You can't have a contest without commotion. There are bound to be many trainers around, many people shouting, many overseers, many spectators."

[32] "But I wanted a quiet life."

"Moan and groan, then, since that's what you deserve. I mean, what greater punishment could there be for someone who remains uneducated and disobedient to God's commandments than feeling distress, grief, envy—in short, than being wretched and miserable? Don't you want to free yourself of all that?"

[33] "How do I go about that?"

"Haven't you repeatedly been told that you must completely eliminate desire,* direct your aversion only toward things that are subject to will, and let go of everything—your body, possessions, status, books, commotion, political power, and lack of political power? If you ever deviate from this path, you see, you become a subservient slave, impeded, constrained, entirely dependent on others. [34] No, you should have Cleanthes's words at hand: 'Lead me, Zeus, both you and Destiny.'* Do you want me to be in Rome? Off I go to Rome. To Gyara? Off I go to Gyara. To Athens? Off I go to Athens. To prison? Off I go to prison. [35] But if you ever think, 'When do I get to go to Athens?' you're lost. At any rate, this desire, if unfulfilled, will certainly make you miserable, and if fulfilled, it will make you vain and proud of things in which you shouldn't take pride—and if you're again prevented from going, you'll be miserable because you're experiencing something you don't want to experience. [36] So let go of all this."

"Well, Athens *is* beautiful."

"But far more beautiful are happiness, equanimity, serenity, and self-reliance."

[37] "Rome's nothing but commotion and salutations."*

"But contentment is worth all the difficulties. So if it's a time of difficulties, why not eliminate your aversion toward them? Why must you bear your burden like a donkey being beaten with a stick? [38] Can't you see that otherwise you'll inevitably and always be the slave of anyone who's able to bring you relief or create all sorts of obstacles for you? You'll have to conciliate him as you would a spirit of bad luck.*

[39] "There's only one path that leads to contentment—and this is a thought you should have at hand morning, noon, and night—and that is to renounce things that aren't subject to will, to think of none of them as yours, to surrender your whole life to the gods and fortune, to entrust the guardianship of your life to them, seeing that they were in fact created by Zeus for that purpose, [40] and to focus exclusively on what's up to you and unimpeded, with this goal as the point of all your reading, writing, and listening to lectures. [41] That's why I find it impossible to call a person hardworking if I hear only that he reads and writes. Even if I'm also told that he stays up all night, I still can't call him that without knowing what his purpose is. You wouldn't call someone hardworking if he stays awake at night over a girl, and by the same token I withhold the title too. [42] If it's fame that keeps a person awake, I call him ambitious, and if it's money, I call him avaricious, but not hardworking. [43] On the other hand, if a person makes his command center the point of all his efforts, with the intention of keeping it in accord with nature throughout his life, then and only then I call him hardworking. [44] After all, you should never praise or blame people for things that may be either good or bad, but for their judgments. These actually belong to a person, and it is they that make his actions wrong or right.

[45] "Bearing all this in mind, enjoy what you have and welcome whatever the moment brings. [46] If you see any of the matters you've studied and researched presenting themselves to you to be put into practice, that should please you. If you've eliminated or reduced the malicious and abusive aspects of your character, your impetuousness, your use of foul language, your aimlessness and inconstancy, and if the things that used to move you leave you unmoved, or less moved than you were before, you're in a position to celebrate a festival every day—today because you did well in one particular set of circumstances, tomorrow because you'll do the same in another. [47] How much better a reason this is for a sacrifice than a consulship or governorship! You have yourself and the gods to thank for these qualities. Just remember in whose gift they are and what kind of people receive them and why. [48] If you acquire the habit of thinking like this, will you still be uncertain where to find happiness and where

you have to be to please God? Wherever we are, aren't we all equidistant from God? Wherever we are, don't we all equally see his works?"

4.5
Against those who are pugnacious and fierce

[1] "A truly good person doesn't get involved in fights himself, and he also does his best to prevent anyone else from doing so. [2] For this, as for everything else, we have before us the example of the life of Socrates, who not only avoided fights himself, whatever the circumstances, but didn't let others fight either. [3] See how many conflicts he resolved in Xenophon's *Symposium*, how patient he was with Thrasymachus, Polus, and Callicles, how he put up with his wife, and with his son, too, who was trying to refute him with sophistic arguments.* [4] He knew, you see, beyond the shadow of a doubt, that no one can be the master of anyone else's command center, and so he didn't wish for anything that wasn't his. What does this mean? [5] That a person shouldn't try to get others to act in accord with nature,† because that isn't up to him, but while others are attending to their own affairs as they see fit, he himself should remain in accord with nature and, merely by minding his own business, should prompt them, too, to live in accord with nature.† [6] This is the constant aim of a truly good person. Does he aim for a praetorship? No, but if he ends up a praetor, he aims to safeguard his command center in those circumstances. Does he aim for marriage? No, but if he ends up married, he aims to keep his command center in accord with nature in those circumstances. [7] But if he wants his son or wife never to be at fault, he's wanting something to be up to him that's not up to him. And the process of education is precisely the process of learning what is and isn't up to us.

[8] "How can there be any trace of pugnacity in such a person? He's not going to be shocked by anything that happens, is he? Nothing can seem strange to him, can it? Doesn't he expect worse and harsher treatment at the hands of bad people than he actually receives? Doesn't he count as it as gain whenever they fall short of the full extent of their wickedness? [9] 'So-and-so railed at me.' I'm very grateful to him for not hitting me. 'But he hit me as well.' I'm very grateful that he didn't injure me. 'But he injured me as well.' I'm

very grateful that he didn't kill me. [10] I mean, has a bad person ever had anyone explain to him that a human being is a tame animal, a sociable creature, and that the very act of doing wrong does a great deal of harm to the wrongdoer? Since he's never learned or become convinced of this, he's bound to follow the course of action that seems to him to be to his advantage. [11] 'My neighbor has thrown stones.' It's not you who've done wrong, then, is it? 'But some things in my house were broken.' Well, are you one of your domestic utensils? No, you are will. [12] So what means have you been given to respond to this situation? If you react like a wolf, you'll bite him back and throw a greater number of stones in your turn. But if you want to react like a human being, examine your resources and see what faculties you were born with. Was ferocity one of them? Was vindictiveness? [13] So when is a horse to be pitied? When it's deprived of its natural faculties—not when it can't crow like a cock, but when it can't run. And what about a hound? When it can't fly? No, when it can't follow a scent. [14] By the same token, then, isn't it the case that a human being, too, will be miserable not when he can't choke lions or hug statues,* because he didn't come into the world equipped by nature with the faculties for doing this, but when he's lost his kindness and trustworthiness?

[15] "This is the person that people should 'gather together to mourn for all the evils he has come into the world to face,' and not, by Zeus, 'the one who's been born' or 'the one who's died,'* but the one who has had the misfortune, while still alive, to lose what is truly his own. That isn't his patrimony, his land and house and guesthouse and slaves, because none of these belong to a person; they all belong to others, and are enslaved, dependent, given by their masters now to one person and now to another. [16] No, it's the qualities that make him human, the imprints with which his mind was impressed when he came into the world. Think of the marks we look for on coins, the presence of which make a coin acceptable and the absence of which lead to its rejection. [17] 'Whose imprint is on this sestertius? Trajan's? Let's have it. Nero's? Throw it away, it's not legal tender, it's not in good condition.'* The same goes for the kind of person we're talking about. What imprints do his judgments bear? 'Kindness, comradeship, patience, sociability.' Let's have him, I accept him, I'll have him as my fellow citizen, I accept him as a neigh-

bor or a travel companion. [18] Just make sure that he doesn't have a Neronian imprint. Is he irascible, wrathful, querulous? 'If he feels like it, he cracks the skulls of people he comes across.'* [19] Why are you calling him human, then? We don't draw conclusions about things merely by their outward appearance, do we? I mean, if so, why not call a ball of wax an apple? [20] No, it must also have the right smell and the right taste; its external shape isn't enough on its own. Likewise, the presence of nose and eyes aren't enough for us to tell whether someone is a human being, but we need to check whether he has human judgments . [21] Here's someone who doesn't listen to reason and doesn't understand when he's been proved wrong: he's a donkey. Here's one whose self-respect has perished: he's a complete waste of space, a sheep† rather than a human being. Here's one who's looking to meet someone, and then to kick and bite him, so he's not a sheep or a donkey but some wild beast.

[22] "What? Do you want me to be despised?"

"By whom? By knowledgeable people? How could knowledgeable people despise someone who's gentle and has self-respect? By ignorant people? Why would you care? I mean, no craftsman cares what people who are ignorant of his craft think of him."

[23] "But they'll pester me all the more."

"Why do you say 'me'? Can anyone damage your will or prevent you from making natural use of the impressions that occur to you?"

"No."

[24] "Then why are you uneasy? Why do you wish to show yourself to be a fearful person? Won't you step up and proclaim that you refuse to fight with anyone, whatever they may do, and that you're especially amused by those who think they're harming you? 'These slaves don't know who I am or where what's good and bad for me is to be found. They're unable to get at what's mine.'

[25] "This is also how the inhabitants of a well-fortified city laugh at their besiegers: 'Why are these people going to all this trouble for nothing? Our wall is safe, we have enough food to last us a very long time indeed, and the same goes for all our equipment in general.' [26] These are the things that make a city strong and impregnable, and for a human soul it's his judgments, that's all. No wall is as strong, no body as impenetrably hard, no possession as safe from theft, no reputation as invulnerable to attack. [27] Everything ev-

erywhere is perishable and easily captured, and anyone who takes it seriously is bound to be uneasy, pessimistic, fearful, and sad. His desires are bound to be frustrated, and his aversions will fail to prevent the occurrence of things he wanted to avoid. [28] Aren't we willing, then, to strengthen the only means of safety that's been granted to us? Aren't we willing to abandon the realm of what's mortal and enslaved and cultivate what's immortal and naturally free? Have we forgotten that no one harms or does good to another person, and that it's always a person's judgment about what's good and what's bad that causes him harm? This is the destructive factor, this is the cause of conflict, civil strife, and war. [29] The conflict between Eteocles and Polynices* was generated purely and simply by their judgment about rulership and exile, that the latter is the worst of evils and the former the greatest of goods.

[30] "It's absolutely natural for everyone to pursue the good and avoid the bad, and to regard anyone who deprives him of the former and involves him in the latter as an enemy, as someone scheming against him, even if he's a brother, a son, a father. And the reason is that nothing is more closely related to us than the good. [31] It follows, then, that if these external things are good and bad, no father is dear to his son, nor brother to brother, but everything everywhere is teeming with enemies, schemers, and informers. [32] But if right use of will is the only thing that's good and wrong use of will the only thing that's bad, how could conflict arise or the trading of insults? What would the fight be about? About things that are nothing to us? Hardly! And whom would we fight? Those who are ignorant, those who are unfortunate, those who hold false beliefs about matters of supreme importance?

[33] "It was because Socrates bore this in mind in his domestic life that he could endure a thoroughly shrewish wife and a rude son. I mean, how did her bad temper manifest? In pouring as much water over his head as she wanted and in stamping on the cake.* But how can that bother me if I believe that these things have nothing to do with me? [34] That's my job, and neither tyrant nor master can impede me against my will, nor can a crowd, though I'm just one man, nor can a stronger person, though I'm weaker, because will has been given to each of us by God to be unimpeded. [35] The products of these ideas are harmony in the household, concord in the state, and

international peace, and they make a man grateful to God and confident that, whatever the circumstances, he's faced with things that are not his and are worthless. [36] But while these are matters that we're capable of writing and reading about, and we can see their importance as we read about them, we're nowhere near being convinced of them. [37] So the saying about the Spartans—'Lions at home, but foxes at Ephesus'*—applies to us too: we're lions in the classroom but foxes outside."

4.6

To those who find the pity of others distressful

[1] "I find it irritating to be pitied," someone said.

"So is being pitied in *your* control or that of the people who are doing the pitying? And is it up to you to make it stop?"

"Yes, it's up to me, if I can convince them that their pity is misplaced."

[2] "But is this at present something that's up to you, your not deserving pity? Or is that not up to you?"

"I think it is. But the people I'm thinking of don't pity others for their mistakes, which are the only things that deserve pity. No, they pity them for their poverty, lack of political power, illness, death, and so on and so forth."*

[3] "So are you ready to convince the mass of ordinary people that none of these things is bad but that happiness is possible even for poor people, those who lack political power, and those who've been disenfranchised? Or will you present yourself to them as a rich and politically powerful man? [4] The second of these two courses is the one a social climber would take, a pointless and worthless person. And look at what it takes to sustain the pretense. First, you have to get hold of some slaves and acquire a few pieces of silverware. Then you have to make sure that people see the slaves and the silverware, while trying your best to disguise the fact that it's the same few things of yours they're seeing over and over again. You'll also need resplendent clothes and all kinds of ostentatious stuff; you'll have to make yourself out to be someone who has the respect of the most eminent members of society† and try to dine with them, or at least get others to believe that you're dining with them; and as for your body, you'll have

to come up with some fraudulent artifice to appear more handsome and noble than you are. [5] These are the dodges you'll have to devise if you want to take the second route to not being pitied.

"As for the first route, it's both impractical and time-consuming to try to do what Zeus was incapable of doing, and convince all humankind what's good and what's bad. [6] This isn't an ability that's been granted you, is it? You've only been granted the ability to convince yourself, and you haven't yet done that. And now you're trying to convince others? [7] But no one spends more time with you than you do with yourself, do they? And whose arguments are you more likely to be persuaded by than your own? Who could be more kindly disposed and closer to you than you are to yourself? [8] So how come you haven't yet persuaded yourself to get an education?

"Everything's topsy-turvy at the moment, isn't it? What is it that you're interested in learning? It's how to be immune to distress, disturbance, and debasement—in other words, how to be free—isn't it? [9] So haven't you heard that there's only one route to that destination? It's letting go of things that aren't subject to will, detaching yourself from them, and acknowledging that they aren't yours. [10] So to which category does someone else's opinion about you belong?"

"Among the things that aren't subject to my will."

"It's nothing to you, then."

"That's right."

"So as long as you're still hurt and disturbed by what people think of you, has the truth about good and bad really sunk in? [11] Shouldn't you leave other people alone, then, and concentrate on yourself, as both pupil and teacher simultaneously? 'If other people find it profitable to go against their natures and live like that, that's their concern, but no one is closer to me than myself. [12] Why, then, is it that, although I've listened to the philosophers' theories and agree with them, in fact my burden hasn't eased at all? Am I really so dense? But I wasn't found to be so very dense in all the other subjects I wanted to tackle. I was quick to learn to read and write, and just as quick when it came to wrestling, geometry, and analyzing syllogisms. [13] Can it be, then, that reasoned argument has failed to convince me? But I gave my approval and allegiance to reason and its works right from the start, and now I read about it, listen to lectures about it, and write about it. Nor have I yet found a stronger argument than this.* [14] So what's the problem? Perhaps I haven't eliminated the contrary judg-ments? Or perhaps my beliefs themselves are untrained and unac-customed to being confronted by the real world, like pieces of stored armor that are becoming rusty and can't even fit me anymore? [15] It's true that when it comes to wrestling or writing or reading, I'm not satisfied with just learning my lessons, but I turn the arguments with which I'm presented over in my mind and devise new ones, and I do the same for changing arguments as well.* [16] But the essential theoretical principles, the prerequisites for being immune to dis-tress, fear, passion, and impediment—for being free—these I fail to exercise. I don't train myself in their practical application as I ought. [17] And so I worry about what other people will say about me, and whether they'll take me to be a person of consequence and one who's achieved happiness.'

[18] "You poor thing! Can't you see what you're saying about your-self? What sort of person do you take yourself to be? What sort of person are you when you think, feel desire or aversion, have an incli-nation, prepare for action, undertake a project, or act in any other way that's typical of human beings? But instead you're bothered by others' pity?"

[19] "Yes, but their pity is unjustified."

"Is that what hurts you? But isn't someone in distress an object of pity?"

"Yes."

"So in what sense is their pity unjustified? The very feelings that being pitied arouses in you are what justify their pity! [20] What does Antisthenes say? You must have been told at some point: 'A king's role, Cyrus, is to do good and be reviled.'* [21] My head's fine and everyone thinks I've got a headache. Why should that bother me? I don't have a fever and everyone's sympathizing with me as though I had one. 'You poor thing! You've had no relief from your fever for ever so long!' I look sad and say, 'Yes, it really has been a long time since I last felt well.' 'What's going to happen, then?' 'That's in God's hands.' And at the same time I'm secretly laughing at them for feel-ing sorry for me.

[22] "Is there anything stopping me from doing the same in the present case too? I have no money, but I have a correct judgment about poverty, so why should it bother me if people pity me for my

poverty? I hold no public office, while others do, but my judgment regarding holding and not holding public office is as it should be. [23]
If people pity me, that's their concern, but I'm not hungry or thirsty
or cold; all they're doing is projecting their hunger or thirst onto me.
What shall I do, then? Shall I go around proclaiming, 'You're wrong,
gentlemen, if you think there's something wrong with me. I don't
care about poverty and lack of political power; I don't care about anything, in fact, except having correct judgments. They're mine and
they're immune to impediment, and I haven't paid anything else any
mind'? [24] But isn't this just nonsense? How could I have correct
judgments if I'm not satisfied with being who I am but get wrought
up about what people think of me?"

[25] "But other people will be better off than me and will be promoted over me."*

"But that makes perfect sense, doesn't it? If people have been intent on something, they're bound to have the advantage in it, the
thing they've worked at, aren't they? They've been intent on ob-
taining political power, while you've been intent on your judgments.
They've been intent on becoming rich, you on how you use your impressions. [26] Look and see if they have the advantage over you in
the areas you've taken seriously and they neglect—if, when they give
their assent to something, it's more in compliance with natural standards; if they're more successful in attaining the objects of their desires and in avoiding the objects of their aversions; if they're better
at hitting the mark in their purposes, intentions, and inclinations; if
they maintain their proper roles as men, sons, parents, and so on for
all the other names they bear that indicate their relationships with
other people. [27] If they have political power, shouldn't you be honest with yourself and admit that while you do nothing in order to gain
such power, that's all they're ever concerned about, and that it doesn't
make sense for someone who gives his attention to something to be
less successful in that field than someone who's neglecting it?"

[28] "All right, but since I'm the one who's concerned with the cor-
rectness of my judgments, isn't it more reasonable for me to be the
one with power?"

"Yes, in the area where you exert yourself, your judgments, but in
any field where others have taken more pains, let them have first
place. Otherwise, it's as if you thought that your true judgments

made you better at hitting a target than an archer, or better at working metal than a smith. [29] So don't be so intent on judgments, give your attention to whatever it is you want to gain, and then shed tears if things don't go well for you, because weeping is all you'll be good for. [30] But in fact you say your focus is elsewhere, that you concern yourself with other things, and, as people rightly say, 'You can't combine two different activities at once.'

[31] "One man gets up in the morning and tries to find someone from the imperial household to greet, or someone to speak honeyed words to, or to send a gift to, or he tries to find a way to gratify a celebrity dancer, or to get into someone's good graces by maligning someone else. [32] When he prays, these are the kinds of things in which he hopes to be successful; when he performs a sacrifice, they are the compensation he hopes for. He has applied Pythagoras's saying, 'Let not slumber approach your weary eyes,' to this enterprise.* [33] '"Where did I go wrong" in my flattery of others? "What did I do?" I hope I didn't behave like someone free or honorable.' And if he finds that he did, he rebukes himself and tells himself off: 'What business did you have saying that? You could have lied, couldn't you? Even the philosophers say that there's nothing to stop us from lying.'*

[34] "But if it's really true that you've concerned yourself only with the proper use of impressions, then when you get up in the morning, ask yourself, 'What do I still have to do to achieve imperturbability and serenity? Who am I? Not my body, my possessions, or my social status, surely? No, I'm none of these things. What am I, then? I'm a rational being.' [35] What demands does this place on you? Review what you've done: '"Where did I go wrong" with regard to becoming content? "What did I do" that was unfriendly or antisocial or unkind? "What duty did I leave undone" in this regard?'

[36] "Given that people are so very different in their appetites, behavior, and hopes, do you still want to be on an equal footing with others in those areas that you haven't been intent on and they have? [37] And are you then surprised if they feel sorry for you and make you irritated? But they don't take it amiss if it's you who's taking pity on them. Why not? Because they're confident that what they're getting is good, while you lack this confidence. [38] That's why what you have isn't enough for you and you long for what they have, while they're satisfied with what they have and don't long for what you have. I mean,

if you were truly convinced that, where good things are concerned, it's you who are in possession of them and they who've gone astray, it wouldn't occur to you to be worried about what they think about you."

4.7
On freedom from fear

[1] "What makes a tyrant an object of fear?"

"His bodyguards and their swords," someone said, "and his chamberlains and the retainers he has who bar people from entering."

[2] "So if you bring a child into his presence when he has his guards with him, why doesn't the child feel fear? I suppose it's because he isn't aware of who they are. [3] Now, if someone knows the guards for what they are and knows that they're armed, but is approaching the tyrant precisely because for some reason he wants to die and is looking for an easy death at someone else's hands, will he find the guards terrifying?"

"No, because he wants the very thing that makes them frightening."

[4] "Imagine someone, then, who's completely indifferent about whether he lives or dies, and willingly accepts his lot: when he comes into a tyrant's presence, what's to stop him doing so without fear?"

"Nothing."

[5] "Now imagine someone who feels the same way about his possessions, children, and wife as that man feels about his body. Imagine he's so crazy and witless that he doesn't care whether or not he has these things. Think of a child playing with shards of pottery, who tries to win the game, but doesn't care about the shards. Like this child, our man has come to consider material things unimportant, but enjoys playing and occupying himself with them. Under these circumstances, is there any tyrant or are there any guards with their swords who could make him afraid?

[6] "So madness can make a person regard these things with indifference, and so can habit: witness the Galileans.* But is no one capable of being taught by reasoned argument that God has created everything in the world and has made the world itself completely unimpeded and self-sufficient, with its parts serving the needs of the whole?* [7] Now, no other part has been given the ability to understand God's governance except the rational animal, which has the

resources to work all this out—to know that he's a part and a part of a particular kind, and to understand that it's right for the parts to yield to the whole. [8] Moreover, since it's in his nature to be honorable, great-souled, and free, he understands that, of the things he encounters, some are unimpeded and up to him, while others are impeded and up to others, and he knows that it's things that are subject to will that are unimpeded, and things that aren't subject to will that are liable to impediment. [9] Hence, if he regards what's good for him and in his best interests as belonging exclusively to the former category, consisting of things that are unimpeded and up to him, he'll be free, content, happy, unharmed, principled, pious, and grateful to God for everything, and he'll never complain about any of his experiences or criticize anyone. [10] However, if he locates the good in things that are external to him and aren't subject to will, he'll inevitably be impeded and obstructed, a slave to those who have power over the things he values and fears. [11] And he'll inevitably be impious because he imagines that he's being harmed by God, unjust because he'll always be trying to get more than his fair share, debased, and petty.

[12] "If someone understands all this, is there anything that could stop him living in a carefree and relaxed way, calmly consenting to everything that might happen to him and accepting what has already happened? [13] Is it your wish that I should be poor? Bring it on, then, and you'll see what poverty is when it finds a good actor to play that part. Is it your wish that I should hold public office? Bring it on. That I should not hold public office? Bring it on. Perhaps you want me to suffer hardship? Bring on hardship as well. [14] Banishment? Wherever I go will be fine with me, because here was fine with me, too, not because of the location but because of my judgments, and I shall take those with me. No one can deprive me of them. They're my only true possessions, no one and nothing can take them from me, and my having them is enough for me wherever I am and whatever I'm doing."

[15] "But let's say that now it's time for you to die."

"Why say 'die'? Don't make a tragedy of it, but tell it as it is: 'Now it's time for your matter to revert once more to the components of which it's made.' Is there anything to fear in that? Is any part of the universe going to perish? Is it in any way an abnormal or strange thing to happen? [25]* Show me the guards' swords. See how long and sharp they are! So what do they do, these long, sharp swords?"

"They kill people."

[26] "And what about fever? What does that do?"

"The same."

"And what about a roof tile? What does that do?"

"The same."*

"So should I stand in awe of all these things, bow down before them, and go about enslaved by them? God forbid! [27] But once I've learned that everything that's born must also die, so that the world doesn't come to a halt or get held up, it no longer matters to me whether it's a fever that sees to my death or a roof tile or a soldier— though if I had to decide between them, I'm sure the soldier would do it less painfully and more quickly.

[16] "Is this why a tyrant is an object of fear? Is this why his guards' swords seem long and sharp? Others may be frightened by these things, but I've thoroughly investigated the matter and found that no one has power over me. [17] I've been set free by God, I know what he enjoins me to do, no one can enslave me any longer, and I have the right kind of manumitter and the right kind of tribunal.* [18] 'Am I not the master of your body?'† What's that to me? 'Am I not the master of your property?' What's that to me? 'Aren't exile and imprisonment within my power?' Again, I leave all this and my body in its entirety in your hands; you can do any of these things whenever you like. Try your power out on me and you'll see how far it extends! [19] Who is there, then, that I can still be afraid of? The chamberlains? In case they do what? Shut me out? If they find me wanting to enter, they're welcome to shut me out."

"So why do you go to the palace door?"

"Because I think it's appropriate for me to take part in the game as long as it lasts."

[20] "Why aren't you shut out, then?"

"Because if I'm not admitted, I don't want to be admitted. Rather, I always prefer what actually happens, because I consider what God wants to take precedence over what I want. I'll be his devoted servant and attendant; his inclinations are my inclinations, his desires my desires. In a word, his wishes are my wishes. [21] Being shut out isn't something that happens to me but to those who try to force their way in. So why don't I use force? It's because I know that nothing good is being handed out to those who've made it inside. No, when I hear someone being congratulated because he's being honored by Caesar, I say, 'What's the outcome for him? Is he actually gaining the kind of judgments that he needs for a governorship? Or the kind he needs to take up a procuratorship?'

"Why, then, should I push my way in for the tidbits that are being tossed around? [22] Children grab tidbits and fight one another over them, but men don't, because they don't consider them important. If shards of pottery are being handed out, even children don't snatch them up. [23] Governorships are being handed out; that interests the children, as do money, praetorships, and consulships. Children are welcome to scramble for them, to be shut out of the palace, to be beaten, to kiss the hands of the giver and his slaves. But to me these are no more than tidbits. [24] But if it so happens that as he's tossing these tidbits around one of them lands in my lap, I'll pick it up and eat it. Even a tidbit can have that much value.* But stooping to pick one up, or tripping someone else up, or being tripped up, and flattering those who have access to the palace—no tidbit is worth it, and neither is anything else that isn't a true good, that the philosophers have persuaded me not to think of as good.

[28] "So since I'm not frightened by anything a tyrant can do to me, and since I don't crave any of the things he can procure for me, why should I stand in awe of him? Why should I admire him? Why should I fear his guards? Why should it make me happy if he speaks kindly to me and makes me welcome, and why should I let others know how he spoke to me? [29] If he were Socrates or Diogenes, his praise would be evidence of my character, but he's not, is he? He's not the kind of person I emulate, is he? [30] No, I go to him because otherwise the game would be ruined, and I serve him as long as he doesn't tell me to do anything stupid or objectionable. If he says to me, 'Go and fetch Leon of Salamis,'* I tell him to find someone else, because I'm pulling out of the game. [31] If he orders me to be taken off to prison, I go along with that because it's intrinsic to the game."

"But you'll lose your head."

"And does *his* head last forever, or the heads of people like you, his obedient servants?"

"But you'll be thrown out unburied."*

"If I'm my carcass, yes, I'll be thrown out. But if I'm not my carcass, you should refine how you talk and tell it like it is, rather than try to frighten me. [32] These things frighten children and fools, but if someone who's entered a school of philosophy doesn't know what he is, he deserves to feel fear and to flatter those he used to flatter before. He hasn't yet learned that he isn't flesh and bone and sinews but the faculty that makes use of these things, that manages and understands impressions."

[33] "Yes, but these arguments make people disrespect the law."

"Really? I can't think of any arguments that do a better job of making people obey the law. There's more to law than what a fool commands. [34] Nevertheless, consider how these arguments get us to behave as we should even toward fools, because they teach us not to oppose them by claiming as our own any arena where they could defeat us. [35] They teach us to surrender our bodies, possessions, children, parents, brothers—to renounce them all and let them go. They exclude only our judgments, and it was the will of Zeus, too, that judgments should be an individual's exclusive property. [36] Is there any breach of law here, anything unreasonable? In any arena where you're superior and stronger, I yield to you. On the other hand, where I'm superior, you give way to me, because I've made it my concern and you haven't. [37] You're concerned to see that you live in rooms faced with marble, and to make sure that your slaves and freedmen serve you, that you wear eye-catching clothes, and that you have many hounds, minstrels, and actors to call on. [38] I don't lay claim to any of these things, do I? So have you ever concerned yourself with your judgments? Or with your rational faculty? Do you know what its constituent parts are, and how they're related and interconnected? Do you know what faculties it has and what they're like? [39] Why does it irritate you, then, if someone else, who's taken an interest in these matters, is superior to you in this respect?"

"But there's nothing more important than these matters."

"Well, is anyone stopping you from getting stuck in and engaging with them? And is there anyone who's better equipped than you with books, spare time, and supportive people? [40] Just give these matters some attention at last, and devote some time, even if it's only a little, to your command center. Consider what it is, this thing that you have, and where it came from*—this faculty that makes use of everything else, assesses everything, selects, and rejects. [41] But as long as you give your attention to externals, you'll have more of them than anyone else, and your command center will be in your preferred condition—dirty and neglected."

4.8
To those who rush to assume the guise of philosophers

[1] "Never praise or blame anyone for things that may be either good or bad, and never ascribe either skill or lack of skill to anyone. Then you'll be untainted by either overhasty judgments or malice. [2] 'He's bathing hurriedly.' Does that mean he's doing it wrong? Not at all. What's he doing? Bathing hurriedly."

[3] "Is *everything* done well, then?"

"No, but any act that's based on correct judgments is done well, and any act that's based on bad ones is done badly. Until you know on what kind of judgment a given action is based, refrain from either praising or criticizing it. [4] It's not easy, however, to form judgments on the basis of outward appearances. 'He's a carpenter.' What makes you think so? 'He's using an adze.' So why does it follow that he's a carpenter? 'He's singing, so he's a professional musician.' Why does that follow? 'He's a philosopher.' What makes you think so? 'He has a threadbare cloak and long hair.' And what do tramps have?

[5] "It's judging by externals that makes people say, when they see one of them disgracing himself, 'Look what the philosopher's doing!' But based on the fact that he's disgracing himself, it would be better for them to deny that he's a philosopher. [6] If having a threadbare cloak and shaggy hair were essential to the concept and profession of philosophy, they'd be right. But if it's being free from error instead, why not deny him the title of philosopher on the ground that he doesn't live up to the profession? [7] After all, that's what happens in the case of the other arts. When we see someone doing bad work with an axe, we don't say, 'Does carpentry serve any useful purpose? Look at the bad work carpenters do.' On the contrary, we say, 'The fact that he's doing bad work with an axe shows that he's no carpenter.' [8] The same goes also if we hear someone singing badly. We don't say, 'See how musicians sing,' but 'He's no musician.' [9] It's

only when it comes to philosophy that people do what I've been saying. When they see someone behaving in a way that conflicts with the profession of philosophy, they don't deny him the title. They assume that he's a philosopher and then infer from the fact that he's disgracing himself that philosophy serves no useful purpose.

[10] "Why is this? It's because we respect our conceptions of a carpenter, a musician, and any other kind of professional, but not that of a philosopher. Instead, because we lack a clear and coherent concept, we judge by externals alone. [11] But there's no other art, is there, that's acquired by adopting the appropriate guise and hairstyle, and lacks principles, material to work with, and objective? [12] So what is a philosopher's material? Not a threadbare cloak, surely? No, it's reason. And what's his objective? It's not to wear a threadbare cloak, is it? No, it's to reason correctly. And what are his principles? They're surely not concerned with how to grow a long beard or have a thick head of hair, are they? No, as Zeno says, it's knowing the elements of reason: what each of them is, how they fit together, and what their consequences are. [13] So shouldn't you first see if someone who's disgracing himself is living up to the profession before you find fault with the enterprise? But at present, when you yourself are behaving decently, on the basis of his apparent misbehavior you say, 'Look at the philosopher!'—as though it were appropriate to call someone who's behaving like that a philosopher—and 'So is that what a philosopher is?' But you don't exclaim 'Look at the carpenter!' when you know that one of them is an adulterer or when you see him guzzling his food, or 'Look at the musician!' [14] In other words, even you understand to a certain extent what it is to be a philosopher, but because you haven't given the matter sufficient attention, you don't have a firm grasp of the concept and you get confused.

[15] "But even those who are called philosophers go about their business in ways that are sometimes good and sometimes bad. No sooner have they taken up a threadbare cloak and let their beard grow long than they say, 'I'm a philosopher.' [16] But no one claims to be a musician just because he's bought a plectrum and a lyre, nor does anyone claim to be a smith just because he's wearing a felt cap and an apron. No, their guise is whatever is suitable for their art, and they gain their title from the art, not from the guise. [17] That's why Euphrates was right to say, 'For a long time I tried to hide the fact

that I was practicing philosophy, and I found it useful to do so. In the first place, it enabled me to know that if I did something well, I was doing it not on account of any people who might be looking on but on my own account. It was for my own sake that I ate properly and made sure that my expression and gait were calm and collected. Everything was for myself and God. [18] In the second place, just as the contest was mine alone, so it was also I alone who incurred the risks. If I ever behaved disgracefully or improperly, the cause of philosophy remained out of danger, and I did no harm to the general populace by going wrong as a philosopher. [19] That's why people who didn't know what I was up to were surprised that, although all the people I consulted and spent time with were philosophers, I wasn't one myself. [20] And what harm was there in letting my actions rather than any external clues mark me as a philosopher?"*

"See how I eat, how I drink, how I sleep, how patient I am, how abstemious, how I help others, how I manage my desires and aversions, how I maintain my social relationships, whether natural or acquired, without confusion or obstruction. Judge me on this basis, if you can. [21] But if you're so deaf and blind that you don't take even Hephaestus to be a good smith unless you see him wearing a felt cap on his head,* what harm is there in not being recognized by such a stupid judge?

[22] "This is how Socrates went unrecognized by most people; in fact, they used to come and ask him for introductions to philosophers!* [23] But he wasn't irritated by this, as we might be, was he? He didn't say, 'Really? I don't seem to you to be a philosopher?' No, he'd just take them off and effect an introduction. He was content with just being a philosopher, and he was pleased to find that it didn't hurt him not to be recognized as one. The point is that he bore in mind what his particular work was. [24] What is the work proper to a truly good person? To have many students? Of course not. That's the concern of those who are intent on it. To thoroughly understand complex theories? That too is the concern of others. [25] In what sphere, then, was he someone of note, and wanted to be so? In the sphere of harm and help. 'If anyone can harm me,' he says,* 'the work I'm engaged in is nothing. If I'm waiting for someone else to help me, I myself am nothing. If I want something and it doesn't happen, I feel sorry for myself.' [26] This was the great arena where he

FIGURE 8. Wall painting from Pompeii (IX I, 7, triclinium e), ca. 75–100 CE, currently held at the Museo Archeologico Nazionale in Naples, Italy, inv. 9529. Hephaestus, the god of metallurgy, is here seen making the golden armor of Achilles for the Trojan War. Note the typical blacksmith's felt cap he is wearing.

issued a challenge to all and sundry, and I don't think he ever yielded first place to anyone in—what do you think? Proclaiming and asserting, 'I'm such-and-such a kind of person?' Hardly! But in simply *being* that kind of person.

[27] "Again, you see, it's a fool and a braggart who says, 'I have equanimity and serenity. I would have you realize, people, that while you're all churned up and in turmoil over things of no worth, I alone have been delivered from all unrest.' [28] Isn't it enough for you to feel no pain yourself, without proclaiming, 'Gather round, all you who suffer from gout and headaches, you who have fevers, the lame, and the blind, and see me in sound health and immune to all disorders.' [29] This a vain and vulgar thing to say, unless, like Asclepius,* you're able immediately to suggest a cure that will immediately make

them, too, free from illness, and you're using your own health as an example for this purpose.

[30] "That's what a Cynic does, one who's been judged by Zeus to be worthy of the scepter and diadem.* He says, 'I want you to see, people, that you're looking for happiness and serenity in the wrong place, where they aren't to be found. [31] Behold! I've been sent by God to you as an example! I have no possessions, no house, no wife or children—not even bedding or tunic or utensils. And see how healthy I am! Put me to the test and you'll find that I have peace of mind. Listen to my remedies and the treatment that has cured me.' [32] What unmitigated kindness and generosity! But be sure you know whose work this is: it is the work of Zeus or of the rare person whom he has judged worthy of this form of service, who is obliged never to disclose anything to the world at large that might invalidate the testimony he gives in support of virtue and against external things. 'Never did his fair face turn pale and no tear did he wipe from his cheeks.'* [33] Not only that, but he must neither long for nor miss anything—no person or place or way of life—as children long for harvesttime or holidays, and under all circumstances he must be equipped with self-respect, as others are with walls, doorways, and doorkeepers.*

[34] "But what happens at the moment is that no sooner do people become attracted to philosophy—think of the attraction dyspeptics have toward food that soon they'll find repulsive—than they lay claim to the scepter and kingship. Such a man lets his hair grow long, assumes a threadbare cloak, leaves his shoulder bare, and quarrels with everyone he meets;* even if he sees someone wearing a warm winter cloak, he picks a fight with him. [35] First put in your winter training,* man! Observe your inclinations to see whether they're those of a dyspeptic or the cravings of a pregnant woman. Start by practicing not being recognized for what you are; do philosophy for a short while just for yourself. [36] That's how fruit is produced: the seed has to be buried for a while and lie hidden, and it must be allowed to grow gradually if it's to come to fruition. But if the ear grows before the stem has become jointed, it doesn't come to maturity— it's the product of a garden of Adonis.*

[37] "That's the kind of plant you are too. You've flowered before your time, and winter will wither you. [38] Remember what farmers say about their seeds when an unseasonably early warm spell oc-

curs. They worry that the seeds will shoot up and then a single frost will grip them and expose their weakness. [39] You too need to be careful, man. You've shot up and rushed to gain a reputation before your time. You think you're somebody when you're a fool among fools. You'll be blighted by frost, or rather you've already been blighted by frost down in your roots, while up above you're still producing a few flowers, which make you think that you're still alive and flourishing. [40] But please leave *us* to mature naturally. Why are you exposing us to the elements? Why are you forcing our growth? We're not yet capable of flourishing in the open air. Let the root system spread, then let the plant acquire its first, second, and third joints, and then the fruit will push its way out naturally,† and there's nothing one can do to stop it.

[41] "The point is that anyone who's pregnant, big with such great ideas, is bound to be aware of his aptitude and incline to act accordingly. [42] Look, a bull isn't unaware of his nature and aptitude; when a dangerous creature appears, he doesn't wait for someone to encourage him, and neither does a hound when it catches sight of a wild animal. [43] If I already have the aptitude of a good person, why would I wait for you to supply me with what I need to carry out my work? But at present I don't have these resources, believe me, so the question is: why do you want me to wither before my time, as you yourself have withered?"

4.9
To someone who had lapsed into shamelessness

[1] "Whenever you see someone in a position of political power, set against it the fact that you have no need of political power. Whenever you see someone making a fortune, see what you have instead of that. [2] If you have nothing to put in its place, you see, you feel sorry for yourself, but if you have no need of wealth, you should realize that what you have is more than what he has and far more valuable. [3] One man longs for a beautiful wife; you have your not longing for a beautiful wife. Does that strike you as insignificant? Yet how much would these very people give—the rich, the powerful, the men with beautiful wives—to be able to regard wealth as unimportant, and political power, and even these wives of theirs whom they love and gain?

[4] You know what thirst is like when you have a fever, don't you? It bears no resemblance to the thirst of a healthy person. Someone in good health has a drink and that ends his thirst. Someone with a fever, however, is only briefly satisfied, and then he feels sick, turns the water into bile, vomits, gets cramps in his stomach, and ends up thirstier than he was before. [5] That's what it's like to be rich, to hold political power, and to have a beautiful woman as one's wife, while not being free of the desire for money, political power, and beautiful women. And then there's the envy they feel as well, the fear of losing what they have, the filthy talk, the filthy thoughts, the indecent behavior."

[6] "And what loss am I incurring?" he asked.

"Man, you used to be a self-respecting person and now you aren't. Have you lost nothing? Instead of Chrysippus and Zeno, you're reading Aristides and Eubius.*† Have you lost nothing? Instead of Socrates and Diogenes, you're impressed by someone if he can corrupt and seduce a large number of women. [7] You want to be attractive and you use artifice to make yourself seem so, even though you're not. You want to appear in resplendent clothes to turn women's heads, and if you happen on some perfume, your day is made. [8] Previously, you didn't give these things a moment's thought; you were thinking of where you might find a decent conversation, an exceptional man, a noble thought. You therefore used to sleep as a man, appear in public as a man, wear manly clothes, and speak as befits a good man. And then you say, 'I've lost nothing'? [9] Are you saying that cash is the only thing people can lose? Can't self-respect and decency be lost? And isn't anyone who loses these things liable to injury? [10] It may be that you no longer think of any of these losses as injurious, but there was a time when you considered such a loss the only real form of injury and harm, and when you were concerned to ensure that no one could dislodge these ways of thinking and behaving from you.

[11] "See? They've been dislodged from you, and no one but yourself is to blame. Resist yourself and claim yourself for decency, self-respect, and freedom. [12] Suppose you were told this about me, that someone or other was forcing me to commit adultery, to wear clothes like yours, and to perfume myself, wouldn't you have gone and murdered him, the person who was mistreating me like that? [13] So shouldn't you be helping yourself now? And see how much easier this

kind of help is. You don't have to kill anyone, tie him up, assault him, or appear in court; you just have to talk to yourself, and there's no one more likely to be persuaded, and no one who's more likely to persuade you than yourself.

[14] "Start by condemning what you've been doing, without letting that self-condemnation make you see yourself as a hopeless case. That is, don't behave like those despicable people for whom to give in once is to surrender themselves completely, and who are swept away by the stream, so to speak. [15] No, learn from the men responsible for boys' physical training. A child has had a fall scored against him. 'Get up,' he says, 'carry on wrestling until you've made yourself strong.' [16] That's what you should do too. You should know that there's nothing more malleable than the human mind. All you need to do is apply your will and the result you want happens, the correction is made. On the other hand, all you have to do is nod off and all is lost. Both ruination and help come from within."

[17] "And do I gain anything good from all this?"

"What greater good can you think of than this? You'll exchange shamelessness for self-respect, immodesty for modesty, untrustworthiness for trustworthiness, licentiousness for decency. [18] If you think there are greater goods than these to be found, carry on doing what you're doing. You're beyond saving, even by a god."

4.10
What we should treat as unimportant and what should matter to us

[1] "Uncertainty and helplessness only ever occur in relation to externals. 'What shall I do? What's going to happen? What will the future hold? I hope I don't encounter this or that.' [2] You only ever hear these expressions from people who are involved with things that aren't subject to will. After all, you never hear people saying, 'How can I not assent to something false? How can I not withhold assent from something true?' [3] If a person is gifted enough to worry about such things, I'll jog his memory. 'Why are you worried?' I'll say. 'It's up to you. Be safe. Don't rush into assent before you've applied the rule of conformity with nature.' [4] And again, if he's worried about his desires and aversions, in case his desires are unfulfilled and disappointed and his aversions fail to prevent the occurrence of what he

wants to avoid, [5] the first thing I'll do is give him a kiss for having let go of the things that other people get worked up about—for having freed himself from their fears—and for being focused instead on his own proper business, where he is himself. [6] And then I'll say to him, 'If you'd like your desires not to be disappointed and your aversions to effectively prevent the occurrence of what you want to avoid, desire nothing that isn't your own and feel aversion toward nothing that isn't up to you. Otherwise, you're bound to be disappointed and to experience what you want to avoid.' [7] How can there be uncertainty here? What room is there for 'What's going to happen?', 'What will the future hold?', and 'I hope I don't encounter this or that'? [8] Now, the fact of the matter is that the future isn't subject to will, is it?"

"No."

"And goodness and badness essentially belong to the class of things that are subject to will, don't they?"

"Yes."

"So whatever the future holds, you're able to make use of it in accord with nature, aren't you? No one can stop you doing so, can they?"

"No."

[9] "So don't say, 'What's going to happen?' Whatever happens, you'll make good use of it and the outcome will be a blessing for you. [10] What would Heracles have been if he'd said, 'How can I make sure that I don't encounter a huge lion or a monstrous boar or savage people?' What's the problem? The greater the boar you encounter, the greater the contest in which you'll be involved. If it's villainous men you encounter, you'll be ridding the world of villains."

[11] "But what if I should die in the process?"

"Then you'll die as a good man, performing a noble deed. After all, since you have to die anyway, you're bound to be doing something when death finds you—working your land, digging a ditch, engaged in some commercial transaction, serving as consul, suffering from indigestion or diarrhea. [12] So what do you want to be doing when death arrives? Speaking for myself, I'd like to be doing something that's proper to a human being—something benevolent, something that contributes to the common good, something honorable. [13] And if I can't be doing something that important when death finds me, I'd like at least to be doing something that can't be impeded by others, something that's been given me to do—improving myself, working on the faculty that makes use of impressions, striving for equanimity, giving my social relationships their due—and if I'm so fortunate, applying myself to the third domain, the one that has to do with unassailability of judgment.*

[14] "If death overtakes me when I'm occupied like this, it will be enough for me if I can raise my hands toward God and say, 'The resources that I received from you to help me understand your governance of the world and act in compliance with it, these I have not neglected. For my part, I have not dishonored you. [15] See the use I've made of my senses; see the use I've made of my preconceptions. Did I ever find fault with you? Was I ever displeased by anything that happened? Did I ever want things to be other than how they were? Did I ever contravene the requirements of my social relationships? [16] I'm grateful to you for having brought me into the world and for the gifts you gave me. The amount of time I've had to make use of them is enough for me. Now take them back again and assign me to whatever new post you see fit. For they are all yours, and it was you who gave them to me.' [17] What more could one want than to depart in this state of mind? Moreover, what life could be better or more decent than that of someone who thinks like this, and what life could come to a happier end?

[18] "But in order for this to happen, one has to put up with a lot and do without a lot. You can't want both a consulship and this; you can't be intent both on owning land and on having this; you can't be concerned for both your slaves and yourself. [19] No, if you want something that isn't yours, what's yours will be lost. That's the way things are: nothing comes for free. [20] Not that there's anything surprising in that. If you want to be consul, you must lose sleep, rush to and fro, kiss people's hands, rot away at other men's doors, say and do a bunch of stuff that's unbecoming for a free man, scatter gifts far and wide, and send some people presents every day. [21] And what's the result? Twelve bundles of rods, a seat three or four times on the tribunal, putting on games in the Circus, and providing people with meals in baskets.* If there's anything more to it than that, I'd be glad for someone to explain it to me.

[22] "So when it's a matter of acquiring equanimity and serenity, of sleeping when you're asleep and being awake when you're awake, of having no fears or worries, do you expect to get it all for free and

without any hardship? [23] If your focus is on these results and you suffer some loss or spend money in vain, or if another person gets something that you should have, will your first reaction to what's happened be irritation? [24] Won't you offset the value of what you're gaining against the value of what you've lost? Do you expect to get things of such importance for nothing? That's impossible: 'two different activities,' remember?* [25] It's impossible for you to take care that you have externals and to take care of your command center. If you want the former, forget about the latter. Otherwise, you'll have neither one nor the other, because you'll be pulled in two directions. So if you want the latter, you must give up the former. [26] My oil will be spilled, my utensils broken, but I'll have equanimity. While I'm out of the house, a fire will break out and destroy my books, but I'll be using my impressions in accord with nature.

[27] "But I'll have nothing to eat. Well, if I'm that badly off, death is my haven. Death is the haven and place of refuge for everyone and everything.* That's why none of our experiences in life is unbearable. You can leave whenever you want and no longer be troubled by smoke.* [28] So why worry? Why stay awake at night? Won't you just work out where what's good and what's bad for you are situated, and say, 'Good and bad are up to me. No one can take my good away from me, and no one can make me experience something bad against my will.' [29] So why don't I throw myself down and snore the night away? What's mine is in no danger, and what's not mine will be the concern of whoever gets it, as and when it's given to him by whoever controls access to it. [30] Who am I to wish that things that aren't mine should be like this or like that? It's not my right to choose, is it? No one has made *me* their director, have they? I'm content with the things that are in my power. I have to make them as fine as possible, and everything else can be however its master wants it to be.

[31] "Does anyone who's aware of all this lie awake at night, 'tossing and turning'?* What does he want? What is he missing? Patroclus? Antilochus? Protesilaus?† I mean, was there ever a time when he thought any of his loved ones immortal? Was there ever a time when he wasn't perfectly well aware that tomorrow or the day after either he or his friend was bound to die? [32] 'All right,' he says, 'but I thought he'd outlive me and bring up my son.' That's because you're a fool and you were counting on something that can't be known for

certain. Why not hold yourself responsible, then, rather than sitting and crying like a girl? [33] 'But he used to serve me my food.' Because he was alive, you idiot! He can't serve you now. But Automedon will serve you instead,* and if Automedon dies, you'll find someone else. [34] If the pot in which your meat is usually boiled gets broken, do you have to die of hunger because you don't have your familiar pot? Wouldn't you send out and buy a new one? [35] 'No,' he says, 'because there's nothing worse than this that I could suffer.'* That's because this is the kind of thing you think of as bad. And then, while clinging to the idea that this is a bad thing, are you angry with your mother for not forewarning you about it and telling you that from then on you would live in misery?*

[36] "What do you people here think? Didn't Homer deliberately compose this episode to enable us to see that the highest birth, great strength, great wealth, and exceptional good looks aren't enough to stop people being miserable and utterly wretched as long as they lack the right judgments?"

4.11
On cleanliness

[1] "Some people doubt whether sociability is an aspect of human nature,* but, I think, even they wouldn't dispute the fact that it's certainly in our natures to want to be clean, and that human beings are distinguished from other animals by this feature above all. [2] That's why, when we see an animal cleaning itself, we typically say in surprise that it's behaving like a human being; and conversely, if someone accuses an animal of being dirty, we usually leap to its defense by saying, 'It isn't a human being, you know.' [3] In other words, we think of cleanliness as a distinctively human quality,* deriving in the first instance from the gods. For since it's in the gods' nature to be clean and pure, the closer people draw to them by means of reason, the more they're attracted to cleanliness and being clean. [4] Since it's impossible, given the materials from which they're composed, for human beings to be altogether clean, reason has been assigned the task and does its best to see to their cleanliness.

[5] "The first and most important kind of cleanliness is that of the soul, and the same goes for uncleanliness. But you'd find that what

makes a soul unclean is different from what makes a body unclean. The only kind of uncleanliness you'd find, in the case of soul, is what soils it for the performance of its functions. [6] Now, the soul's functions are inclination and disinclination, desire and aversion, aptitude, purposiveness, and assent. [7] So what is it that makes the soul dirty and unclean in its performance of these functions? When it judges badly, that's all. [8] It follows that uncleanliness of the soul consists in bad judgments, what it takes to clean it is the introduction of the right kind of judgments, and a clean soul is one that has the right kind of judgments. Only such a soul is immune to confusion and contamination in the performance of its functions.

[9] "We should do our best to achieve something similar for the body as well. Given the human constitution, it's impossible for there not to be flux of mucus.* That's why nature made hands, and the nostrils themselves as channels through which to discharge the fluids. So if someone sucks the mucus back down again, in my opinion he's not behaving as a human being should. [10] It's impossible for our feet not to get muddy or otherwise dirty as we make our way through this kind of muck. That's why nature provided us with water and hands. [11] It's impossible for some dirt not to remain on our teeth after eating, and so nature tells us to clean our teeth. Why? To show you're a human being and not a wild beast or a pig. [12] It's impossible for our bodies not to have some dirt left on them and not to need cleaning as a result of the fact that we sweat and our clothes stick to us. That's why we have water, oil, hands, washcloths, strigils, natron, and sometimes a whole lot of other equipment for cleaning the body.* [13] You don't bother? But a smith cleans rust off his tools and has implements that have been made especially for this, and you yourself wash your plate before eating, unless you're a disgustingly filthy person. So won't you wash and clean your body?"

[14] "What's the point?" he said.

"I'll tell you again. Above all, it's so that you can act as is proper for a human being, but it's also so that you don't offend people you meet. [15] In fact, you're smelling a bit here today, though you don't realize it. You think you deserve to smell.* All right; so be it. But surely the people who sit next to you, share a couch with you, or greet you with a kiss don't deserve your smell, do they? [16] Take yourself off to a desert somewhere, and live there alone, smelling yourself. That's what you deserve. It's only right that you and you alone should en-joy your filthiness. But what kind of person behaves so thoughtlessly and inconsiderately in a city, do you think? [17] If nature had en-trusted a horse to you, would you have ignored it and neglected it? Well, think of your body as a horse that you've been entrusted with. Wash it, wipe it, make it such that no one will draw away or turn aside from you. [18] And who doesn't turn aside from a person who's dirty and smelly, and whose skin has the hue of spattered dung or worse? Someone spattered with dung smells because of something external with which he happens to have come into contact, but a smell that's due to lack of care comes from within, from a person who, one might say, has become rotten inside."

[19] "But Socrates didn't often bathe."*

"All the same, his body gleamed. It was so attractive and charm-ing that the most desirable and well-born men were in love with him, and wanted to go to bed with him more than they did with the best-looking men.* He might have neither bathed nor washed—that was his choice—but the few occasions on which he did so were effective."

[20] "But Aristophanes says, 'I'm referring to those whey-faced, barefoot men.'"*

"Yes, and he also says that Socrates 'trod the air' and stole clothes from the wrestling school. [21] I mean, look, Aristophanes's evi-dence is directly contradicted by everyone who wrote about Socrates. Everyone else says that it was a pleasure to see him as well as to listen to him. And they say the same about Diogenes too. [22] The point is that we shouldn't let even our outward appearance scare people away from philosophy but should show ourselves to be joyful and serene in all respects, including where our bodies are concerned. [23] 'Do you see, people? I have nothing and I need nothing. See how, even though I have no house or city, even though I may perhaps live away from the country of my birth and have no place to call home, I live a more se-rene and content life than any highborn or wealthy man. And look at my body as well. See how it's not being spoiled by my austere way of life.' [24] But if I heard these words from someone who had the ap-pearance and look of a condemned criminal, could any god persuade me to have anything to do with philosophy, if that kind of person is its product? Hardly! Even the prospect of attaining wisdom wouldn't tempt me.

[25] "By the gods, I'd prefer a young man who's just starting to be drawn to philosophy to come to me with carefully styled hair rather than with a wasted and filthy body, because he'd be showing that he had some impression of beauty and a desire for decency. He's exercising his ingenuity on the place where he thinks beauty is to be found. [26] All that remains to do is set him straight. 'Young man,' I'd say, 'it's good that you're looking for beauty. You should know, then, that its location is the part of you where reason lies. Look for it where your inclinations and disinclinations are, where your desires and aversions are. [27] That's the special part of you, but in itself your body is just clay. Why take futile pains over it? If you learn nothing else, you will in time come to see that the body is worthless.'

[28] "But if he comes to me filthy and dirty, with facial hair down to his knees, what can I say to him? What common ground do we have which could act as a starting point for me to bring him on? [29] What has ever aroused his enthusiasm that bears any resemblance to beauty and that would enable me to change his mind by saying, 'Beauty isn't located there, but there'? Should I say, 'Beauty isn't to be found in being filthy, but in reason'? I mean, is he interested in beauty? Does he have any conception of it? You might as well go and argue with a pig, to try to get it to stop wallowing in mud. [30] That's why Xenocrates's words got through even to Polemo, because he was a young man who loved beauty. He came to the school with glimmerings of an interest in beauty, but he was looking for it in the wrong place.*

[31] "I mean, look, nature didn't make even animals that live alongside humans dirty. Does a horse live in the dirt? Does a first-class hound? No, but pigs do, and horrid geese, worms and spiders—all creatures that are kept as far away as possible from human company. [32] Don't you, a human being, aspire to be even one of these domestic animals rather than a worm or a spider? Won't you take a bath sometime, however and wherever you want? Won't you wash yourself in cold water if warm isn't to your liking? Won't you come here clean, so that people can enjoy your company? Are you going to be like this even when you join us on our excursions to temples? Even spitting and blowing one's nose are forbidden there, and you're nothing but spit and snot.

[33] "So where are we? Is anyone requiring you to beautify your-

self? Far from it—except when it comes to beautifying that which is our true nature: reason and its judgments and activities. As far as your body is concerned, we're asking no more than that you keep it clean and stop it giving offense. [34] But if someone tells you that it's wrong to wear a purple-trimmed toga, you feel obliged to go off and smear your everyday toga with dung and rip holes in it."

"But how can I have a nice toga?"

[35] "You have water, man. Wash it. Look, here's a lovable young man and here's an old man who deserves to love and be loved in return. He's someone to whom people entrust the education of their sons, to whom daughters and teenagers will come, perhaps. Do they expect to hear him deliver his lectures from a dung heap? [36] Hardly! Every eccentricity springs from some quirk of human nature, but yours comes close to not being human at all."

4.12
On paying attention*

[1] "When you relax your attention for a little while, don't imagine that you'll recover it whenever you choose, but bear in mind that because of the mistake you've made today, you're bound to be worse off in everything you do in the future. [2] To start with the most serious issue, it becomes habitual not to pay attention. Secondly, it also becomes habitual to put off paying attention, and then you can be sure that from one moment to the next you'll constantly be putting off contentment, decency, and a life that is and remains in accord with nature. [3] Now, if procrastination works to your advantage, completely giving these things up will be even more advantageous. But if it brings no advantage, why not maintain your attention unceasingly? [4] 'Today I'd like to have fun.' So what's preventing you from doing so while paying attention? 'I want to sing.' So what's preventing you from doing so while paying attention? Are any aspects of life excluded—any that are out of reach of attention? I mean, is there anything that you'll do worse by paying attention and better by not paying attention? [5] In fact, is there anything in life that's goes better in the hands of inattentive people? Does an inattentive carpenter do more accurate work? Does an inattentive helmsman steer more safely? And what about less important tasks? Are any of

them accomplished better by lack of attention? [6] Don't you realize that, once you let your mind wander, it's no longer in your power to recall it and have it focus on decency, self-respect, and composure? Instead you simply follow your predilections and do whatever comes into your head."

[7] "What should I pay attention to, then?"

"In the first place, to those universal principles of ours. You should have them at hand, and without them you shouldn't go to sleep, wake up, drink, eat, or mingle with others. The principles I mean are that no one is the master of someone else's will, and that good and bad are to be found nowhere else but in will. [8] It follows that no one has the power either to procure something good for me or to make me experience something bad. I myself am the only one who has power over myself in these respects. [9] With these principles as my secure foundation, what reason do I have to be troubled by external things? How could a tyrant, illness, poverty, or an indictment frighten me?

[10] "But I've displeased so-and-so. Well, he's not an action of mine, is he? Nor a judgment of mine? No. So why should I care? But he's widely regarded as an important person. [11] That's his concern, and the concern of those who think him so. However, there *is* a certain being whom I'm obliged to please, submit to, and obey, and that's God—and myself, secondarily. [12] God has made me responsible for myself and has subordinated my will to no one but me, giving me standards to enable me to use it correctly. When I follow these standards, I pay no attention to anyone who contradicts me if the topic is syllogisms, and I don't concern myself with anyone at all if the topic is changing arguments. [13] So why, where matters of greater importance than arguments are concerned, do I get annoyed when people criticize me? What's the reason for this agitation? It must be because I'm a novice in this domain. [14] I mean, knowledge in all its forms despises ignorance and ignorant people, and this goes not just for the sciences but for the arts and crafts as well. Take any cobbler you like, or any carpenter, and you'll find that he despises the common run of people when it comes to his own work.

[15] "First, then, we should have these principles at hand and do nothing without them. Our souls should be intent on this objective: to pursue nothing external, nothing that isn't ours, but, as the Almighty has ordained, to go all out in pursuit of things that are subject

to will and accept everything else as it is given to us. [16] Moreover, we must remember who we are and the names that we bear, and try to direct our behavior into appropriate forms according to the demands of our social relationships. [17] What's the right time for singing or having fun, and in what company? What will be out of place? How can we make sure that our companions don't despise us or we despise ourselves? When is mockery appropriate? Whom should we laugh at and for what? When should we seek company and with whom? And finally, when we're with others, how do we keep ourselves safe?* [18] Whenever you err in any of these respects, you pay for it immediately, and the penalty doesn't come from outside but from the action itself.

[19] "Well now, is it possible to get it all right straightaway? No, but what's possible is to be unceasingly intent on not going wrong. We must be satisfied if we never relax our attention and thereby avoid a few mistakes, at least. [20] You should know that, at the moment, what you mean when you say, 'I'll pay attention tomorrow,' is 'Today I'll be immoral, importunate, odious. It will be possible for others to hurt me. Today I'll be angry and envious.' [21] Do you see how many evils you're letting yourself get away with? But if it's good for you to pay attention tomorrow, how much better would it be to do so today? If it's in your best interests tomorrow, it's far more so today. That way, you'll be able to pay attention tomorrow as well, and not put if off once again to the next day."

4.13
On those who too readily share personal information

[1] "Whenever we think that someone has talked openly with us about his personal affairs, we're somehow tempted to confide in him ourselves, and we think of this as honesty. [2] The primary reason for this is that it seems unfair for us to have been told our neighbor's business and not to reciprocate by sharing some of ours with him too. Secondly, it's due to the fact that we think we'll give people the impression of not being open if we keep quiet about our own affairs. [3] And indeed one often hears people say,* 'I've told you everything about myself. Why are you reluctant to tell me anything about yourself? What kind of behavior is that?' [4] Then another factor is that we think it safe to trust someone who's already trusted us with his

confidences, because we suppose that he'd never reveal what we've told him out of a concern that we might sometime reveal what he told us. [5] That's how unwary people are caught by soldiers in Rome. A soldier sits down next to you in civilian clothing and begins to speak ill of Caesar, and then, as if you'd received a pledge of good faith from him because it was he who initiated the disparagement, you in your turn speak your mind—and then you're bound and taken off to prison.

[6] "We experience something similar in everyday life as well. He felt himself safe in trusting me with his personal information, so I don't† tell all and sundry what I've been told. [7] No, I keep what I've been told to myself—or at any rate I do if that's the kind of person I am—but after he's left, he tells everyone what I said. And then, if I find out what he did, and if I'm the kind of person he is, I want to retaliate and I reveal to others what he's told me in confidence. And so I defile and am defiled. [8] However, if I bear in mind that one person can't harm another but that an individual is both harmed and benefited by his own actions, I manage not to act like him, but I've still suffered what I've suffered because of my own unguarded talk."

[9] "Yes, but it *is* unfair for someone to have been told confidential information by his neighbor and not to reciprocate by sharing some of his with him."

[10] "But I didn't invite your confidences, did I, man? You didn't make your confiding in me conditional on my confiding in you in return, did you? [11] If you're a blabbermouth and take everyone you meet to be a friend, would you have me do the same? It may have been all right for you to have confided in me, but if it's not all right for me to confide in you, why should I be incautious? [12] It's as though I had a watertight storage jar, but yours had a hole in it, and you came and entrusted your wine to my keeping, so that I could store it in my jar, and then you got cross because I'm not entrusting my wine to you as well. But that's because you have a leaky jar!

[13] "Under these circumstances, then, how is the exchange fair? You confided in someone trustworthy and self-respecting, and someone who regards only his own actions as being harmful or beneficial, while nothing external to him can either harm or benefit him. [14] Would you have me trust you, when you've dishonored your will

and want so badly to get money or political power in some form or advancement at court that you're prepared to do a Medea and murder your children?* Where's the fairness in that? [15] Show me that you're trustworthy, self-respecting, and reliable. Show me that your judgments make you a friend of mine and that your jar isn't leaky, and you'll see that I won't wait for you to confide in me, but I'll come of my own accord and ask if I can tell you my secrets. [16] I mean, who refuses to use a sound jar? Who spurns an adviser who's kind and trustworthy? Who doesn't welcome someone who's prepared to share the burden of his problems and thereby to lighten his load?"

[17] "Yes, but I'm trusting you while you aren't trusting me."

"Well, in the first place you're not really trusting me either. It's just that you're a blabbermouth and that makes you incapable of keeping things to yourself. I mean, if what you say is true, make me the sole recipient of your confidences. [18] But the fact is that whenever you see *anyone* who's not otherwise engaged, you sit down beside him and say, 'Brother, there's no one who's more kindly disposed toward me than you, no one who's a better friend, so please let me tell you about my affairs.' And you do this to complete strangers! [19] And even if you do trust me, that's obviously because you see me as a trustworthy and self-respecting person, not because I've told you about my affairs.

[20] "So get me to think the same way as you. Prove to me that if a person tells someone else about his affairs, that makes him a trustworthy and self-respecting person. If that were true, I'd go around telling everyone about my affairs, if that was what it took to make me a trustworthy and self-respecting person. But it isn't true: what it takes is judgments of an uncommon kind. [21] At any rate, if you see someone who's intent on things that aren't subject to will and has subordinated his will to them, you may be sure that this is a person who is constrained and impeded by thousands upon thousands of people. [22] You don't need pitch or a wheel to get him to divulge what he knows.* All it takes is a nod from a pretty girl, let's say, to shake the information out of him, or a friendly gesture from a member of Caesar's inner circle, or his longing for political power or an inheritance, or countless other things of that sort. [23] Remember, then, that in general confidential information requires trustwor-

thiness and corresponding principles, and it's not easy to find these qualities nowadays. [24] Or can anyone here give me a current example of a person who's such that he can say, 'I care only for what's mine, which cannot be impeded and is naturally free. This, which is the essence of goodness, I have, and as for everything else, what will be will be. It makes no difference to me.'"

Fragments

1

"Does it make any difference to me," he asked, "whether things are made out of atoms or particles or fire and earth?* Isn't it enough to know what is essentially good and bad, the limits of desire and aversion, and of inclination and disinclination, to use these as rules to manage our lives, and to bid farewell to things that are beyond us? Such things are in any case probably not comprehensible by the human mind, and even if one assumes that they are fully comprehensible, the question still remains whether there's anything to be gained by comprehending them.* Shouldn't we say that people who insist that it's crucial for a philosopher to know such things are just creating unnecessary work? What about the Delphic commandment, then, to know yourself?* Is it redundant as well?"

"No, that certainly isn't," someone said.

"So what does it mean? If one told a choral dancer to know himself, wouldn't he respond to the instruction by paying attention to the other members of the chorus and to singing in harmony with them?"

"Yes."

"And likewise for a sailor? A soldier? Do you think that a human being has been made to live all by himself or with others?"

"With others."

"By whom?"

"By nature."

"What nature is, how it governs the universe, even whether or not there really is such a thing—in that case, are these matters with which there's no need to concern oneself?"

2

"Anyone who's dissatisfied with the circumstances assigned him by fortune is unskilled in the art of living, while anyone who nobly endures his circumstances and makes reasonable use of what they have to offer deserves to be called a good person."

3

"Everything obeys and serves the universe—earth, sea, sun, all the other heavenly bodies, and the flora and fauna of the earth. The human body, too, is its servant, in sickness and health (which is as the universe wills), in youth and old age, and in the course of all the other changes that the body goes through. It is therefore reasonable to suppose that what is up to us—that is, our faculty of judgment—cannot be the one thing that resists the universe. The universe is powerful and superior to us, and it has done a better job of taking thought for us than we can, by including us along with everything else[†] in its governance. Besides, to act against it is not only to align oneself with the irrational, but it is unproductive of anything except a futile struggle, and only causes us pain and grief."[*]

4[*]

"God has made some things up to us and other things not up to us. The best and most important thing is up to us—it is, in fact, what perfects even God's life—and that is making use of impressions. When right use is made of impressions, the consequences are freedom, contentment, joy, self-possession, and in addition justice, obedience to the law, self-discipline, and virtue in general. Everything else he made not up to us. So we too should be of one mind with God. In keeping with the way he has divided things up, we should do all we can to lay claim to things that are up to us but give authority over things that are not up to us to the universe and gladly surrender to it whatever it may need, which may even be our children, our homeland, or our lives."

5

"Is there anyone here who isn't impressed by the famous words of Lycurgus of Sparta?* When he lost the sight of one of his eyes thanks to a fellow citizen, the people turned the young man over to him for punishment as he saw fit, but instead of punishing him, he gave him an education, made a good man of him, and then presented him to the assembled citizens. The Spartans were surprised, but he said, 'When you handed this person over to me he was contemptuous and unruly. I'm returning him to you well behaved and a model citizen.'"

6

"But this is nature's primary function: to bind and adapt our inclinations to our view of what's fitting and useful."

7

"Thinking that others will despise us if we don't do everything we can to hurt our chief enemies is typical of particularly debased and ignorant people. I mean, it's commonly said that one of the marks of a despicable person is his inability to cause harm, whereas it's much more his inability to do anyone good."

8

"Universal nature was and is and will be like this, and it's impossible for things to happen differently than they do now. And it's not only human beings and all the other creatures of the earth who've been subject to this alteration and change, but even the gods. And, by Zeus, the four elements themselves are altered and changed up and down: earth becomes water, water becomes air, air in its turn changes into fire, and there's the same process from above downward.* Anyone who undertakes to turn his mind in this direction and to persuade

himself to accept the inevitable of his own accord will live a very measured and harmonious life."

9

A famous Stoic philosopher extracted from his satchel the fifth book
of the *Discourses* of the philosopher Epictetus, which were arranged
by Arrian and which are undoubtedly compatible with the work of
Zeno and Chrysippus.* In that book we find—written in Greek, of
course*—the following idea:

Things that appear to the mind (φαντασίαι is the technical term
in philosophy)—that is, things by which our consciousness is immediately struck, as soon as it has an image of something that gets
through to the mind—are neither subject to our will nor up to us but
force themselves, by a certain power of their own, upon our attention.
However, assents (the term is συγκαταθέσεις), whereby these impressions are identified, are subject to our will and up to us. Consequently,
when some terrifying sound occurs, from the heavens or from a collapsing building,* or when news suddenly arrives of some imminent
danger, or anything else of that kind happens, even a sage's mind is
bound to be moved a little, to contract* and be frightened, not from
any anticipatory judgment that something bad is about to happen
but because of certain rapid and unconscious motions that forestall
the proper functioning of the mind and the rational faculty.* Soon,
however, the wise man withholds his assent (this is οὐ συγκατατίθεται
οὐδὲ προσεπιδοξάζει)* from τὰς τοιαύτας φαντασίας (that is, the terrifying mental impressions), and instead rejects and repudiates them,
and finds nothing in them to make him frightened. And this, they
say, is how the minds of a fool and a wise man differ: a fool thinks
that things which, when they first strike his mind, seem to be harsh
and terrible really are like that, and then, as if they were truly frightening, he goes on to give them his assent and προσεπιδοξάζει (this is
the word the Stoics use in their discussions of this issue), whereas
a sage experiences a brief and slight alteration of color and expression, but then οὐ συγκατατίθεται [withholds his assent], and instead
retains his conviction and the strength of the opinion he has always
held about such impressions, as things that are not really frighten-

ing in the slightest but cause us fear with their misleading appearances and empty alarms.

This is the idea, based on the teachings of the early Stoics, that we
find expressed by the philosopher Epictetus in the work I mentioned.

10

I have heard Favorinus* say that the philosopher Epictetus described
most people who are taken to be philosophers as philosophers ἄνευ
τοῦ πράττειν, μέχρι τοῦ λέγειν (which means "only as far as words go,
without putting them into practice"). Epictetus was also given to an
even more forceful way of expressing the same point, and Arrian has
left us a record of it in the books he composed about Epictetus's discourses. He says that whenever Epictetus noticed someone who had
no sense of shame, who put his energy to inappropriate uses, who
was morally corrupt, brazen, and given to outrageous remarks, and
who paid attention to everything apart from his soul—whenever, Arrian says, he saw that kind of person appropriating the precepts and
teachings of philosophy, taking up physics, studying logic, and embarking on the investigation of philosophical theories by the dozen,
he would call on gods and men to witness the travesty and would often interrupt this appeal by exclaiming, "Where are you putting all
these teachings, man? Check whether the vessel is clean. I mean, if
you put them in the vessel of opinion, they're ruined, and once rotten
they turn into piss or vinegar or perhaps something worse." Surely
there could be nothing with more authority or more truth than these
words, employed by the greatest of philosophers to assert that the
writings and teachings of philosophy, when poured into the foul
and filthy vessel that is a depraved impostor, are altered, changed,
spoiled, and (as he puts it κυνικώτερον [in a rather Cynic way]) turn
into urine or something more vile than urine.

Again, Favorinus informs us that Epictetus used to say that there
are two vices which are far more serious and offensive than all the
others: lack of fortitude and lack of self-control—that is, when we
fail to tolerate or endure the wrongs that we ought to endure, or when
we fail to resist things and pleasures that we ought to resist. And so,
Epictetus says, if someone were to take to heart the following two

words and make them his watchwords for governing and observing himself, he will, for the most part, be free of imperfections and will live a life of tranquility. And these two words, he used to say, were ἀνέχου and ἀπέχου [bear and forbear].

10a*

When what's at stake is the safety of our souls and our self-respect, we may have to act even without stopping to think about it, as Arrian approvingly quotes Epictetus as saying.

11*

"Now, when Archelaus* invited Socrates to his court, promising to make him rich, Socrates sent back the following message: 'In Athens, four quarts of barley meal sell for an obol and water flows from springs.' The point being that even if what I have is unsatisfactory, I can make it satisfactory by being satisfied with it. Do you think that when Polus played the part of Oedipus in Colonus, a beggared outcast, he pleased his audience's ears less or gave them less enjoyment than when he played Oedipus the king?* Then shall an honorable person make a worse showing than Polus, rather than making a good job of playing whatever role God assigns him? Won't he imitate Odysseus as well, who was just as remarkable in his rags as in his close-woven, purple-dyed toga?"*

12

"There are some people who are bad-tempered but keep it to themselves. They do exactly the same as those who are completely carried away by rage, but they do it calmly and apparently without a hint of anger. We need to be on our guard against such people. Their inconspicuousness is far worse than violent anger, because in the latter case, people quickly have their fill of retaliation, whereas the kind of person we're talking about nurses his anger for ages, like people with a mild fever."

13

"But," someone said, "I see people who are honorable and good dying from hunger and cold."

"But what about those who are dishonorable and bad? Don't you see them dying from luxury, pretentiousness, and vulgarity?"

"All right, but it's demeaning to be dependent on others."

"And is anyone entirely self-sufficient, you scoundrel? Only the universe is self-sufficient.* I mean, to find fault with providence because bad people go without punishment thanks to their power and wealth is no different from saying that bad people who've become blind haven't been punished because their fingernails are in good condition. And, personally, I'd say that there's more of a difference between goodness and possessions than there is between eyes and fingernails."

14

"...* people who introduce into the discussion those dour philosophers who think that pleasure isn't natural but an epiphenomenon on things that are natural, such as justice, moderation, and freedom.* Why, then, does the soul find 'pleasure and peace,' as Epicurus puts it, in bodily goods which are relatively unimportant, but not in its own goods, which are of critical importance? Even so, I've also been endowed by nature with self-respect, and I often blush when I feel that I'm saying something disgraceful. It's this feeling that stops me from counting pleasure as good and the goal of life."

15

"In Rome, the women engage with Plato's *Republic* because of his claim that women should be held in common. But they pay attention only to the man's words, not his meaning. It's not that he recommends that people should marry and live together, one man with one woman, and then proposes that women should be held in common. No, he does away with regular marriage altogether and replaces it with another kind. It is generally true that people like to find excuses for their own transgressions.* After all, philosophy tells us that we shouldn't even extend a finger aimlessly."

16

"It's worth appreciating that it isn't easy for a person to form a judgment unless he says and hears the same ideas day after day, and at the same time puts them to work in his life."

17

"When we're invited to a banquet, we address ourselves to what's on offer. If someone were to ask his host to serve up fish or cakes instead, that would be thought outrageous. Yet in life we ask the gods for things they don't give us, and do so even though there are plenty of things that they have given us."

18

"It's charming," he said, "how some people preen themselves on qualities that aren't up to us. 'I'm better than you,' says one, 'because I own many plots of land, and you're starving.' Another says, 'I'm of consular rank.' Another, 'I'm a procurator.' Another, 'I have gorgeous hair.' But one horse doesn't say to another, 'I'm better than you because I've got a large field to graze in, plenty of barley, golden bridles, and embroidered caparisons.' No, it says, 'I'm faster than you.' The same goes for every creature: they're better or worse because of the virtues or vices that are peculiar to their species. Are human beings, then, the only creatures that don't have a virtue of their own? Must we count on our hair, our clothes, and our ancestors?"

19

"A doctor's failure to give advice angers people who are ill; they think he's given up on them. Why shouldn't we regard a philosopher in the same way and think that he's given up expecting us to come to our senses if he's stopped telling us anything useful?"

20

"People whose bodies are in a good condition can endure heat and cold, and in the same way, people whose souls are in a good condition can put up with anger, grief, joy, and all the other passions."

21

"That's why Agrippinus deserves our praise, because, although he was a man of the very highest caliber, he never praised himself but used to blush even if someone else was praising him. Typically, when faced with any difficulty, he'd write in praise of it. If he had a fever, he'd eulogize fever; if he was out of favor, he'd eulogize being out of favor; if he was sent into exile, he'd eulogize exile. Once, in fact, when he was about to eat his breakfast, someone came with the news that Nero had banished him, and he said, 'Then we'll eat breakfast in Aricia.'"*

22

"When Agrippinus was serving as a governor, he used to try to persuade the people he sentenced that it was right for them to be sentenced. 'It's not because I hate them or want to steal from them that I cast my vote against them,' he said, 'but because I'm their custodian and guardian. I'm like a doctor, who reassures the patient he's cutting open and persuades him to submit.'"

23

"Nature is wonderful and, as Xenophon says, benevolent toward its creatures.* At any rate, there's nothing nastier and more foul than the human body, and yet we love our bodies and look after them. I mean, if we had to tend to our neighbor's body for just five days, we wouldn't be able to stand it. Just think what it would be like to get up in the morning, clean someone else's teeth, and then, after he had done† the necessary, wash his nether regions. It's truly amazing that we love something that demands so much of us every day. I stuff this sack of mine, and then I empty it. What could be more tedious? But I'm duty bound to serve God, and so I live on and put up with washing, feeding, and covering this wretched body. And when I was younger, it required something else of me as well, and yet I put up with it. So why do you find it intolerable when nature, which gave you your bodies, takes them away?"

"Because I love my body," someone said.

"Well, but as I was saying just now, this too, the very love that you feel for your body, is a gift of nature. And it's nature again that says, 'Let your body go now and it won't be a nuisance anymore.'"

24

"If someone dies young, he blames the gods <because he's being taken before his time. And if someone lingers on into extreme old age, he too blames the gods,>* because he's afflicted with complaints at a time when he ought to have been able to rest. Despite this, at the approach of death, he wants to stay alive; he sends for the doctor and begs him to do all he can and give him his best attention. It's quite remarkable," he said, "to see how people want neither to live nor to die."

25

"Whenever you lay into someone and threaten him, remember to tell yourself beforehand that you're no wild animal, and then you'll get through life without having done anything savage that you'd later regret and pay for."

26*

You're a pathetic little soul sustaining a corpse, as Epictetus used to say.

27

He said that we must discover an art of assent* and, in the domain of inclination, must pay careful attention to make sure that every inclination is conditional,* contributes to the common good, and is commensurate with the value of what it's an inclination for. He also said that we should avoid desire altogether and apply aversion to nothing unless it's up to us.

28

"So," he said, "the contest is for no trivial prize; what's at stake is madness or sanity."*

28a*

"Socrates used to say, 'What do you want to have? The souls of rational or non-rational creatures?'

'Rational creatures.'

'What kind of rational creatures? Sound or corrupt?'

'Sound ones.'

'Then why don't you make that your aim?'

'Because we already have them.'

'Then why are you fighting and quarreling?'"

28b

"'It's my rotten luck that this has happened to me.' On the contrary: 'It's my good luck that, although this has happened to me, I feel no distress, since I'm unbruised by the present and unconcerned about the future.' What happened could have happened to anyone, but not everyone could have carried on without letting it distress him. So why regard the incident as a piece of bad luck rather than seeing your avoidance of distress as a piece of good luck? Do you generally describe a person as unlucky when his nature worked well? Or do you count it as a malfunction of a person's nature when it succeeds in securing the outcome it wanted? Well, you know from your studies what it is that human nature wants. Can what happened to you stop you from being fair, high-minded, moderate, conscientious, unhasty, honest, self-respecting, self-reliant, and so on—from possessing all the qualities which, when present, enable a person's nature to be fulfilled? So then, whenever something happens that might cause you distress, remember to rely on this principle: this is not bad luck, but bearing it valiantly is good luck."

Notes

Conventions: A reference such as 1.12 refers to an entire discourse (in this case the twelfth discourse of the first book); sections of discourses are referred to as 1.12.7 or 4.6.13, for instance. References to the *Handbook* and Fragments use simple numbers, such as *Handbook* 1 or Fragment 12, but some of the longer *Handbook* entries have subsections that are referred to as, for instance, *Handbook* 1.3. The symbol § has been used to indicate sections within the discourse currently being annotated.

Handbook

1.1: *inclination, desire, aversion*: "Desire" and "aversion" are technical terms in Stoicism. Desire is a strong inclination to possess what seems good, and aversion a strong inclination to avoid what seems bad. On "inclination," see the note to *Handbook* 2.2. The sentence assumes the three domains or phases of practical training: the first domain is concerned with desire/aversion, the second with inclination/disinclination, and the third with judgments; see the introduction, 30–33.

1.1: *our own doing*: Official positions are not up to us even if we work for them, because, like reputation, they are given us by others. We can want to be elected, but we cannot choose to be elected.

1.2: *unimpeded... not ours*: The things that are up to us are unimpeded just because they are entirely up to us; no one or nothing from outside can obstruct us, and we take no orders from outside, like a slave. But see also the note to *Handbook* 2.2 on reservation.

1.3: *remember this*: Many times in the *Handbook*, Epictetus urges his students to remember or to bear something in mind, or to have a precept at hand. In his commentary, Simplicius put a nice spin on this, suggesting that Epictetus was directly addressing the rational soul, which has been "degraded to forgetfulness" by its engagement with the external world, and so constantly needs to be reminded to "remember" (*On Epictetus's Handbook* 226).

1.4: *fail to get the former*: See also 4.10.25.

2.2: *things that are contrary to nature among the things that are up to us*: Things such as negative emotions and wrongdoing. See also Handbook 48b.2.

2.2: *desire... for the time being*: As a temporary measure, until desire is under one's control and aims only for things that are in accord with nature and up to us (see 4.1.84). Many of Epictetus's remarks are designed for relative beginners. See further the note to 1.4.1.

2.2: *inclination and disinclination*: The terms *hormē* and *aphormē* (often translated "impulse" and its opposite) refer to the mental faculty that leads us to do something, to act. Non-rational animals are moved entirely by their inclinations, but mature human beings have the ability to use reason to direct their inclinations: they can choose to assent or not to the impression that leads to an inclination to act.

2.2: *reservation... detachment*: Things in the external world are not "up to us" or subject to our will. Because we cannot be certain that any of our actions will come out exactly as planned—other people or events (i.e., fate) may thwart us—a Stoic proceeded "with reservation" (that is, accepting that he may have to adapt himself to prevailing conditions: see *Handbook* 4) and "with detachment" (that is, without being concerned if the outcome was not exactly what he set out to do). His intentions matter more than the action itself, and by easily avoiding obstacles in this way, he attains contentment, a smoothly flowing life. The basic principle is enunciated at 4.7.20: "I always prefer what actually happens, because I consider what God wants to take precedence over what I want."

3: *attractive, useful, or lovable*: "These three—pleasure, utility, and the affection that is a necessary part of our nature—rivet the soul to mortal unpleasantness." Simplicius, *On Epictetus's Handbook* 235.

3: *upset if they die*: See also *Handbook* 11, 16; *Discourses* 1.1.14, 3.3.15, 3.24.85–88, 4.1.111–112, 4.7.5.

4: *resent what's happening*: Being annoyed by external events is contrary to nature because it shows a lack of acceptance of what universal nature throws your way. It was a Stoic exercise to foresee difficulties before encountering them, to make them easier to handle. On Epictetus's concept of will, see the introduction, 26–27.

5a: *Socrates would have thought it so*: Epictetus is thinking of a famous passage of Plato's *Apology of Socrates* (40c–41c), in which Socrates suggests that death is either extinction or relocation to a better place, and that in either case there is nothing to fear.

5b: *what a fully educated person does*: Two entries from Marcus Aurelius's *Meditations* cast light on this entry. "The gods are not to be blamed, because they do no wrong, either deliberately or involuntarily. Nor are men to be blamed, because they do no wrong that isn't involuntary. So don't blame anyone" (12.12). And "There's no point in assigning blame, because either you can set the person straight, in which case you should do that, or, if you can't do that, you should straighten out the business itself. And if you can't do that, what's to be gained by assigning blame?" (8.17). As usual, when Epictetus talks of "education," he means education in philosophy. A "fully educated" person is a Stoic sage.

7: *bulbs*: Hyacinth bulbs are still commonly eaten around the Mediterranean.

7: *like the sheep*: Perhaps because the sheep were the last to be taken on board, and so the wayward passenger would be caught up among them. Perhaps also, metaphorically, because sheep were supposed to be gluttonous (*Discourses* 2.9.4), and if the traveler refused to give up his snacks, he would be behaving like a sheep.

7: *left behind*: So the "captain" in the metaphor is Zeus or God, the rational providence that steers all things and determines the length of an individual's life. In *Handbook* 11 the same power is called "the donor." In *Discourses*, Epictetus often refers obliquely to God as "someone else."

12: *Start with trivial things, then*: See also 1.18.18, 3.13.20–21, 3.24.84–88; 4.1.111–114; *Handbook* 3, 15, 26.

12: *different from what you want*: This is the same exercise as in *Handbook* 4: foreseeing possible trouble, so that you are not surprised or angry when it happens.

14b: *what he wants or doesn't want*: See also 1.4.19, 2.2.26, 3.20.8, 4.1.59–60, 4.1.85.

15: *Heraclitus*: It is not impossible that we should read "Heracles" here rather than "Heraclitus": L.-A. Dorion, "Héraclite ou Héraklès? À propos d'Épictète, *Manuel* 15," *Revue de Philologie* 89, no. 1 (2015): 43–63. Both were greatly admired by the Stoics.

15: *godlike men*: Diogenes of Sinope, the founder of Cynicism, scorned all the things of the world, including political office. The Presocratic thinker Heraclitus of Ephesus is mentioned because he, too, according to tradition, refused high office when he was offered it (Diogenes Laertius, *Lives of the Eminent Philosophers* 9.2). Along with Socrates, Diogenes and Heraclitus were considered paradigms by the Stoics.

16: *inwardly as well*: So a Stoic displays sympathy, but does not feel it, because that would be to arouse a passion in his soul. See the introduction, 24–25, on passion. Does this make a Stoic a hypocrite? No, because he is doing what he always does in relation to other people: playing a role. See the introduction, 28–29, on roles.

17: *role was chosen by someone else*: The theatrical metaphor recurs at 1.29.46, 4.1.165, and 4.7.13. The "someone else" is, as often elsewhere, God.

18: *croaks ominously*: The flight and calling of birds were, if unexpected or occurring at a significant moment, frequently taken to be meaningful. Stoics explained such omens by their theory that everything in the world is interconnected, even if the connection between a raven's croak and, say, your falling ill is not immediately obvious.

19a: *isn't up to you*: Once more, Epictetus refers to one of his favorite topics, the Stoic teaching of adaptation or reservation (see the note to *Handbook* 2.2). The wording is close to *Discourses* 3.6.5. See also 3.22.102.

20: *bide your time*: See also *Handbook* 34, *Discourses* 1.20.7–12, 2.18.24, 3.3.14–17, 3.12.15.

23: *to think so*: See 2.1.36, 4.8.17–20, and *Handbook* 46.1.

24.3: *self-respect*: Epictetus often stresses the importance of self-respect—and often pairs it, as here, with trustworthiness (integrity, honesty) as the two fundamental qualities an aspirant should have. The Greek is *aidōs*, and it makes people see what they do as a reflection of what they are. It is therefore closely related to Epictetus's emphasis on the role or roles one plays (see the introduction, 28–29). People are spurred to act if the action is appropriate to their idea of themselves, or otherwise to avoid the action. *Aidōs* determines "how much you're worth to yourself and at what price you sell yourself" (*Discourses* 1.2.11). It combines the notions of sense of shame, conscience, and self-respect; its opposite is having no sense of shame—nothing that would make one stop acting inappropriately. It was Democritus, in the fifth century BCE, who introduced this sense of *aidōs* as shame in one's own eyes (see Fragments 84, 244, and 264 Diels/Kranz).

24.4: *everyone does their own job*: This is the social principle that underlies the theoretical ideal state of Plato's *Republic*.

25.2: *a patron's door*: In Rome, a rich and powerful man had dependents; he was the "patron," they were his "clients," and his prestige was measured in part by the quantity and quality of his clients. Clients were expected to wait in the morning by the patron's doorway until being admitted into the interior of the house, where, forming the "reception line" mentioned by Epictetus, they would greet and salute their patron before he set the agenda for the day. In return, a client might expect his patron to help him in various ways, especially financial and political. Some of this *Handbook* entry seems to be based on 3.24.48–49.

27: *badness isn't a natural feature of the world*: A rather elliptical entry. It is the nature of the world that it is perfect (according to Stoicism), and it is the nature of a target to be hit. The only bad things in the world are introduced by human beings, who miss the target in the sense that they think they are doing what is good for them, when it may in fact be bad. Or perhaps the meaning is that, since badness does not occur naturally, it cannot be an end or target and so constitute something's nature. See further G. Boter, "Epictetus, *Encheiridion* 27," *Mnemosyne* 45, no. 4 (1992): 473–81.

29: This entry is a doublet, with a few differences, of all of *Discourses* 3.15 except the ending. The earliest manuscript of the *Handbook* does not include it, nor was it in the copy that Simplicius drew on for his commentary in the sixth century, so it was added in a subsequent edition and therefore not by Arrian himself. It is an introductory talk, so it was perhaps added by someone who recognized the introductory nature of the *Handbook*. The differences between this entry and *Discourses* 3.15, though minor, are puzzling. Why are there two versions of this talk? Where did the different readings come from?

29.2: *wield a spade*: Perhaps the athletes helped prepare the ground for some of the events. This is just one of the "undignified" consequences of wanting to be a champion athlete.

29.2: *flogged*: Flogging was the standard punishment for infringements at the Olympic Games—a very undignified punishment that was otherwise reserved for slaves.

29.4: *Euphrates*: The manuscripts of the *Handbook* give us "Socrates" here, but Euphrates of Syria is the philosopher in the parallel passage of *Discourses* (3.15.8), and his eloquence is noted by others as well. Socrates is mentioned so often by Epictetus that it would have been easy for a scribe to write his name here by mistake. Euphrates was active in the first and early second centuries CE.

29.6: *think you can*: The received text at this point does not quite make sense. I think that a scribe omitted a few words because his eye skipped from one "you can" to the next, so I have added the relevant clause as it is found in the parallel passage of *Discourses* (3.15.10).

29.7: *imperial procurator*: An imperial procurator was usually the chief financial officer of a province, but in small provinces, where the chief issue was taxation, not defense, he might be the governor as well.

29.7: *command center*: A Stoic term for the mind. The term originated with Plato, at *Protagoras* 352b. The command center is so called because "it centralizes, unifies, and interprets what goes on in the rest of the soul." J. Annas, *Hellenistic Philosophy of Mind* (University of California Press, 1992), 64.

30: *appropriate for us to take*: In Stoicism, an "appropriate" action is one that has a reasonable justification. These are often actions that conform with our nature as human beings, such as helping others; but there may be occasions when it is not appropriate to help others. Another way of looking at appropriate actions is that they are those that a sage would do, and so our actions may be appropriate even though we are not fully virtuous sages.

30: *our relationships*: See the introduction, 28–29, on roles.

31.4: *sole rule is a good thing*: See 2.22.13–14 and 4.5.29. In legend, Eteocles and Polynices were the sons of Oedipus. When they inherited the throne of Thebes, they decided to share it, each ruling for one year and then handing over to his brother. Eteocles went first, while Polynices was in exile in Argos, but at the end of the year Eteocles refused to cede the throne, so Polynices raised an army, headed by the famous Seven against Thebes, to seize power. He failed, and the two brothers killed each other in single combat.

31.4: *inextricably linked*: See also 1.27.14.

32: This *Handbook* entry is based on *Discourses* 2.7.

32.1: *something that isn't up to us*: Otherwise, you would not be consulting the seer in the first place but acting as a self-reliant agent.

32.3: *Socrates's approval*: See Xenophon, *Memorabilia* 1.1.6–9.

32.3: *the matter in question*: This probably means (see also 2.10.5) "situations where the individual seeks to bring his desires into accordance with nature, but is unable to determine the direction towards which nature or fate is leading." G. Gabor, "When Should a Philosopher Consult Divination? Epictetus and Simplicius on Fate and What Is Up to Us," in *Fate, Providence, and Moral Responsibility in Ancient, Medieval and Early Modern Thought*, ed. P. D'Hoine and G. van Riel (Leuven University Press, 2014), 325–42, at 338–39. Moreover, no one, however fully rational, can anticipate everything, and there are occasions when forewarned is forearmed. See also E. MacGillivray, "Reassessing Epictetus' Opinion of Divination," *Apeiron* 53, no. 2 (2020): 147–60.

32.3: *being killed*: The story is told by Aelian, at *Historical Miscellany* 3.44, and by Simplicius in his commentary on this passage (*On Epictetus's Handbook* 395–396). Three friends were on their way to consult Apollo's oracle at Delphi when they were set upon by thieves. One ran away, and the other two fought back, but one of them was accidentally killed by the other during the fight. The oracle refused to hear the question of the man who ran away and pardoned the one who had accidentally killed his friend.

33.1: *other people*: The bullet points (so to speak) that follow constitute a kind of basic training, a laying of the foundation for the establishment of one's "role," or the identity one takes on as a philosopher, that determines the way one presents oneself to others (see, e.g., *Handbook* 37, *Discourses* 1.2).

33.2: *compare them to others*: This seems to be drawn from 3.16.4.

33.5: *Avoid swearing oaths … as much as you can*: Stoics avoided swearing oaths for two reasons. First, the future is uncertain, so you may have to break your promise. Second, in oaths you commonly call on the gods to assist you in something that should be up to you alone. However, in the ancient world oaths were used when signing contracts, for instance, so that no one could expect to get through life without having to swear oaths; hence Epictetus's "as much as possible." At the end of 1.14 he outlines an acceptable kind of oath: one of allegiance to God and acceptance of all that he has in store for you.

33.6: *happens to be clean*: This is based on *Discourses* 3.16.3.

33.10: *moral improvement*: Much of this paragraph is reminiscent of *Discourses* 3.4.

36: *conjunction*: In Stoic logic, a disjunctive statement is "Either it is day or it is night," where if one proposition is correct, the other cannot be. A conjunctive statement (here a meaningless one) has the form "It is both day and night." See also *Discourses* 2.9.8.

39: *measure of his property*: The same idea is otherwise expressed at *Handbook* 33.7. How much you possess and what you possess should be determined by actual bodily needs and by no other criterion.

39: *walking off a cliff, so to speak*: You will not know when to stop.

40: *self-respecting*: This is the basis of the "role" (in Epictetus's sense of the word) that women should play if they are to fulfill their potential and be happy.

45: *'hurriedly'*: Compare 4.8.2.

45: *cognitive impressions*: A cognitive impression in Stoicism is one to which assent is fully justified. It accurately represents a real state of affairs, it is molded and impressed on the mind according to that reality, and it could not represent a non-actual object or fact. Skeptically inclined thinkers doubted whether such an impression could exist.

46.1: *introduce them to philosophers*: See Plato, *Theaetetus* 151b, *Laches* 200d, *Protagoras* 310a–311a, 316a–c for this Socratic practice. Epictetus mentions it also at *Discourses* 3.5.17, 3.23.22, and 4.8.22–23. Nowadays, however, scholars tend to see this practice not as a denial by Socrates that he was a philosopher but as an ironic reflection on the would-be student: he lacks what it takes to be a philosopher, so Socrates introduces him to a sophist.

47: *Don't hug statues!*: According to Diogenes Laertius, *Lives of the Eminent Philosophers* 6.23, Diogenes the Cynic used to hug statues in freezing weather to develop physical and mental endurance. But the feat was not exclusive to Diogenes, and despite the fact that Diogenes is one of his heroes, Epictetus either ridicules the practice (as here), or considers it not worth the effort (*Discourses* 3.12.2, 4.5.14). Here, Epictetus's point is also that others are bound to see you doing it.

47: *without telling anyone*: See 3.12.17.

48b.2: *rid himself of every desire*: As a temporary measure: see *Handbook* 2.2. A progressor, someone just setting out on the Stoic path, lacks the ability to know which things are real goods, and it is only real goods that one should desire.

49: This entry combines elements of *Discourses* 1.17 and 2.19.

49: *feel proud about*: Chrysippus of Soli was the third head of the Stoic school in the third century BCE. He was chiefly responsible for the theoretical side of Stoicism and is frequently referred to by Epictetus as such—often, as here, with the spin that there is no point in knowing Chrysippus's theories if you cannot put them into practice. The unclarity of Chrysippus's writing was notorious.

52.2: *prove that we shouldn't lie*: This threefold division of philosophy is not quite the same as Epictetus's usual distinction of three phases of philosophical training (on which see the introduction, 30–33). It does, however, reflect the three parts of philosophy that the Stoics recognized: ethics, physics, and logic. Not lying clearly belongs to ethics. Analyzing proofs belongs to logic. The second "aspect" belongs to physics because the ultimate justification for not lying depends on the study of human nature, which is one of the jobs of physics.

53: *the following sentiments*: The first excerpt is from Cleanthes, the second head of the Stoic school, meaning that one cannot resist one's foreordained destiny. The second is a fragment of one of Euripides's plays (fragment 956 Nauck²). The third is from Plato, *Crito* 43d (with an insignificant modification). The fourth is a paraphrase of Plato, *Apology of Socrates* 30c–d;

Anytus and Meletus were two of Socrates's prosecutors in his trial. The first three excerpts in effect say the same thing.

Discourses

Preface: *Lucius Gellius*: Possibly L. Gellius Menander, a contemporary Corinthian known from an inscription (*Corpus Inscriptionum Latinarum* III 7269).

1.1: *What is and is not up to us*: This discourse makes a suitable start to the whole collection. It enunciates several of Epictetus's central themes, and it also forms the first entry in the *Handbook*, albeit in a boiled-down version.

1.1.1: *see whether or not it's acceptable*: Compare the start of 1.20, 1.17.1–3, and 2.23.5–15.

1.1.3: *whether or not you should be writing to your friend*: The idea that the governing art is the one that tells you whether or not you should be doing something originated with Plato, at *Statesman* 304b–c.

1.1.12: *inclination and disinclination*: See the note to Handbook 2.2.

1.1.16: *steward of the winds*: See the beginning of Homer, *Odyssey* 10.

1.1.17: *As God wishes*: Epictetus frequently speaks monotheistically, of "God" or "Zeus," but he also talks of "gods" in the plural—the traditional Greco-Roman pantheon. There is no incompatibility, because the Stoics were pantheists (as well as theists): see K. Algra, "Epictetus and Stoic Theology," in *The Philosophy of Epictetus*, ed. T. Scaltsas and A. Mason (Oxford University Press, 2007), 32–55. So Epictetus assumes that God pervades everything, even the gods. In Judaism and Christianity, angels are perhaps the equivalent of the gods as Epictetus conceives them. They are agents of the single God. At *Handbook* 31.5, Epictetus also approves of traditional religious practices such as libation and sacrifice.

1.1.18: *decapitated today*: The final third of the discourse illustrates the point that the body is not "up to us": although Lateranus and the other Stoic members of the conspiracy against Nero were killed or sent into exile, they were able to accept their punishments with dignity and with their wills intact, which was "up to them."

1.1.19: *as Lateranus did*: Plautus Lateranus was executed in 65 CE as an accomplice of Gaius Calpurnius Piso in his conspiracy against the emperor Nero.

1.1.20: *speak to your master*: On Epaphroditus, Epictetus's former master, see the introduction, 3–4.

1.1.25: *train themselves*: It was a Stoic exercise, perhaps stemming originally from Musonius Rufus, to keep a notebook handy in which to write down important precepts and ideas, so that you could consult it and quickly refresh your determination to continue on the path of virtue. We have an example of such notebooks: Marcus Aurelius's so-called *Meditations*.

1.1.27: *idiotic choice*: Since the future is uncertain in any case, and since both exile and death are indifferents, there is no good reason to choose a worse option. Epictetus approved of suicide only in extreme cases (when "a life in accord with nature is humanly impossible" [3.24.101, with 1.2.25 as an example]), but otherwise not (1.9.10–17). It is the ultimate expression of the idea that "death is nothing to us." Publius Clodius Thrasea Paetus, a Stoic martyr to the cause of restoring the Roman Republic in the face of sole rule, was forced to commit suicide by the emperor Nero (as was Seneca).

1.1.28: *Agrippinus used to say*: Paconius Agrippinus was a Stoic philosopher who was banished by Nero at the same time as Thrasea's suicide. The Stoics were not opponents of sole rule *per se*, but of tyrannical abuse of power. See P. Brunt, "Stoicism and the Principate," in *Studies in Stoicism*, ed. M. Griffin and A. Samuels, with M. Crawford (Oxford University Press, 2013), 275–309.

1.1.30: *have breakfast there*: Agrippinus clearly had property in Aricia, a cool and pleasant hill town not far from Rome. Epictetus returned to this story in a later discourse, some of which is preserved as Fragment 21.

1.2: *role in every situation*: See the introduction, 28–29, on "roles" in Epictetus.

1.2.2: *reasonable thing to do*: A rite of passage for Spartan teenagers involved their trying to steal cheeses from the altar of Artemis Orthia while avoiding whip-wielding adults. By Roman times, this had become a spectator sport, with banked seats from which the audience could watch the blood flow.

1.2.6: *preconceptions... with nature*: On preconceptions, see 1.22, 2.11.1–12, 2.17.1–13, and 4.1.41–45.

1.2.8: *happen to him*: One of the ex-slave's frequent references to slavery. See the introduction, 4.

1.2.9: *someone else's doing it*: In a story told by the Stoic Seneca the Younger, a Spartan boy killed himself by running headfirst into a wall rather than fetch someone's chamber pot (*Letters* 77.14).

1.2.12: *Nero's theatrical spectacle*: The emperor Nero had both athletic and literary pretensions, and he seems to have written whole tragedies himself and contributed songs to others' compositions. We do not know who Florus was; for Agrippinus, see the note to 1.1.28.

1.2.18: *fair and lovely*: A common kind of Roman toga was made out of white wool, but its border was dyed purple. The dye was extracted with great labor from the murex shellfish, and its expense made a purple-dyed robe a sign of prestige.

1.2.20: *bound to ask you*: Because he was a senior member of the Senate. The presiding magistrate of the Senate, in this case the emperor, raised an issue and asked the senators for their views in order: the leader of the Senate, then the consuls, then ex-consuls, then praetors, and so on. Helvidius Priscus was a praetor.

1.2.21: *leave without grieving*: Helvidius was indeed sent into exile in 75 by the emperor Vespasian, and he had earlier been exiled by Nero (he was the son-in-law of Thrasea [note to 1.1.27]). Vespasian subsequently had him killed.

1.2.25: *true to himself and died*: Athletics was all about manhood, and in the gymnasium one exercised naked.

1.2.26: *Baton's gymnasium*: Athletes oiled their bodies before competing. This served as pre-exercise massage (much as nowadays we stretch our muscles), and it apparently helps conserve body moisture, but it was not done just for these limited practical purposes. Nor was the point, for a wrestler, to make his body slippery; wrestlers were obliged to sprinkle sand over their bodies after they had oiled themselves, to allow their opponents to get a grip. The main reason for oiling the body was to display oneself, fit and gleaming, to one's peers and admirers. "Baton's gymnasium" just means "the local gym." So it was part of what Epictetus is calling this athlete's "role" that he was an internationally recognized star.

1.2.29: *No, I won't*: Romans were generally clean-shaven, so that a beard, a Greek habit, became one of the badges of a philosopher, especially if it was a full beard (see also 2.23.21, 3.1.24, 4.8.12). The philosopher-mystic Apollonius of Tyana, an older contemporary of Epictetus, was said to have had his beard forcibly shaved off by orders of the emperor Domitian as a punishment.

1.2.32: *Winter training is called for*: In antiquity, armies generally stood down and even disbanded for the winter, so to undergo winter training was to train the whole year long, showing special determination.

1.2.37: *Milo... neglect my body*: Milo of Croton (in Greek southern Italy) was an almost legendary wrestler of the sixth century BCE.

1.2.37: *Croesus... neglect my possessions*: Croesus, king of Lydia in the mid-sixth century BCE, became a byword for great wealth. We still say "As rich as Croesus." But his glorious reign ended in defeat, death, and the incorporation of his kingdom into the growing Persian empire of Cyrus the Great.

1.3.3: *a wretched and lifeless thing*: This is rhetorical exaggeration. For Stoics, the body cannot be lifeless (until it actually dies) because, like everything else, it is imbued and held together by *pneuma*, spirit. Here he is saying that if *per impossibile* we could take the body on its own, it would be inert and lifeless (see also 3.10.15, 3.22.41, and Fragment 26). Epictetus occasionally speaks in this way, as though he separated mind and body in a dualistic fashion (perhaps most markedly at 1.3.3 and 1.29.16), but it is always only for rhetorical and educational effect. He is trying to get his students to see the body as of no true value and to reorient their attention to the soul rather than the body. Further discussion is to be found in T. Brennan, "Stoic Souls in Stoic Corpses," in *Body and Soul in Ancient Philosophy*, ed. D. Frede and B. Reis (De Gruyter, 2009), 389–408.

1.3.4: *most people do*: By security in the use of impressions, Epictetus means the ability to identify things and their values correctly, "even when asleep, drunk, or in a black mood" (2.17.33; see also 3.2.5). On "self-respect," see the note to *Handbook* 24.3.

1.4: *On progress*: Since Stoics believed that every human being, qua rational, was a fragment of God, it followed that perfection was possible for us all. The concept of progress toward that state was therefore important to them (as it was to Epicureans as well). In this talk Epictetus stresses, as often elsewhere, that progress is not made by reading books and listening to his lectures but by putting into practice the content of the books and lectures.

1.4.1: *the philosophers*: Throughout the book, when Epictetus says "the philosophers," he invariably means Stoics, and when he says "philosophy," he invariably means Stoicism.

1.4.1: *uprooted desire . . . and set it aside*: The injunction to avoid desire altogether is repeated at 3.22.13, 4.1.175, 4.4.33, Fragment 27, and *Handbook* 2 and 48b. Of course, the Stoics recognized good desires, such as the desire to be a person of moral integrity (see, e.g., 4.1.84). But this discourse (along with many others in the book) is addressed to relative beginners, who need to eliminate all desire for a time, to make sure they have eliminated base desires; when they have reached a point where they know what is good and can choose what use to make of the faculty of desire (i.e., only on things that are up to them), desire can be reintroduced (3.13.21). Until then, their desires will target things that seem to be good, even if in fact they are not good.

1.4.6: *Chrysippus's treatises*: The contrast between real moral progress and knowing philosophical theory is recurrent in the discourses. Theory and putting the theory into practice need to go together. On Chrysippus, see the note to *Handbook* 49.

1.4.11: *to avoid being deceived*: See 3.2 and the introduction, 30–33, for the training of desire, inclination, and assent.

1.4.24: *until my hair was gray*: Hemlock was the poison that killed the elderly Socrates after he had been condemned to death by an Athenian court in 399 BCE, and the quotation is a slightly altered version of a sentence spoken by Plato's Socrates at *Crito* 43d.

1.4.25: *speak that way*: Priam was the legendary king of Troy at the time of the Trojan War. Oedipus was in legend a king of Thebes.

1.4.27: *a life of contentment and tranquility*: The "deception" that Epictetus is talking about is being taught a lesson by the fictions of tragedy.

1.4.29: *harmony with nature*: I take it that the slightly awkward language of this sentence is a semihumorous imitation of Chrysippus himself, who was notoriously difficult to read (*Handbook* 49, *Discourses* 1.17.16, 3.21.7).

1.4.30: *cultivated crops*: See the Homeric *Hymn to Demeter*. In legend, Triptolemus was a scion of the Eleusinian royal family who was taught agriculture by the goddess Demeter and then traveled around the world teaching others.

1.4.32: *vine and wheat*: Dionysus (Bacchus) and Demeter (Ceres), respectively.

1.5: *Against the Academics*: In Epictetus's time, there was no Academy as such. The school started by Plato in the fourth century BCE had been destroyed early in the first century BCE, during the sack of Athens by the Roman general Sulla. For much of its history, the Academy had not been given to the dogmatic perpetuation of Platonism but, while still claiming descent from Socrates and Plato, taught a skeptical philosophy. It is this period of the Academy's history that Epictetus is looking back to in describing them, as in this discourse, as Skeptics, for whom nothing can be known for certain.

1.5.3: *refuses to abandon his inconsistencies*: So some Academics refuse to accept that some impressions are reliable (the first kind of necrosis), while others shamelessly exploit invalid arguments.

1.5.5: *strength of character*: Or obstinacy, at any rate.

1.5.7: *fire or steel*: The analogy with physical necrosis continues: "fire" is cautery and "steel" is incision, the two most common surgical procedures.

1.6: *On providence*: On the Stoic concept of divine providence and determinism, see also 1.12, 1.14, 1.16, 3.17, and the introduction, 22–23. The ancestor of their position is given by Socrates in Xenophon, *Memorabilia* 1.4 and 4.3. There are echoes of Xenophon in Epictetus here, but they are perhaps due only to the fact that the terms of the argument from design (briefly: if there is a program, there must be a programmer) had become standardized over the centuries. See, e.g., Cicero, *On the Nature of the Gods* 2.18–22.

1.6.7: *by accident*: The Epicureans held that each and every thing was simply a chance conglomeration of atoms.

1.6.10: *in some way related*: In other words, the mind not only receives sense impressions but is also able to think about them, manipulate them, create new content, and move from one thought to another by association.

1.6.11: *accidentally and by chance*: The Epicureans did have such an explanation: everything is an accidental concatenation of atoms that will last for a greater or lesser time.

1.6.23: *Phidias*: Phidias of Athens became famous for his cult statue of Athena in the Athenian Parthenon, and was then commissioned to make the statue of Zeus for his temple in Olympia, which became one of the Seven Wonders of the Ancient World. W. Stephens extracts a Stoic "philosophy of travel" from this and Epictetus's other incidental remarks on travel in "The Providential Tourist: Epictetus on How a Stoic Travels," in *From Ancient Greek to Asian Philosophy*, ed. E Hoppe and R. Weed (Athens Institute for Education and Research, 2007), 127–40.

1.6.28: *greatness of soul*: This is a somewhat obscure virtue, but a standard one since the time of Aristotle (*Nicomachean Ethics* 4.3). Essentially, a great-souled person expects great things of himself. Epictetus includes it among the virtues also at 1.6.43, 1.9.32, 1.12.30, 2.16.14, 2.16.41, 3.8.6, and 4.1.109.

1.6.29: *grief and sorrow*: So external events should be seen as no more than inconveniences, not as the source of evil or good. "Epictetus gives at least five different reasons why one should not be disturbed by any event, outcome, or happening, past, present, or future: (1) since any worldly occurrence is external to one's own [will], it is neither good nor bad but indifferent; (2) natural events are rational, and to the rational being the rational is always endurable; (3) Zeus ordains everything that happens and his providence is superior to what I will, so I can keep my mind in harmony with fate by conforming my will to his divine intent; (4) I am so equipped that I am free to bear all that happens without being disturbed; (5) it is possible to turn every event into something beneficial, e.g. by using it to strengthen one's patience, magnanimity, fortitude, resilience and the like." W. Stephens, *Stoic Ethics* (Continuum, 2007), 66.

1.6.33: *comfort*: Heracles was a model for Cynics and Stoics for his perseverance and good works.

1.7: *all such arguments*: Epictetus refers to what he calls "hypothetical arguments" elsewhere as well, and gives us examples at 1.25.11–12 and 1.29.51. It is not easy to determine exactly what he means by the term, but see J. Barnes, *Logic and the Imperial Stoa* (Brill, 1997), 85–98, and S. Bobzien, "The Stoics on Hypotheses and Hypothetical Arguments," *Phronesis* 42, no. 3 (1997): 299–312. It is even harder to determine what he means by "changing arguments." They were arguments the premises of which could change truth-value (§20), but beyond that it is not easy to see their importance. See Barnes, *Logic*, 99–125; P. Crivelli, "Epictetus and Logic," in Scaltsas and Mason, *Philosophy of Epictetus*, 20–31; and J.-B. Gourinat, "Épictète et la logique," in *Mélanges de philosophie et de philologie offerts à Lambros Couloubaritsis*, ed. M. Broze, B. Decharneux and S. Delcomminette (Vrin, 2008), 435–46. What Epictetus says at 4.12.12 suggests that they might have been sophisms, exploiting equivocation. It was not Epictetus's job to provide any kind of textbook on Stoic logic, and he leaves few clues as to the nature or importance of these arguments. But nothing in the discourses is spoiled by our not knowing exactly what they are, because Epictetus usually mentions them in passing as examples of theoretical subjects studied in his school, when he wants to stress that theory must be supplemented by practice. We do, however, know what he means by "question and answer": dialectical arguments of the kind made famous by Socrates, in which propositions and counterpropositions are discussed and analyzed.

1.7.18: *But if they don't, we don't have to*: At this point an early editor detected a lacuna in the text and filled it with a sentence made up by himself, which constituted §18. But probably all that is needed to fill the gap is what I have written.

1.7.25: *to infer something impossible*: Whatever exactly hypothetical arguments are, this was clearly felt to be the source of their trickiness: see 3.2.17.

1.7.32: *burned down the Capitol*: The Capitol or Capitoline Hill was densely occupied by buildings, including the two most important temples of ancient Rome, to Jupiter and Juno. It was considered the sacred and symbolic heart of the city. The temple of Jupiter burned in 69, so it is possible that Epictetus witnessed it. The rebuilt temple burned down again in 80, but that was an accident, whereas Epictetus is assuming a deliberate act.

1.8.1: *epicheremes and enthymemes*: An epichereme is an argument that is based on probabilities rather than truths, and therefore belongs more to rhetoric than to logic. An enthymeme was a form of deductive argument adapted for rhetorical use. In the example that follows, the "If... then" argument is typical of deductive arguments as the Stoics saw them, and the looser statement is an enthymeme. On enthymemes, see (in brief) H. Yunis, introduction to *Aristotle: The Art of Rhetoric*, trans. R. Waterfield (Oxford University Press, 2018), xxxiv–xliii; and (at length) M. Burnyeat, "Enthymeme: Aristotle on the Logic of Persuasion," in *Explorations in Ancient and Modern Philosophy*, vol. 1 (Cambridge University Press, 2012), 152–201.

1.8.3: *enthymeme is an incomplete syllogism*: For argument against this view of enthymemes, see Burnyeat, "Enthymeme." He shows that it originated with the Stoics and does not represent Aristotle's position.

1.8.11: *wasn't Plato a philosopher*: Plato is brought in at this point because he combined argumentative with rhetorical and other writerly skills. None of the medical treatises that have come down to us under the name of Hippocrates, the founder of scientific medicine in the fifth century BCE, display the same graces as Plato's writing, but they are at least often lucid.

1.9.1: *citizen of the universe*: Socrates attracted apocryphal stories like this; it is not based on anything he says in the surviving records of his conversations, but it also occurs in writers other than Epictetus, such as Musonius Rufus, *Discourses* 9.

1.9.4: *father or grandfather*: A child's characteristics were commonly believed to come from the father and to be sown by his "seeds," while the mother provided little more than nurture.

1.9.5: *by their rational faculties*: Some of this sentence may be a quotation or paraphrase of the somewhat unorthodox Stoic thinker Posidonius, who lived and wrote voluminously in Rome in the first century BCE. At any rate, in his fragment 14 Edelstein/Kidd, he speaks of a "community of made up of human beings and gods," but he might have learned the phrase from an earlier thinker, probably Chrysippus.

1.9.11: *depart to their kin*: The Stoics approved of suicide in extreme cases—if there was absolutely no chance of continuing to make progress toward virtue or otherwise to fulfill one's roles—but being bound to a body was not a good enough reason in itself. "Departing to their kin [i.e., the gods]" is just a metaphor; Epictetus does not believe in any form of afterlife. On suicide, see also notes to 1.1.27, 1.9.16, and 2.10.6.

1.9.13: *indifferents*: On indifferents, see the introduction, 19–20.

1.9.16: *your service here on earth*: Compare Plato, *Phaedo* 61b–62e: suicide is permitted only when it is clearly the gods' will. The metaphor of our lives here as a form of military service, continued in the next sentence, also stems from Socrates, at Plato, *Apology of Socrates* 28b–e. On the ambiguity and unclarity of responding to such a "signal from God," see the notes to 2.10.6 and 3.26.29.

1.9.20: *the door is open*: A recurrent metaphor for suicide. See also 1.24.20,

1.25.18, 2.1.19–20, 3.8.6, 3.13.14, and 3.22.34, with W. Stephens, "Epictetus on Fearing Death," *Ancient Philosophy* 34, no. 2 (2014): 365–91.

1.9.24: *by a god*: This is a paraphrase of some of Plato, *Apology of Socrates* 28b–30a. It is a stretch for Epictetus to claim that it says anything about Socrates's kinship with God.

1.9.30: *same result from you*: The purpose of his plea to Epaphroditus would be to make Epictetus's life tolerable, but Epictetus was tolerating it anyway.

1.10.8: *so-and-so reads*: It seems that one of the practices of Epictetus's school was that a student would read a preselected passage and Epictetus would expound it. See further the introduction, 12.

1.11: *On family affection*: This discourse is the starting point for two wide-ranging papers by R. Salles, "*Oikeiosis* in Epictetus" (§§1–26) and "Epictetus and the Causal Conception of Moral Responsibility" (§§27–40).

1.11.2: *family life*: What follows bears comparison with those dialogues of Plato's (often called the dialogues of search) where he has Socrates investigate an issue by closely questioning an interlocutor. The course of the argument is dictated by similar triggers (such as the interlocutor's confession of ignorance) and Epictetus's tactics are all typically Socratic. The chief difference is that Epictetus more overtly steers the conversation, and that his interlocutor, though more of a character than most of the interlocutors in other discourses, is even more of a cipher than those of Socrates, so that Epictetus rarely has to develop a complex argument in the way that Socrates did. But the underlying assumption is the same: that the interlocutor already knows the truth, and it is the job of the questioner to elicit it from him. Or, in terms of Epictetus's theory of preconceptions (1.22, 2.11.1–12, 2.17.1–13, 4.1.41–45), we could say that that it is the questioner's job to get the interlocutor to apply his preconceptions correctly to particular circumstances.

1.11.5: *a natural reaction*: So Epictetus will argue that, in the case of human beings, an action can only be natural if it is reasonable or rational.

1.11.7: *make mistakes*: The only person who would never make mistakes is a Stoic sage, and the Stoics themselves acknowledged that such a person was "as rare as a phoenix" (Alexander of Aphrodisias, *On Fate* 196–197). Even Zeno, Cleanthes, and Chrysippus did not claim to be sages. Stoics looked back to Socrates and Diogenes of Sinope, the truest representative of Cynicism, as possible sages. For a thorough study, see R. Brouwer, *The Stoic Sage: The Early Stoics on Wisdom, Sagehood and Socrates* (Cambridge University Press, 2014). Epictetus's focus is less on sagehood and more on making progress in that direction.

1.11.13: *the others aren't*: If (as is likely from a parallel passage, 1.22.4) Epictetus is thinking of the prohibition on eating pig meat, he is a bit muddled, because it was prohibited at the time equally among Jews, Syrians, and Egyptians (or at least upper-class Egyptians). See R. Lobban, "Pigs and Their Prohibition," *International Journal of Middle East Studies* 26, no. 1 (1994): 57–

75. But perhaps here he is just making a general point about different dietary practices, not just about eating pig meat.

1.11.17: *natural and good*: Having argued—or implied—that the interlocutor's leaving his child was unnatural, Epictetus now turns to a second argument, that his action contradicted his affection for the child.

1.11.18: *family members*: It follows that Epictetus did not consider affection to be a "passion," because no passion is compatible with reason. See the introduction, 24–25, on passion.

1.11.23: *fond of her*: A child-minder (*paidagōgos*) was a household slave who accompanied young children when they left home to go to school or somewhere, and in general made sure that they behaved well.

1.11.23: *didn't care for her*: In Stoic terms, as Epictetus often makes clear, the child's death is a matter of indifference, but our natural affection for our children makes us prefer a child to be alive rather than dead. There is no incompatibility between these two propositions, provided that the actions that we take to preserve a child's life are carried out "with reservation" (on which see the note to *Handbook* 2.2).

1.11.31: *right to grieve*: In Homer's *Iliad* it is the death of his close friend Patroclus that snaps Achilles out of his sulk and returns him to the battlefield.

1.11.33: *our beliefs and judgments*: The difference between a belief and a judgment is that a belief (*hypolēpsis*) is a settled opinion, whereas a judgment (*dogma*) is just an opinion. So every belief is a judgment, but not every judgment is a belief.

1.12.1: *any care or forethought*: This second position is that of the Epicureans.

1.12.3: *go on my way*: Odysseus's words at Homer, *Iliad* 10.279–280, addressed to the goddess Athena. For Socrates on the omnipresence of God, see Xenophon, *Memorabilia* 1.1.19, 1.4.18, and 4.3.12. Like Heracles, Odysseus was a Stoic hero for his endurance of hardship.

1.12.5: *to follow the gods*: A common Stoic formulation of the goal of life, but with a long history dating back to Plato and possibly Pythagoras.

1.12.15: *to want everything to happen as it does happen*: The rational acceptance of what we are given is a recurrent theme in Epictetus. It is impious not to accept what we are given, because it is given us by God. These things are not up to us, but where things are up to us, we should be active agents rather than passively accept our lot.

1.12.23: *Socrates wasn't in prison*: While awaiting execution after his conviction, Socrates spent some time in prison, and Plato's dialogues *Crito* and *Phaedo* are set there.

1.12.24: *my poor crippled leg*: Epictetus could be talking to himself, since he was lame (1.8.14, 1.16.19).

1.12.25: *the thread of your destiny*: One of the three Fates in traditional Greek religion was Clotho, the weaver. The other two were Atropos (the implacable) and Lachesis (she who allots).

1.13.5: *corpse-laws*: That is, laws designed by people whose focus was on the body, not the soul. Epictetus liked to suggest that the body in itself was inert, no more than a carcass (e.g., 2.19.27) or "clay" (e.g., 4.11.27).

1.14.2: *heavenly things are in a sympathetic relationship with things on earth*: This understanding (perhaps originally that of Posidonius) of how the universe is physically unified was also, incidentally, the basis of the Stoic advocacy of astrology. This form of divination was so widespread in the Roman world in Epictetus's time that it is not surprising to find his anonymous interlocutor immediately agreeing with the proposition.

1.14.10: *causes it to revolve*: On the ancient earth-centered conception of the universe, the sun, along with all the other heavenly bodies, revolved around the earth. Extremely complicated models had to be invented to explain the apparent motion of the heavenly bodies.

1.14.12: *guardian spirit*: Another term for what elsewhere is called the "command center" or rational faculty or god within. It derives, as far as we can tell, from Plato (see especially the great myth that concludes his *Republic*), but it may be Pythagorean in origin. It is not immediately clear whether this guardian spirit is indwelling (as in Marcus Aurelius or 2.8.11–14) or external. The last sentence of the discourse suggests the former: if the guardian spirit is indwelling, and is in a sense our true self, then in swearing an oath of loyalty to it we are swearing loyalty to ourselves.

1.16.2: *for service*: It was common at this time, and for many subsequent centuries, to view the world as a *scala naturae*—a great chain of being from inanimate objects, to plants, animals, human beings, and finally to gods. Many were also inclined to add that each lower group existed to serve the next higher. See also 1.6.18 and 2.8.7.

1.16.4: *tribune*: Not to be confused with the tribune of the people (*tribunus plebis*), a military tribune was a senior officer in the Roman army. The tribunes of 1.19.24 and 3.14.12 are probably *tribuni plebis*.

1.16.14: *not discard them*: In other words, men should not shave! See also 1.2.29.

1.17.3: *interminable regress*: Skeptics argued that Stoics were committed to precisely this regress; Epictetus insists that reason can look at itself.

1.17.7: *what a modius is*: A modius was a Roman dry measure, the equivalent of about thirteen liters in our terms.

1.17.9: *just a piece of wood*: That is, it is a precisely sized barrel into which grain was poured.

1.17.11: *Only Chrysippus, Zeno, and Cleanthes*: That is, "only the Stoics." These three—in the order Zeno, Cleanthes, Chrysippus—were the first three heads of the school in the third century BCE and were always looked back on as the founding fathers of Stoicism.

1.17.12: *doesn't Antisthenes say so too*: Antisthenes was a disciple of Socrates and a prolific author, but none of his work survives, except as reported by others. Since he was one of the teachers of Diogenes, Cynics came to regard him as a forerunner. Their lineage went: Socrates—Antisthenes—Diogenes—Crates—Zeno.

1.17.12: *Socrates say as much*: In a number of dialogues, Plato has Socrates conduct a close examination of the meaning of terms such as "courage" and "justice."

1.17.12: *the meaning of everything*: Xenophon was writing about Socrates: *Memorabilia* 1.1.16, 4.6.1.

1.17.14: *all wrongdoing is involuntary*: This was one of Socrates's fundamental axioms, taken over by the Stoics. Wrongdoing is involuntary because it harms the wrongdoer and no one wants to be harmed.

1.17.16: *written in Latin*: Given the notorious obscurity of Chrysippus's Greek, I suppose the implication here is that Latin is a more lucid language than his Greek.

1.18.3: *anger or pity*: Epictetus is not really recommending that we pity them, because pity, along with anger and all the other passions, was to be avoided, according to Stoicism. See 2.17.26, 3.22.13, 3.24.43, and 4.1.4. He is saying that mistaken judgments deserve pity more than anger, but best of all is to show people where they have gone wrong. We should probably interpret 1.28.9 in the same way.

1.18.9: *hate him*: Due to damage in the primary manuscript (which dates from the eleventh century), the text of the rest of the paragraph is in places very uncertain. It was this that enabled scholars to identify the primary manuscript (usually called "S" because the manuscript used to belong to the Saibanta family in Verona), since it is damaged (an ink blot obscures the text), but all the other manuscripts show a lacuna, proving that they were written later. The most recent attempt to uncover some of the original text is J. Sellars, "Epictetus, *Dissertationes* 1.18.10," *Classical Quarterly* 66, no. 1 (May 2016): 410–13.

1.18.15: *one of clay*: This became one of the most widely known stories about Epictetus. According to Lucian, writing in the second half of the second century, the iron lamp was later sold for a huge sum of money to someone who wanted a souvenir of the famous philosopher (*The Ignorant Book Collector* 14).

1.18.16: *Only things we possess can be lost or ache*: There is an implied reference here to a feeble sophism called the Horned Man: "What you have not lost you still possess; you have not lost horns; so you still possess them."

1.18.17: *Know yourself*: See the note to 3.1.18.

1.19.6: *Fever has an altar in Rome*: According to Valerius Maximus (*Memorable Deeds and Sayings* 2.5.6), Fever had three temples in Rome. The point of praying to Fever was to avert it, so Epictetus is implicitly saying to the tyrant, "Stop plaguing me!"

1.19.11: *It does everything for itself*: This was standard Stoic doctrine; see also 2.25.15–16. Stoics saw a person's responsibilities in terms of ever-increasing concentric circles: from preservation of the self to care for family, for extended family, for fellow citizens, for fellow countrymen, and finally for the whole human race. That is, what you "appropriate to yourself," or consider as belonging to yourself, gradually expands as you become more rational. But preservation of the self was and remained the fundamental motive. On "appropriation," see also *Handbook* 30, *Discourses* 2.22.15, and the introduction, 21–22.

1.19.20: *Felicio, my very dear friend*: Felicio was a slave's or freedman's name.

1.19.24: *lamps being lit for him*: A thanksgiving ritual; see also 2.17.37.

1.19.26: *priesthood of Augustus*: After his death in 14 CE, the emperor Augustus was deified, and the priest of his cult was always an important figure in society. Nicopolis, where Epictetus lived, had been founded by Augustus, and so his cult was particularly prominent there.

1.20: *On reason and its ability to examine itself*: Compare 1.1, 1.17.1–3, and 2.23.5–15.

1.20.17: *a plausible thing to say about a human being*: Epicurus founded his school in Athens at much the same time that Zeno was introducing Stoicism there. Although they shared some common assumptions, their worldviews were very different, and the rivalry between the schools continued for centuries. For further criticism of Epicureanism, see 1.23, 2.20, 2.23.20–22, 3.7.

1.20.19: *so many books*: His books occupied three hundred papyrus rolls, according to Diogenes Laertius, *Lives of the Eminent Philosophers* 10.26. Each roll could contain up to thirty thousand words. There are similar arguments against Epicurus at 2.20.15–16 and 2.23.21–22.

1.21.2: *swallowed a skewer*: I suppose that swallowing a skewer, rather than the meat, was proverbial for being unsatisfied.

1.21.4: *you usually call mad*: Epictetus's invisible interlocutor in this exchange is already a would-be Stoic, and it was common for Stoics to describe everyone except an enlightened sage (of whom there were very few, perhaps only Socrates and Diogenes) as insane. See also the end of 1.28.

1.22.3: *he's out of his mind*: Reckless insanity can pass for courage.

1.22.3: *That's how conflict occurs between people*: In general terms, a preconception is a kind of latent thought, which when triggered turns into an articulated thought. Suppose I see a tabby cat; the bare sense-impression itself is not enough for me to say, "That's a tabby cat," but the sense-impression plus the preconception of a cat is. According to orthodox Stoics, a person's mind at birth is a tabula rasa. Through experience, we gain concepts of things, and these concepts form a set of reliable preconceptions by means of which we identify things in the world; taken as a whole, one's preconceptions amount to one's belief system. We also gain true and reliable moral concepts in this way. Members of rival schools attacked the Stoics for saying that these concepts are reliable and true, by pointing to the frequency of disagreements among people over concepts. Epictetus seems to be responding to this attack and attempting to circumvent the problem by saying (a) that our preconceptions, at least of moral and theological concepts, are innate, in the sense that we have an innate capacity to develop them (this position has been called "dispositional innatism"); and (b) that they are reliable in themselves, and it is only in their application to particular instances that disagreement arises (1.22.2–4; 2.17; 4.1.41–45). So there is no conflict among the restricted set of moral concepts—they are, after all, very general and vague intuitions, such as "What is good is beneficial"—though there may be among non-moral concepts. For more on preconceptions, see 2.11.1–12, 2.17.1–13, and 4.1.41–45. For the significance of (b) for Epictetus's educational and argumentative techniques, see A. A. Long, *Epictetus: A Stoic and Socratic Guide to Life* (Oxford University Press, 2002), 80–85. See also D. Scott, "Innatism and the Stoa," *Proceedings of the Cambridge Philological Society* 34 (1988): 123–53, for a clear discussion of the issues.

1.22.4: *holy or unholy*: See 1.11.12–13, with the note.

1.22.5: *Agamemnon and Achilles as well*: For the context of what follows, see the first book of Homer's *Iliad*.

1.22.8: *without a war prize*: A prose rendering of *Iliad* 1.118–119.

1.22.17: *in labor*: A reference either to Plato, *Theaetetus* 148e–151d, where the image occurs of people being pregnant with ideas, or to Plato, *Symposium* 208e–209e, where people may be pregnant with the virtues.

1.23: *Against Epicurus*: On Epicurus and Epicureanism, see T. O'Keefe, *Epicureanism* (University of California Press, 2010), and J. Warren, ed., *The Cambridge Companion to Epicureanism* (Cambridge University Press, 2009).

1.23.1: *anything that contradicts this*: For the suggestion that Epicurus's practice contradicts his theory about the lack of innate sociability among human beings, see also 2.20.

1.23.3: *not natural for us to feel affection for our offspring*: Affection for offspring is an aspect of being "social," or capable of thinking and caring for others than ourselves. The Epicurean denial that such affection was natural was one of the most controversial points of their doctrine.

1.23.4: *mouse… causes him distress*: See also 3.7.19. Epictetus is saying that a child should be as unlikely to upset someone as a mouse, but many of his listeners would remember also that Epicurus was known to have a slave called "Mouse," who had presumably been raised in Epicurus's household.

1.23.5: *impossible for us not to love it and care for it*: A Stoic can love his child while he has it but lets it go without grieving if it dies (3.24.11, 3.24.84–87, 4.1.111–112, *Handbook* 3, 7, 11, 14a).

1.23.8: *Wolves don't abandon their offspring either*: This is an unfair move by Epictetus. There is a big difference between not having children in the first place and abandoning them. A mother's love for and defense of her offspring constitute, for Stoics, the most primitive example of how it is natural for us to care for others as well as ourselves. But these two dispositions in us can clash (2.22.15–17), and in the case of such conflict, self-preservation will always win out, unless we operate entirely from will (2.22.18–20).

1.24.2: *Olympic victor*: Epictetus liked the analogy with the Olympics. It occurs most extensively in *Handbook* 29 and 51.2, and *Discourses* 3.15 and 3.25. In the Olympics, however, one competes against others, whereas in working on oneself a student competes against himself—his inertia, laziness, ingrained bad habits, false beliefs, bad judgments, and so on. According to Plato, Socrates compared himself to an Olympic victor, at *Apology of Socrates* 36d–e.

1.24.6: *a different report*: Diogenes of Sinope was the founder of Cynicism. With this discourse, which inclines strongly toward Cynicism, see also 3.22 and 4.8.30–33. Epictetus did not pluck the image of Diogenes as a spy out of thin air. In a famous story, told by Diogenes Laertius, *Lives of the Eminent Philosophers* 6.43 (and alluded to by Epictetus also at 3.22.24–25), Diogenes tells Philip II of Macedon that he has come to spy on his insatiable greed. Diogenes crops up often in the discourses as a paradigmatic philosopher; for translations of further anecdotes about him, see R. Dobbin, *The Cynic Philosophers from Diogenes to Julian* (Penguin, 2012), or R. Hard, *Diogenes the Cynic: Sayings and Anecdotes* (Oxford University Press, 2012). The spy metaphor is usefully unpacked by M. Schofield, "Epictetus: Socratic, Cynic, Stoic," review of *Epictetus: A Stoic and Socratic Guide to Life*, by A. A. Long, *Philosophical Quarterly* 54, no. 216 (July 2004): 448–56, at 452–55. When Epictetus says that he is sending one of his students off to Rome as a spy, he means just that this student is leaving the school and going out into the real world.

1.24.6: *he says*: These are quotations or paraphrases of famous sayings of Diogenes.

1.24.12: *he says*: This is something only the emperor could say.

1.24.16: *O Cithaeron, why did you receive me?*: From Sophocles, *Oedipus the King* 1391. Oedipus has realized that he was exposed as a child on mount Cithaeron, and that it must be he who murdered his father and married his mother, and brought divine punishment down on Thebes. The previous quotation is from an unknown play.

1.24.20: *take your leave*: Epictetus liked the analogy between life and a game: see also 1.25.7–8, 2.5.17, 2.16.37, 4.7.19, and 4.7.30–31. Another metaphorical way in which he encouraged a light, detached approach to the world was to compare life to a festival: 1.12.21, 2.14.23, 4.1.104–109, 4.4.24–27.

1.25.3: *Hasn't Zeus offered you guidance already?*: There was discussion within the Stoic school about how specific ethical instruction should be. In what follows, Epictetus sides with those who thought it best to avoid specifics.

1.25.6: *If you keep his commandments, do you need any others?*: Epictetus speaks of God's commands or commandments in several other places. Elsewhere he speaks of God's laws, which are also to be obeyed (1.29.4, 2.16.28, 3.11.1–3)—which, since they are the laws of the world, we cannot help but obey. We are naturally attracted to what is good for us; but God made only a very limited set of things good for us (i.e., those that are up to us); therefore, to obey his ordinances is to be attracted only to things that are good for us and to treat everything else as bad or indifferent (4.3.10). There is no conflict between this obedience and the requirement that a Stoic should be as autonomous as possible, because God is nature, and nature is reason, and reason-in-us is a fragment of the reason that is God and nature. So to follow God is to follow the commands of one's reason.

1.25.7: *the Saturnalia*: A major Roman festival in honor of the god Saturn, held in December and famous for its carnival-like atmosphere.

1.25.10: *Agamemnon and Achilles*: See the first book of Homer's *Iliad* for context.

1.25.13: *someone else*: Zeus or God, as often in the discourses.

1.25.15: *Mysia*: Mysia was a region of northwest Asia Minor; the Romans had not fought there in recent history. But there was a view in antiquity that Moesia, in central Europe, was the original home of the Mysians, and that the two words "Mysia" and "Moesia" were variants of the same name. The Romans fought several wars in Moesia between 86 and 106 CE.

1.25.19: *Gyara*: A small and arid island in the Aegean that was used by several Roman emperors as a place to send undesirables. Epictetus's teacher, Musonius Rufus, was sent there by Nero. It was a byword for a horrible place to live. Successive Greek governments in the twentieth century continued the tradition by building a prison on the island (called Gioura today) for political prisoners.

1.25.22: *Demetrius said to Nero*: Demetrius was a Cynic philosopher of the first century CE.

1.25.32: *Philosophers speak in paradoxes*: These concluding sentences seem an afterthought rather than an integral part of the discourse, so I have separated them out. See the note to 3.8.7.

1.25.33: *the truths of philosophy seem paradoxical to the ignorant*: The Stoics (like Socrates) were fond of making startling claims. In the first century BCE, Cicero even devoted a whole work to trying to explain six fundamental Stoic paradoxes: virtue is the only good; virtue is sufficient for happiness; all virtues and all vices are equal; ignorance is madness; only the sage is free; only the sage is rich. The book is known simply as *Stoic Paradoxes*. However, Epictetus on the whole is not given to such extreme expressions.

1.26.11: *Epaphroditus's knees in supplication*: On Epaphroditus, see the introduction, 3–4.

1.26.18: *the unexamined life was not worth living*: One of Socrates's most famous sayings, from Plato, *Apology of Socrates* 38a.

1.27.1: *and yet appear to exist*: "Exist" in this sentence could equally be replaced by forms of "be the case": "Either things that are the case appear to be the case," etc.

1.27.2: *Pyrrhonists and Academics*: The two schools of Skepticism. Pyrrho of Elis lived from c. 360 to c. 270 BCE.

1.27.7: *death is unavoidable*: Epictetus allows the conclusion—that we should therefore accept death or at least resign ourselves to it—to be implicit.

1.27.8: *echo his noble words*: What follows is a paraphrase of Homer, *Iliad* 12.328: "Let us go on and win glory for ourselves, or yield it to others" (Richmond Lattimore's translation). It is not so clear in Epictetus's paraphrase, perhaps, but Sarpedon was hoping either to win glory by victory or to die at the hands of another glorious fighter.

1.27.10: *wanting something and not getting it*: See also 2.17.18 and 3.2.3. For the Stoic view of passion, see the introduction, 24–25.

1.27.18: *I never take it there, but here*: One of the features of Arrian's stenographic recording of Epictetus's talks is that their performative aspects have been lost. Here, for instance, Epictetus must have gestured toward his mouth. Gestures, meaningful silences, changes of tone of voice: readers have to supply these features themselves.

1.28.3: *I can't*: See also the start of 2.16: whether the stars are odd or even in number was a standard question to which any definite answer was bound to be unverifiable, prompting one to suspend judgment on the matter.

1.28.4: *deprived of the truth*: The sentence does not occur in any of Plato's published works, though the sentiment occurs at *Republic* 413a and *Sophist* 228c–d. Epictetus mentions it again at 2.22.36.

1.28.7: *counsels are ruled by anger*: Euripides, *Medea* 1078–1079. "The woman" is Medea, who plans to punish her husband, Jason, by killing their children. Medea was a favorite exemplar for philosophers and a starting point for discussion of how one could intentionally act contrary to one's best judgment. See J. Dillon, "Medea among the Philosophers," in *Medea: Essays on Medea in Myth, Literature, Philosophy, and Art*, ed. J. Clauss and S. Johnston (Princeton University Press, 1997), 211–18.

1.28.9: *if that's the case*: See the note to 1.18.3 on pity.

1.28.13: *not only the Iliad but the Odyssey as well*: Homer's *Iliad* consists of episodes in the legendary Trojan War, which was caused by Paris's theft of beautiful Helen, Menelaus's wife. The *Odyssey* tells the often fantastic story of the return home from the war of one of the Greek heroes, Odysseus.

1.28.28: *preconceptions*: For both Stoics and Epicureans, preconceptions were reliable and true, and could therefore serve as standards or reference points. On preconceptions, see 1.22, 2.11.1–12, 2.17.1–13, and 4.1.41–45.

1.28.32: *The Hippolytus*: Sophocles, Ion of Chios, and Euripides all wrote plays called *Phoenix*. The *Hippolytus* is by Euripides.

1.29.18: *so be it*: The two quotations are actually paraphrases, the first of Plato, *Apology of Socrates* 30c, and the second of Plato, *Crito* 43d. Anytus and Meletus were two of Socrates's three prosecutors in his trial.

1.29.21: *lost my lamp*: See 1.18.15.

1.29.29: *his commanding officer*: "Sounding the retreat" is Epictetus's metaphor for God's indicating that it is time to die, perhaps by one's own hand: 3.13.14, 3.24.101, 3.26.29–30.

1.29.31: *the Saturnalia*: See the note to 1.25.7.

1.29.34: *how to reduce syllogisms*: In Stoic logic, all syllogisms (formally valid arguments) are either "indemonstrable" (elementary syllogisms that need no further validation) or non-indemonstrable. The way that the formal validity of a non-indemonstrable argument is demonstrated is by analyzing it into indemonstrable stages, so that it is reduced to indemonstrable arguments. So to reduce or analyze syllogisms is to prove or disprove their validity.

1.29.37: *Caesar's gladiators*: In Epictetus's time, the main gladiatorial schools were owned by the emperor.

1.29.38: *my favorite contestant*: Perhaps a former student.

1.29.40: *this kind of compound proposition to analyze*: In Stoic logic, a compound proposition (*tropikos*) was one that was either conjunct or disjunct— either "It is day and light," or "Either it is day or it is night."

1.29.54: *Oh, the injustice of educated men!*: I take this to be a quotation, with which Epictetus immediately and clearly shows that he disagrees.

1.29.65: *A noble spirit, to have wept for us*: A paraphrase of Plato, *Phaedo* 116d. What follows is a paraphrase of 117d, when one of his own followers, not just the jailer, was weeping.

1.30.2: *he asks you*: What follows is a concise summary of the core of Epictetus's thought.

2.1.8: *run from them*: Ropes hung with brightly colored feathers were stretched across woodland pathways to drive deer into hunters' nets.

2.1.13: *It's not dying that's dreadful, but dying in disgrace*: A line from an unknown tragedy.

2.1.15: *bogeys*: At *Crito* 46c Plato has Socrates describe death and execution as bogeys with which to frighten people; see also *Phaedo* 77e.

2.1.17: *separated before*: "Spirit" translates *pneuma*, the vital principle that, in Stoicism, pervades and organizes the whole universe and every part of it. It permeates material things so thoroughly that it and they are separable only in thought, not in reality. It can also be called "God" or the divine reason. Death is the separation of *pneuma* from the body, and at the first inbreath after birth, *pneuma* is taken into and animates the body. Epictetus does not mean to imply that the soul is immortal, just that *pneuma* and the elements that make up the body existed separately before birth and will do so again after death.

2.1.18: *been and gone*: Since there is nothing outside the universe (only void, no thing), the matter of the universe is constant in quantity and, in the form of the four elements (earth, water, air, fire), it is constantly being recycled. So the universe is "self-sufficient" (4.7.6; Fragment 13). When things come to an end, their elements return to their primary positions in the universe (in concentric circles around the world, according to their density) and the generative principle of the universe then draws on this stock to create the next generation of things, and so on forever. See also 3.24.10, 3.24.87, 3.24.94, and Fragment 8. At 4.1.100 this is called "the cosmic cycle."

2.1.19: *smooth ones*: Smooth bodily motions cause pleasant sensations and rough ones unpleasant.

2.1.26: *in front of the praetor*: Turning the slave was part of the ritual of manumission in Rome; it symbolized that an outsider was in the process of becoming an insider.

2.1.32: *no one wrote more*: Socrates famously wrote nothing, but it will turn out shortly that Epictetus means metaphorical writing—the writing of internal dialogues in his mind. We are presumably supposed to think that, in asking his question, Epictetus's interlocutor is displaying complete ignorance of Socrates and Socratic literature.

2.2: *On tranquility*: Tranquility (*ataraxia*, also quite often translated "peace of mind" or "serenity") was the stated goal of both Stoicism and Epicureanism.

2.2.7: *epilogue*: These were all standard parts of a forensic speech.

2.2.9: *individual or the state*: A very free paraphrase of Xenophon, *Apology of Socrates* 3.

2.2.14: *find truth also*: Along with all editors, I have omitted a sentence that follows in the manuscripts. With its mention of caution and confidence, it has clearly drifted from the previous lecture. It does not make much sense either: "Where truth and nature are found, there is caution; where truth is found, there is confidence, where nature is."

2.2.15: *they cannot harm me*: A paraphrase of Plato, *Apology of Socrates* 30c, and one of Epictetus's favorite quotations, which occurs also at 1.29.18 and 3.23.21. Anytus and Meletus were two of the men who prosecuted Socrates at his trial in 399 BCE.

2.2.18: *provoke the judges*: See Xenophon, *Apology of Socrates* 23, and for Socrates as a kind of Stoic suicide, see R. Waterfield, "Xenophon on Socrates' Trial and Death," in *Xenophon: Ethical Principles and Historical Enquiry*, ed. F. Hobden and C. Tuplin (Brill, 2012), 269–305.

2.2.21: *ridiculous to say 'Give me some advice'*: See also 1.25.3. Epictetus does, of course, constantly give advice. The person he's addressing at this point must be a complete beginner, to judge by what follows, and seems to have come to Epictetus with a question similar to the one that triggers 1.15.

2.2.25: *this general principle*: As often at the end of a meandering talk, Epictetus addresses the issue raised at the beginning. Here, then, the "general principle" is that, in trials both literal and metaphorical, one should safeguard one's will, the only thing that is genuinely ours.

2.3.4: *to recognize successful syllogisms*: On the reduction or analysis of syllogisms, see the note to 1.29.34.

2.4.8: *common property*: Epictetus's interlocutor is trying to use a Stoic argument to defeat the Stoic Epictetus. In his *Republic*, Plato floated the idea that, within the class of philosopher-rulers of his ideal city, women should be shared, and the founder of Stoicism, Zeno of Citium, adopted the idea in his *Republic* as well, probably for all citizens, not just for a limited class as in Plato's city.

2.4.8: *a Socratic kind of guest*: Plato and Xenophon both wrote works called *Symposium*, featuring Socrates at a dinner party. Since his behavior was urbane and cultured, Epictetus is being sarcastic.

2.4.10: *Archedemus*: Archedemus of Tarsus was a prominent Stoic philosopher of the second century BCE.

2.5.16: *any ball I throw*: See the discussion of Epictetus's ball-playing analogy in T. Brennan, *The Stoic Life* (Oxford University Press, 2005), 146–51.

2.5.18: *how to play in the law court*: What follows is a free and brief paraphrase of Plato, *Apology of Socrates* 26e–28a, where, however, Socrates is addressing Meletus, not Anytus. The word here translated as "superhuman being" is *daimōn*, and Socrates uses it because he was charged, among other things, with "introducing strange new *daimonia*," so that Meletus is caught in the trap of accusing Socrates of atheism in the course of trial in which he was charged with believing in superhuman beings. If he was an atheist, he was innocent of the charge!

2.5.19: *but not donkeys*: A mule being half donkey, half horse.

2.5.24: *either in accord with nature or contrary to nature*: See the introduction, 19–20, on preferred and dispreferred indifferents.

2.5.24: *Otherwise, it isn't a foot*: Epictetus is echoing an argument of Chrysippus's that he quotes at 2.6.9–10. See also 2.10.4–5.

2.5.26: *a small copy of the universal city*: It was Stoic doctrine that all rational beings (gods and fully mature human beings), by virtue of their rationality share membership of a higher community than the particular states on earth where they are born and live. This is the origin of the Stoic idea of cosmopolitanism—that we are "citizens of the world" rather than just Romans or Athenians. Like earthly cities, the universal city has laws—effectively, the unwritten laws governing moral behavior—and some maintained that these laws and that spiritual community deserve our allegiance more than our earthly homes.

2.5.29: *Don't forget that*: Also at 3.18.7. The risk (see 4.1.123) is presumably that of compromising his integrity, or thinking that by condemning someone to death or exile he is doing something significant.

2.6: *On indifference*: This discourse seems a bit of a miscellany, and I have divided it up accordingly. The first chunk (§§1–2) is on the same topic as the previous discourse.

2.6.1: *A conditional*: Such as "If it is day, it is light."

2.6.10: *being muddied*: This is probably a verbatim quotation of Chrysippus.

2.6.15: *more relevant than having his way*: Chrysantas's story is told in Xenophon, *Cyropaedia* 4.1.3.

2.6.18: *Hades*: As an orthodox Stoic, Epictetus did not believe in any form of afterlife. Talk of "descending to Hades" after death is a concession to popular usage, while Epictetus's true position is given at 3.13.15: "There's no Hades."

2.6.26: *taking Socrates as our model*: See Plato, *Phaedo* 60c–61c.

2.7: *The correct way to go about divination*: On divination, see also the note to *Handbook* 32.3.

2.7.3: *one or the other*: By "signs" Epictetus means propositions such as "What is good is always beneficial." We are innately disposed to form certain moral conceptions. On preconceptions, see 1.22, 2.11.1–12, 2.17.1–13, and 4.1.41–45.

2.7.4: *entrails or birds*: One of the most common methods of divination was the examination of the entrails, especially the liver, of a sacrificed animal, to look for any oddities that needed interpretation. You bought and brought the creature, so it was assumed that the state of its innards was relevant to you. Another method was to interpret the flight of birds, especially birds of prey. The Stoics approved of divination because it was compatible with their view of divine providence, causation, and determinism.

2.7.8: *preferable to my not sending them*: Gratilla was the wife of a Roman senator called Arulenus Rusticus. Both were Stoics, and Rusticus was condemned to death by the emperor Domitian during the upheavals that also saw the banishment of Epictetus. Rusticus's grandson, Quintus Junius Rusticus, was the first philosophy teacher of Marcus Aurelius.

2.8.18: *spectacle of yourself in public*: On Phidias and his statues, see the note to 1.6.23.

2.8.26: *Nothing I do shall be vain or revocable*: Zeus speaking at Homer, *Iliad* 1.526 (Richmond Lattimore's translation).

2.9.8: *fulfills its potential*: A conjunction has the form "It is day and light." A disjunction has the form "Either it is day or it is night." See also the note to *Handbook* 36.

2.9.15: *wealth, health, and status*: There is a very similar mocking of mere rote knowledge of ethics at 2.19.12–14.

2.9.19: *when you're Greek*: This is one of many places in the discourses where Epictetus tries to instill in his students *aidōs* (see the note to *Handbook* 24.3)—the "self-respect" that will make them act in accordance with their roles and not claim to be other than they are. See R. Kamtekar, "*Aidōs* in Epictetus," *Classical Philology* 93, no. 2 (1998): 136–60.

2.9.20: *as well as being called one*: Christians were commonly called "Jews" in Epictetus's time, so he might be talking about Christians here, but baptism is also practiced within Judaism—for admitting non-Jews to the faith, for example—so it is not certain.

2.9.22: *the rock of Ajax*: At Homer, *Iliad* 7.268, Ajax picks up an enormous rock to hurl at the Trojan hero Hector.

2.10: *appropriate for him*: The names we bear indicate our roles in life. See the introduction, 28–29.

2.10.4: *as if he were an isolated entity*: On our lack of isolation, see 2.5.24–26.

2.10.6: *we were born for*: One might think that Epictetus is here contradicting his regular position on suicide, that it is always an option in extreme circumstances. Since we lack foreknowledge, how can we ever kill ourselves? But the Stoic who chooses suicide does not base his decision on the future; he has certain knowledge in the present that the continuation of life is unreasonable for him. But then, how does he know that the conditions that are making him contemplate suicide are not just another test from God (1.24.1)? A Stoic who chooses suicide has to be really certain that there is no other option for him.

2.10.24: *someone who's injured me*: It was a traditional feature of Greek popular morality that good should be repaid with good, and harm with harm. Epictetus sneers at people who are guided by this principle at 2.14.18 and 4.1.167.

2.11.1: *matters of supreme importance*: Note how in this discourse Epictetus presents "the starting point of philosophy" in perfectly general terms, with scarcely a hint of Stoicism. This is his usual method with beginners.

2.11.6: *our own particular views*: For Epictetus on preconceptions, see also 1.22, 2.17.1–13, and 4.1.41–45. When he says these concepts are "innate," he probably means that we have an innate capacity to form certain moral and religious beliefs, not that we come into the world with fully formed concepts like Platonic Forms, or with knowledge of self-evident truths. See, for example, 2.17.1, where he denies that people have knowledge: knowledge is a result of philosophical training. Moral preconceptions are innate because they are formed naturally (on the basis of a natural predisposition to form them) as a result of our development as moral creatures by the process of appropriation (see the introduction, 21–22). Our experience and developing rationality will then allow us to transform this innate capacity into articulated or elucidated concepts, as 2.17.10 suggests, which can then act as standards or reference points to guide our moral development.

2.11.16: *there must be a standard*: The standard, or reference point, must be our set of preconceptions (1.22, and the start of the present discourse); preconceptions are designated such standards at 1.28.28. In orthodox Stoicism, the criterion of truth was what they called a "cognitive impression"—an impression the truth of which, or its correspondence with the facts, cannot be doubted. Epictetus seems to be suggesting that our innate preconceptions in the moral sphere carry that degree of cognitive certainty.

2.11.21: *scarcely unchanging*: On the indeterminacy of pleasure, see especially Plato's *Philebus*.

2.11.22: *unworthy of even the scales*: Epictetus is punning. The word for "scales" is also (for obvious reasons) the word for the "yoke" on an oxcart. So he's saying, "I'll consider you lower than a dumb beast."

2.12.5: *he was able to say*: What follows is a paraphrase of Plato, *Gorgias* 472b–c or 474a, as also at 2.26.6.

2.12.7: *envious of bad things*: Epictetus is inventing typical snatches of Socratic dialogue to make his point, but there is an echo of Plato, *Philebus* 48b–50a, on envy. See also Xenophon, *Memorabilia* 3.9.8.

2.12.9: *the definiendum*: In a definition, the thing to be defined is the *definiendum*, and the *definiens* is the term or terms that define it.

2.12.16: *even a great dispute*: Hesiod, *Theogony* 87, translated by Martin West. The reference to Socrates's resolving conflicts in Xenophon's *Symposium* is repeated at 4.5.3. Presumably Epictetus is thinking of passages such as *Symposium* 3.6 and 4.5, where Socrates pours oil on argumentative waters, but it is not a particularly profound way of viewing *Symposium*.

2.12.21: *the soul*: "Soul," here and throughout the book, translates the Greek *psykhē*, which is notoriously impossible to translate, since it corresponds with no single thing in English. It is the "soul," the animating part of a person and the true self; it is the conscious self or "mind," which thinks, remembers, feels, imagines, etc.; sometimes it is "temperament" or "character." It is a blanket term for the inner, conscious and unconscious parts of a person, and hence is frequently distinguished from and coupled with the body. It is important to try to capture the capaciousness of the Greek term, and so I have mostly used "soul," but sometimes "mind" (and occasionally "heart," as in "wholehearted").

2.12.25: *ended up where I am today*: I take this to mean that Epictetus's teaching style in Rome was different. There, he was more of a Cynic street preacher ("the messenger, the spy, the herald of the gods," as he describes a Cynic at 3.22.69), liable to accost people and try to persuade them to mend their ways; in Nicopolis, however, he had a regular school.

2.13.13: *firmly on both feet*: Homer, *Iliad* 13.281 (Richmond Lattimore's translation), of a man waiting nervously in ambush for the enemy to arrive. In the surrounding lines, Homer also mentions chattering teeth and turning pale.

2.13.15: *the approval of a non-expert*: Antigonus Gonatas was the king of Macedon from the mid-270s until 239 BCE. As a young man, he had attended Zeno's lectures in Athens, and later he invited him to come to Macedon to be one of his court philosophers and the tutor to his son. As Socrates had done before him (see the note to Fragment 11), Zeno refused the invitation.

2.13.24: *Socrates . . . the tyrants*: The so-called Thirty Tyrants who ruled Athens as Spartan puppets for a few months at the end of the Peloponnesian War. Epictetus may be thinking of the Leon episode (for which see the note to 4.1.160) or Xenophon, *Memorabilia* 1.2.33–38.

2.13.24: *who bought him as a slave*: See also 3.24.66 and 4.1.115–117, with Diogenes Laertius, *Lives of the Eminent Philosophers* 6.38, 6.43, and 6.74.

2.13.25: *Leave speaking as a philosopher*: These words are a guess, written to fill a gap in the received text.

2.13.26: *someone to lead the state*: A line from an unknown tragedy.

2.14.1: *a certain Roman*: Presumably the Naso mentioned by Arrian in the title, but we cannot identify him.

2.14.8: *son, father, . . . and subject*: Epictetus often stresses the importance of maintaining one's social relationships or roles as son, father, brother, citizen, and so on (see the introduction, 28–29. Part of the point is to remind his students that they already had these roles before they turned to philosophy. Maintaining these roles therefore grounds them in the real world and acts to counter a tendency toward spiritual pride—the common fault of thinking that, as a philosopher, one is better than other people.

2.14.17: *three wars*: He mentions this achievement because service on a minimum of three military campaigns was required by Roman law before a man could be a candidate for high office. See also 4.1.39.

2.14.23: *what their intention was*: The festival analogy was often ascribed to Pythagoras, the philosopher-mystic of the sixth century BCE. In his *Lives of the Eminent Philosophers*, Diogenes Laertius says, "Pythagoras claimed that life is like a festival: some go there for the athletic competitions, some to buy or sell, but the best people go as spectators. Likewise, in life, some men are naturally servile, hunters of fame or profit, but a philosopher's quest is for the truth" (8.8). A typical Greek festival included athletic competitions as well as what we might call a "fair," and festivals differed in how much weight they gave to one aspect or the other.

2.15.10: *both cities, the great and the small*: See the note to 2.5.26.

2.15.14: *the more hellebore they need*: Hellebore was commonly used in antiquity to treat insanity. It is a strong purgative, and deadly in large quantities.

2.15.20: *now in this direction and now in that*: In a healthy body, the four humors (black bile, phlegm, yellow bile, blood) are in equilibrium. Disease is an imbalance of the humors, when one dominates the others. This causes a flux of the dominant humor; typical examples brought up by ancient medical writers are the flux of blood during menstruation, and the flux of phlegm that marks a head cold.

2.16.9: *cheers and jeers*: This repeats some of 2.10.

2.16.17: *slept in a temple to find out what to do*: It was common practice for people to sleep in temples to receive an oracular dream from the god. This was especially common practice in temples of the healing god Asclepius, in the hope of receiving a dream that hinted at or expressed a cure.

2.16.30: *worse than Dirce's*: Dirce's Spring was in Thebes. The Marcian aqueduct, built in the middle of the second century BCE, and about 90 kilometers long, was one of the four main aqueducts supplying Rome.

2.16.31: *The Baths of Nero and the Marcian water*: A parody of Euripides, *Phoenician Women* 368: "The gymnasia where I was schooled, and the water of Dirce"—places which Polynices, the speaker, misses because of his exile from Thebes.

2.16.36: *Susa . . . or Ecbatana*: Important cities in Central Asia, neither of which was part of the Roman Empire.

2.16.44: *Eurystheus rather than Heracles*: Eurystheus was the cowardly king of Argos to whom Heracles was indentured as a punishment and for whom he carried out his famous twelve labors.

2.16.45: *Procrustes and Sciron*: Two monstrous brigands eliminated by Theseus.

2.17.5: *obsessed with definitions*: Theopompus of Chios, working in the fourth century BCE (and so contemporary with Plato), is more famous today as a historian, though he was just as celebrated in his day as an orator. The point he makes against Plato is sound, because Plato's insistence that we have to be able to define a concept before employing the term is too restrictive.

2.17.7: *instances are to be assigned to each of them*: See further 1.22, 2.11.1–12, and 4.1.41–45 on preconceptions.

2.17.8: *empty noises we were making*: Hippocrates of Cos (fifth century BCE) was taken to be the founder of scientific medicine.

2.17.16: *the first domain*: See §§29–32, 3.2, 3.12, and the introduction, 30–33, for the three domains and the training of desire, inclination, and assent.

2.17.20: *what do I care?*: See also 1.28.7–9 on Medea's choice, a favorite topic for thinkers interested in moral psychology, ever since Euripides's brilliant play. Seneca, one of Epictetus's most important Stoic predecessors, also wrote a *Medea*.

2.17.33: *these lofty ambitions make you a god*: If the student mastered the third domain as well as the other two, he would be a Stoic sage. In calling him a god, Epictetus is acknowledging, as all other Stoics did, too, that sagehood is extremely rare. The point is to keep aiming for it.

2.17.34: *treatise On the Liar*: The simplest formulation of the Liar Paradox—perhaps the only true paradox—is "This statement is a lie." Chrysippus is said to have written extensively on the paradox (Diogenes Laertius, *Lives of the Eminent Philosophers* 7.196). Epictetus refers to it again at 2.18.18, 2.21.17, 3.2.6, and 3.9.21. See M. Mignucci, "The Liar Paradox and the Stoics," in *Topics in Stoic Philosophy*, ed. K. Ierodiakonou (Oxford University Press, 1999), 54–70.

2.17.40: *Antipater and Archedemus*: On Archedemus, see the note to 2.4.10. Antipater of Tarsus became head of the Stoic school in the mid-second century BCE.

2.18.8: *As soon as you've conceived a desire for money*: Since, as the title of this discourse shows, it is meant to be about impressions, we should understand all these statements as, for instance, "As soon as you have the impression that money is something desirable."

2.18.11: *not thoroughly erased*: According to Seneca, Zeno said that they can never be completely erased: "Even in the wise man's mind a scar will remain when the wound [caused by the passions] has healed" (*On Anger* 1.16.7).

2.18.17: *trickier than the Master Argument*: See 2.19.1–10, with the notes. The philosopher in question is Diodorus Cronus (late fourth/early third centuries BCE).

2.18.18: *the Liar Paradox or the Silent Man*: For the Liar Paradox, see the note to 2.17.34. The Silent Man seems to be a way of referring to the sorites paradox. The sorites paradox is: at what point does a pile become a heap? If 50 grains make a heap, 49 grains make a heap; if 49 grains make a heap, 48 grains make a heap ... and so on until we arrive at the absurd conclusion that 5 grains of sand are a heap. The paradox only arises because of a certain vagueness with which it is set up, but that was its point: it was a Skeptical way of suggesting that we cannot know the meaning of any term. Chrysippus's solution was just to fall silent at a certain point, in response to the question: so if I remove one more grain ... ? See S. Bobzien, "Chrysippus and the Epistemic Theory of Vagueness," *Proceedings of the Aristotelian Society* 102 (2002): 217–38. The sorites puzzle may be pretty pointless on its own, but it becomes more interesting when brought to bear on other predicates. Is there a point at which a child becomes an adult (as all modern societies assume)? Is there a point at which a chimpanzee or a dolphin becomes rational?

2.18.21: *alive or dead*: A vague echo of Plato, *Laws* 854b–c, although Plato was talking about temple robbery, not sexual temptation.

2.18.22: making light of his allure: Plato, *Symposium* 218c–219a.

2.18.22: *the heirs of Heracles*: In legend, at the first Olympics, instituted by him, Heracles won both the wrestling and the pancratium. This feat was repeated only seven times in the history of the games. The names of those who achieved it were written on a special list as the "heirs of Heracles" and they were hailed as "men of wonder."

2.18.22: *pancratiasts*: Pancratium was a kind of violent combination of boxing and wrestling. Its closest equivalent today is mixed martial arts, which is sometimes called "modern pancratium." Boxing and pancratium were two of the most popular Olympic events in Roman times.

2.18.28: *to win a kingdom*: For the philosopher as king, see the notes to 3.21.19 and 3.22.49.

2.18.29: *the Dioscuri*: these "sons of Zeus" were Castor and Pollux. As deities, they were considered to respond to emergency pleas, and especially to the prayers of sailors in danger.

2.18.32: *constantly wrestling with blights*: Hesiod, *Works and Days* 413, translated by Martin West.

2.19.1: *unless it is or will at some point be the case*: Diodorus Cronus is most famous for the Master Argument, but he was also one of Zeno's teachers. A plausible reconstruction of the Master Argument (for which Epictetus is our chief witness) goes as follows: "If a sea battle will not be fought tomorrow, then it was also true in the past that it would not be fought. And since (by the first proposition in Epictetus's text) everything past that is true is necessary, it was necessarily the case in the past that the battle would not take place, and necessarily false that it would take place. Thus it was impossible that the sea battle would take place. And since (by the second proposition) an impossibility cannot follow a possibility, it was impossible from the first moment of time that the sea battle would take place. Therefore, if something will not be the case, it is never possible for it to be the case. And thus the third proposition in the text is proven false, and shown to be logically incompatible with the other two propositions. The conclusion that remains is that nothing, in fact, is possible which is not either true, or going to be true." R. Dobbin, *Epictetus: Discourses and Selected Writings* (Penguin, 2008), 263.

2.19.2: *in agreement with him*: The Stoics probably became interested in the Master Argument because of their belief in a predetermined universe. Cleanthes of Assos was the second head of the school after Zeno; on Antipater, see the note to 2.17.40.

2.19.5: *Panthoides*: A philosopher belonging to the same "Megarian" or "dialectical" school as Diodorus Cronus.

2.19.7: *Hellanicus... on the subject*: Hellanicus of Lesbos was a historian in the Herodotean mold (that is, he included ethnography and mythography) of the fifth century BCE. His remarks on these Trojans would have come in his *On the Trojan War*.

2.19.8: *those who've written on it*: Plutarch too says that people used the Master Argument to show off at parties (*Moralia* 614f–615a [*Table Talk*]).

2.19.12: *A wind bore me from Troy to the Cicyonians*: Homer, *Odyssey* 9.39. Epictetus is mocking the mere rote learning of information from books.

2.19.14: *Diogenes's account in his Ethics*: This Diogenes is not Diogenes of Sinope, whom Epictetus frequently mentions, but Diogenes of Babylon, a prominent Stoic of the third and second centuries BCE.

2.19.20: *albeit in a loose sense*: Epicureans held that pleasure was the good for man; Peripatetics (the Aristotelian school) held that health, wealth, and so on were not indifferents but contributed to human happiness. Most of us are therefore unthinking Epicureans and Peripatetics.

2.19.26: *a construct of ivory and gold*: On Phidias and his statues, see the note to 1.6.23.

2.19.31: *here's the carpenter, here are the materials*: Epictetus is the carpenter, his students are his materials.

2.20.3: *If any proposition is universal, it is false*: The objector has contradicted himself: his proposition "Nothing is universally true" is itself a universal statement, and therefore ex hypothesi false.

2.20.8: *why do you care?*: Epicurus contradicts himself because he cares enough about us to want to convert us to his teachings, when care is the mark of a social being.

2.20.9: *error of thinking that the gods care for people... other than pleasure*: Two cardinal points of Epicurean doctrine.

2.20.15: *reluctant and complaining though they may be*: As in Cleanthes's hymn at *Handbook* 53.1, and in the following famous image: "They too [Zeno and Chrysippus] affirmed that everything is fated, with the following model. When a dog is tied to a cart, if it wants to follow it is pulled and follows, making its spontaneous act coincide with necessity, but if it does not want to follow it will be compelled to do so in any case. So it is with people too: even if they do not want to, they will be compelled in any case to follow what is destined." Hippolytus, *Refutation of All Heresies* 1.21.

2.20.17: *kept from sleeping*: In Greek legend, Orestes and his sister Electra took it upon themselves to avenge the murder of their father Agamemnon by killing the perpetrators, their mother Clytemnestra and her lover Aegisthus. For the crime of matricide, Orestes was then hounded by the Furies.

2.20.17: *the Galli*: Priests of Cybele, the Anatolian Mother Goddess. They were given to extreme forms of ecstatic devotional behavior, including self-castration (§19). The city in Phrygia where Epictetus was born was a center for the worship of Cybele.

2.20.22: *What do you say, philosopher?*: In this paragraph, Epictetus turns from attacking the Epicureans to the Academics. It is true that the Epicureans, too, denied the existence of benevolent gods, but the form of argument outlined here—arguing both sides of a case—is typically Academic and Skeptic. They argued that if good arguments could be found for both sides of a case, neither side could reliably be held to be true.

2.20.23: *to frighten people and deter wrongdoing*: This position was famously first floated in the surviving fragment of a play written at the end of the fifth century BCE by either Critias or Euripides. Text in J. Diggle, ed., *Tragicorum Graecorum Fragmenta Selecta* (Oxford University Press, 1998), 177–79; translation in R. Waterfield, *The First Philosophers: The Presocratics and the Sophists* (Oxford University Press, 2000), 305–6.

2.20.26: *Lycurgus*: A semilegendary wise man, held to have singlehandedly created Sparta's political, legal, and military institutions.

2.20.26: *abandon their city*: In 480 BCE (after the battle of Thermopylae), and again the following year, the Athenians abandoned their city and let it be burned and plundered by the invading Persian army rather than submit to "slavery"—to becoming subjects of the Persian empire.

2.20.27: *the Pythia*: The priestess at Delphi in Greece who went into a trance and delivered Apollo's messages to those who consulted the oracle in this way.

2.20.28: *your mouth or your eye*: This point is also used against Skeptics at 1.27.18, and in general it was common to argue that Skeptics refute themselves because to carry out the simplest of daily tasks, such as crossing a road, it is necessary to suspend skepticism. Otherwise: "That may or may not be a bus bearing down on me," says the Skeptic as he steps out into the road.

2.20.30: *vinegared fish any more than it's porridge*: This was a standard Skeptical argumentative ploy: something is no more this than that. They also—an easier argument—standardly denigrated the reliability of the senses, as Epictetus-as-slave goes on to do.

2.20.32: *Demeter, a Maiden, a Pluto*: Epictetus is thinking of the myth of the abduction of Persephone (here, as often, called the Maiden) by Pluto, the god of the underworld. After Demeter got her daughter back (for some of the year, at any rate), she gave humans the gift of grain cultivation. See the note to 1.4.30 on Triptolemus.

2.20.35: *insolence toward them*: Similar arguments at 1.22.14 and 3.7.10–16.

2.21.22: *ulcers*: Amoebic dysentery is often accompanied by ulceration of the intestines.

2.22: *On friendship*: The reader should not be surprised to find in this discourse talk not only of friends but also of family members: the Greek word translated "friendship" (*philia*) covers both kinds of affective relationship. Epictetus's doubts in this discourse about the possibility of true *philia* for anyone except a Stoic sage are fully in line with traditional Stoicism.

2.22.11: *Do you think your father doesn't?*: A slightly altered version of Euripides, *Alcestis* 691.

2.22.13: *same mother and father*: For Eteocles and Polynices, see the note to *Handbook* 31.4.

2.22.14: *look at what they said*: Euripides, *Phoenician Women* 621–622. Eteocles is the first speaker, his brother the second.

2.22.15: *every creature is appropriated above all to its own interest*: On "appropriation," see the introduction, 21–22.

2.22.15: *beloved, or lover*: The terminology is that of male homoerotic love: the "beloved" (*erōmenos*) was typically the younger object of the affection of the "lover" (*erastēs*).

2.22.17: *the death of his beloved*: Alexander the Great's male beloved was Hephaestion. When Hephaestion died in 324, Alexander's grief knew no bounds, and the alleged burning of the temple of the healer god Asclepius in Ecbatana, for his failure to cure Hephaestion, was only one of its manifestations. But the story is implausible, and Arrian himself doubts it at *The Anabasis of Alexander* 7.14.5.

2.22.20: *maintain my various family relationships*: In other words, "If morality and other people's interests are to have a secure claim on me, they must not be in any competition with what I want for myself; and hence, to assure that, it is necessary to identify oneself and one's interests with the moral point of view." Long, *Epictetus*, 223.

2.22.21: *no more than a conventional idea*: This exact sentiment does not appear in Epicurus's extant works, but it is the kind of thing he might have said.

2.22.22: *the Trojan War*: Epictetus refers in order to the Peloponnesian War of 431–404 BCE between the Athenians and Spartans; the ascendancy of Thebes over both these two states in the 360s; the Persian Wars of the early fifth century; the Macedonian conquest of Greece, culminating in the battle of Chaeronea in 338 and the Macedonian conquest of the Persian empire by Alexander the Great; the Roman wars against the Getae; and the legendary Trojan War, initiated by Paris's treachery to Menelaus (see also 1.28.11–13). The Getae or Dacians were a Thracian people, occupying land around the mouth of the Danube; those living south of the river had been pacified and incorporated into the Roman province of Moesia many decades earlier, while Augustus was emperor, but in Epictetus's lifetime both Domitian (in 86–88) and Trajan (in 101–102 and 105–106) had been involved in warfare with them.

2.22.26: *sharing the same minder*: A child-minder (*paidagōgos*) was a household slave who accompanied young boys when they left home to go to school or somewhere, and in general made sure that they behaved well.

2.22.32: *a necklace came between them*: The story of Amphiaraus and Eriphyle is part of the legend of the Seven against Thebes (see the note to *Handbook* 31.4). Amphiaraus could see the future and knew the expedition was doomed, but he was persuaded to join it by his wife Eriphyle, who had been bribed with a fabulous necklace by Polynices, who was eager to have a hero of Amphiaraus's stature by his side as he attempted to effect his return to Thebes.

2.22.36: *no soul is willingly deprived of the truth*: The saying does not occur in any of Plato's published works, though the sentiment occurs at *Republic* 413a and *Sophist* 228c–d. We have already met it at 1.28.4.

2.23.2: *speech itself*: The five senses, speech, and reproduction were considered by Stoics the fundamental aspects or functions of soul.

2.23.3: *reaches far out*: Among the senses, only vision and hearing are effective at a distance from their objects and so need special explanation. Hearing was correctly explained by Stoics as sound waves impinging on the organ; for vision, see the next note.

2.23.4: *thanks to its tension*: In Stoicism, the soul pervades the whole body and, as it were, extends into the organs of sensation. In vision, the spirit (*pneuma*) that is the soul is imprinted with the shape, color, and other characteristics of visible things, as follows: "Stoics say that we see when the light between our visual faculty and the object is stretched into the shape of a cone.... The tip of the cone in the air is at the eye, the base at the object seen. Thus the thing seen is communicated to us by the tension of the stretched air." Diogenes Laertius, *Lives of the Eminent Philosophers* 7.157.

2.23.16: *the underlings to the king*: This seems not just a strange question in itself, but a strange one to raise at this point in the discourse. But in what follows Epictetus hints at its relevance as he talks of the subservience of the body to the will. So, by means of parallel cases, the questioner is asking, "What if the body, the servant, is superior to the will, which you're saying is the master?"

2.23.21: *On the End, Physics, and On the Canon*: Three of Epicurus's many books. Epictetus makes the same point against Epicurus at 1.20.18 and 2.20.15–16.

2.23.21: *beard grow long*: A full beard was a sign of a philosopher. See J. Sellars, *The Art of Living*, 2nd ed. (Bristol Classical Press, 2009), 15–19.

2.23.21: *a blessed day*: The letter of Epicurus from which this is extracted can be found at Diogenes Laertius, *Lives of the Eminent Philosophers* 10.22.

2.23.30: *cowardly*: So, having dealt with impiety, Epictetus turns to the second charge he brought in §2, that of cowardice.

2.23.32: *Helen... as an ordinary woman*: Ugly and supposedly lowborn Thersites features in the second book of Homer's *Iliad* and elsewhere also is used by Epictetus as an example of ignobility. Helen is "Helen of Troy," the most beautiful woman in the world.

2.23.33: *swept off their feet*: By Helen's beauty or the persuasiveness of rhetoric. The opponents Epictetus has in mind are Skeptics, who argued that nothing is absolutely what it is.

2.23.41: *the Sirens*: See the twelfth book of Homer's *Odyssey* for these beguiling creatures.

2.23.42: *both you and Destiny*: See *Handbook* 53 for the next three lines of the passage, from one of Cleanthes's poems.

2.24: *did not have what it takes*: Epictetus acknowledged that plenty of people might be superficially attracted to philosophy, but few will stick with it (2.14.23–29, 3.6.9). As well as turning away students, he regularly discouraged visitors (e.g., 1.11.39, 1.15.8).

2.24.6: *it certainly takes skill*: This last exchange between Epictetus and his hapless interlocutor is not in our manuscripts. But there is a gap in the text that needs filling, since in each case Epictetus is establishing skill on both sides, the active and the passive (so to speak). That way he can infer the conclusion he wants, that listening takes skill, and overcome the interlocutor's earlier doubt, expressed by his "Apparently." All this is very reminiscent of Plato's Socratic dialogues.

2.24.13: *use a demonstrative argument on you*: A demonstrative argument is one that leads to knowledge rather than opinion. Its premises are known to be true, and then it demonstrates by deductively evident steps that its conclusion follows from the premises.

2.24.21: *the rift between Agamemnon and Achilles*: One of Epictetus's stock examples (see also 1.22.5–8 and 1.28.24) of conflicting opinions, or, as he would put it, of the inability to apply preconceptions correctly to particular cases. Since this is the starting point of philosophy (1.22.9, 2.11.13), he feels himself unable to make a start with this interlocutor.

2.24.23: *many cares*: Homer, *Iliad* 2.25.

2.24.23: *a clever priest . . . get the better of you*: Calchas, a seer, explained that to end the plague that was racking the Greek camp, Agamemnon had to return Chryseis, whom he had captured and taken as his concubine, to her Trojan father, a priest of Apollo. Despite being furious with him, Agamemnon returned Chryseis—but took Achilles's concubine (his "war prize") for himself, provoking the quarrel that is the central story of the *Iliad*.

2.24.24: *Not richer than Agamemnon, though, surely*: The purpose of the comparisons that follow with Agamemnon and Achilles is to drive home the point that taking material things and worldly honors to be good did not do them any good, and they had more of these so-called goods than the imaginary interlocutor.

2.24.25: *as Hector or Ajax could*: Hector's rock features at *Iliad* 8.320–328, Ajax's at *Iliad* 7.268–272.

2.24.25: *mother ... father a descendant of Zeus*: Achilles's mother was the sea-goddess Thetis, and his father, Peleus, was a grandson of Zeus.

2.24.26: *reduced them to silence*: In Book 9 of the *Iliad*, Odysseus and Phoenix (along with Ajax) form a delegation to try to persuade Achilles to stop sulking and return to help the Greeks defeat the Trojans. Achilles's speech occupies lines 308–429.

2.25.2: *a demonstrative argument*: See the note to 2.24.13.

2.25.3: *whether or not it's necessary*: The argument echoes a famous one by Aristotle, that to determine whether or not one should study philosophy, one should already be a philosopher (fragment 51 Rose).

2.26.4: *protreptic and refutational arguments*: A protreptic speech was one designed to encourage the audience to change their lives for the better or, generally, to instruct rather than to refute. But the distinction between the two kinds of argument is not hard-and-fast, since Epictetus himself frequently uses refutation as a form of instruction, and he seems to believe that an interlocutor, chastened by refutation, would then be open to protreptic.

2.26.6: *Socrates ... used to say*: What follows is a paraphrase of Plato, *Gorgias* 474a. See also 2.12.5.

3.1.5: *a hideous wrestler, wouldn't he?*: There was considerable discussion in athletic training manuals as to what the best physique was for each of the athletic disciplines, and what special abilities were required. On pancratium, see the second note to 2.18.22. The five events of the pentathlon were discus, long jump, javelin, sprint, and wrestling.

3.1.7: *human excellence*: The word translated "excellence" (*aretē*) is also the word for "virtue," so when Epictetus subsequently introduces virtue, it is not an illegitimate move in the argument. "Human excellence" is just another way of saying "virtue."

3.1.14: *youthful debauchery*: Polemo of Athens was the fourth head of the Platonic Academy, from 314 until 269 BCE. It was he who came up with the formula for the good life that was adopted by Stoicism: "living in accord with nature."

3.1.16: *take no notice of the oracle*: In legend, Apollo's oracle told Laius that he was destined to father a child who would kill him and marry Jocasta, Laius's wife and the child's mother. Laius therefore abstained from sex with Jocasta, until one night when he got drunk. The child who was born was Oedipus, and he fulfilled the prophecy in all respects.

3.1.18: *no one pays them any mind*: Along with a number of other moral maxims (e.g., "Die without regrets" and "Nothing in excess"), the famous "Know yourself" was inscribed by the entrance to the temple of Apollo at Delphi in Greece.

3.1.19: *as he himself says*: What follows is a paraphrase of Plato, *Apology of Socrates* 28e and then 29c–30a.

3.1.23: *different from them*: See 1.2.18 and 22 for the analogy with the purple trimming of a toga, and 1.2.30 and 4.8.42 for the image of the lion and the bull.

3.1.24: *In any case*: Epictetus picks up the thread from §§10–11.

3.1.24: *threadbare cloak*: Along with a bushy beard, the other mark of a philosopher was a *tribōn*, a coarse, thin cloak, worn all the year round to demonstrate ascetic hardiness and disdain for worldly affairs. Professional philosophers generally presented a public image that stressed poverty, or at least frugality, as a way of advertising the success of their teaching: they themselves had moved beyond the superficial values of the world, and they could teach others to do so as well.

3.1.28: *what are we to make of him?*: Compare 1.16.10–14, with its conclusion: "Insofar as it's up to us, we shouldn't confuse the sexes, but keep them distinct."

3.1.34: *president of the games*: Epictetus's interlocutor presumably has Corinthian citizenship. The Isthmian Games, one of the greatest international athletic festivals, was hosted by Corinth. The cadet force was made up of young men aged about nineteen, who underwent various forms of training in their future military and civic responsibilities.

3.1.36: *usually doesn't speak to anyone*: Epictetus is always speaking to his students, of course, but perhaps he had a reputation for being less open with the more casual visitors: see the beginning of 2.24. Nevertheless, there are a several occasions when he speaks to them as well: 1.10, 1.11, 1.15, 1.19.26–29, 2.2, 2.4, 2.6.20, 2.14, 2.24, 3.4, 3.7, 3.9. As often, it is not easy to assess Epictetus's tone of voice. Could this be an ironic joke?

3.1.37: *matters of supreme and essential importance*: For the philosopher as God's messenger, see also 3.22.23; as a witness for God, 1.29.46–49, 3.24.112–113, 3.26.28, 4.8.32; as a servant of God, 3.22.69, 3.22.82, 3.22.95, 3.24.65, 3.24.98, 3.24.113–114, 3.26.28, 4.7.20, 4.8.32. For discussion, see K. Ierodiakonou, "The Philosopher as God's Messenger," in Scaltsas and Mason, *Philosophy of Epictetus*, 56–70.

3.1.38: *the poet… says*: Homer, *Odyssey* 1.37–39. Zeus is recalling how he sent Hermes, the messenger god, to Aegisthus to warn him not to have an affair with Clytemnestra or kill her husband, Agamemnon. Then, in the next sentence, Epictetus draws on Hermes's epithets from *Odyssey* 1.84.

3.1.42: *Try to be beautiful*: A reminiscence of Plato, *First Alcibiades* 131d.

3.2.2: *the domain of assent*: See also 3.12 and the introduction, 30–33, for the training of desire, inclination, and assent.

3.2.8: *finished working at the other domains*: If he had finished working in the first two domains, he would be a good man, and then the third domain would secure his goodness. The earlier discourse 2.17.31–33 is a bit clearer on this point.

3.2.11: *pointing at him with his middle finger*: Another anecdote about Diogenes of Sinope, the founder of Cynicism. Diogenes Laertius, *Lives of the Eminent Philosophers* 6.34, reveals that the "sophist" (i.e., orator) was Demosthenes, the famous Athenian speechwriter and statesman. Pointing with the middle finger was considered impolite.

3.2.15: *Crinis*: An obscure Stoic philosopher—and not a very good one, in Epictetus's opinion.

3.3.6: *That's why . . . irrelevant*: The sentence is counterfactual. Goodness is not different from honor and justice, and so good people maintain their relationships: 2.14.8, 2.22.18–21, and later in the present discourse at §8. The Epicureans are probably Epictetus's targets, since for them pleasure was the good, which therefore had nothing to do with honor and justice.

3.3.12: *come to the province*: It was traditional in Rome for a man, after his year of consulship, to be sent out to govern one of the provinces of the empire as proconsul. It was not uncommon for proconsuls to see the position as an opportunity to enrich themselves.

3.3.13: *leaves him no choice*: As elsewhere in *Discourses* (1.25.13, 1.30.1, 2.5.22, 3.1.43, 3.13.13, 4.1.103), "someone else" is God, here because it is he who has established that everyone prefers what he regards as good.

3.3.18: *pernicious judgments we need to eliminate*: So we are not to feel pity for someone who is destitute? That is not quite what Epictetus is saying. He is saying that, rather than automatically feel pity, we should consider what we can do for him by way of kindness. Only our reaction to his poverty is our responsibility and, as the events of life always do, the beggar therefore offers us an opportunity for appropriate and virtuous behavior. On pity, see also the note to 1.18.3.

3.3.22: *the spirit that contains them*: "Spirit" translates *pneuma*, which is used here almost as a synonym for "soul" (as also at 2.1.17). The human soul is made of pure *pneuma*, which is at the same time the stuff that permeates all creation and maintains it. Hence, in Stoicism, it is sometimes equated with God.

3.4.1: *governor of Epirus*: Nicopolis, where Epictetus lived, was the capital city of the Roman province of Epirus. The governor may be Gnaeus Claudius Pulcher.

3.4.5: *a paradigm of correct audience behavior*: In other words, as Epictetus puts it elsewhere, he has to be true to his role. See especially 1.2. At 1.29.44 he says in brief what he is here telling the governor: " 'Accept a governorship.' I accept it, and use the role to display how an educated person behaves."

3.4.6: *you wanted someone else*: In ancient times, it was common for plays to be put on as part of a contest. Originally, in fifth-century BCE Athens, the playwrights competed for the prize; in the fourth century, prizes were introduced for actors as well, and this became the primary contest, especially since, as the centuries passed, the plays that were staged had often been written by long-dead playwrights, whose work remained popular.

3.4.9: *Sophron gets the crown*: Probably Marcus Julius Sophron, a comic actor who was born in Hierapolis, the same city in Phrygia that Epictetus came from. The contest was probably part of the Actia (see the note to 3.22.52). See C. Jones, "Sophron the Comoedos," *Classical Quarterly* 37, no. 1 (1987): 208–12.

3.5.14: *I'm becoming a better person*: There is nothing exactly like this in the extant Socratic literature. It is somewhat reminiscent of Xenophon, *Memorabilia* 1.6.8–9.

3.5.17: *knew anything or taught anything*: Socrates's disavowal of knowledge was one of his most famous features (see also 3.23.22), though it is peculiar to Plato's Socratic works (and to a fragmentary dialogue written by Aeschines of Sphettus), not Xenophon's. As an argumentative ploy, it enabled him to ask questions, to elicit others' views and find flaws in them, rather than assert anything himself.

3.5.17: *Protagoras or Hippias*: Protagoras of Abdera and Hippias of Elis were two prominent members of the sophistic movement of the fifth century BCE. See the note to *Handbook* 46.1.

3.6.8: *common to everyone*: These common resources are presumably the preconceptions of 1.22 and elsewhere, and the sense organs (see 3.5.8, 3.13.13, and 4.10.15).

3.6.9: *pick up soft cheese with a fishhook*: If the saying was not proverbial, it may have originated with the Cynic Bion of Borysthenes (third century BCE). Diogenes Laertius reports him as having said, "You can't reel in soft cheese with a fishhook" (*Lives of the Eminent Philosophers* 4.47).

3.7.1: *the Corrector*: The job of a Corrector was to assess the way the free cities of Greece were administered and to suggest reforms where necessary. He was a high-ranking Roman and a personal appointee of the emperor, with wide-ranging powers.

3.7.3: *to see him on his way*: In ancient times, sailing in winter was particularly hazardous. We cannot identify this Maximus, but Cassiope is probably the village in the north of the island of Corcyra (modern Corfu). Perhaps Maximus's son was being sent into exile in this remote place. But Epictetus's point is clear: can it be for bodily reasons that people behave honorably? And then the main point of the discourse is that it makes no sense (on Epictetus's hostile interpretation of Epicureanism) for an Epicurean such as the Corrector to behave honorably.

3.7.7: *we've discovered the essence of goodness*: The Stoics were suspicious of pleasure, because it arises when we get something we want, and they considered most of what we want to be indifferents, and therefore to feel pleasure in relation to them is the result of incorrect judgments. But they did allow, as Epictetus does here, that acting virtuously was accompanied by a kind of gentle and reasonable pleasure.

3.7.11: *an official . . . to refrain from doing so*: It very soon turns out that the official Epictetus has in mind is the Corrector himself.

3.7.12: *Don't steal*: Epicurus said no such thing, of course; this is Epictetus's distortion of Epicurus's assertion that people are obliged to be just and honest only insofar as it is in their interest to do so. What Epictetus omits is that an Epicurean agent's interest, properly understood, would not lead him to steal.

3.7.19: *taking part in public life*: See also 1.23 and 2.20 on these aspects of

Epicureanism. In general, Epictetus's diatribes against Epicureanism need to be taken with a pinch of salt. Epicurus did not, for instance, ban marriage and procreation altogether, but he did not think they were good for people unless they were ready for the responsibilities that go with them, which few people were.

3.7.19: *superintendent of the cadet force or gymnasiarch*: On the cadets, see the note to 3.1.34. The gymnasiarch was in charge of a gymnasium, which acted as a school for the physical education of boys and was one of the centers of elite community life. People went there not just to exercise but also to meet and socialize and to listen to lectures.

3.7.19: *young Spartans and Athenians used to receive*: Their education is also held to have been exemplary at 2.20.6. It appears that even in the second century CE, Greeks used to look back with rose-colored glasses on their classical past, six hundred or so years earlier.

3.7.22: *tendency to attract and overcome people*: Epictetus generally says that the cause of wrongdoing is self-deception—the mistaken judgment that something bad is good. Here (and see also 1.27.3, 3.8.1), he gives the corollary: so-called pleasure entices us into mistaken judgments. And he invites the Epicurean Collector to become a Stoic.

3.7.23: *what will the outcome be?*: Epictetus answers the question at 2.20.34–35.

3.7.25: *of three kinds*: The tripartite division adumbrated in the sentence remains obscure because Epictetus does not develop it anywhere else in the extant discourses. The first class of appropriate actions must be those that preserve a person's (or a creature's) life, because the Stoics believed that was every creature's primary motivation. The second class may consist of those that preserve one's role as a human being. The third class, as §26 shows, is concerned with the many particular roles that one has.

3.7.31: *Whose antechamber did you sleep in?*: Symphorus and Numenius were clearly freedmen with considerable influence in the imperial court. Sleeping in someone's antechamber was a way to be among the first to greet him in the morning.

3.8.4: *a cognitive impression of it*: See the note to *Handbook* 45.

3.8.7: *listen to this*: It is hard to find a connection between this last paragraph and what preceded it. The endings of 1.25, 2.6, 3.3, 3.10, 3.13, and 3.15 involve similarly abrupt changes of topic. Since we have discourses that are simply entitled "A Miscellany" (3.6, 3.11, 3.14), it seems possible that Arrian gave each of these discourse a title that reflected the dominant theme of the opening paragraphs but that they, too, are in a sense miscellanies. It is not clear what these unattached paragraphs are, since they are not full discourses. Could they be all that Arrian could recover of some talks?

3.8.7: *pointed at me*: The point of the anecdote is presumably that Italicus was anxious not to be thought of as a philosopher because of the poor reputation they had in Rome. This Italicus may be Silius Italicus (c. 28–c. 103), but he was known as a poet rather than a philosopher.

3.9: *for a lawsuit*: The chief interest of this discourse is that it shows Epictetus talking to someone with no philosophical training or aspirations. For a historical analysis of the discourse, see J. Nicols, "Epictetus, the Rhetorician from Cnossos, and the Practice of Civic Patronage in the Principate," *Historia* 58, no. 3 (2009): 325–35.

3.9.3: *the Cnossians*: Cnossus was the largest city in Crete, and it would be a prestigious position to be its representative in Rome.

3.9.9: *took to be your equal*: That poor judgments lead to poor behavior is a constant refrain of Epictetus's, but here he adds a new twist—that it may be arrogance that prevents one from examining one's judgments and improving them where necessary.

3.9.16: *you'll be poorer than I am*: An echo of the argument in Xenophon, *Oeconomicus* 2.

3.9.18: *a patron*: A patron in Rome was typically a wealthy and powerful individual. He attracted a number of "clients," and the relationship between them, which was enshrined in law, was essentially one of mutual assistance. See the note to *Handbook* 25.2. As in §3, a whole town or community could have a patron, who was expected to represent its interests in Rome and in return received the support of its citizens.

3.9.21: *Liar... murrhine ware... Denier*: On the Liar Paradox, see the note to 2.17.34. The Denier was probably a similar paradox. Murrhine ware was made from a mineral, fluorspar, which had bands of various colors. A cup made from it was thought to improve the taste of wine; it was beautiful and extremely rare and expensive.

3.10.1: *those that are relevant to bed*: The "judgments" Epictetus has in mind are chiefly short and memorable precepts, compatible with Stoicism, that can act as immediate reminders as to how to behave. See §18, 4.12.7, and *Handbook* 8 for examples, and Marcus Aurelius's *Meditations* is full of them. The verses that follow, from *The Golden Verses of Pythagoras* (40–44), serve much the same purpose. The *Golden Verses* were not written by Pythagoras; they were written at some point within the Pythagorean school to summarize the rules by which their communities lived and the exercises they practiced.

3.10.4: *'Paean Apollo!' is*: A paean was a hymn to Apollo, invoking him under the title "Paean Apollo." It was so familiar, Epictetus seems to be suggesting, that it had become more or less meaningless.

3.10.6: *keeps being hit*: On pancratium, see the second note to 2.18.22.

3.10.8: *obeyed your trainer*: These are typical questions that the officials at the Olympic Games put to contestants.

3.10.13: *to await death well and in the right way*: As in 3.5 and elsewhere, the assumption that having a fever might well lead to death is a telling reminder that ancient medicine lacked many cures that we take for granted nowadays.

3.11.4: *the poet's words concerning strangers*: Homer, *Odyssey* 14.56–58. Eumaeus, the swineherd, is speaking (though he does not know it) to his master, Odysseus, who is disguised as a particularly shabby beggar.

3.12.2: *hug statues*: We can only guess what spectacular trick "setting up a palm tree" was; §9 suggests it might have been a feat of strength, perhaps pushing a tree-sized pole into an upright position, or climbing up the pole once it has been set up. On hugging statues, see the note to *Handbook* 47.

3.12.9: *palm tree... tent... mortar and pestle*: See the previous note on "setting up a palm tree." The rest of the sentence perhaps refers to the Cynic practice of carrying around all their belongings, which both kept them fit and encouraged them to reduce their belongings. But, as Epictetus says, that would be pointless for someone attending his school.

3.12.13: *inclination and disinclination*: On the three domains and the training of desire, inclination, and assent, see also 3.2 and the introduction, 30–33

3.12.15: *an unexamined life*: Socrates's famous assertion that the unexamined life is not worth living comes at Plato, *Apology of Socrates* 38a.

3.12.15: *if it's to be accepted*: That is, if it is a "cognitive impression," on which see the note to *Handbook* 45.

3.12.17: *without telling anyone*: This Apollonius might be Apollonius of Tyana, a mystical teacher of the first century CE who recommended ascetic practices.

3.13.4: *the conflagration*: Stoics believed in eternal recurrence—that the physical universe goes through an endless sequence of cycles, each ending after an immensity of time in total conflagration, followed by regeneration, with exactly the same events happening in each cycle. God survives the conflagration by withdrawing into himself, so that he is able to initiate the next sequence; but the gods in the plural will perish, along with everything else, at the time of the conflagration, because they have particular functions relating to the maintenance of the universe. See A. A. Long, "The Stoics on World-Conflagration and Everlasting Recurrence," in *From Epicurus to Epictetus: Studies in Hellenistic and Roman Philosophy* (Oxford University Press, 2006), 256–82.

3.13.5: *people... enjoy one another's company*: The premise is fully Stoic: see the introduction, 21–22, on "appropriation."

3.13.9: *no wars anymore*: We have no way of knowing in what year this talk was delivered, but whenever it was, it is likely that there was warfare on the borders of the empire. Epictetus is referring to the general Pax Romana in the heartland of the empire, the countries bordering the central and eastern Mediterranean.

3.13.13: *senses and preconceptions*: "Senses and preconceptions" go together because it is our preconceptions that enable us to identify what our senses perceive. On preconceptions, see 1.22, 2.11.1–12, 2.17.1–13, and 4.1.41–45.

3.13.14: *the elements*: The Stoics held that human beings are composed of the four elements (earth, water, air, and fire). At death, these elements separate and return to their natural abodes, conceived as four concentric circles, from the heaviest at the center to the lightest at the outer rim of the universe.

3.13.15: *no Hades . . . no Pyriphlegethon*: Acheron, Cocytus, and Pyriphlegethon were three of the rivers of Hades, the underworld where it was conventionally held that we (in some sense of "we") went after death.

3.13.20: *as best we can*: The remainder of this discourse seems to have little to do with what preceded it, and there is no reference for "such things." See the note to 3.8.7.

3.14.9: <. . . >: There is a gap in the text. There might have been more on Socrates's argumentative style, and then another description of diffidence as the feeling that something is not doable under the circumstances.

3.15: All this discourse, except for the short last paragraph, is repeated, with minor variations, as *Handbook* 29. See the first note there.

3.15.4: *wield a spade*: Perhaps the athletes helped prepare the ground for some of the events.

3.15.4: *swallow . . . sand, be flogged*: Flogging was the standard punishment for infringements at the Olympic Games—a very undignified punishment that was otherwise reserved for enslaved people. Some events took place in a sand pit, but the most likely opportunity for swallowing sand would have been when a wrestler or pancratiast sprinkled sand over himself to enable his opponent to get a grip.

3.15.8: *Euphrates*: Euphrates of Syria was a Stoic philosopher active in the first and early second centuries CE.

3.15.14: *Galba was assassinated*: Galba was emperor for about three weeks, from December 68 to January 69. This final paragraph is another which seems to have little or no connection with the rest of the discourse. See the note to 3.8.7.

3.15.14: *governed by providence*: On the Stoic concepts of divine providence and determinism, see 1.6, 1.12, 1.16, 3.17, and the introduction, 22–23.

3.17: *On providence*: On the Stoic concepts of divine providence and determinism, see also 1.6, 1.12, 1.16, and the introduction, 22–23.

3.17.4: *Sura*: Probably L. Licinius Sura, a three-time consul early in the second century. We happen to know that he had a freedman called Philostorgus.

3.18.4: *guilty of impiety*: What is the backstory here? Has the father committed the son for trial for impiety? Is the father also the "judge," in a metaphorical sense? Piety was correct behavior toward not just gods but also one's elders, and especially one's father.

3.18.7: *just as great a risk*: Compare 2.5.29.

3.20.5: *Menoeceus . . . from his death*: In legend, Menoeceus was a highborn Theban who sacrificed himself to ensure that Thebes would not fall to the Seven against Thebes (on whom see the note to *Handbook* 31.4).

3.20.7: *Admetus*: Admetus's father, Pheres, refused to die in place of his son even though he was already close to death from old age. See also 2.22.11.

3.20.10: *the heavier the pestle, the more I'm benefited*: The word "pestle" here clearly refers to something like a barbell.

3.20.12: *what the magic wand of Hermes promises*: Hermes was, among other things, the god of trickery and hence of magic. His wand, called a caduceus, was a winged stick with two snakes entwined around it.

3.20.19: *I know nothing*: Epictetus's tone is heavily ironic. It looks as though Lesbius was his slave.

3.21.13: *the mysteries*: Plato had established the analogy between taking up philosophy and being initiated into the mysteries, and between making progress in philosophy and progressing through the stages of a mystery cult. The most famous and best-attended mystery cult was that of the cereal goddesses, Demeter and Persephone, at Eleusis, a coastal town northwest of Athens. The hierophant, herald, and torchbearer were all senior functionaries at Eleusis.

3.21.14: *The promises are the same*: The promises made by Stoicism and by the mysteries were similar only at a very general level: "You'll be a better person."

3.21.19: *Socrates… Diogenes… Zeno… doctrine*: Socrates, Diogenes, and Zeno were all said to have been prompted to become philosophers by the oracle of Apollo at Delphi. In assigning refutational argument to Socrates, Epictetus is thinking of the methodology of Plato's Socratic dialogues. Diogenes of Sinope, the founder of Cynicism, is awarded "kingship and reproof" because it was his job to correct people's morals in a peremptory fashion; for the philosopher as king, see also the note to 3.22.49. Zeno of Citium is awarded the realm of instruction and doctrine because, as the founder of Stoicism, he established at least in outline both its doctrines and its teaching methods. To Epictetus, all three thinkers essentially held the same views, or were representatives of the same philosophy, but their roles and teaching methods differed.

3.22: *On Cynicism*: As this discourse shows (see also 1.24.6–9 and 4.8.30–33), Epictetus was far from dismissing Cynicism as useless. Its devotion to the lifelong quest for personal virtue was congenial to Stoics, and they were in agreement that virtue by itself is sufficient for happiness and is entirely up to us. Moreover, Epictetus in particular appreciated the fact that a Cynic could retain hardly any features of his previous life. You could not even think of being a Cynic unless you were prepared to change radically. But whereas Epictetus thought Stoicism could be usefully practiced by everyone, he did not think Cynicism could or should have such a wide appeal (see 4.8.32). His brand of Stoicism was not so ascetic. On Cynicism, see W. Desmond, *Cynics* (University of California Press, 2008).

3.22.2: *take our time… he said*: This is the third longest discourse in the collection, after 4.1 and 3.24.

3.22.4: *in this great city too*: The great city that is the world: see the second note to 2.5.26.

3.22.8: *witnesses*: On Thersites, see the note to 2.23.32. Epictetus's point is that you have to know your role in life, and that a Thersites should not aim too high.

3.22.10: *a threadbare cloak these days*: See the note to 3.1.24.

3.22.13: *eliminate desire altogether*: See the note to 1.4.1.

3.22.15: *out in the open*: A true Cynic had little or no property. He lived as a homeless person and worked as a street preacher.

3.22.23: *The next step for the true Cynic*: Having covered the training of the Cynic, in what follows Epictetus outlines three topics: the messages that are conveyed by a Cynic's moral values (§§23–44), his way of life (§§45–89), and his personality (§§90–106). The discourse is the earliest coherent outline that we possess of the Cynic way of life and its prerequisites.

3.22.24: *battle of Chaeronea*: Fought in 338 BCE, this was the battle that decisively delivered mastery of the Greeks to Philip II of Macedon, and then to his heirs. In this apocryphal story, Diogenes told Philip that he had come "to spy on his insatiable greed" (Diogenes Laertius, *Lives of the Eminent Philosophers* 6.43). See also 1.24.6–10 for Diogenes as a spy.

3.22.26: *echo Socrates's words*: The first words, and the tone of voice, echo Socrates's words (as retold by Cleitophon) at Plato, *Cleitophon* 407a–b. Plato too (if *Cleitophon* was written by Plato) imagines Socrates as proclaiming the words on the tragic stage.

3.22.27: *Myron or Ophellius*: Presumably famous athletes of the day, whose vocation led to suffering of some kind. For Croesus, see the note to 1.2.37.

3.22.30: *Nero... Sardanapallus*: The emperor Nero killed himself in 68 after a troubled reign. In the historical tradition to which Epictetus is referring, Sardanapallus was the last king of the Assyrian empire, who lived a vile and decadent life and then burned himself to death along with all his wealth rather than fall into the hands of his enemies.

3.22.30: *pounding in my chest*: Homer, *Iliad* 10.15, 91, 94–95. Half of *Iliad* 18.289 shortly follows.

3.22.35: *'shepherd' is perfect for you*: In Homer's poems, it is common to call a king a "shepherd of his people."

3.22.38: *our messenger and spy*: Epictetus puts the following dialogue into Diogenes's mouth, all the way until §49. This is indicated in the Greek by a switch from you-singular (the student whom Epictetus is addressing) to you-plural (the "us" of §38), and also by what Epictetus says at the start of §50, when he returns to his student.

3.22.49: *king and master*: The true Cynic deserves this designation because he is answerable to no one else, because he has the interests of his fellow citizens at heart (§72), and because he has the moral authority that makes it his job to reprimand others in a lordly fashion (§§93–96).

3.22.50: *devouring... everything you give him*: Hard-core Cynics lived as beggars.

3.22.50: *a fine shoulder*: A Cynic typically wore his cloak with one shoulder exposed (see also 4.8.34) to demonstrate his endurance of cold and as a nod toward the ideal of complete nakedness—that is, the complete rejection of society's conventions.

3.22.52: *Nicopolitans*: Actually, a famous international athletic and musical festival called the Actia was celebrated every four years at Nicopolis, but it is true that all the international festivals paled beside the Olympics.

3.22.52: *swallowing a lot of sand*: On being flogged and swallowing sand, see the note to 3.15.4. The Olympic festival was held at the height of summer, hence the heat and thirst.

3.22.54: *lashed like a donkey*: It appears to be true that Cynics were occasionally flogged, as a punishment for their more outrageous views. They held, for instance, that stealing was not wrong—that, in fact, since ownership of property was bad for the owner, a thief was doing him a favor.

3.22.55: *haul them off to the proconsul*: The proconsul in Roman provinces was ultimately responsible for seeing that the law was carried out.

3.22.57: *trained by Eurystheus*: On Eurystheus and Heracles, see the note to 2.16.44. Heracles was a Cynic hero for his endurance and moral mission.

3.22.58: *fight and kill one another*: There were occasional deaths at the Olympic Games over the centuries it was run, as at other festivals. They were caused by heat exhaustion, by the violence of the boxing and wrestling events, or by the hazards of the chariot races. Diogenes is getting at the spectators' half-hopeful desire to witness some such accident.

3.22.60: *what does he say about poverty, death, pain?*: For the answers, see 1.24.6–7.

3.22.60: *the Great King*: The king of the vast Achaemenid empire, which still existed in Diogenes's day (before its conquest by Alexander the Great) was commonly referred to simply as the Great King, and to ordinary thinking was a byword for happiness.

3.22.62: *should I accept his invitation?*: That is, should he, as a would-be Cynic, accept physical comfort in any form? And should he not be entirely self-reliant?

3.22.63: *Diogenes became a friend of Antisthenes, and Crates of Diogenes*: For Antisthenes, see the note to 1.17.12. Crates of Thebes (c. 365–c. 285 BCE) was a Cynic follower of Diogenes, and was one of the teachers of Zeno of Citium, the founder of Stoicism.

3.22.65: *stop you shivering*: Rotting compost and manure generate heat. The mention of manure is not—or not just—one of Epictetus's gratuitous insults. Manure is rich in antibiotics, and wrapping an affected limb—or, in the case of fever, the whole body—in animal manure was held to be efficacious and is still recommended by some alternative medical practitioners, at least in the form of poultices.

3.22.67: *valuable in themselves*: Epictetus's answer for non-Cynics is given at 3.7.26.

3.22.71: *adding up already*: In one of the famous stories about Diogenes, he had reduced his possessions until the only utensil he had was a cup. One day he saw a boy using his hands to drink water from a stream—so he threw away his cup.

3.22.72: *the people's guardian, laden with responsibilities*: Homer, *Iliad* 2.25, said of Agamemnon.

3.22.74: *better for him to have exposed them at birth than to kill them by neglect*: Though the exposure of infants was little talked about, it was a not uncommon practice in the ancient world. Some were found and reared as slaves in other homes, but not all. Seriously deformed children were more likely to be exposed; a second son was at risk because if two sons lived, the estate would be divided between them, with the possibility of making it too small to be viable, or of dropping a rung on the status ladder; a second daughter was at risk, or even a first, because of the need to give her a dowry in due course of time and her negligible economic value meanwhile.

3.22.76: *Crates was married*: Diogenes Laertius tells the story at *Lives of the Eminent Philosophers* 6.96. Hipparchia fell in love with Crates, and no one, not even Crates himself, could dissuade her from wanting to marry him. Eventually, he stripped to show her that, as a Cynic, he owned nothing and insisted that, if she was to be his wife, she had to be a Cynic as well. The couple became notorious for living as beggars and even having sex in public. Shocking passersby was one of the Cynics' teaching methods.

3.22.78: *Epaminondas, who died childless*: Epaminondas was the liberator of Thebes from Spartan dominance and military occupation, and then the chief architect of Thebes's brief dominance in mainland Greece from 371 until his death in 362 BCE.

3.22.78: *Priam... Danaus... Aeolus*: Priam was the legendary king of Troy at the time of the Trojan War. So far from being "trashy," his eldest son, Hector, is actually portrayed by Homer as a good person and a true hero (as Epictetus acknowledges at 3.22.7). Danaus had fifty daughters (and his twin brother Aegyptus had fifty sons). Aeolus, keeper of the winds, had six sons and six daughters.

3.22.80: *dogs of the table, guards of the gate*: Homer, *Iliad* 22.69. "Cynic" means literally "doglike." The name may have started as an insult, but it was adopted by the Cynics in the sense that they felt themselves to be the watchdogs of people's morals.

3.22.88: *just by his physique*: See also 1.24.8.

3.22.92: *laden with responsibilities*: Alexander quoted Homer, *Iliad* 2.24, and Diogenes responded with the next line (which we have already met, at §72). Both descriptions ("counselor" and "king") are perfectly apt.

3.22.95: *so be it*: The first is an oft quoted line from one of the hymns written by Cleanthes of Assos, the second head of the school in the third century BCE. See *Handbook* 53 for the next three lines of the hymn. The second quotation, also beloved of the Roman Stoics, is from Plato, *Crito* 43d. We have already seen it at 1.4.24 and 1.29.18.

3.22.103: *blind by comparison*: Argus was a mythical giant who was said to have a hundred eyes.

3.22.106: *empty inside*: For the mask metaphor, see also 2.1.15-20.

3.22.108: *especially me*: The first sentence is a made-up paraphrase of Homer, *Iliad* 6.490-492; the second sentence is a direct quotation of lines 492-493. These lines occur toward the end of the most poignant scene in the *Iliad*, between Hector and his wife Andromache (6.369-502).

3.23.11: *It was extraordinarily good*: Although Epictetus's interlocutor is a philosopher (§§9, 15), he clearly made use of the rhetorical technique known as *ekphrasis*, the re-creation in words of a real or imagined work of art. Epictetus contrasts this with the teaching style of a true philosopher, which is more austere but more productive.

3.23.17: *much better than Dio's*: Dio of Prusa, named "Chrysostom" (the golden-tongued), was a famous lecturer (or "sophist," in the terminology of the time), who died c. 115 CE. Since, like the interlocutor of this discourse, he too was well versed in philosophy, he makes a perfect point of comparison and Epictetus scarcely disguises the fact that he is attacking Dio himself as well as all others of his ilk. It is probable that, like Epictetus, Dio had studied with Musonius Rufus. A student of Dio's, Favorinus of Arelate, wrote a now lost treatise *Against Epictetus*.

3.23.20: *written by Lysias or Isocrates*: Epictetus's meaning is that his interlocutor has not read the Socratic literature as philosophy but as consisting of "fine phrases" (2.1.30-33). Lysias and Isocrates were famous orators, whose lifetimes overlapped that of Socrates.

3.23.20: *that flows better*: "I have often wondered what arguments" are the first words of Xenophon's *Memorabilia*, one of the chief sources for Socrates. So Epictetus is imagining someone reading the work just for its style, not for its philosophy—and even trying to improve its style (and in a particularly trivial way), when Xenophon was considered one of the best prose stylists in the language.

3.23.21: *the argument that strikes me on reflection as being the best*: The first quotation, one of Epictetus's favorites, is from Plato, *Apology of Socrates* 30c. Anytus and Meletus were two of the prosecutors at Socrates's trial. The second is a slightly altered version of Plato, *Crito* 46b.

3.23.22: *take them off and introduce them*: See *Handbook* 46.1 and the note there.

3.23.23: *Quadratus's house*: "Quadratus" is probably just a placeholder name for the kind of rich Roman in whose house recitations and lectures might be held.

3.23.25: *as though I were a teenager*: Plato, *Apology of Socrates* 17c.

3.23.27: *the sun draws its nourishment to itself*: It was a Stoic view that the rays of the sun were lines of vapor drawn up to the sun to feed its fires.

3.23.33: *a critical style and a didactic one*: Compare the threefold division of types of philosophical instruction at 3.21.19, with "protreptic" and "refutational" implicitly identified, as at 2.26.4. For discussion, see G. Boter, "Epictetus 3.23.33 and the Three Modes of Philosophical Instruction," *Philologus* 153, no. 1 (2009): 135–48.

3.23.33: *an epideictic one*: For protreptic, see the note to 2.26.4. "Epideictic" was a kind of speaking that was designed above all for praise and blame, things which Epictetus considers not worth a philosopher's attention. He seems to be implying that his interlocutor's speeches fall into the epideictic category, rather than being protreptic.

3.23.35: *how Achilles died*: Clearly, the philosopher to whom Epictetus is speaking used to pepper his talk with moral examples from Homer. Epictetus does exactly the same, but his point is that his interlocutor focuses more on entertaining the audience than getting across the moral lesson.

3.23.38: *Xerxes... battle of Thermopylae*: Xerxes was the ruler of the Persian empire at the time of the Persian invasion of Greece in 480 BCE and personally accompanied the expedition. The first land battle of the war took place, famously, at Thermopylae in northern Greece.

3.24.3: *what is essentially good and bad... up to us*: Echoing earlier discourses: "the essence of goodness lies in the use of impressions, and the essence of badness likewise, and... things that aren't subject to will don't take on the qualities of either badness or goodness" (2.1.4); "Goodness is essentially a certain state of will, and so is badness" (1.29.1).

3.24.10: *while others come into being*: See the note to 2.1.18.

3.24.13: *learned their minds*: Homer, *Odyssey* 1.3.

3.24.13: *obedience to law*: Homer, *Odyssey* 17.487, with the verb adapted for a single subject (Heracles) rather than Homer's original "gods."

3.24.14: *leaving them orphaned*: To the ancient Greek and Roman way of thinking, a child was an orphan if he lacked a father, because the mother had no or few legal rights.

3.24.16: *took him into account in all he did*: In myth, Heracles had two fathers simultaneously, because both Zeus and his mortal father Amphitryon slept with his mother, Alcmene, on the same night.

3.24.18: *wept as he sat on a rock*: Homer, *Odyssey* 5.82.

3.24.38: *Epicureans and bum boys*: This is perhaps the source of the assertion in Diogenes Laertius, *Lives of the Eminent Philosophers* 10.6, that "Epictetus called Epicurus a promoter of anal sex between men." The Greek word *kinaidos* strictly referred to the passive or penetrated partner in sex between men (as at 2.10.7), but it was also used as a more general insult (as at 1.5.10, 2.20.37, 3.1.32, and 4.2.9).

3.24.44: *are you saying that I should curry his favor?*: We are completely unprepared for this question. It appears that the interlocutor has come to Nicopolis from Athens (where his family is and where he wants to live) to consult Epictetus on how to persuade some power possessor in Rome, presumably the emperor, to let him stay in Athens (§§75–77). For the practice alluded to in "make my way to his door," see the note to *Handbook* 25.2. For more on patrons and clients, see also the note to 3.9.18.

3.24.52: *Olympic crown*: The Olympic crown of olive twigs was indeed worthless in itself, but in fact Olympic victory was also invariably translated into more tangible rewards back home.

3.24.61: *counterpenalty as well*: There were certain classes of suit in classical Athens where the prosecutor and the defendant could both propose a penalty, and the jury decided which to adopt. Socrates's proposal was notorious: claiming that he was a benefactor of the city, he suggested that he be treated as such and be fed at public expense for the rest of his life. Subsequently, he was persuaded to suggest a modest fine, but by then his cheekiness had alienated so many of the jurymen that the prosecutors' proposal of the death penalty was the one they chose, albeit by a fairly slim majority.

3.24.66: *the whole world rather than any particular place*: So ideally one's loyalty is to the world at large, the Great City, rather than to a particular city such as Rome. But given that we fall short of Diogenes's standard, Epictetus also values normal patriotism, as fulfilling one's role as a citizen (e.g., 2.5.26).

3.24.66: *he'd have done the same there as well*: The Perrhaebians lived in the far north of Greece, where it borders on Macedon.

3.24.67: *Antisthenes set me free*: On Antisthenes, see the note to 1.17.12.

3.24.70: *the Great King*: The king of the Persian empire. Perdiccas III was the king of Macedon before Philip II and Alexander III (also known as Alexander the Great). Their reigns coincided with Diogenes's lifetime.

3.24.70: *must first . . . be subjugated by things*: Epictetus frequently distinguishes these two stages (e.g., 1.4.19, 4.1.59, 4.1.85). It is our attachment to things that puts us in the power of the people who can procure them for us or deny them to us.

3.24.71: *spitting . . . and departing*: There is probably an implicit reference here to a famous story about the philosopher Anaxarchus. When a tyrant, Nicocreon of Cyprus, threatened to cut out Anaxarchus's tongue, he bit it off himself and spat it at Nicocreon (Diogenes Laertius, *Lives of the Eminent Philosophers* 9.59). "Departing," as often, means departing from this life.

3.24.73: *the Acropolis*: Epictetus expresses disdain of the sights of Athens also at 2.16.32–33, where he calls the Acropolis, beloved of tourists then as now, "blocks of stone and a prettified rock." Piraeus was, as it still is, the port that served Athens; the Long Walls, built in the fifth century BCE, connected Athens to Piraeus, so that even in wartime (before the days of siege warfare) goods could reach the city from the sea.

3.24.76: *What kind of manumitter can you present him with?*: There were several ways in which Roman slaves could be manumitted. Here Epictetus is talking about "manumission by the rod," whereby a third party (the manumitter) claimed, fictitiously, that a certain enslaved person was in fact free, and touched him or her with a rod. If the slave owner had no objection, the magistrates (for the plural, see "tribunal" at 4.7.17) who were supervising the procedure declared the slave free. To judge by the next sentence (see also 2.16.41–42 and 4.1.151), eye contact was also an aspect of the ritual. For more on manumission, see 2.1.26.

3.24.77: *stroll in the Lyceum*: The Lyceum was a wooded park in ancient Athens, with a temple to Apollo and a famous gymnasium. It was a favorite haunt.

3.24.85: *remind them of their humanity*: A triumph was considered the apex of a Roman's military career, and in order not to let it go to his head, a slave might travel in the triumphal chariot, standing behind the general, and whisper to him, "Look behind you! Remember that you are human!"

3.24.89: *words of ill omen*: It is bad luck to speak about death, because that might attract its attention.

3.24.89: *just so long as they do good*: The mention of incantations that use negative words for good results is puzzling. Epictetus is probably referring not to formal incantations chanted by magicians but to the less formal kind chanted over babies, for instance, by nurses. As in our nursery rhyme "Rockabye Baby," negative things might be mentioned, but in an apotropaic fashion—to make sure that they do not happen to the baby. This is implied by §90. I owe this understanding of the sentence to correspondence with Radcliffe G. Edmonds III.

3.24.93: *death... a change... from what is now, not to what is not, but to what is not now*: This is perhaps Epictetus's primary reason for not fearing death: it is a perfectly natural process, and the recycling of the elements that made up our constitution is essential for the perpetuation of the universe (4.7.15).

3.24.99: *before abandoning it*: Epictetus is referring to Plato, *Apology of Socrates* 28d–29a.

3.24.105: *an important reminder*: It was a famous saying, and over the centuries it was attributed to a variety of people who were considered wise, starting with Anaxagoras of Clazomenae in the fifth century BCE.

3.24.117: *take the auspices*: Newly appointed Roman magistrates took the auspices on the Capitol.

3.25.3: *the most blessed or the most wretched person in the world*: At few of the major games were there second prizes. You either won or lost.

3.25.5: *as quails do when they run away*: Quail fighting was popular in antiquity, as it still is in Afghanistan and elsewhere. There were a great many athletic festivals around the Mediterranean in Roman times, and professional athletes traveled from one to another. The most famous athletes could command substantial appearance fees.

3.26.7: *guarding someone's doorway*: These are all jobs that would typically be done by enslaved people.

3.26.13: *What is there left for me to do?*: By impressions that are hard to bear, Epictetus is thinking of something like the imminent death of one's child: see the parallel passage, 2.21.18–21.

3.26.14: *the last of the domains*: See 3.2, 3.12, and the introduction, 30–33, for the three domains and the training of desire, inclination, and assent.

3.26.23: *a drawer of water at the same time*: Cleanthes was so determined to study with Zeno that he worked after school watering gardens (Diogenes Laertius, *Lives of the Eminent Philosophers* 7.168). As in the New Testament, a "drawer of water" was a very lowly slave.

3.26.29: *the signal to retreat*: Every time Epictetus employs the metaphor of God's sounding the retreat (see also 1.9.16, 1.29.29, 3.13.14, 3.24.101), it is ambiguous. Here, for instance, is Epictetus suggesting that we accept a death by starvation, or anticipate it by suicide? The same ambiguity occurs also at, e.g., 3.5.10, 3.24.96–98.

3.26.33: *Like a mountain lion*: Homer, *Odyssey* 6.130.

3.26.37: *ill like Manes*: According to Musonius Rufus (*Discourses* 18A), when Zeno was ill, he refused delicate food and said, "Treat me as you would treat Manes"—that is, as you would treat an enslaved person, "Manes" being a common slave name.

4.1: *On freedom*: This is the longest discourse by quite a margin, but it is very focused: freedom depends on knowing that nothing is important except what is up to us.

4.1.14: *Thanks be to the Fortune of Caesar!*: Fortune was a powerful deity, recognized especially in the Hellenistic and Roman periods. Cities acknowledged Fortune as the presiding deity of their particular destiny, and if an individual was a person of destiny, as a Roman emperor was, he too had Fortune as his tutelary deity.

4.1.19: *possibly more even than you*: Thrasonides is a fictional character, the protagonist of a comedy written by Menander of Athens (end of the fourth century BCE) called *The Hated Man*, of which we have only fragments. Getas was his slave. A man falling for an unsuitable woman and receiving advice and help from an enslaved person was a common plot for plays of the New Comedy.

4.1.22: *Getas refuses to give it to him*: Thrasonides was presumably intending to kill himself.

4.1.30: *in a letter to the Persian king he says*: We have fifty-one letters attributed to Diogenes (though this one is not among them), but none of them is genuine, and the earliest of them were probably composed in the first century BCE.

4.1.33: *the 5 percent tax*: See also 2.1.26: the tax seems generally to have been paid by the slave himself from his savings, rather than the owner.

4.1.38: *the right to wear rings*: Members of the equestrian order, second in rank to patricians, had the right to wear gold rings. It was the highest social rank to which an ex-slave could aspire. Despite what Epictetus says in §40, no former slave could become a senator, though his children could.

4.1.39: *a second campaign, and a third*: Service on a minimum of three military campaigns was required by Roman law before a man could be a candidate for higher office.

4.1.41: *haphazardly to particular entities*: On preconceptions, see especially 1.22. The Socrates reference is Xenophon, *Memorabilia* 4.6.1.

4.1.51: *the resources to discover the truth*: As elsewhere, these "resources" are our preconceptions, once they have been articulated by mature reasoning.

4.1.53: *the acquiring of property by commercial means, that is*: In other words, we are no longer talking about literal slavery, just the metaphorical kind.

4.1.53: *if the Great King is unhappy, he isn't free*: The Great King is the king of the Persian or Achaemenid empire. There was no such person in Epictetus's time, but he is looking back to classical texts, perhaps especially the *Gorgias*, where Plato denies the king's happiness. See *Gorgias* 470d–e and 524e–525a.

4.1.57: *twelve fasces*: Fasces were bundles of rods, sometimes surrounding an axe. Junior officials called lictors carried them in procession before senior Roman officials. Only consuls had the right to be preceded by twelve fasces.

4.1.58: *the Saturnalia*: On the Saturnalia, see the note to 1.25.7. During the festival, enslaved people were allowed far more freedom than usual.

4.1.88: *daggers against other people*: If the tyrants are my false judgments about wealth, health, and so on—that they are good things and to be pursued—and the bodyguards are wealth, health, pretty girls, and so on, then having eliminated the false judgments, wealth and so on can stay because they no longer have any effect on me. The image of internal tyrants originates with Xenophon (*Oeconomicus* 1.18–23) and Plato (*Republic* 560b–c).

4.1.91: *an ambassador, a quaestor, a proconsul*: These three officials are specified because they would be accompanied by an armed guard.

4.1.100: *its place in the cosmic cycle*: Everything is made up of the four elements in different proportions, and when something comes to an end, its elements are recycled as other objects or used to make other creatures.

4.1.102: *gifts from my father*: In antiquity, it was commonly thought that all a person's qualities were inherited from the father, while the mother provided no more than a safe space for the embryo to develop.

4.1.106: *the rites to be prolonged*: On the mysteries, see the note to 3.21.13.

4.1.107: *I want my children and wife to be with me*: This is a response to Epictetus's statement at §99 that one should want what God wants.

4.1.113: *as you do there*: Presumably Epictetus gesticulated at this point in the direction of a nearby gymnasium. It was common for philosophers to teach in or near a gymnasium, which was the center of education in Greek cities.

4.1.113: *the right to manumission*: See the note to 3.24.76.

4.1.114: *could no longer be enslaved by anyone*: See also 3.24.67, and 3.24.66 for the pirates.

4.1.118: *he can have me flogged*: The "he" is presumably the emperor (as at 1.24.12 and 2.13.17–22). This is confirmed by §145.

4.1.123: *Helvidius… the man who killed him did*: See also 1.2.19–21 on Helvidius Priscus. It was the emperor Vespasian who killed him.

4.1.124: *exhausted by its running*: Here we see how close the notion of happiness is to that of fulfilling one's function.

4.1.131: *ordained for me*: Two lines of a hymn written by Cleanthes. Two more lines are quoted at the end of the *Handbook*.

4.1.146: *Aprulla won't let me*: Aprulla is presumably one of the old women Epictetus is claiming his interlocutor cultivates, probably (see §148) in the hope of being remembered in her will.

4.1.150: *Felicio*: Felicio (see also 1.19.17–22) is a slave's or freedman's name.

4.1.151: *to look my masters in the eyes*: See the note to 3.24.76. This is the only place in which Epictetus implies that petitionary prayer has some use, and it is probably just a concession to popular ways of speaking. Given the kind of predetermined universe in which the Stoics believed, petitionary prayer is nonsensical, and even blasphemous, since it is asking for the world to be other than what it is (Fragment 17). The kind of prayer of which Epictetus could approve is illustrated in *Handbook* 53.

4.1.151: *even though it isn't*: Epictetus was lame (1.8.14, 1.16.20).

4.1.152: *because they weren't*: Diogenes's parents were freeborn (as Epictetus acknowledges at §157), so Epictetus is using "free" in the psychological sense.

4.1.156: *Archidamus of Sparta*: Archidamus III was the senior of the two Spartan kings during much of Diogenes's lifetime. He ruled from 360 until 338. Quite a few works were attributed to Diogenes, including the spurious letters that we have encountered before in §§30–31, but it is uncertain how many of these works are genuine.

4.1.158: *the law is everything to me*: He does not mean man-made laws, of which the Cynics were highly contemptuous, but natural law, the fundamental moral principles that are dictated to us by nature and that form or should form the basis of man-made legal codes. We are given examples of such laws at 1.26.1, 1.29.4, 2.16.28, and 3.17.6 (= 1.29.13); we discover them for ourselves when we live in accord with nature. But when he mentions Socrates and the law in the next paragraph, that *is* man-made law, the law of Athens.

4.1.160: *without a thought for his own safety*: Epictetus derives his remarks about Socrates's bravery on the battlefield from Plato's accounts at *Apology of Socrates* 28e, *Laches* 181a–b, and *Symposium* 219e–221b. For Socrates's military experience, see also the beginning of Plato's *Charmides*.

4.1.160: *he would very probably be put to death*: Leon of Salamis (the island was Athenian territory) was a prominent democrat in Athens toward the end of the fifth century BCE. After the Athenians lost the Peloponnesian War (431–404), a narrow oligarchy of thirty men (the notorious "Thirty Tyrants") was imposed on the city by the victorious Spartans. The Thirty set about killing their opponents and at one point ordered Socrates (whose relationship with the Thirty was ambiguous at best) to join the detachment that was to arrest Leon. Socrates refused to obey the order, while the others carried out the arrest, and Leon was duly killed. Socrates avoided arrest himself perhaps only because the regime of the Thirty soon collapsed. The story is told by Plato, at *Apology of Socrates* 32c–d, and is mentioned by another contemporary source (Andocides, *On the Mysteries* 94), and then, as a famous story, by many later writers.

4.1.163: *he said*: Epictetus paraphrases Plato, *Crito* 47d.

4.1.164: *calling on him to do so*: Another famous episode in Socrates's life. He happened to be the chairman of the Assembly meeting on a day when the Athenians wanted to hold an illegal vote. His refusal did not come to much, however, since he was not chairman the following day, and his successor gave in to the Athenians' demands. The fullest account of the episode is Xenophon, *Hellenica* 1.7, but see also Plato, *Apology of Socrates* 32b, and Xenophon, *Memorabilia* 1.1.18.

4.1.164: *treated the tyrants with contempt*: See the note to 4.1.160, and Xenophon, *Memorabilia* 1.2.33–37.

4.1.166: *no one to take care of them*: A paraphrase of Plato, *Crito* 54a.

4.1.168: *they'd still have been in Athens, wouldn't they?*: As a stand-in for Socrates, Epictetus focuses on the circle of friends and disciples he had gathered in Athens, rather than thinking that he could have helped people in Thessaly as well. But the text of this sentence is not entirely secure.

4.1.172: *prepare yourself...for death*: Plato, *Phaedo* 64a and 67d–e.

4.1.177: *standing in his doorway*: For the practice to which Epictetus is alluding, see the note to *Handbook* 25.2.

4.2.9: *loudly acclaim the dancer*: See also 3.4 and *Handbook* 33.10. Epictetus seems to take this as a sign of attachment to worldly values, lack of decorum, and being carried away by impressions.

4.3.12: *Masurius and Cassius*: Masurius Sabinus and Gaius Cassius Longinus were colleagues, both eminent Roman jurists in the first half of the first century CE. For God's laws, see the note to 1.25.6.

4.4.3: *salutations and public office*: Salutations were an important feature of Roman social life. Every morning, the clients of a patron (see the notes to 3.9.18 and *Handbook* 25.2) met at the entrance to his house and formally greeted him as he emerged. Salutations preserved the hierarchy, then, and Epictetus brackets them with high office because it would be a holder of high office who received salutations.

4.4.5: *contentment... isn't subject to interruption or obstruction*: This is more straightforward in the Greek, since the word for "contentment," *euroia*, means literally "the state of flowing smoothly." It was Zeno, the founder of Stoicism, who first defined happiness as a smoothly flowing life. This is the origin of Epictetus's insistence that, when it is working properly, will cannot be impeded.

4.4.7: *making the same mistakes*: At this point, the manuscripts add two further sentences: "So how am I to stop making these mistakes? I used to make them in the past, but no longer, thanks to God." Since they make no sense in this context, I think they must be a marginal note by a Christian scholar that crept into the text. I do not think it is a case of Epictetus's apostrophizing himself, because it is not at all the kind of thing Epictetus would say; he is modest about his accomplishments.

4.4.12: *sprinkled sand*: see the note to 3.15.4.

4.4.13: *both cognitive and non-cognitive impressions:* See the note to *Handbook* 45 on cognitive impressions.

4.4.21: *so be it*: Plato, *Crito* 43d, slightly altered. See also 1.4.24, 1.29.18, 3.22.95, and *Handbook* 53.3.

4.4.21: *marched off to war as often as he did*: On Socrates's military record, see the note to 4.1.160. Both the Lyceum and the Academy were wooded parks where people liked to stroll; both were also frequented by philosophers and their students. Plato favored the Academy and Aristotle the Lyceum.

4.4.22: *compose hymns of praise in prison*: See Plato, *Phaedo* 60c–61c.

4.4.33: *completely eliminate desire*: See the note to 1.4.1.

4.4.34: *Lead me, Zeus, both you and Destiny*: A line from a hymn composed by Cleanthes; see the end of the *Handbook*.

4.4.37: *commotion and salutations*: On salutations, see the note to 4.4.3.

4.4.38: *as you would a spirit of bad luck*: In other words, he would try to keep him at bay. See also the note to 1.19.6 on the worship of Fever at Rome.

4.5.3: *sophistic arguments*: The idea that Socrates resolves conflicts in Xenophon's *Symposium* crops up also at 2.12.15. Thrasymachus is Socrates's interlocutor in the first book of Plato's *Republic*, and Polus and Callicles are the two main interlocutors in Plato's *Gorgias*. There are a number of stories, all apocryphal, on the theme of Socrates's domestic troubles with his wife Xanthippe (see §33), but in the extant Socratic literature there is no conversation such as the one mentioned here between Socrates and one of his sons, though he does converse with his son Lamprocles at Xenophon, *Memorabilia* 2.2.

4.5.14: *hug statues*: See the note to *Handbook* 47.

4.5.15: *the one who's died*: Epictetus is referencing some famous lines from Euripides's *Cresphontes* (fragment 452 Nauck^2). The character in the play claimed that we should mourn people at their birth, because of all the evils of the world, and by the same token celebrate someone's death.

4.5.17: *not in good condition*: Nero was emperor from 54 until 68, Trajan from 98 until 117, so he was probably the emperor at the time of this lecture by Epictetus. I may have overtranslated this sentence. It might just be no more than "Throw it away: it's bad, worthless." But Nero's coinage was still valid all over the empire, and there is no evidence of local suppression in Nicopolis: hence my translation is an attempt to make sense of the sentence.

4.5.18: *cracks the skulls of people he comes across*: According to the (not always reliable) biographer Suetonius, a contemporary of Epictetus, Nero once cracked the skull of a praetor (*The Lives of the Caesars: Nero* 26).

4.5.29: *Eteocles and Polynices*: See the note to *Handbook* 31.4.

4.5.33: *stamping on the cake*: The cake in the story was a gift from Alcibiades, Socrates's lover, so Xanthippe stamped on it in jealousy.

4.5.37: *Lions at home but foxes at Ephesus*: Ephesus is located on the west coast of Asia Minor, and the Spartans were always less successful campaigning in Asia Minor than on the Greek mainland.

4.6.2: *so on and so forth*: It seems that the interlocutor this time is no callow youth but someone who has been a philosopher for some time.

4.6.13: *a stronger argument than this*: It is not clear what argument he is referring to. I think it is probably what Epictetus said in his own voice at §9 about the "only route" to the destination of freedom.

4.6.15: *changing arguments as well*: See the note to 1.7.

4.6.20: *A king's role, Cyrus, is to do good and be reviled*: On Antisthenes, see the note to 1.17.12. This is his fragment 86a Prince. Cyrus the Great was the king of Persia in the sixth century BCE. Antisthenes wrote two books titled *Cyrus*, offering advice on ideal kingship.

4.6.25: *promoted over me*: The question picks up on Epictetus's talk of lack of political power, but it is still abrupt.

4.6.32: *this enterprise*: See 3.10.2, where Epictetus quotes a bit more of these lines from *The Golden Verses* of Pythagoras. Here, of course, he is saying that it is a travesty for someone who is mired in the world of indifferents to make use of these salutary verses. Proper use of them is made by the moral person of §35.

4.6.33: *nothing to stop us from lying*: Actually, the Stoics said that only an enlightened sage could legitimately lie under certain circumstances, such as helping a friend. Plato seeded the idea, at *Republic* 414b–415d.

4.7.6: *the Galileans*: Followers of Jesus of Galilee. Since the early Christians expected the imminent end of the world, they scorned death, even when unarmed and facing lions in the arena. At Titus 3:12, Saint Paul reveals his intention to spend a winter in Nicopolis, sometime in the early 60s; it is not clear that he did so, but Epictetus might have had firsthand experience of the Christian community there, assuming there was one in his day.

4.7.6: *the needs of the whole*: The Stoic universe is self-sufficient because there is nothing outside it, and all its "parts," the things of the world, are broken down on death into the four elements, which are then recycled, so that "the parts serve the needs of the whole."

4.7.25: It seems that §§25–27 became displaced and should properly belong here.

4.7.26: *The same*: Apart from the danger of loose tiles falling off, tiles were commonly hurled from roofs during street fighting. King Pyrrhus of Epirus, for instance, was killed by one in Argos in 272 BCE.

4.7.17: *the right kind of tribunal*: See the note to 3.24.76 for the process of manumission of a slave that Epictetus is assuming.

4.7.24: *Even a tidbit can have that much value*: For Stoics, worldly things are indifferent, in that they are not good, but they have value in that some may be preferred to others—health over sickness, for instance. See the introduction, 19–20. So Epictetus counsels glad acceptance and proper use of these things if they are given to one: see, e.g., 1.1.17, 1.1.27, 2.16.28, 3.10.16, 4.3.11, 4.10.30, *Handbook* 15.

4.7.30: *Leon of Salamis*: See the note to 4.1.160.

4.7.31: *thrown out unburied*: This was the final punishment for serious crimes. Unburied people did not lie with their ancestors and existed only as aimless ghosts, excluded from an afterlife existence in Hades.

4.7.40: *where it came from*: The "command center," or rational mind, was considered by Stoics to be a spark in us of the divine Reason that governs the whole universe.

4.8.20: *mark me as a philosopher*: Despite his approval of Euphrates's behavior, Epictetus was attached to his philosopher's beard (1.2.29). But he was not concealing the fact that he was a philosopher.

4.8.21: *felt cap on his head*: The chief province of the god Hephaestus (Vulcan to the Romans) was metallurgy in all its forms.

4.8.22: *introductions to philosophers*: See *Handbook* 46.1 and the note there.

4.8.25: *he says*: This is not a quotation from the Socratic literature; Epictetus is putting words into Socrates's mouth.

4.8.29: *Asclepius*: The god of healing.

4.8.30: *scepter and diadem*: For the Cynic as king, see the notes to 3.21.19 and 3.22.49.

4.8.32: *wipe from his cheeks*: Homer, *Odyssey* 529–530.

4.8.33: *walls, doorways, and doorkeepers*: See 3.22.14–16: the true Cynic lives in the open, with no house to hide him from sight.

4.8.34: *quarrels with everyone he meets*: Four characteristics often attributed to Cynics; for the bare shoulder, see the note to 3.22.50.

4.8.35: *winter training*: See the note to 1.2.32.

4.8.36: *a garden of Adonis*: Before the Adonia festival, seeds of quick-growing plants such as lettuce were planted in pots; these were the "gardens of Adonis." During the festival, these pots were exposed to the sun on rooftops, where the plants would quickly wither, while women lamented the early death of beautiful Adonis, beloved of both Aphrodite and Persephone. Regarding the joints of grain stems: "In the winter, cereals remain in the blade, but as the weather begins to warm up, they send up a stem . . . and it becomes jointed. And the outcome is that the ear very soon appears in the third, or sometimes the fourth joint." Theophrastus, *Inquiry into Plants* 8.2.4.

4.9.6: *Aristides and Eubius*: Writers of pornography.

4.10.13: *unassailability of judgment*: For the three "domains," see especially 3.2 and 3.12 but also 2.17.14–18, 2.17.29–32, and the introduction, 30–33.

4.10.21: *meals in baskets*: On the bundles of rods (fasces), see the note to 4.1.57; only a consul had the right to be preceded by twelve such bundles. The tribunal was a raised platform from which praetors passed judgments. It was also the praetors who were required to arrange public entertainments. Patrons (see the notes to 3.9.18 and *Handbook* 25.2) were expected to hand out food in baskets to their clients.

4.10.24: *'two different activities,' remember*: The proverb is quoted in full at 4.6.30: "You can't combine two different activities at once."

4.10.27: *Death is the haven and place of refuge for everyone and everything*: This should not be taken to imply an afterlife, since death is merely the separation of body and soul (e.g., 2.1.17), or dissolution into our constituent elements (e.g., 3.13.14). He means only that we can retire to death if we so choose.

4.10.27: *troubled by smoke*: See 1.25.18–20.

4.10.31: *tossing and turning*: Homer, *Iliad* 24.5, of Achilles after the death of Patroclus. The other two people mentioned, Antilochus and Protesilaus, were also friends of Achilles who died.

4.10.33: *Automedon will serve you instead*: Automedon was Achilles's charioteer, and after Patroclus's death he became Achilles's closest friend.

4.10.35: *nothing worse than this that I could suffer*: Homer, *Iliad* 19.321. Achilles is mourning Patroclus's death.

4.10.35: *live in misery*: Achilles's mother was the goddess Thetis, and it was she who told him of his fate, that he could either live a long and inglorious life or a short and glorious one.

4.11.1: *sociability... an aspect of human nature*: Epictetus is thinking of Epicureans; see 1.23.1 and 2.20.6–7.

4.11.3: *distinctively human quality*: So the main point of this discourse is that an unclean person does not fulfill his role as a human being. In general, Epictetus does not despise the body so much as consider it yet another gift from God that it is therefore a person's duty to attend to, while falling well short of becoming attached to it (1.2.37).

4.11.9: *flux of mucus*: Since the human body consists of four humors (black bile, phlegm, yellow bile, blood), there are bound to be times when the humors are out of balance, and that is always indicated by some kind of flux. A head cold is a flux of phlegm or mucus.

4.11.12: *equipment for cleaning the body*: A strigil, a kind of scraper, was used to clean off olive oil that had been massaged into the body. Taking off the oil simultaneously took off accumulated dirt. Natron is a naturally occurring mixture of sodium carbonate and sodium bicarbonate; mixed with oil, it made a kind of soap.

4.11.15: *You think you deserve to smell*: Probably because he feels himself to be spiritually advanced enough to ignore his body.

4.11.19: *Socrates didn't often bathe*: Plato, *Symposium* 174a.

4.11.19: *the best-looking men*: Epictetus is thinking chiefly of Alcibiades: Plato, *Symposium* 217a–219d. Socrates was notoriously ugly.

4.11.20: *whey-faced, barefoot men*: Aristophanes was an Athenian writer of comedies, contemporary with Socrates. In his play *Clouds*, produced in 423 BCE, he made Socrates a catch-all figure to enable him to mock current intellectual trends. The quotation is line 103 of the play. Intellectuals were mocked as pale because of the time they spent indoors, poring over books. In his response, Epictetus refers to lines 225 and 179.

4.11.30: *looking for it in the wrong place*: Polemo, the fourth head of the Platonic Academy (see also 3.1.14), was notorious for having lived a promiscuous life as a young man, until being converted to philosophy by Xenocrates, the third head of the school. So he was presumably locating beauty in the female form.

4.12: *On paying attention*: For discussion of what Epictetus means by "attention," see J. Sellars, "Roman Stoic Mindfulness," in *Ethics and Self-Cultivation*, ed. M. Dennis and S. Werkhoven (Routledge, 2018), 15-29. For Epictetus, the point is to pay attention to one's ethical principles in order to make progress toward virtue. He is not really recommending the kind of general mindfulness that might form part of Buddhist or some such practice, though there may be a hint of this at §§4-5.

4.12.17: *how do we keep ourselves safe?*: This is the theme of 3.16.

4.13.3: *people say*: It emerges shortly that this is what Epictetus's interlocutor in this discourse has said.

4.13.14: *murder your children*: See the note to 1.28.7 on Medea.

4.13.22: *divulge what he knows*: It is not quite clear how pitch was used for torture in the ancient world. Was it simply the application of boiling pitch to some part of the body, or was it "pitchcapping," whereby hot pitch was made to form a kind of cap on the victim's head, and then allowed to cool, so that when it was removed it tore off both hair and skin? As for the wheel, the victims were tied to large cart wheels and then beaten with clubs, the gaps between the spokes of the wheel guaranteeing that bones would be broken.

Fragments

1: *atoms or particles or fire and earth*: The Epicureans held that the world was composed of atoms that came together by chance, the Stoics that the world was an orderly, designed, ever-changing arrangement of the four elements. This fragment is very important, in that it gives us our only direct evidence for Epictetus's view of the value of studying physics. See the introduction, 11-12, and for a tempting alternative view of the fragment, Barnes, *Logic*, 25-27.

1: *anything to be gained by comprehending them*: Epictetus is echoing Socrates on the unimportance of detailed knowledge of physics, as expressed by Xenophon at *Memorabilia* 1.1.11-16 and 4.7.5-6.

1: *the Delphic commandment ... to know yourself*: See the note to 3.1.18.

3: *causes us pain and grief*: This seems to be a strong statement of determinism (on which see the introduction, 22-23). Irrationality exists, and even though it seems to set one against the will of the universe, which is rational, that is not so: even the irrational is part of the cosmic plan.

4: Fragments 4-8 are passages where Epictetus quoted, or at least drew heavily on, his teacher Musonius Rufus. Each of them has a headline: "Rufus. From Epictetus on friendship." They therefore also count as "fragments" of Rufus, and are numbered 38-42 in Lutz's collection. The headline was written by John of Stobi, who preserved them in his fifth-century *Anthology*, as he did the previous three fragments as well.

5: *Lycurgus of Sparta*: See the note to 2.20.26.

8: *the same process from above downward*: In Stoic physics, the four elements, in their natural state, occupied four concentric circles around the earth: earth down in the center, then water, then air, and then fire. But the elements change into one another, and so Epictetus (or Rufus) describes the motion as "up and down."

9: *Zeno and Chrysippus*: Zeno of Citium and Chrysippus of Soli were the first and third heads of the Stoic school. The writer who preserves this fragment is suggesting that what Epictetus said in the second century CE can inform us about the views of the earliest Stoics in the third century BCE. Given the loss of most of the work of the early Stoics, this is an assumption modern scholars often have to make as well.

9: *in Greek, of course*: This fragment and the next were preserved by Aulus Gellius in the second century, in his anthology called *Attic Nights*, written in Latin.

9: *a collapsing building*: An unpleasantly common event in ancient Rome, most familiar, perhaps, from Juvenal, *Satires* 3.190–204.

9: *to contract*: "Distress is an irrational contraction." Andronicus, *On Passions* 1.

9: *forestall the proper functioning of the mind and the rational faculty*: A Stoic sage was not supposed to react with fear to anything; he was above such passions, because he had rid himself of all the judgments that cause such passions. But no one can stop an involuntary reaction to sudden frightening noises and so on. So the Stoics had to explain how even a sage was liable to these involuntary reactions. The technical term for such an instinctive reaction was *propatheia*. For useful commentary on this fragment, see M. Graver, *Stoicism and Emotion* (University of Chicago Press, 2007), 85–88.

9: οὐ συγκατατίθεται οὐδὲ προσεπιδοξάζει: Gellius's translation omits the second of the two Greek verbs: "he does not give his assent *or attach an extra opinion* [to the impressions]." But he returns to the missing verb a few lines later.

10: *Favorinus*: Favorinus of Arelate was a famous lecturer and author working in the first half of the second century CE.

10a: This fragment is preserved by Arnobius, a Christian writer of the early fourth century.

11: With fragments 11–25 we return to the invaluable anthology compiled by John of Stobi in the fifth century.

11: *Archelaus*: King of Macedon 413–399 BCE, and a famous patron of artists and intellectuals. Socrates declined the invitation (because, Epictetus suggests, he had no need of riches), but others, including the Athenian playwright Euripides, did not.

11: *Oedipus the king*: The reference is to Sophocles's two Oedipus plays, *Oe-*

dipus the King and *Oedipus at Colonus*. Polus of Aegina was a famous tragic actor of the fourth century BCE.

11: *rags . . . purple-dyed toga*: Toward the end of Homer's *Odyssey*, Odysseus returns home to Ithaca but disguises himself as a beggar, hiding his true nobility, to get the better of the suitors who were plaguing his wife and taking over his estate.

13: *Only the universe is self-sufficient*: In Stoic physics, there was nothing outside the universe and always the same amount of matter inside it, which was constantly being recycled.

14: This fragment starts in midsentence.

14: *such as justice, moderation, and freedom*: The "dour philosophers" are almost certainly the Stoics themselves, so Epictetus's tone is ironic. In describing them thus, he has in the back of his mind a passage of Plato's *Philebus* (written well before Stoicism existed) where a different position on pleasure (that it is no more than release from pain) is attributed to "dour" thinkers.

15: *excuses for their own transgressions*: The women were presumably using *Republic* to justify sleeping around.

21: *eat breakfast in Aricia*: See *Discourses* 1.1.28–30 for a fuller explanation of this saying and for information about Agrippinus.

23: *Nature is . . . benevolent toward its creatures*: Xenophon, *Memorabilia* 1.4.7.

24: *blames the gods*: There is a gap in the text which must have contained something like the words I have supplied.

26: The last few fragments are all from Marcus Aurelius's *Meditations*.

27: *an art of assent*: See the introduction, 23–24.

27: *every inclination is conditional*: The Stoic teaching of proceeding "with reservation." See the note to *Handbook* 2.2.

28: *madness or sanity*: Perhaps the madman here is one who refuses to accept the life that he has been allotted, while the sane man accepts every experience. But in their more extreme and paradoxical moments, Stoics tended to say that only the enlightened sage was sane, while everyone else without exception was mad.

28a: Despite the lack of mention of Epictetus, this is almost certainly a fragment from *Discourses*. See J. Sellars, "A Disputed Fragment of Epictetus in Marcus Aurelius," *Mnemosyne* 71, no. 2 (2018): 331–35. It does not correspond to anything in extant Socratic literature.

Textual Notes

Here, for scholars and those who may be comparing different translations, I list all the places where the text I translate differs from those of the editions I have used (for which see p. xiii). They are marked in the translations by an obelisk, or dagger (†). The punctuation of the discourses is frequently so difficult, and decisions about it so subjective, that I have not listed those places where I differ from the texts in this respect—where, for instance, I read a sentence as a question, not a statement; or where I extend or shorten a stretch of direct speech.

Handbook

16: I retain τινὰ with the majority of the manuscripts.

24.1: I assign this sentence to an interlocutor and divide up the entry accordingly.

24.2: Reading μοι for σοι with Meibom.

29.1: Reading αἰσχρῶς with *Discourses* 3.15.1.

29.2: Reading παρορύσσεσθαι with *Discourses* 3.15.4.

29.7: Reading τὸ σαυτοῦ with the best manuscripts.

33.2: Reading λέξον μέν.

36: I read τοῦ … φυλαχθῆναι.

Discourses

1.1.19: Deleting τις ἐν Ῥώμῃ with Upton.

1.2.36: Retaining οὐ with the manuscripts, but the text here is a bit of a mess and remains uncertain even after many editorial suggestions.

1.4.29: Reading ἀκολουθά with Schenkl.

1.7.1: Reading τῷ ἠρωτῆσθαι with one manuscript and most recent editors.

1.8.2: Punctuating with Barnes.

1.9.25: Reading οὕτω... οὕτως with Schweighäuser.

1.13.1: Reading ἴσως καὶ with some manuscripts and the majority of the editors.

1.13.3: I suggest reading ὥστε instead of ὥσπερ, a not uncommon scribal error.

1.21.1: Reading προθέσει with some manuscripts; see 1.4.14.

1.22.8: Following Wolf, I fill the supposed ellipsis with ἀγέραστος.

1.28.31: I see no reason for Souilhé's added μόνῳ.

2.1.14: Reading ἀμελὲς with Kronenberg

2.1.33: Reading καὶ "ἦ δ' ὅς," "ἦν δ' ἐγώ," with Kronenberg.

2.6.6: I do not read Schenkl's added ἀσπάζομαι, favored by all editors, and accordingly distribute the following sentences differently.

2.9.21: Reading παραβαπτιστοί with Saumaise.

2.13.18: I read οὔκουν for νῦν οὐκ.

2.15.18: Reading κἄν με οὐδὲν ἀναγκάζῃ with Reiske.

2.16.39: Deleting γραῶν ἀποκλαύματα.

2.17.13: Reading ἱκανῶς with Schweighäuser.

2.17.26: Reading ταλαίπωρε with the majority of the manuscripts.

2.17.33: I read ἔχειν with some manuscripts.

2.22.28: Reading τὰς ἀγορὰς καταλαμβάνειν ὡς τὰς ἐρημίας ἢ τὰ ὄρη with Coraes.

3.1.11: Reading Πῶς δ' οὐχὶ with Upton.

3.2.3: Reading φόβους with Reiske.

3.2.6: Reading τῷ ἠρωτῆσθαι with Schweighäuser, as at 1.7.1.

3.2.14: Reading ἀνθρωπάριον with Reiske.

3.4.11: I omit Νέμεα, Πύθια, Ἴσθμια, Ὀλύμπια ("the Nemean, Pythian, Isthmian, and Olympic festivals"). These four festivals were not particularly known for their acting prizes, and the words fit neither the grammar nor the syntax of the sentence. They look like a marginal gloss that has crept into the text.

3.5.3: Reading εὐθενήσεται with Elter.

3.6.9: Adding μαλακὸν before τυρὸν, or perhaps ἁπαλὸν, which is Bion's word.

3.7.25: I have transferred this somewhat obscure sentence from its place in the manuscripts, just before "The same goes for a human being as well."

3.9.20: Reading ἢ ἀλύετε with Salmasius.

3.10.5: I read the sentence as a question, starting therefore with ποῦ.

3.10.10: Reading this as a statement, not a question, with Upton.

3.10.16: Reading τὸ τὰ with Schenkl.

3.13.20: Reading ἀλλὰ... ἀλλ' with the manuscripts and assuming, with most editors, that there is a lacuna in the text, to be filled by something like the words I have supplied.

3.14.5: With Wolf, I omit διὰ... πίνειν.

3.16.15: Reading ἀποκρίνομαι with some manuscripts.

3.17.8: Reading ἔξωθεν with manuscript S.

3.22.50: Reading ὃ ἂν δῷς with Schenkl.

3.22.94: Reading παρέχει with Wolf.

3.23.4: Reading εἰκῇ ἐπιεικῶς with Reiske.

3.23.33: Reading ἐπιπληκτικός with Boter.

3.23.35: Reading πούλπιτον with Wolf.

3.23.36: Reading ἀποτρεπτικώτερον with Reiske.

3.24.8: Deleting μηδ᾽ . . . ἀποδημῶμεν with Oldfather.

4.1.50: Reading ἀναλθὴς with Oldfather.

4.1.164: I read τοσαῦτα.

4.5.5: Reading κινῇ οὗτος τι with S.

4.5.5 (end): Retaining ἐξάξει with the manuscripts.

4.5.21: Reading πρόβατον for πάντα, with Salmasius.

4.6.4: Reading ἐπιφανεστάτων with Elter.

4.7.18: Reading τοῦ σώματος σου κύριός εἰμι with Schweighäuser.

4.8.40: I suggest the reading κατὰ τὴν φύσιν.

4.9.6: Reading Εὔβιον with Wilamowitz.

4.10.31: Emending "Menelaus" to "Protesilaus" with Oldfather.

4.13.6: Reading οὐ γὰρ with Schenkl.

Fragments

3: I read τῶν ἄλλων.

23: I read ποιήσαντος.

Recommended Reading

Since the readership for this book will range from professionals in ancient philosophy to people with no knowledge of Greek or philosophy, I have indicated those works that are particularly accessible, and I have largely restricted the entries to works written in English. Every section of the bibliography has been tailored for readers of Epictetus, so it should not be taken to be a thorough bibliography on Stoicism, for instance. In addition to works listed here, some publications that illuminate narrower themes are mentioned as appropriate in the notes to the introduction and the translations.

Epictetus's Historical Environment

The two best recent general histories of Rome are M. Beard, *SPQR: A History of Ancient Rome* (Profile, 2015), and G. Woolf, *Rome: An Empire's Story* (Oxford University Press, 2012). Some of Epictetus's personal history is revealed by P. Weaver, "Epaphroditus, Josephus, and Epictetus," *Classical Quarterly* 44, no. 2 (1994): 468–79.

Epictetus's Philosophical Environment

Stoicism arose early in the Hellenistic period (323–30 BCE), along with other schools and trends, of which Epictetus was clearly aware. They can all be studied with the help of K. Algra, J. Barnes, J. Mansfeld, and M. Schofield, eds., *The Cambridge History of Hellenistic Philosophy* (Cambridge University Press, 1999). Shorter, and eminently readable, is J. Sellars, *Hellenistic Philosophy* (Oxford University Press, 2018). A brilliant introductory survey is R. Sharples, "Philosophy for Life," in *The Cambridge Companion to the Hellenistic World*, ed. G. Bugh (Cambridge University Press, 2006), 223–40. Another good introduction is C. Gill, "Stoic Writers of the Imperial Era," in *The*

Cambridge History of Greek and Roman Political Thought, ed. C. Rowe and M. Schofield (Cambridge University Press, 2000), 597–615.

See also:

J. Annas, *Hellenistic Philosophy of Mind* (University of California Press, 1992).

J. Annas, *The Morality of Happiness* (Oxford University Press, 1993).

P. Brunt, "Stoicism and the Principate," in *Studies in Stoicism*, ed. M. Griffin and A. Samuels, with M. Crawford (Oxford University Press, 2013), 275–309.

W. Desmond, *Cynics* (University of California Press, 2008).

J. Dillon, "The Social Role of the Philosopher in the Second Century CE: Some Remarks," in *The Platonic Heritage: Further Studies in the History of Platonism and Early Christianity* (Routledge, 2012), 29–40.

M. Frede, *A Free Will: Origins of the Notion in Ancient Thought*, ed. A. A. Long, foreword by D. Sedley (University of California Press, 2011).

P. Hadot, *What Is Ancient Philosophy?* trans. M. Chase (Harvard University Press, 2002).

C. Kahn, "Discovering the Will: From Aristotle to Augustine," in *The Question of "Eclecticism": Studies in Later Greek Philosophy*, ed. J. Dillon and A. A. Long (University of California Press, 1988), 234–59.

A. A. Long, *Hellenistic Philosophy: Stoics, Epicureans, Sceptics*, 2nd ed. (University of California Press, 1986).

M. Nussbaum, *The Therapy of Desire: Theory and Practice in Hellenistic Ethics* (1994; repr., with new introduction, Princeton University Press, 2009).

G. Reydams-Schils, "Human Bonding and *Oikeiōsis* in Roman Stoicism," *Oxford Studies in Ancient Philosophy* 22 (Summer 2002): 221–51.

G. Reydams-Schils, "Philosophy and Education in Stoicism of the Roman Imperial Era," *Oxford Review of Education* 36, no. 5 (2010): 561–74.

G. Reydams-Schils, *The Roman Stoics: Self, Responsibility, and Affection* (University of Chicago Press, 2005).

J. Sellars, "Roman Stoic Mindfulness: An Ancient Technology of the Self," in *Ethics and Self-Cultivation: Ancient and Contemporary Perspectives*, ed. M. Dennis and S. Werkhoven (Routledge, 2018), 15–29.

R. Sharples, *Stoics, Epicureans, and Skeptics* (Routledge, 1996).

R. Sorabji, *Emotion and Peace of Mind: From Stoic Agitation to Christian Temptation* (Oxford University Press, 2000).

R. Sorabji, *Self: Ancient and Modern Insights about Individuality, Life, and Death* (University of Chicago Press, 2006).

R. Sorabji and R. Sharples, eds., *Greek and Roman Philosophy, 100 BC–200 AD*, 2 vols. (Institute of Classical Studies, 2007).

G. Striker, *Essays on Hellenistic Epistemology and Ethics* (Cambridge University Press, 1996).

M. Trapp, "Philosophical Authority in the Imperial Period," in *Authority and Expertise in Ancient Scientific Culture*, ed. J. König (Cambridge University Press, 2017), 27–57.

M. Trapp, *Philosophy in the Roman Empire: Ethics, Politics and Society* (Ashgate, 2007).

M. Trapp, "Visibly Different? Looking at *Philosophi* in the Roman Imperial Period," in *Philosophari: Usages romains des savoirs grecs sous la République et sous l'Empire*, ed. P. Vesperini (Garnier, 2000), 353–69.

Sourcebooks

The most thorough sourcebook on Hellenistic philosophy is A. A. Long and D. Sedley, *The Hellenistic Philosophers*, 2 vols. (Cambridge University Press, 1987). This book is indispensable for every serious student; the first volume contains translations and commentary, the second the Greek and Latin texts. More handy is the excellent shorter collection by B. Inwood and L. Gerson, *Hellenistic Philosophy: Introductory Readings*, 2nd ed. (Hackett, 1997).

Stoicism

A learned introduction to Stoicism is readily available on the internet: D. Baltzly, "Stoicism," in *Stanford Encyclopedia of Philosophy* (Stanford University, 1997–), article published April 15, 1997; last modified April 10, 2018, https://plato.stanford.edu/entries/stoicism/. B. Inwood's *Stoicism: A Very Short Introduction* (Oxford University Press, 2018), is exemplary, and so is J. Sellars, *The Pocket Stoic* (University of Chicago Press, 2020). Somewhat longer, but clearly written throughout, are F. Sandbach, *The Stoics* (Chatto & Windus, 1975), and J. Sellars, *Stoicism* (University of California Press, 2006). In addition, the early chapters of Brennan's book (in the list that follows) serve as a very accessible introduction. Then there is an invaluable collection of essays by various hands: B. Inwood, ed., *The Cambridge Companion to the Stoics* (Cambridge University Press, 2003). A dedicated reader is B. Inwood and L. Gerson, eds., *The Stoics Reader* (Hackett, 2008).

See also:

J. Annas, "Ethics in Stoicism," in *Ancient Ethics*, ed. J. Hardy and G. Rudebusch (V & R Unipress, 2014), 309–31.

D. Baltzly, "Stoic Pantheism," *Sophia* 42, no. 2 (2003): 3–33.

S. Bobzien, *Determinism and Freedom in Stoic Philosophy* (Oxford University Press, 1998).

T. Brennan, "Reasonable Impressions in Stoicism," *Phronesis* 41, no. 3 (1996): 318–34.

T. Brennan, "Reservation in Stoic Ethics," *Archiv für Geschichte der Philosophie* 82, no. 2 (2000): 149–77.

T. Brennan, *The Stoic Life: Emotions, Duties, and Fate* (Oxford University Press, 2005).

J. Cooper, "Stoic Autonomy," in *Knowledge, Nature, and the Good: Essays on Ancient Philosophy* (Princeton University Press, 2004), 204–44.

M. Graver, *Stoicism and Emotion* (University of Chicago Press, 2007).

B. Inwood, *Ethics and Human Action in Early Stoicism* (Oxford University Press, 1985).

M. Jackson-McCabe, "The Stoic Theory of Implanted Preconceptions," *Phronesis* 49, no. 4 (2004): 323–47.

A. A. Long, ed., *Problems in Stoicism* (Athlone, 1971).

A. A. Long, *Stoic Studies* (Cambridge University Press, 1996).

J. Rist, *Stoic Philosophy* (Cambridge University Press, 1969).

J. Rist, ed., *The Stoics* (University of California Press, 1978).

R. Salles, *God and Cosmos in Stoicism* (Oxford University Press, 2009).

R. Salles, *The Stoics on Determinism and Compatibilism* (Ashgate, 2005).

S. Sambursky, *Physics of the Stoics* (Routledge & Kegan Paul, 1959).

M. Schofield, *The Stoic Idea of the City*, 2nd ed. (Cambridge University Press, 1999).

D. Scott, "Innatism and the Stoa," *Proceedings of the Cambridge Philological Society* 34 (1988): 123–53.

J. Sellars, *The Art of Living: The Stoics on the Nature and Function of Philosophy*, 2nd ed. (Bristol Classical Press, 2009).

S. White, "Stoic Selection: Objects, Actions, and Agents," in *Ancient Models of Mind: Studies in Human and Divine Rationality*, ed. A. Wilson Nightingale and D. Sedley (Cambridge University Press, 2010), 110–29.

J. Wildberger, *The Stoics and the State: Theory, Practice, Context* (Nomos, 2018).

Epictetus and Stoicism

A good introduction is M. Graver, "Epictetus," in *Stanford Encyclopedia of Philosophy* (Stanford University, 1997–), article published December 23, 2008; last modified June 15, 2021, https://plato.stanford.edu/entries/epictetus/. Other than this, the only accessible introductory essays are the introduction to this book and those that introduce other volumes of translations of Epictetus.

The most important recent book-length treatment of Epictetus is A. A. Long, *Epictetus: A Stoic and Socratic Guide to Life* (Oxford University Press, 2002). There are two collections of essays by various hands: D. Gordon and D. Suits, eds., *Epictetus: His Continuing Influence and Contemporary Relevance* (Rochester Institute of Technology Press, 2014), and T. Scaltsas and A. Mason, eds., *The Philosophy of Epictetus* (Oxford University Press, 2007). I have not separately listed essays included in these collections, but the latter publication constitutes one of the best scholarly books on Epictetus.

See also:

E. Asmis, "Choice in Epictetus' Philosophy," in *Antiquity and Humanity: Essays on Ancient Religion and Philosophy*, ed. A. Collins and M. Mitchell (Mohr Siebeck, 2001), 385–412.

J. Barnes, *Logic and the Imperial Stoa* (Brill, 1997).

A. Bonhöffer, *Epictet und die Stoa: Untersuchungen zur stoische Philosophie* (F. Enke, 1890).

A. Bonhöffer, *The Ethics of the Stoic Epictetus*, rev. ed., trans. W. Stephens (Peter Lang, 2021). First published 1894 as *Die Ethik des stoikers Epictet*.

P. Bosman, "Utopia, Domestication and Special Status: Marriage and Family in the Stoic Tradition," *Acta Patristica et Byzantina* 21, no. 2 (2010): 5–18.

G. Boter, "Evaluating Others and Evaluating Oneself in Epictetus' *Discourses*," in *Valuing Others in Classical Antiquity*, ed. R. Rosen and I. Sluiter (Brill, 2010), 323–51.

R. Braicovich, "Critical Assent, Intellectualism and Repetition in Epictetus," *Apeiron* 45, no. 4 (2012): 314–37.

R. Braicovich, "Freedom and Determinism in Epictetus' *Discourses*," *Classical Quarterly* 60, no. 1 (2010): 202–20.

R. Braicovich, "On the Notion of Ethical Exercises in Epictetus," *Prometeus: Filosofia em revista* 7 (February 2014): 126–38.

P. Brunt, "From Epictetus to Arrian," in *Studies in Stoicism*, ed. M. Griffin and A. Samuels, with M. Crawford (Oxford University Press, 2013), 331–59.

C. Cosans, "Facing Death Like a Stoic: Epictetus on Suicide in the Case of Illness," in *Bioethics: Ancient Themes in Contemporary Issues*, ed. M. Kuczewski and R. Polansky (MIT Press, 2000), 229–49.

R. Dobbin, *Epictetus: Discourses, Book 1* (Oxford University Press, 1998).

R. Dobbin, "Προαίρεσις in Epictetus," *Ancient Philosophy* 11, no. 1 (1991): 111–35.

H. Dyson, "The God Within: The Normative Self in Epictetus," *History of Philosophy Quarterly* 26, no. 3 (2009): 235–53.

J.-B. Gourinat, "Épictète et la logique: Une variation sur le thème des vertus dialectiques du sage," in *Mélanges de philosophie et de philologie offerts à Lambros Couloubaritsis*, ed. M. Broze, B. Decharneux and S. Delcomminette (Vrin, 2008), 435–46.

J.-B. Gourinat, "La *prohairesis* chez Épictète: Décision, volonté ou personne morale?" *Philosophie Antique* 5 (2005): 93–133.

M. Graver, "Not Even Zeus: A Discussion of A. A. Long, *Epictetus: A Stoic and Socratic Guide to Life*," *Oxford Studies in Ancient Philosophy* 25 (Winter 2003): 345–61.

J. Hershbell, "Epictetus: A Freedman on Slavery," *Ancient Society* 26 (1995): 185–204.

J. Hershbell, "Epictetus and Chrysippus," *Illinois Classical Studies* 18 (1993): 139–46.

J. Hershbell, "Plato and Epictetus: Philosophy and Politics in Ancient Greece and Rome," in *Griechenland und Rom*, ed. E. Schmidt (Tbilisi University Press, 1996), 476–84.

J. Hershbell, "The Stoicism of Epictetus: Twentieth-Century Perspectives," in *Aufstieg und Niedergang der römischen Welt*, part 2, vol. 36, sec. 3, ed. W. Haase (De Gruyter, 1989), 2148–63.

B. Hijmans, "Epictetus and the Teleological Explanation of Nature," *Proceedings of the African Classical Associations* 11, no. 2 (August 1959): 15–21.

B. Inwood, "L'*oikeiōsis* sociale chez Épictète," in *Polyhistor: Studies in the History and Historiography of Ancient Philosophy*, ed. K. Algra, P. van der Horst, and D. Runia (Brill, 1996), 243–64.

B. Johnson, *The Role Ethics of Epictetus: Stoicism in Ordinary Life* (Rowman & Littlefield, 2014).

R. Kamtekar, "*Aidōs* in Epictetus," *Classical Philology* 93, no. 2 (1998): 136–60.

A. A. Long, "Epictetus," in *The Meaning of Life and the Great Philosophers*, ed. S. Leach and J. Tartaglia (Routledge, 2018), 79–86.

A. A. Long, "Epictetus on Understanding and Managing Emotions," in *From Epicurus to Epictetus: Studies in Hellenistic and Roman Philosophy* (Oxford University Press, 2006), 377–94.

A. A. Long, "Seneca and Epictetus on Body, Mind and Dualism," in *From Stoicism to Platonism: The Development of Philosophy, 100 BCE–100 CE*, ed. T. Engberg-Pedersen (Cambridge University Press, 2017), 214–30.

E. MacGillivray, *Epictetus and Laypeople: A Stoic Stance toward Non-Stoics* (Rowman & Littlefield, 2020).

S. Magrin, "Nature and Utopia in Epictetus' Theory of *Oikeiosis*," *Phronesis* 63, no. 3 (2018): 293–350.

R. Salles, "Epictetus and the Causal Conception of Moral Responsibility and What Is *Eph'hēmin*," in *What Is Up to Us? Studies on Agency and Responsibility in Ancient Philosophy*, ed. P. Destrée, R. Saller, and M. Zingano (Academia, 2014), 169–82.

R. Salles, "Epictetus on Moral Responsibility for Precipitate Action," in *Akrasia in Greek Philosophy from Socrates to Plotinus*, ed. C. Bobonich and P. Destrée (Brill, 2007), 249–63.

R. Salles, "Epictetus on What Is in Our Power: Modal versus Epistemic Conceptions," in *Fate, Providence, and Free Will: Philosophy and Religion in Dialogue in the Early Imperial Period*, ed. R. Brouwer and E. Vimercati (Brill, 2020), 49–63.

R. Salles, "*Oikeiosis* in Epictetus," in Oikeiosis *and the Natural Basis of Morality: From Classical Stoicism to Modern Philosophy*, ed. A. Vigo (Georg Olms, 2012), 95–120.

M. Schofield, "Epictetus: Socratic, Cynic, Stoic," review of *Epictetus: A Stoic and Socratic Guide to Life*, by A. A. Long, *Philosophical Quarterly* 54, no. 216 (July 2004): 448–56.

M. Sharpe, "It's Not the Chrysippus You Read: On Cooper, Hadot, Epictetus, and Stoicism as a Way of Life," *Philosophy Today* 58, no. 3 (Summer 2014): 367–92. https://doi.org/10.5840/philtoday20145225.

G. Stanton, "The Cosmopolitan Ideas of Epictetus and Marcus Aurelius," *Phronesis* 13, no. 2 (1968): 183–95.

W. Stephens, "Epictetus on Fearing Death: Bugbear and Open Door Policy," *Ancient Philosophy* 34, no. 2 (2014): 365–91.

W. Stephens, "Epictetus on How the Stoic Sage Loves," *Oxford Studies in Ancient Philosophy* 14 (1996): 193–210.

W. Stephens, *Stoic Ethics: Epictetus and Happiness as Freedom* (Continuum, 2007).

M. Tremblay, "Digestion and Moral Progress in Epictetus," *Journal of Ancient Philosophy* 13, no. 1 (2019): 100–119.

E. Tsalla, "Epictetus on Plato: The Philosopher as an Olympic Victor," *Philosophical Inquiry* 32, issue 1/2 (2010): 21–42.

J. Wildberger, "Delimiting a Self by God in Epictetus," in *Religious Dimensions of the Self in the Second Century CE*, ed. J. Rüpke and G. Woolf (Mohr Siebeck, 2013), 23–45.

J. Xenakis, *Epictetus, Philosopher-Therapist* (Martinus Nijhoff, 1969).

J. Xenakis, "Logical Topics in Epictetus," *Southern Journal of Philosophy* 6, no. 2 (Summer 1968): 94–102.

Epictetus's Appropriation of Socrates

T. Brennan, "Socrates and Epictetus," in *A Companion to Socrates*, ed. S. Ahbel-Rappe and R. Kamtekar (Blackwell, 2006), 285–97.

J.-B. Gourinat, "Le Socrate d' Épictète," *Philosophie Antique* 1 (2001): 137–65.

B. Johnson, "The Syncretic Socrates of Epictetus," in *Brill's Companion to the Reception of Socrates*, ed. C. Moore (Brill, 2019), 266–92.

Epictetus's School and Teaching Style

B. Hijmans, *Askēsis: Notes on Epictetus' Educational System* (Van Gorcum, 1959).

R. Hock, "'By the Gods, It's My One Desire to See an Actual Stoic': Epictetus' Relation with Students and Visitors in His Personal Network," *Semeia*, no. 56 (1991): 121–42.

B. Wehner, *Die Funktion der Dialogstruktur in Epiktets Diatriben* (Steiner, 2000).

The *Handbook*

Naturally, works listed earlier cover the *Handbook* as well as *Discourses*, but here are some dedicated works. There are two really good introductions: A. A.

Long, *How to Be Free: An Ancient Greek Guide to the Stoic Life* (Princeton University Press, 2018), and J.-B. Gourinat, *Premier leçons sur le Manuel d' Épictète* (Presses Universitaires de France, 1998). Both include translations of the work.

See also:

G. Boter, *The Encheiridion of Epictetus and Its Three Christian Adaptations: Transmission and Critical Editions* (Brill, 1999).

G. Boter, "From *Discourses* to *Handbook*: The *Encheiridion* of Epictetus as a Practical Guide to Life," in *Knowledge, Text and Practice in Ancient Technical Writing*, ed. M. Formisano and P. van der Eijk (Cambridge University Press, 2017), 163–99.

T. Brennan and C. Brittain, *Simplicius: On Epictetus' Handbook 27–53* (Duckworth, 2002).

C. Brittain and T. Brennan, *Simplicius: On Epictetus' Handbook 1–26* (Duckworth, 2002).

A. Gavrilov, "Who Wrote the *Encheiridion* of Epictetus?" *Hyperboreus* 20 (2014): 295–316.

Modern Stoicism

Stoicism has been rediscovered in recent decades as a serviceable way of life for modern times. Many books, blogs, podcasts, and conferences perpetuate the ideas and offer practical advice. Out of this plethora of publications, I pick just four books to recommend. They are D. Fideler, *Breakfast with Seneca: A Stoic Guide to the Art of Living* (Norton, 2021); M. Pigliucci, *How to Be a Stoic: Using Ancient Philosophy to Live a Modern Life* (Basic Books, 2017); D. Robertson, *Stoicism and the Art of Happiness: Practical Wisdom for Everyday Life* (Hodder & Stoughton, 2013); and N. Sherman, *Stoic Wisdom: Ancient Lessons for Modern Resilience* (Oxford University Press, 2021).

Index

This index covers the major concepts and themes, and the proper names, that occur in the *Handbook*, *Discourses*, and Fragments. It does not reference the introduction or the notes. H = *Handbook*, D = *Discourses*, and F = Fragments, but where references are prefaced with no such letter, they are all pointing to *Discourses*. Note that because many of the discussions in the discourses sprawl in a conversational manner, and because Epictetus's main topics all intersect with one another, it is not always easy to determine where a topic begins and ends. In many cases, then, the surrounding contexts need to be read as well as the precise passages indicated in the index.

Dioscuri, 2.18.29

Dirce, 2.16.30

disfavor, 1.24.6, 1.30.2, 2.1.10, 2.1.35, 2.19.18, 2.19.24

disinclination. *See* inclination/disinclination

distress, H 5a, 12.1, 16, 24.1, D 1.2.4, 1.6.29, 1.9.7, 1.23.3–4, 1.25.17, 2.18.14, 2.22.6, 3.2.16, 3.11.2, 3.13.11, 3.22.48, 3.22.61, 3.24.23, 3.24.43, 3.24.90, 3.24.116–117, 4.1.84, 4.3.7, 4.4.32, 4.6.8, F 28b

divination, omens, H 18, 32, D 1.17.18–21, 1.17.28–29, 2.7, 2.10.5–6, 2.16.16–17

doctors, H 29.2, D 2.13.12, 2.14.21, 2.15.15, 2.17.8–9, 3.3.1, 3.10.9, 3.10.13–15, 3.15.3, 3.16.12, 3.20.14, 3.21.20–21, 3.22.73, 3.23.27–30, 3.25.7, 4.1.148, F 19, 22, 24. *See also* Hippocrates

domains (*topoi*), the three, 1.4.11, 1.17.22–24, 1.21.2, 2.17.15–16, 2.17.31–33, 3.2.1–8, 3.12.13–14, 3.26.14, 4.1.69–81, 4.4.13, 4.10.13, F 27. *See also* assent, desire/aversion, inclination/disinclination

Domitian, 2.7.8

eating, as an opportunity for virtue, H 15, 29.6, 33.7, 36, 41, 46.1, D 1.4.20, 1.13.1, 1.16.16–17, 2.4.8, 2.8.12, 2.8.15, 3.10.1, 3.13.21–23, 3.15.10–11, 3.21.4, 4.1.55, 4.4.8, 4.8.20, 4.12.7

Ecbatana, 2.16.36

Egyptians, 1.11.12–13, 1.22.5, 2.9.20, 2.11.15

elements, the four, 3.13.14–15, 4.7.15, F 1, 8

Eleusis, 3.21.13

endurance, patience, tolerance, H 10, 13, 30, 33.13, 47, D 1.6.27–28, 1.6.34, 1.6.40, 1.9.17, 1.14.16, 1.15.7, 2.1.19,

2.10.23, 2.12.14, 2.16.14, 2.16.18, 2.16.38, 2.22.20, 2.22.36, 3.4.12, 3.8.3, 3.8.6, 3.12.10, 3.13.23, 3.20.9, 3.21.5, 3.21.9, 3.22.100, 4.1.18, 4.1.109, 4.1.127, 4.4.18, 4.5.3, 4.5.17, 4.5.33, 4.8.20, F 2, 9, 20

envy, jealousy, H 19b, D 1.9.20, 2.12.7–8, 2.16.45, 2.17.26, 2.19.26, 2.21.3, 2.21.7, 2.21.12, 2.22.6, 2.23.44, 3.2.3, 3.2.16, 3.11.2, 3.13.10, 3.22.13, 3.22.61, 3.22.104, 3.24.43, 4.1.4, 4.4.10, 4.4.32–33, 4.9.5, 4.12.20

Epaminondas, 3.22.78

Epaphroditus, 1.1.20, 1.19.19–22, 1.26.11–12

Ephesus, 4.5.37

Epicurus, Epicureans, 1.20.17–19, 1.23, 2.9.19, 2.19.20–22, 2.20, 2.22.21, 2.23.21–22, 3.7, 3.24.38, F 14

Epirus, 3.4.1

Eriphyle, 2.22.32

Eteocles and Polynices, H 31, D 2.22.13, 4.5.29

Eubius, 4.9.6

Euphrates, H 29.4, D 3.15.8, 4.8.17

Euripides, 1.28.32

Eurystheus, 2.16.44, 3.22.57, 3.26.32

exile, H 21, 32, D 1.1.22, 1.1.26, 1.1.30, 1.2.21, 1.4.24, 1.10.2, 1.11.33, 1.24.4, 1.29.6, 1.30.2, 2.1.10, 2.1.38, 2.5.19, 2.6.22, 2.7.8, 2.16.19, 2.16.38, 2.19.18, 2.19.24, 3.3.17, 3.22.22, 3.24.29, 3.24.105, 4.1.60, 4.1.172, 4.5.29, 4.7.14, 4.7.18, F 21. *See also* Gyara

externals, material things, H 13, 16, 29, 33, D 1.2.7, 1.2.14, 1.4.18, 1.4.26–27, 1.15.2–3, 1.18.12, 1.22.16, 1.29.1, 2.2.10–15, 2.2.25, 2.5.1–9, 2.5.21–24, 2.6.2, 2.13.11, 2.16.11, 2.16.18, 2.22.19, 2.22.28, 3.3.8, 3.7.2, 3.10.16, 3.12.6, 3.15.12, 3.20,